SHARING THE JOURNEY

SHARING THE JOURNEY

*Support Groups and America's
New Quest for Community*

ROBERT WUTHNOW

THE FREE PRESS
New York   London   Toronto   Sydney   Tokyo   Singapore
1994

The Free Press
A Division of Simon & Schuster Inc.
1230 Avenue of the Americas
New York, N.Y. 10020

Printed in the United States of America

printing number

2 3 4 5 6 7 8 9 10

Library of Congress Cataloging-in-Publication Data

Wuthnow, Robert.
   Sharing the journey : support groups and America's new quest for community/Robert Wuthnow.
      p.   cm.
   ISBN 0-02-935625-3
   1. United States—Religion—1960– 2. Small groups. 3. Self-help groups—United States. 4. Community life. 5. United States—Social life and customs—1971–
BL2525.W885 1994   93-27320
302.3'4—dc20   CIP

CONTENTS

PART TWO
HOW SMALL GROUPS FUNCTION

PART FOUR
THE SOCIAL SIGNIFICANCE OF THE
SMALL-GROUP MOVEMENT

PREFACE

For as long as most Americans can remember, our society has been described to us as being composed of individualists. As children, we were taught to be independent. We learned about rugged pioneers who went off by themselves to seek their fortunes. Later, we learned that our social fabric was breaking down, that families were eroding, that communities were dying, and that more and more people were facing life on their own, heroically insisting on their independence and remaining uncommitted to anybody but themselves. Having learned these lessons so well, many of us are therefore likely to be surprised by the results presented in this book. I have been confronted over and over again with expressions of disbelief as I have discussed its conclusions with colleagues and friends.

But the standard wisdom needs to be challenged. Bible studies, prayer fellowships, self-help groups, twelve-step gatherings, therapy sessions, recovery groups—all have been gaining increasing importance in recent years, as both sources of emotional support and settings in which millions of Americans are seeking spirituality. Many proponents of the support-group movement now regard it as the most likely means for revitalizing American religion. Some observers also regard it as a way of saving American society as well: redeeming individuals from destructive addictions, drawing us out of narrow and selfish interests, and turning our attention more toward the needs of others. Critics suggest that the support-group movement, while increasingly pervasive in numbers, may be at best artificial, contributing more to a narcissistic obsession with self than to a more responsible society.

The problem has been that no reliable research examining the strength and implications of the support-group movement had been done. Whole sections of large bookstores are filled with popular treatises encouraging people to join recovery and support groups. Countless writings have been devoted to telling prospective leaders how to organize such groups. Training sessions, retreats, and conferences on the topic abound. All of these can provide valuable information, especially relating to personal experiences. But little effort has been made to gauge the dimensions of the entire movement.

How many people are involved in small supportive groups? What motivates them to become active in these groups? What kinds of groups do they join? How do these groups actually function? What do their members like most? What do they like least? How is spirituality influenced, if at all, by these groups? Is the wider society being influenced by them as well?

These questions are the concern of this book. It represents more than three years of research by a team of fifteen scholars. The research included a survey of a representative sample of the American public in which more than a thousand members of small groups were identified and questioned about their personal backgrounds, their groups, and the nature and consequences of their involvement in these groups. In addition, more than a hundred members, group leaders, and clergy were interviewed at length with open-ended questions about their groups. A dozen groups in which these people were involved were chosen for intensive study. Researchers attended group meetings regularly from at least six months to as long as three years, traced the history of these groups, took notes on a standard set of topics, and talked informally with group members and leaders. Information also was collected through interviews with members of other kinds of groups and with local and national leaders of the movement, through attendance at conferences and training sessions, and through the reading of stacks of articles, pamphlets, and books.

This book presents a dispassionate summary of what we found. It describes the extent of involvement in small groups in American society, examines the nature of this involvement, discusses the major varieties of small groups, considers their relationship to churches and other social institutions, discusses what goes on in group meetings, and teases out the consequences members attribute to their involvement.

Besides attempting to portray the dimensions of the small-group movement, the book also is centrally concerned with several larger questions that this phenomenon raises about the character of our society and, indeed, about American character itself. Is the small-group movement a response to the alleged breakdown of community in American society? How do people in small groups reconcile the strong individualistic tendencies that exist in American culture with the demands of being a responsible group member? Are small groups in any significant way altering the character of American religion? What do they tell us about the balance between private life and public commitments in our society?

Although the perspective from which the book is written is largely that of the academician, this study includes a deeply personal dimension as well. Reared by church-going parents in the Midwest, I cannot remember a time when I was not a member of one small group or another. As a child, I was regularly involved in Sunday school classes, youth groups, scouts, and activity groups at school. During college, small groups played a significant role in my life, and as a graduate student I was a founding member of a movement aimed at revitalizing mainline Protestant churches through the formation of small groups. Much of the time since then, I have been a member of various kinds of small groups, and served as a host and leader. I have helped in planning and coordinating them. My experience with small groups frankly has been mixed. I have been nurtured and supported by them, but I have also been frustrated and disappointed on many occasions. It is perhaps this mixture of experiences that has led me to want to understand all sides of the movement in greater depth.

The opportunity to pursue this interest as a research study came several years ago when George Gallup, Jr., asked me to serve on the board of the George H. Gallup International Institute in Princeton, New Jersey. Founded in memory of the pioneer of modern polling techniques, the Gallup Institute was organized to carry on the late Dr. Gallup's interest in contributing to the social betterment of American society by conducting research, particularly in the areas of religion, education, the environment, and health. Through the Gallup Institute, George Gallup, Jr., and I learned more about each other's interest in small groups, and with the advice and assistance of fellow board members Kenneth Briggs—former religion editor of *The New York Times*—and Dr. Nicholas Van Dyck—president of Religion in American Life—we decided to seek funding for a research project on this topic. This funding was made available through a generous grant to the George H. Gallup International Institute from the Lilly Endowment, and the entire project was administered through the Gallup Institute.

In addition to George Gallup, Jr., Kenneth Briggs, and Nicholas Van Dyck, I wish to thank a number of other people who helped bring the present volume to fruition. Robert Corman, who at the time was executive director of the Gallup Institute, played a large role in administering a planning grant from the Lilly Endowment that led to the eventual research study. Corinne Kyle and Marie Swirsky of the Gallup Institute assisted with all financial aspects of the project. Curt Coffman, vice-president of Gallup, Inc., also a board member of the Gallup Institute, assisted with administrative details involving the survey. Dawn Balmforth in the Lincoln, Nebraska, office of Gallup, Inc., supervised the field work. Wendy Young served as project coordinator for the ethnographic phase of the study and assisted with many other tasks as well, including tracking down and photocopying articles, interviewing religious leaders and group members, and attending conferences. Gray Wheeler did a literature review and an initial round of interviews with clergy. Tim Dowd served as chief programmer and computer consultant to the project.

Throughout the volume I have used the editorial "we" quite deliberately to alert readers to the fact that the book draws heavily on the work of the fifteen field researchers who conducted the qualitative interviews and did the participant-observation studies of particular groups: Lynn Davidman, Elaine Friedman, Douglas Jardine, Kathleen Joyce, Matthew P. Lawson, Robert C. Liebman, Daniel Olson, Natalie Searl, George Thomas, R. Stephen Warner, Elfriede Wedem, Brad Wigger, Diane Winston, Sara Wuthnow, Wendy Young.

A companion volume—*Small Groups and Spirituality* (Eerdmans, 1994)—presents chapter-length reports on the groups that we studied in the ethnographic phase of the project. That volume is intended to give the reader more of an inside look at the functioning of specific small groups than can be done in the present book. We have, however, drawn from both the survey and the field observations for both volumes. By agreement with our respondents, we have disguised the identity of their groups and altered names and some features of individuals' biographies to keep their identities confidential. I gratefully acknowledge the cooperation of both the respondents and the field researchers in allowing me to use some interview and observation material in this volume. In the interest of maintaining respondents' anonymity, I make this acknowledgment here rather than by footnoting specific quotations.

I also wish to acknowledge the advice and helpful suggestions we received from numerous scholars, clergy, leaders of self-help groups, and other experts on the subject. Roberta Hestenes, Gareth Icenogle, Edward J. Madara, Lorette Piper, David Stark, and Chavah Weissler were especially generous in this regard. Special thanks go to Jeanne Knoerle and Craig Dykstra at the Lilly Endowment for their interest in the topic and their support during the process of carrying out the research, and to Susan Arellano at The Free Press for her fine editorial advice. If support and encouragement are the hallmarks of small groups, then this research truly has been the beneficiary of this spirit.

1

INTRODUCTION

The Small-Group Movement

In the driveway across the street, a vintage silver Porsche sits on blocks as its owner tinkers with the engine. Next door, a man with thinning gray hair applies paint to the trim around his living room window. But at 23 Springdale something quite different is happening. About two dozen people are kneeling in prayer, heads bowed, elbows resting on folding chairs in front of them. After praying, they will sing, then pray again, then discuss the Bible. They are young and old, men and women, black and white. A teenage girl remarks after the meeting that she comes every week because the people are so warm and friendly. "They're not geeks; they just make me feel at home."

At the largest gothic structure in town, several people slip hastily through the darkness and enter a small door toward the rear of the building. Inside is a large circle of folding chairs. On the wall a felt banner reads "Alleluia Alleluia" (the two As are in red). Before long all the chairs are filled and an attractive woman in her late thirties calls the group to order. "Hi, my name is Joan, and I'm an alcoholic." "Hi, Joan," the group responds. After a few announcements, Betty, a young woman just out of college, tells her story. Alcohol nearly killed her. Then, close to death in a halfway house, she found God. "I thought God hated me. But now I know there is a higher power I can talk to and know."

1

These are but two examples of a phenomenon that has spread like wildfire in recent years. These cases are so ordinary that it is easy to miss their significance. Most of us probably are vaguely aware of small groups that meet in our neighborhoods or at local churches and synagogues. We may have a coworker who attends Alcoholics Anonymous or a neighbor who participates in a Bible study group. We may have scanned lists of support groups in the local newspaper and noted that anything from underweight children to oversexed spouses can be a reason to meet. Members of our family may have participated in youth groups, couples groups, prayer groups, book discussion clubs, or Sunday school classes at one time or another. Perhaps we attend one ourselves. But we may not have guessed that these groups now play a major role in our society.

Groups such as these seldom make the headlines or become the focus of public controversy. They are not the stuff that reporters care very much about. Few people are involved in small groups because they are trying to launch a political campaign or attract the attention of public officials. These groups have little to say about tax initiatives, the national debt, or the public school system. They are not staging protest marches or picketing the nation's capital. Seldom, if ever, do members of small groups appear on talk shows to make scandalous statements about sex, politics, or religion. They are, for the most part, off in the wings when others are clamoring about abortion rights or attempting to challenge the Supreme Court. With the exception of a few lobbying groups, they are not trying to initiate public policy. Nor are they soliciting funds, selling stock, distributing products, or earning a profit. They are simply the private, largely invisible ways in which individuals choose to spend a portion of their free time. In an era when television networks and national newspapers increasingly define what is important, it is thus easy to dismiss the small-group phenomenon entirely.

To overlook this trend, however, would be a serious mistake. The small-group movement has been effecting a quiet revolution in American society. It has done so largely by steering clear of politics, business, and the national news media. Its success has astounded even many of its leaders. Few of them were trying to unleash a revolution at all. They simply were responding to some need in their own lives or in the lives of people they knew. They started groups, let people talk about their problems or interests, and perhaps supplied them with reading material. The results were barely perceptible. The most noticeable

were the addictions that people recovered from and the occasional suicide that may have been prevented. Far more common were the ordinary words of encouragement, the prayers that people recited, their
remarks about good days and bad days, and the cups of lukewarm coffee they consumed. What happened took place so incrementally that
it could seldom be seen at all. It was, like most profound reorienta-
tions in life, so gradual that those involved saw it less as a revolution
than as a journey. The change was concerned with daily life, emotions,
and understandings of one's identity. It was personal rather than public, moral rather than political. For most participants, the larger movement was not something they cared much about, or were even aware
of; they were focused on the movement going on in their own group.
Except for some of the leaders who saw its potential, few thought
about how widely the phenomenon was spreading, and even its most
devoted champions would have been surprised to know just how widespread it was becoming.

This book argues that the small-group movement is beginning to
alter American society, both by changing our understandings of community and by redefining spirituality. Its effects cannot be calculated
simply at the individual level. Once all the individual testimonies are
put together, something of much larger significance is still left to be
understood. What is important is not just that a teenager finds friends
at a prayer meeting or that a young woman named Betty finds God in
Alcoholics Anonymous. These stories have to be magnified a hundred
thousand times to see how pervasive they have become in our society.
They must also be examined closely to see that what is happening now
has never occurred at any previous time in history. Not only are small
groups attracting participants on an unprecedented scale, these groups
are also affecting the ways in which we relate to each other and how
we conceive of the sacred. Community is what people say they are
seeking when they join small groups. Yet the kind of community they
create is quite different from the communities in which people have
lived in the past. These communities are more fluid and more concerned with the emotional states of the individual. The vast majority
of small-group members also say that their sense of the sacred has
been profoundly influenced by their participation. But small groups
are not simply drawing people back to the God of their fathers and
mothers. They are dramatically changing the way God is understood.
God is now less of an external authority and more of an internal presence. The sacred becomes more personal but, in the process, also

becomes more manageable, more serviceable in meeting individual needs, and more a feature of group processes themselves. Support groups are thus effecting changes that have both salutary and worrisome consequences. They supply community and revitalize the sacred. But, for some of their members at least, these communities can be manipulated for personal ends, and the sacred can be reduced to a magical formula for alleviating anxiety.

At present, four out of every ten Americans belong to a small group that meets regularly and provides caring and support for its members. These are not simply informal gatherings of neighbors and friends, but organized groups: Sunday school classes, Bible study groups, Alcoholics Anonymous and other twelve-step groups, youth groups and singles groups, book discussion clubs, sports and hobby groups, and political or civic groups. Those who have joined these groups testify that their lives have been deeply enriched by the experience. They have found friends, received warm emotional support, and grown in their spirituality. They have learned how to forgive others and become more accepting of themselves. Some have overcome life-threatening addictions. Many say their identity has been changed as a result of extended involvement in their group. In fact, the majority have been attending their groups over an extended period of time, often for as long as five years, and nearly all attend faithfully, usually at least once a week.

But the small-group movement has not grown simply by meeting the needs of its individual members. It is thoroughly American. It reflects and extends the most fundamental dilemmas of our society. The fact that it is well organized, has a national leadership structure, and commands huge resources is tremendously important. Yet the movement as a whole is deeply populist. It attracts people who are fed up with large-scale institutions and prefer to help themselves. The way it draws people together is also thoroughly American. It stands in the tradition of voluntary associations and it emulates the work of churches and synagogues. In this sense, the small-group movement is a champion of traditional values. Yet its existence depends on the changing structure of the American family and the community. How it performs its functions is thoroughly American as well. It rejects the received wisdom embodied in formal creeds, doctrines, and ideologies, often diminishing the importance of denominational distinctions, theological tradition, or the special authority of the clergy. But it offers a pragmatic approach to solving one's problems by suggesting that the best proof of God's existence is whether one has received an answer to some personal problem or by asserting that the Bible is true because it works in everyday life. These groups apply spiritual technology to the life of the soul, implying that the sacred can be realized by following simple guidebooks or formulas, and they often substitute powerful unstated norms of behavior, focusing especially on the value of being a group member and on achieving happiness as part of one's spirituality, for the formalized creeds and theological ideals of the past. The group is often able to define what is right or wrong, encouraging members to pay attention to their feelings, but also evoking these feelings and helping members to interpret them in certain ways. Thus, the movement makes faith more relevant but also risks turning belief into something that people can manipulate for their own selfish purposes.

Understanding the small-group movement therefore requires us to examine it closely by subjecting it to critical scrutiny from the inside while viewing it from the outside as well. Its dramatic growth in recent decades can only be explained by considering the social context in which it has arisen. The movement's potential to alter our conceptions of ourselves cannot be understood apart from what we know about American culture at the end of the twentieth century. Ours is a highly fluid society. Many of us lead anonymous lives. We no longer live in the same neighborhoods all our lives or retain close ties with our kin. The small-group movement clearly is rooted in the breakdown of these traditional support structures and in our continuing desire for community. We want others with whom we can share our journeys. Its appeal extends even beyond this desire, tapping into our quest for the sacred itself. But how? And why? How are these desires being met? Why have small groups become the way of meeting them? And with what consequences?

Providing people with a stronger sense of community has been a key aim of the small-group movement from its inception. There is a widespread assumption that community is sputtering to an undignified halt, leaving many people stranded and alone. Families are breaking down. Neighbors have become churlish or indifferent. The solution is thus to start intentional groups of like-minded individuals who can regain a sense of community. Small groups are doing a better job than many of their critics would like to think. The communities they create are seldom frail. People feel cared for. They help one another. They share their intimate problems. They identify with their groups and participate regularly over extended periods of time. Why they do so is important to understand, especially because some groups generate bonds of attachment better than others.

But in another sense small groups may not be fostering community as effectively as many of their proponents would like. Some small groups merely provide occasions for individuals to focus on themselves in the presence of others. The social contract binding members together asserts only the weakest of obligations. Come if you have time. Talk if you feel like it. Respect everyone's opinion. Never criticize. Leave quietly if you become dissatisfied. Families would never survive by following these operating norms. Close-knit communities in the past did not, either. But small groups, as we know them, are a phenomenon of the late twentieth century. There are good reasons for the way they are structured. They reflect the fluidity of our lives by allowing us to bond easily but to break our attachments with equivalent ease. If we fail to understand these reasons, we can easily view small groups as something other than what they are. We can imagine that they really substitute for families, neighborhoods, and broader community attachments that may demand lifelong commitments, when, in fact, they do not.

The quest for spirituality is the other objective that has animated much of the small-group movement. A majority of all small-group members say they joined because they wanted to deepen their faith. Nearly two-thirds of all small groups have some connection to churches or synagogues. Many have been initiated by clergy. Many devote their meetings to studying the Bible or to discussing other religious texts. Most include prayer. Embarking on a spiritual journey is a common theme among members. Some would argue that this trend is indicative simply of thirst in the human heart for a relationship with God. But why now? Why has the small-group movement become the vehicle for expressing this desire? Why not churches? Or religious television? Or individual devotional readings and meditation?

The standard answer is that the churches have become weak. People want to know God but find no guidance when they attend religious services. The small-group movement is thus a way of revitalizing American religion, stemming the tide of secularity, and drawing the faithful back to God before the churches slide into oblivion. But the standard answer is wrong on two counts. The small-group movement is flourishing in American society, not because the churches are weak, but because they are strong. People do not join groups simply because their hearts tell them to. They join because groups are available, because they have direct exposure to these groups, and because someone encourages them to attend. Groups are available because churches and synagogues sponsor them. Members of the clergy initiate them as part of an explicit plan for the future of their church or synagogue. They enlist leaders, create mechanisms for recruiting members, purchase study guides, and provide meeting space. In this sense, the small-group movement is an extension of the role that organized religion has always played in American society.

The standard view is also wrong, though, in suggesting that small groups are stemming the tide of secularity. To be sure, they encourage people to pray and to think about spiritual truths. Nevertheless, they do little to increase the biblical knowledge of their members. Most of them do not assert the value of denominational traditions or pay much attention to the distinctive theological arguments that have identified different variants of Christianity or Judaism in the past. Indeed, many of the groups encourage faith to be subjective and pragmatic. A person may feel that his or her faith has been deepened, but in what way is largely in the eye of the beholder. Biblical truths may be more meaningful, but the reason is that they calm anxiety and help one make it through the day. The deity of small groups is a God of love, comfort, order, and security. Gone is the God of judgment, wrath, justice, mystery, and punishment. Gone are concerns about the forces of evil. Missing from most groups even is a distinct interest in heaven and hell, except for the small heavens and hells that people experience in their everyday lives.

Indeed, it does not overstate the case to suggest that the small-group movement is currently playing a major role in *adapting* American religion to the main currents of secular culture that have surfaced at the end of the twentieth century. Secularity is misunderstood if it is assumed to be a force that prevents people from being spiritual at all. It is more aptly conceived as an orientation that encourages a safe, domesticated version of the sacred. From a secular perspective, a divine being is one who is there for our own gratification, like a house pet, rather than one who demands obedience from us, is too powerful or mysterious for us to understand, or who challenges us to a life of service. When spirituality has been tamed, it can accommodate the demands of a secular society. People can go about their daily business without having to alter their lives very much because they are interested in spirituality. Secular spirituality can even be put to good use, making people more effective in their careers, better lovers, and more responsible citizens. This is the kind of spirituality being nurtured in many small groups today.

The small-group movement is thus the latest in a series of cultural realignments. At the start of the eighteenth century, American religion underwent its first period of realignment. The state churches that colonists imported from Europe were disestablished. Denominational pluralism, later protected by a constitutional separation between church and state, was the result. During the nineteenth century a second major realignment took place. The hegemony of a few Protestant denominations was undermined. Faith became more democratic and more thoroughly American. New denominations proliferated, congregational autonomy and diversity were strengthened, and Catholics and Jews gained a place alongside Protestants. Now, at the end of the twentieth century, denominational structures are waning considerably. Increasing numbers of people have switched from tradition to tradition to tradition. Clergy are under increased pressures to compete with other congregations for members. And the basis of competition has altered significantly, from doctrinal or liturgical distinctions to programmatic appeals. Small groups provide greater variety and allow greater freedom in selecting the religion of one's choice than ever before. They make faith more fluid, championing change itself, and creating modular communities that can be established and disbanded with relative ease.

But this discussion is simply a preview. The assertions I have made in these opening pages need substantiation. We need to understand more clearly what kinds of people have become involved in small groups. Are the participants a distinct category of the American population—differing from others in their personal backgrounds, interests, and needs—or are they much like everyone else? We need to examine the varieties of these groups and their connections with religious organizations. Certainly a local prayer group must be sharply distinguished from a meeting of Alcoholics Anonymous. Yet we must consider carefully how the two are similar as well. Even the fact of diversity is important for us to consider. How is it possible for the small-group movement to contain such diversity? What does this tell us about American society? We also need to consider how community is fostered and how spirituality is nurtured. We must listen carefully to what those in small groups have discovered there and pay special attention to the caring they have received, the spiritual insights they have gained, and the group processes by which these deeply personal transformations have been effected. Only then can we turn to the question of whether small groups are also transforming American culture.

THE SMALL GROUPS RESEARCH PROJECT

To accomplish these tasks I undertook a national research project on small groups and spirituality, and its results form the core of this book. As a first step in the project, I invited approximately a dozen religious leaders and scholars with knowledge of small groups to participate in a working conference to help me identify the central issues needing to be addressed. This conference, hosted by the George H. Gallup International Institute in Princeton and funded by a grant from the Lilly Endowment, generated a rich menu of researchable questions and tentative insights. Following the conference, we conducted a preliminary survey of the American public, interviewed a number of clergy, and thoroughly reviewed the published literature. Then, with a major research grant from the Lilly Endowment to the Gallup Institute, I launched a three-year project that included both an extensive opinion survey of the American public and in-depth case studies and personal interviews with more than a hundred members of a dozen selected groups in various parts of the country.

The conclusions presented in this book, therefore, are based on two kinds of primary evidence. The national survey screened a representative sample of the American public to identify persons who were currently involved in any small group that met regularly and provided caring and support for its members. This procedure yielded approximately 1,000 people who were asked a long list of questions about the nature of their group, why they became involved, what its activities were, how well they liked it, and what they had received from it. For comparative purposes, we also surveyed more than 900 people to find out why they had not become involved in a small group. The second kind of evidence is qualitative. With the assistance of more than a dozen fellow researchers, I collected information from people who were deeply involved in small groups; we asked them to tell their stories in their own words and observed the groups in which they were involved firsthand. We also interviewed a number of men and women who have risen to national prominence as leaders of the small-group movement, spoke to pastors and community representatives (who were sometimes critical of the movement), and collected huge stacks of study guides, directories, newsletters, and bibliographies. (Methodological detail is presented in the appendix.)

Given the vast numbers of people involved, it is not surprising that numerous books already have been written about small groups. Rummage through any library and you will find short books telling how to run a group, how to be a good group member, how to live a more successful life by getting involved in groups, and how to make your business or church more successful by starting up a small-group program. Most of these books offer practical advice gleaned from their authors' experiences in leading a group. Some speak candidly of pitfalls to avoid. A great number draw general principles from the Bible and counsel their readers that their groups will be successful if they only follow these principles. Most speak glowingly of the work small groups are already accomplishing and of the tremendous mission they can fulfill. With few exceptions, however, these books are not based on systematic evidence. They reflect their authors' views and personal experience, but do not provide any way of knowing how representative these views may be. They also suffer from being written at such close ideological proximity to the movement itself. Some are quite honest in discussing the shortcomings of small groups. But the overwhelming majority are written by small-group advocates. They see enormous potential in the movement, but fail to consider it in relation to broader questions about what is happening in American society as a whole.

The aim of this book thus is to present a more sober assessment of small groups than is currently available in the literature on this phenomenon. I adopt this stance, not from mean-mindedness, but because it is time our hopes and opinions were informed by some knowledge of how these groups actually work. Many of the groups work remarkably well, providing their members with personal support and encouraging them to think, more than they might otherwise, about spiritual issues; others do not work as well, failing either to retain their members' interest or to encourage open discussions of personal needs. What makes the difference? Many of the groups that work, moreover, do so for reasons other than the ones found printed in the handy do-it-yourself manuals. Thus, we need to consider some hard evidence about groups and, on the basis of that evidence, to confront some difficult issues that must be raised if we want small groups to be better understood and better utilized in the formation of spirituality and the cultivation of community.

The survey and in-depth interviews in combination provide a strong basis for accomplishing this task. The survey makes it possible to provide, for the first time, a reasonable estimate of the number of people in the United States who presently are involved in small groups or who have been involved at some time previously in their lives. It permits us to determine which kinds of groups are currently most popular, and it allows us to make comparisons among the members of these various kinds of groups. Because nearly all the members we surveyed were able to give knowledgeable information about their groups, their answers allow us to compare an unbiased sample of nearly a thousand small groups located all across the United States. The present data is thus a considerable improvement over research studies in the past that have tried to draw conclusions by comparing only a few small groups in one or two geographic areas. Indeed, with the help of advanced statistical techniques, we can systematically examine why some groups function better along various dimensions than others and what best differentiates members who are satisfied with their groups from members who are dissatisfied; we can also control for other differences among types of groups or types of members. Using the same procedures, we can also assess not only how often members report receiving care and encouragement but which kinds of members are most likely to benefit from such care and encouragement. Similarly, we can see how many members feel their lives have been deeply influenced—psychologically and spiritually—by their groups and what specific group activities have been most instrumental in effecting these changes. The qualitative evidence permits us to interpret the conclusions suggested by the survey in greater detail. We can see more clearly what specific individuals gained from their participation and, by having observed small groups directly, we can show how the interaction developed.

In the chapters that follow, I report what group members told us in their own words and summarize the vast amount of statistical data provided by the survey (details of which have been reserved for the appendix). It is important, however, for readers to understand my interpretive framework as well. I did not bring a preconceived theory to bear on the process of collecting and interpreting the evidence. I have, however, developed some guiding arguments in the course of the research itself. These arguments bear heavily on the questions of community, spirituality, and cultural change to which I have already alluded. It will be helpful to outline each of these arguments briefly before we turn to a consideration of the small-group movement itself.

THE ISSUE OF COMMUNITY

My argument about community is that small groups are both providing community and changing our understanding of what community is. In view of all the criticisms that have depicted Americans as a society of lonely, self-interested individualists suffering from isolation, disrupted families, a lack of friends, difficulty in establishing intimate relationships, and the demeaning anonymity of large-scale institutions, the small-group movement poses a rather different picture of our society. The large number of people who are involved in small groups, the depth of their involvement, the extent of their caring for each other, and even the degree to which they reach out to others in the wider community all suggest that the social fabric has not unraveled nearly to the extent that many critics have suggested. In short, small groups are a significant feature of what holds our society together. And their prevalence means that society does have mechanisms to hold it together. Small groups draw individuals out of themselves, pull them out of their isolated personal lives, and put them in the presence of others where they can share their needs and concerns, make friends, and become linked to wider social networks. Small groups provide a way of transcending our most self-centered interests; they temper our individualism and our culturally induced desire to be totally independent of one another. The attachments that develop among the members of small groups demonstrate clearly that we are not a society of rugged individualists who wish to go it entirely alone but, rather, that we are a communal people who, even amidst the dislocating tendencies of our society, are capable of banding together in bonds of mutual support.

Nevertheless, we must also understand that the kind of community generated by small groups is clearly different from that which has characterized families, neighborhoods, ethnic groups, and tribes throughout most of human history. We can see how different these two forms of community are if we pause for a moment to consider a few of the contrasts. Small groups are in one sense similar to families because both tend to consist of relatively few people who interact intimately and shape each other's primary identities. As families have come to embrace fewer people in these ways, either because of divorce and fewer children or because of geographic dislocations among extended family members, small groups may be functioning as surrogate sources of intimacy and primary identity. Yet it is also important to recognize that small groups differ from families in several basic ways. The members of small groups are seldom related to each other biologically. They thus do not share the imagined heritage, destiny, or physical traits and personality characteristics that unite individuals who are related by blood. Most families are also economic units that

bear legal responsibilities for their members' shelter, clothing, education, and medical support, and these economic responsibilities generally extend over long periods of time, usually for at least several
generations. Small groups clearly do not function as families in this
respect. Their members seldom incur any financial obligations on
behalf of other members or the group as a whole. Neighborhoods, ethnic groups, and tribes differ from small groups in other important
ways. The community provided in these settings generally has an
important physical dimension. People live in the same area, see each
other informally in the course of their everyday lives, and identify
themselves with the help of certain buildings, streets, parks, culinary
customs, or distinctive clothing. The social unit is primary in the sense
that an individual can live in only one neighborhood or be a member
of only one tribe. There is also a sense of inevitability about such identities. Adults may have chosen their neighborhoods, but throughout
much of history they chose to remain in the community of their birth,
and their ethnic or tribal identity was ascribed to them, rather than
being chosen at all. Small groups are, by comparison, far less associated with physical proximity and decidedly more purposive, intentional,
and voluntaristic.

When people say they are finding community in a small group, and
even when they describe their group as a family, therefore, they mean
something quite different from the connotations that words like
"community" or "family" have had in the past. Whether they recognize it or not, their sense of community now means something over
which they have a great deal of control. They have chosen to join one
particular group, rather than any of dozens they might also have been
exposed to, and they may be involved in more than one, certainly if
their involvement over a lifetime is considered. Moreover, their dependence on the group is far more likely to involve emotional care than
physical or economic support, and this care may be given quite spo-
radically. Certainly the encouragement received in a group can be
powerful, but it is still limited to an evening a week, compared with
the continuous by-play that takes place among families who share the
same dwelling. Members' obligations to each other and to the group
as a whole also are likely to carry a distinct meaning. Participants seldom incur serious financial responsibilities in order to sustain the
group. They may donate a share of their time to it over an extended
period of time, but they can also extricate themselves from the group
with relative ease.

These characteristics of community are, of course, increasingly typical in other sectors of modern society as well. Members of families choose to leave each other with greater frequency now than at any time in the past—filing for divorce or moving away from parents and siblings—and dual-career couples may feel less economic responsibility to each other than in earlier times. Geographic mobility makes neighborhoods more a matter of choice than birth. Ethnic identities gradually erode as a result of intermarriage, mobility, and norms of cultural pluralism, so that an individual's identity can be more a function of what he or she chooses to emphasize. Religious affiliation has become more voluntaristic. Clubs, community associations, and jobs have also encouraged individuals to be more purposive in creating their own networks.

If small groups reflect wider changes in the definition of community, they also reinforce these tendencies. They do so because their members are exposed not only to networks of care and support in these groups but to an ideology or set of beliefs that emphasizes the value of certain kinds of relationships rather than others. Emotional support is emphasized far more than physical or monetary support. In many groups, for example, it is acceptable to lean on other members for encouragement or a kind word, but individuals are expected to be rigorously independent when it comes to taking care of themselves medically or financially. Emotional support is defined to mean encouragement rather than criticism or guidance. The group tells its members they are okay, but refrains from offering constructive advice. Serious or long-term emotional difficulties are unlikely to be dealt with in most small groups at all. Tolerance of diversity is another norm championed in the ideology of most small groups. Caring for someone is more likely to be defined by this norm as not criticizing them rather than as trying to help them come to a different understanding. Choosing a group on the basis of what one can get out of it is another such norm. Members are, to turn a familiar statement on its head, more likely to ask what the group can do for them than what they can do for the group.

Community, then, becomes more intentional as a result of the small-group movement. People recognize the differences between their groups and their families, neighborhoods, and churches. Yet their involvement in small groups also influences how they think about these other settings and what aspects of community they value. It becomes entirely possible to think of oneself as an intensely communal, caring person by virtue of being in a group. Yet the group itself may function more as a place where each individual comes to think about himself or herself than where genuine concern about others triumphs over individual needs. Even to suggest that individual personal needs should be put in a secondary place runs against the ideology of many groups. When community becomes intentional, other concerns also necessarily become more important. Members of the same tribe may gripe about one another, but know they must work out their differences because they have little choice but to live with each other. Small-group members are more likely to recognize that they can move on to another group. Rather than confronting fellow members with their complaints, it is easier to exit the system entirely. At the same time, intentionality also places an added burden on group members. While they are still part of the group, they cannot so easily blame fate of birth for bringing them there. They have to decide whether they really want to be involved, listen to their feelings for cues, and worry about whether they are getting enough to make the time worthwhile. It is thus not surprising that groups have come to champion the importance of paying attention to one's feelings. The problems reinforced by group involvement are the same ones that groups aim to resolve.

These considerations are terribly important because the basic fabric of society depends on how individuals structure their relationships with one another. This is not to say that economic wherewithal or political arrangements are unimportant. But community always lies at the intersection of individual needs and institutional structures. If small groups are altering the ways in which we conceive of community, their impact may well be greater than even their most deeply involved members may realize. The changes at the individual level may seem overwhelmingly positive. Person X says that she has been cared for, encouraged, given a better self-concept, and strengthened to make it through the day. That result is all to the good. But in the process we must also be mindful of what she is not saying or be aware that these needs would not have occurred to people in many other social circumstances. She is not saying, for example, that she plans to devote her life to this group. She is not saying that she will alter her career plans for the group. She may make small sacrifices for other group members, but if she finds the group burdensome or unfulfilling, she may extricate herself. And, in talking about how she can share her innermost feelings with these strangers and feel supported by them, she is saying something that her grandmother would have found difficult to understand.

Thus, we must adjust our perspective of the small-group movement and ask why it is defining community the way it is. We must not expect more of it than it can provide. The movement may help us adapt to the emotional pressures of living in a diverse, individualistic society, but it cannot truly replace the traditional communities that we have lost. Instead, small groups enable us to pry ourselves loose from such moorings. We would perhaps find them constraining anyway, getting in the way of our career aspirations and our changing personal interests. Small groups make it possible for us to survive, even as market pressures, jobs, and disrupted personal relationships make greater demands on our lives. They help us adapt to these pressures, but, for most of us, do not fundamentally shield us or cause us to lead our lives in a different way. To their credit, they provide us with small, portable sources of interpersonal support. Their weakness lies in their inability to forge the more enduring bonds that many of us would like or to strongly resist the fragmenting forces in our society.

THE SEARCH FOR THE SACRED

My argument about small groups and spirituality is similar to the one I have just suggested about community. By their own accounts at least, members of small groups frequently joined because they were interested in deepening their spirituality, and many of them say this quest has been fulfilled. Their faith has become a more important part of their lives, and they have found others with whom they can pray and share their spiritual interests. I would go so far as to say that the small-group movement cannot be understood except in relation to the deep yearning for the sacred that characterizes much of the American public. To be sure, this generalization does not apply to some individuals and types of groups. But a great deal of the momentum for the movement as a whole comes from the fact that people are interested in spirituality, on the one hand, and from the availability of vast resources from religious organizations, on the other hand. Small groups have been championed by many religious leaders as a way of revitalizing their congregations. And there is evidence that small groups do encourage people to become more actively involved in their congregations. Yet the more important fact, in my view, is that small groups are also redefining how Americans think about the sacred.

We can imagine at the outset why this redefinition might be occurring if we remember that there is often a close connection between how people understand their relationships with each other and how they approach God or some other conception of the sacred. I do not mean, of course, that the one necessarily serves as an exact template for the other. But societies organized around the authority of kings and lords, for example, are more likely to employ figures of kingship and lordship in metaphoric ways when they try to speak about God than societies organized in different ways. Similarly, religious traditions in which an intimate, emotion-laden relationship with God is valued are quite likely to emphasize the importance of intimacy in human relationships as well. At present, therefore, it would not be surprising to find that small groups oriented toward the intentional cultivation of caring relationships might also be especially interested in helping individuals cultivate such relationships with the divine as well.

It is, however, the intentionality of these relationships that is worth considering, not whether they emphasize caring. In many cultures it would be unthinkable to engage in activities with the explicit purpose of discovering the sacred. Divine providence, grace, and the inscrutability of God would be emphasized instead. God would seek out the individual, like Yahweh capturing Moses's attention through the burning bush. But it would be less likely for the individual to set out to find God—and certainly unthinkable that deep spirituality could be found by following a set of prespecified guidelines or steps. Such quests are, of course, quite common in American culture, and they have been throughout our nation's history. Prayer and the reading of sacred texts, for example, are prescribed ways of drawing closer to God. Nevertheless, the small-group movement elevates the degree to which such activities are planned, calculated, and coordinated.

Most small groups that have anything to do with spirituality do not simply let the sacred emerge as a byproduct of their time together. Instead, they prescribe activities for growing closer to the sacred. Books are studied and prayers are recited, sometimes in unison, and generally according to a formula indicating what is appropriate to think about and to say. Study guides spell out a sequence of steps that people can follow in order to find God or to know the will of God. The notion of discipline becomes more important because seekers are supposed to exercise control over their time, thoughts, and, increasingly, even their feelings as they embark on the quest for God. Being disciplined in one's spiritual life is regarded as a good thing, just as being disciplined about one's health habits, weight, physical exercise, mental health, and use of time is a good thing. The sacred comes to be associated with the process or activities by which it is pursued. The object after which one seeks may remain somewhat mysterious or intangible, but group members know clearly that they are on the right track because they are following a rational set of procedures.

The sacred is also being redefined by the small-group movement's emphasis on achieving practical results for everyday living. The image of a spiritual journey might suggest that seekers are on their way to the promised land—perhaps the heavenly realm that believers enter after death or perhaps a millennial kingdom that will eventually replace the present world. The dominant impulse in the small-group movement, however, is to emphasize the joys of the journey itself. Seekers often have no idea where they are headed, only that they are on the road. Thus, the important principle is to cope with life as fully as possible from day to day. The signs of spiritual growth follow naturally from this logic. The signs of the sacred are all pragmatic. They reveal themselves in feelings of peace, happiness, and a good self-image. The sacred, above all, *works*. It helps people get along better on the job, behave better with their families, and feel better about themselves.

Coping more effectively with everyday life is, of course, a desirable aim. But the contemporary redefinition of spirituality falls short on two counts. All too often it serves more to comfort people—allowing them to feel better about things as they are and helping them to be happy—than to challenge them to move significantly beyond their present situation, especially if such movement involves definite sacrifices or discomforts. Rather than encouraging people to seek higher goals, it can inoculate them against taking the risks that may be necessary for true growth. A small group helps its members adapt to the demands of everyday life rather than providing a sense of transcendence that casts a new perspective on everyday life. It also makes the individual the measure of all things. At one time, theologians argued that the chief purpose of humankind was to glorify God. Now it would seem that the logic has been reversed: the chief purpose of God is to glorify humankind. Spirituality no longer is true or good because it meets absolute standards of truth or goodness but because it helps us get along. We are the judge of its worth. If it helps us find a vacant parking space, we know that our spirituality is on the right track. If it leads us into the wilderness, calling on us to face dangers we would rather not deal with, then it is a form of spirituality we are unlikely to choose. To be sure, there are significant exceptions to these patterns. Small groups sometimes challenge their members to undertake painful processes of spiritual growth. But the more common pattern seems to be a kind of faith that focuses heavily on feelings and on getting along rather than encouraging worshipful obedience to or reverence toward a transcendent God.

Pragmatism of this kind is so common in American culture that it may seem good to consider the sacred in this way. But pragmatism is also a way of escaping the difficulties of defining absolute truth in an age of relativism. A small group may combine a dozen people from a dozen different religious backgrounds. They very likely will be unable to agree on specific religious doctrines or theological arguments. What they can agree on is that God helped them through the day. And yet, being helped may be so personal and subjective that nobody could prove or disprove whether it happened or not. Rather than struggling hard to determine what truth may be or trying to learn how it has been understood throughout the centuries, therefore, they simply take a live-and-let-live attitude toward each others' opinions.

The most general way in which small groups are redefining the sacred, therefore, is by replacing explicit creeds and doctrines with *implicit* norms devised by the group. Throughout the centuries, religious bodies have devoted much of their energy to hammering out doctrinal statements. They have sent representatives to church councils to debate the wording of creeds, and they have formed organizational structures around varying concepts of ecclesiastical authority. Making things explicit incurred huge costs, to be sure, including much sectarian strife and even religious wars, but believers assumed that it was important to know specifically what was right and what was wrong. The small-group movement is changing all of that. Group members still have a sense of the importance of knowing what is right or wrong, but their groups seldom study religious history or formal theological statements. Rather, they discuss small portions of religious texts with an eye toward discovering how these texts apply to their personal lives. Personal testimonies carry enormous weight in such discussions, but these stories are also subject to group norms. These norms include implicit assumptions about whether one can be instructed directly by God, whether it is important to read the Bible to receive wisdom, what the role of intuition is, and how prayer should be understood.

Implicit norms vary widely from one group to the next. What makes them so powerful in all cases, however, is the fact that they remain implicit. Because they are unacknowledged, these norms cannot be directly challenged. Someone who feels uncomfortable for having violated a group norm is likely to leave and join a different group. Otherwise people simply do what seems comfortable within the context of their own group. The process can be like the blind leading the blind. In other cases, old-timers define what is appropriate for people to believe and say. And in a few cases, strong leaders are able to exercise virtually unlimited control over their groups.

In a very real sense, then, the group can become a manifestation of the sacred. Its members feel power within the group. They feel closer to God when they are gathered than when they are apart. They are sure the deity approves of the way they meet. They may be less sure that people can find God apart from the group. The group then encourages people to think about spirituality, but in the process it channels their thinking so that only some ideas about the sacred are acceptable. Spirituality becomes a matter of sincere seeking and of helping each other, all the while respecting whatever idiosyncratic notions of the sacred one's peers may develop. Moreover, God becomes a relational deity who somehow needs to be triune in order to have heavenly companionship.

If such a redefinition of the sacred is taking place as a result of the small-group movement, it is surely important to understand how people in small groups are thinking about spirituality and how they are pursuing it. The sacred is, of course, central to religious organizations. Insofar as many religious organizations are actively promoting small groups in hopes of drawing people into greater religious involvement, these organizations may find themselves paying an unexpected cost. The groups they are sponsoring may be promoting a new, pragmatic definition of the sacred even as they encourage people to become more interested in their spiritual development. There may be wider consequences, too. One of the hopes that many religious leaders attach to the rediscovery of the sacred is that other values will be strengthened as well—a commitment to family, for example, or a greater desire for peace and justice. Some of these values may, indeed, be reinforced by the small-group movement. Yet the means of attaining them may be the most important single message being reinforced. Indeed, the great variety of small groups competing with one another may result in so many different values being nurtured that the overall effect is difficult to discern. But if all groups are encouraging their members to believe that they can only find God by discussing the sacred with others, that this process must involve the application of rational techniques, such as studying the Bible one verse at a time or expanding the group by one new member every six months, and that practical personal consequences are the litmus test of true spiritual development, then these implicit norms may be the big winners overall.

SOCIETY IN TRANSITION

America at the end of the twentieth century is fundamentally a society in transition. We are acutely aware that the technological developments of the past century have had profound effects on the way we live. We know we cannot retreat to the life of small towns, farms, and national isolation. It is far from clear what kind of society we will have in the next century. One thing is clear, however: the search for community and for the sacred will continue to characterize the American people. These quests will animate our values and the ways in which we relate to our friends and neighbors. But values and personal relationships will have to be selected in an increasingly uncertain world. There will be a greater array of options from which to choose and fewer authoritative grounds on which to make these decisions. Discretion will have to be exercised in an increasing number of situations, and it will be necessary for decisions to be revocable, so that different courses of action can be pursued. Sensing this fact, individuals will invest less of their energy in large-scale institutions and expect less of these institutions. Such entities will still be called upon to govern and to deal with broad issues affecting the entire society, such as providing for national security or protecting the environment through legislation. They will, however, be considered restrictive if they try to impinge too closely on the day-to-day activities of the individual. For these activities, we will look increasingly to social units of more modest proportions, such as informal networks of colleagues in the work place, classes that meet for a few months to transmit new skills, and task groups designed to solve short-term problems. The small-group movement will be an important part of these developments.

It should be evident by now that this book does not simply describe the small-group movement; it also views broader changes in American culture through the lens of the movement. My argument about cultural change is that the small-group movement has been successful because it fits so well with trends already at work in American society, and that its success will, in turn, further these trends. This argument runs against the grain of standard ways of thinking about the movement. The common view is that small groups are successful because they fill needs otherwise unmet in contemporary society; these needs include emotional support, friendship, and ways to develop spiritually. By filling such needs, the small-group movement is seen to be stemming the tide. I do not deny that many individuals who participate in small groups feel that their groups are meeting such needs. The data show that group members do feel this way. But the mistake is to infer then that small groups are fundamentally at odds with larger societal trends and are working mainly to counter them. It makes more sense, in my view, to see that small groups are helping people adapt to these trends.

I do not flesh out this argument in detail here because it receives careful attention in all of the chapters that follow. To illustrate the main point, however, let us consider the simple fact that small groups are enormously diverse. Indeed, they are diverse in at least three important ways. There is wide variation among different types of groups. For example, Bible studies, twelve-step groups, and book discussion groups may all provide caring and support and yet do so for people with very different interests. Within particular types, there is also wide variety: for example, Bible studies for teenagers, for young single people, for married couples with children, and for retired people. And then, within most particular groups, there is likely to be a highly varied membership: perhaps people of different ages, from different religious backgrounds, and with different political views. Later, we consider evidence showing the range and limits of this variety more precisely. But for now the question is: So what? What do we make of this fact?

The variety evident among small groups is, in my view, indicative of how the movement has adapted to a larger development in American society. I have already reviewed some of the ways in which traditional forms of community are changing. Geographic mobility uproots families from neighborhoods and kin. Occupational mobility exposes them to values and interests different from those of their parents. Intermarriage transcends ethnic and religious lines. If spirituality is one of the driving forces behind small groups, we might ask why churches and synagogues are unable to supply the vehicles in which to pursue spirituality. But the strength of churches and synagogues has depended on the stability of these traditional forms of community. People were Presbyterians or Catholics or Jews because their parents were and because previous generations had emigrated from certain countries and settled near particular ethnic groups. Once the distinctive reasons for being Presbyterian or Catholic or Jewish erode, then churches and synagogues have no special hold over the quest for the sacred. That is, people may still pursue spirituality by attending religious services (we know that they do), but the resources and appeals of organizations sponsoring these services may diminish.

But smaller groups have an enormous advantage in adapting to a more fluid social environment. They require virtually no resources, other than the time their members devote to them each week, so they can start with relative ease and disband just as easily. The hidden resources that help them grow, such as trained leadership, meeting space, or study guides, moreover, can readily be obtained from churches and synagogues, at least if most of these groups purport to foster the same kind of spirituality taught in the churches and synagogues and, therefore, encourage people to return to these organizations. In addition, there are likely to be pockets of like-minded people who can populate a group that requires only twenty members to operate, whereas the same might not be true if two hundred members were required. Besides, someone interested in slightly different issues can simply start another group. In short, small, relatively fluid, low-budget groups have an adaptive advantage in a heterogeneous environment such as the contemporary United States. The success of the movement is thus partly attributable to this adaptive advantage, not simply to whether individual members' needs are being met.

To end the discussion at this point would be to suggest that small groups are driven by larger social forces over which they have little control. The truth of the matter is more complex. Individual group leaders play a very active role in identifying a particular niche in which a new group can form, and the group plays an active role in meeting the needs of those who attend. Otherwise, the group is likely to disband. On a larger scale, however, the environment does exercise a strong influence over the aggregate behavior of many groups. Still, at this level, it is also appropriate to say that the small-group movement reinforces cultural developments, rather than simply adapting to them. We can see how this may be the case by taking our considerations of diversity a step further.

The availability of hundreds of thousands of small, highly diverse groups permits American society to loosen itself from its traditional moorings and become even more mobile and fluid. People can move to new communities more easily because they know they can join support groups there; they can shift their religious affiliation to a new denomination for the same reason; or they can enter a new line of work, withstand the trauma of leaving a spouse, or become interested in a new political cause. This point perhaps can be seen more clearly by imagining a hypothetical situation in which no such groups existed. Under such conditions, individuals might become so distraught at the prospect of living their lives in lonely isolation that they would cling more tightly to their families of origin or to their local neighborhoods. Were that not possible, they might increasingly turn to government agencies to protect their neighborhoods or to provide them with mental health programs or to guide economic development in a way that would encourage corporations to take better care of their employees. Indeed, Germany or Japan might provide the models for such a society. The fact that small groups exist on a large scale, therefore, means that American society can move ahead without adopting some of these alternative patterns.

In short, the small-group movement has taken familiar organizational forms and adapted them to new social conditions. Voluntary associations have long been a favored way of meeting needs in the United States rather than depending on government programs or trying to create traditions that were not strong here in the first place. Small groups carry on the voluntaristic emphasis. They also adapt it to meet new challenges, such as helping individuals cope with addictions, helping them find spirituality when large religious organizations fail to do so, or rebuilding their personal identities after families and other primary groups have become inadequate to the task. Many small groups help to maintain the social equilibrium. They extend trends that are already under way, but do not set forth visions of a better world that would radically transform the way things are. And in extending these trends, small groups may also contribute to some of the problems inherent in such developments. Rather than putting the brakes on marital dissolution, for example, they may make it easier for spouses to separate and remarry, or they may even make it possible for employers to put greater pressures on working women because there will be support groups to pick up the pieces.

When I say that the small-group movement is effecting a quiet revolution in American society, therefore, I mean that it is adding fuel to the fires of cultural change that have already been lit. The small-group movement may be providing community for people who feel the loss of personal ties and it may be nurturing spirituality in an otherwise secular context. But it is not succeeding simply by filling these gaps. It is succeeding less because it is bucking the system than because it is going with the flow. It does not offer a form of community that can be gained only at great social or personal cost. Instead, it provides a kind of social interaction that busy, rootless people can grasp without making significant adjustments in their lifestyles. It allows bonding to remain temporary. It also provides a form of spirituality that is thoroughly adaptable to the complex, pluralistic world in which we live. We need not cling to traditional ethnic communities or religious traditions. Indeed, it is no longer essential even to know very much about the claims of these traditions. Rather, we can find spirituality that is suitably rational or sufficiently well-thought-out to seem legitimate in a fairly well-educated society and yet have no fear that this spirituality will do much to upset our daily routines.

If small groups are the glue holding together American society (as some argue), they are then a social solvent as well. They provide a way out of the traditional attachments that formerly may have bound people tightly to their communities. Former Mennonites who have grown weary of church customs and moved to urban areas can leave the fold more comfortably, not having to become pure secularists or isolated individualists, by joining a prayer fellowship in their neighborhood. Adult children who have fled the dysfunctional families of their youth can get along without kin networks by spending time each week attending a twelve-step group. The solvent helps people slip away from previous forms of social organization. At the same time, it facilitates the enormous adjustments required. Group members are, indeed, making a journey, quite literally into the unknown. It helps to share the journey. And it helps to focus on the process itself. This is why technique, talk, storytelling, and group support become so important.

None of these observations should be construed to suggest that the small-group movement is in any way failing its members. Social institutions seldom do much more than help populations adjust to a changing environment. They solve day-to-day problems and work with envisioned realities, but do not change reality as fundamentally as visionary leaders would like to think. The individual who finds God is no less blessed; the person who recovers from an addiction is no less important. But from a broader perspective, the same forces that have created these needs are at work in shaping the groups that help respond to them.

A CRITICAL JUNCTURE

Having summarized some of the broader arguments of the book, let me hasten to say that I have written it primarily for the interested reader who cares to understand better what is happening in American society at the end of the twentieth century—whether that reader is currently involved in a small group, a leader, thinking about joining one, concerned about small groups' possible ill-effects, or simply curious about them. The small-group movement is at least as important to understand as the political system or the economy. Those who are involved in small groups often claim that these groups have influenced how they think about political and economic issues; for example, raising their interest in questions of peace and social justice, or, in the case of conservative religious groups, generating ire about abortion and gay rights. These members also know that there is far more to group life than these issues. The people with whom they relate form a primary means of identity. The fact that members are able to tell stories about their lives makes these groups far more significant to participants than the fact that they are a Republican or a Democrat. In the telling of personal stories, members gradually become a different people, individuals whose identities depend in subtle ways on the feedback given by other members. Those who are not in groups can well imagine the importance of such processes. Many of these people have been in groups in the past, have participated in informal networks that functioned in the same ways, or at least have experienced families, classes, and work groups that served as primary sources of identification.

In my view, the small-group movement is now at a critical juncture in its development. To date, despite the various criticisms I have already raised, its social effects have been largely beneficial. The movement has provided caring and support for millions of Americans who were suffering from addictions, personal crises, loneliness, and self-doubt and has helped them rebuild their lives. It has been a source of vitality for many religious organizations by providing reasons for people to join these organizations and to start thinking about their spiritual journeys. The movement has skillfully deployed its resources to reach virtually all segments of the population. It probably has exacerbated some of the problems associated with individualism in American society at the same time that it has tried to encourage people to care more deeply for others. To be sure, there are some worrisome signs concerning the ways in which it is redefining community and spirituality, but the movement's failings reflect more on broader trends in our society than on the movement itself. In responding to social and personal needs, the movement has been able to grow enormously. Consequently, it is now poised to exercise even greater influence on American society in the next decade than it has in the past two decades. The resources are there: models have been developed, leaders have been trained, national networks have been established, and millions of satisfied participants are ready to enlist their friends and neighbors. What it will do with these resources is thus an important question for its members and leaders to consider.

The movement stands at an important crossroads in its history, a turning point requiring it to choose which of two directions it will go. It can continue on its present course. Or it can attempt to move to a higher level of interpersonal and spiritual quality. Given its success over the past two decades, it can easily maintain the same course. It can draw millions of participants by making them feel good about themselves and by encouraging them to develop a domesticated, pragmatic form of spirituality. By helping people feel comfortable, it can perhaps even expand its numbers. The other option will require it to focus less on numerical success and more on the quality of its offerings. Besides comforting its members, the movement may find itself challenging them at deeper levels—to make more serious commitments to others who are in need, to serve the wider community, and to stand in worshipful, obedient awe of the sacred itself.

Many of the movement's leaders, both locally and nationally, recognize that this crossroads has been reached. One of the leaders we interviewed put it especially well: "What worked for us in the 1970s and 1980s isn't going to work in the 1990s and beyond. We have to evolve and be attentive to the social context." Some want to see an ever more diverse variety of support groups established. Some are hoping to harness the movement for political ends. Others are promoting it as a way to make big churches grow bigger. The movement's successes have made many converts. Religious organizations that once scorned the idea of small groups are now championing them as the wave of the future. But the movement has also generated opponents. Social observers, as I have indicated, worry that it may be contributing to a narcissistic obsession with the self rather than encouraging greater concern for others. Clergy sometimes express fear that small groups are turning people into conformists who simply follow the latest spiritual fads rather than being interested in the accumulated wisdom of religious traditions. Some members of the clergy fear that their own authority is being undermined by small groups. And, among proponents and opponents alike, there is often a sense that hard, evaluative questions must be asked. The movement is too powerful—and its potential too great—for these questions not to be addressed. Thus, the time is ripe to seek a better understanding of small groups. We will want to listen to what members themselves have to say, but first we must set the stage more carefully by tracing the roots from which the movement has arisen and by establishing more precisely how it is currently situated in the American population.

PART ONE

THE DIMENSIONS OF THE MOVEMENT

2

THE QUEST FOR COMMUNITY

Social and Cultural Contexts of the Small-Group Movement

From whence does the small-group movement originate? Why has it arisen at this particular moment in history? To answer these questions we must turn directly to the role of spirituality in American culture, to the quest for community, and to the complex interplay between the two. It is in this vortex that the small-group movement has emerged and acquired its distinctive appeal. The movement is a response both to the intense yearning for the sacred that characterizes the American people and to the breakdown of communities, neighborhoods, families, and other sources of personal support. As people try to rediscover the sacred, they are led to ask questions about community. And as they seek community, they are led to ask questions about the sacred. Both quests are propelling their interest in small, intimate groups. The current strength of the movement is thus a function of the fact that it arises from two prevailing characteristics of American society. The fragmented lives that many of us lead provide an *incentive* to seek community in support groups. But the religious traditions that are so much a part of American culture *legitimate* this quest by telling us that community is important, and, indeed, by leading us to believe that community is also the way to find spirituality and transcendence. A brief examination of these two features of our society will help us understand the forces currently propelling the small-group movement.

YEARNING FOR THE SPIRITUAL

The contemporary quest for the sacred is not new. Americans always have been intense seekers of spirituality. The first settlers prayed for divine guidance and beseeched God to bless their journey to the New World. Subsequent generations found spirituality to be as essential to their lives as the bread they ate. They read the Bible, prayed, and sought God's blessings as they planted their crops, bore their children, experienced the joy of living, and faced illness and death.[1] They pursued the sacred in their private—and vastly differing—ways, for the spiritual then, as now, was a matter of individual conscience.

But this personal faith was only part of the story: Americans have always expressed their religious convictions in communities as well as individually. The Puritans may have sought spirituality deep within their own souls, but they were a communal people who met regularly in corporate acts of worship. The pioneers who journeyed westward were known for their rugged individualism, yet they planted churches everywhere they went. As the nation grew, popular piety grew apace, fostered by Methodist class meetings and Baptist Bible studies.[2] People may have been converted individually in the revival meetings that swept through farming areas and cities alike, but they started fellowship groups, attended ladies' aid societies, and swelled the ranks of Sunday school classes.[3]

Spirituality went hand in hand with group life for historic, theological, and practical reasons. The historic reason was that personal piety had been expressed in this way for as long as anyone could remember. Even the earliest Christians met in groups, forming churches in their homes and subjecting their interests in spirituality to the authority of their fellow believers.[4] The theological reason was that Christianity encouraged believers to come together and form bonds of love and fellowship like those taught by their Lord. The practical reason was that believers found they needed one another for support. Without the affirmation of others, their faith was weakened.

We are still a deeply spiritual people. Despite all the material progress that was supposed to take our minds off God, and despite all the scientific advancement that was going to undermine our faith that God even existed, most Americans continue to express a need in one way or another for spirituality in their lives. Some people realize this need when they struggle to understand themselves and feel drawn to the spiritual insights of poets and religious writers. Many people see it when they are caught up in anxiety and find comfort in uttering a prayer. Others may be drawn to the spiritual by the beauty of nature or by the cry of a newborn baby.

Opinion surveys show just how widespread the search for spirituality is in our society. In a recent study, 79 percent of the American public said they think about their relation to God "a lot" or "a fair amount" of the time. In the same study, 82 percent gave the same answers to questions about how much they think about the basic meaning and value of their life. And 68 percent said they think this much about developing their faith. In this study, as in other studies, only about one person in twenty seemed to consider the sacred unimportant.[5]

Other evidence demonstrates that the search for spirituality is more than a casual response to the latest public opinion pollster. As a nation, we purchase more Bibles per capita than in any other industrialized society. The market for religious and devotional books is a billion-dollar-a-year industry. So is religious television. Virtually everyone claims to believe in God, and the vast majority pray to this God regularly.[6] Philosophers who once were content to write that life had no inherent meaning are now devoting increasing attention to questions about the meaning and purpose of human existence. Hundreds of thousands of college students flock each year to courses in religious studies departments.[7] Meditation appears to be at an all-time high. Even political figures and business leaders claim to seek divine guidance in making important decisions.

THE LOSS OF COMMUNITY?

This interest in spirituality is, in many ways, like that of our ancestors. But the deep ties with community that sustained people in their faith and in their lives over the centuries, argue many social observers, may now be on the verge of collapse.[8] The villages and farming communities where most people lived at the start of the twentieth century have become virtually extinct. A century ago, nearly three-quarters of the American population lived in small towns and in rural areas. Today, fewer than one-quarter reside in these locales. Nationally, the vast majority of people live in metropolitan areas. If the South is excluded, these areas now include more than 80 percent of the population. The composition of urban areas has also changed dramatically over the past century. At one time, urban neighborhoods—reinforced by a com-

mon ethnic heritage, language, customs, local shops, and schools—
provided community, but these, too, mostly have been lost. People
now live anonymous lives in suburban housing developments or in
high-rise apartment buildings. Instead of feeling a common bond with
our neighbors, we fear them.[9]

To be sure, the situation has not become as bad as some gloomy
forecasts predicted. In the 1950s, when television first became popular,
many commentators worried that Americans would simply retreat into
their living rooms, watch sitcoms with abandon, and never come out
again. Harvard sociologist David Riesman, in his widely read book *The
Lonely Crowd*, envisioned a society in which people were thrown
together in shallow ways, but had neither the courage to be themselves nor the desire to share intimately with anyone else.[10] Others predicted the rise of widespread mental illness because people would be
isolated and have no friends. Most of these forecasts have failed to
come true. People do not sit at home watching television all the time
(although they spend an enormous amount of time doing so). They
still go to work, make sure their children go to school, and find time
on weekends to attend ball games and go shopping. People have not
become nameless faces in the crowd. Instincts to blend into the herd
notwithstanding, people still jealously guard their individuality, and
often do so by cherishing their family heritage, their ethnic identity,
and their national origins.[11] Instead of being entirely isolated, most
people still have close friends, and many of these friends live in the
same community.[12]

But genuine community entails more than simply having friends
with the same zip code. We may know some of our neighbors well
enough to wave as they whiz by on their way to work in the morning.
We may stop to chat once in awhile or take them pumpkin bread at
Christmas as a neighborly gesture. We may even consider them our
friends. It is more doubtful that we have ever discussed our most cherished values with these neighbors. It is equally doubtful that these
neighbors can help us recover from addictions or dysfunctional family
backgrounds or that they can help mentor us when we are uncertain
about the core of our identity. The same may be true of the people we
know at church. Sitting together in the pews on Sunday morning, we
may feel that there is much in common among us. But do we know
that? Skeptics, at least, ask: Have we ever opened up to these people
by admitting our fears, discussing our deepest anxieties, or sharing our
most basic dreams and aspirations?

In other ways, personal experience in contemporary society often leads us to see evidence all around us of the breakdown of community. The smile and "hello" that used to greet us at the grocery store have been replaced by the pallid face of an automaton who busily passes our items across a bar-code scanner. Work was once a place where people did the same things, knew the same skills, and shared a common destiny. Now the boss may be miles away, linked to us by satellite and computer networks, and our coworkers may have become our most bitter competitors. If we are lucky, we may have some close friends at work—after all, we spend an increasing share of our waking hours in the workplace. But we also know that the hectic pace of everyday life makes it harder to keep up with our friends, and we know that the large-scale institutions that make up our society do not make the quest for community any easier. Faced with impersonality, bureaucratic red tape, and incessant competition, we may be sorely tempted to launch a full-scale retreat from public life.

Social observers worry that we may be making these conditions worse, rather than better, by retreating more and more into our private lives. Individualism, they remind us, once meant being responsible for ourselves *and* our neighbors. But we have replaced this traditional concept with a more radical individualism that looks out for number one at the expense of everyone else.[13] In the 1970s this radical individualism came to be associated with the Me Generation, as people struggled to find themselves and turned inward. This period was followed by the Decade of Greed: failing to find anything deep within themselves, people seemed to give up and merely opted for the chance to collect as many toys for themselves as they could before dying.

Most people, however, seem to believe at some level that this self-centered individualism is no way to live. They may not have the security of a tight-knit neighborhood, but they want it. They may not enjoy the comfort of a warm family, but they wish they could. They value their individual freedom, but go through life feeling lonely. They desire intimacy and wonder how to find it. They cling to the conviction that they have close friends who care about them, but they frequently feel distant from these friends. They worry what would happen if they were truly in need.[14] Wanting community, and not being able to find it, they turn to other solutions, some of which become their worst enemies.

In the case of Betty, the young woman at the Alcoholics Anonymous group mentioned in the last chapter, the intense loneliness in her first year away from home at college led her to drink. For a time she was able to tell herself that she would never be lonely again. The bottle would always be her friend. Others tell themselves the same thing about their work. As long as they can stay head-over-heels in love with their projects, they will never need anyone else.

Religious leaders, sensing the dysfunctional behavior and pain that come when people lack the care and support they need, increasingly are pointing out how desperately the American public needs to rediscover community. As the rector of a church populated mostly by busy suburban professionals lamented recently, "What community we used to enjoy has slowly been taken away as people are off commuting to work in another city, and the children are all in different school districts, and the whole family is following a different schedule." Even the church, he felt, was being undermined by these centrifugal forces. "Before, you already knew people from your neighborhood, and therefore you would know them in church. But now we have to reinvent ways to get [community] back."

Rebuilding community, then, is the challenge, at least according to many religious leaders and social observers alike. For each of us, as individuals, can we find the caring and supportive communities we so deeply desire, and can these communities nurture us on our spiritual journeys in the ways they have done in the past? Or must people of our time go the distance alone, facing the ultimate questions of their existence in the lonely solitude of their hearts? And for us, as community and religious leaders or simply as responsible citizens, can we reinvent ways to find community? Or must we see our society driven ever more by the fragmenting forces of the marketplace, the mass media, and the impersonal demands of bureaucratic organizations? Certainly, this yearning for community is one of the significant forces behind the recent rise of the small-group movement.

THE TURN INWARD

The lack of community may be serious in its own right, but it is even more serious when we consider how closely spirituality has always been linked to community. Indeed, many observers wonder if spirituality can survive the challenges of our society if it is not connected again in some meaningful way with the power and support of caring communities. Spirituality, they fear, will retreat so far inside the individual that it may never come out again. And if it does not, is it really spirituality?

Even to suggest this possibility is likely to arouse some disagreement. Isn't spirituality, after all, fundamentally a matter of the heart? Mustn't it be the individual who seeks the sacred, explores the mysteries of life, and comes up with answers that are uniquely and individually satisfactory? How genuine can a conviction be if it doesn't touch the inner being of the individual?

We can answer all these questions in a way that upholds the value of the individual and of a deep inner spirituality. And yet we can still ask whether spirituality is becoming such a private affair in our time that it loses much of its power. We can certainly question a spirituality that fails to result in any love of neighbor. We can also ask how well a purely inward spirituality may function for the individual as a person. Doesn't that person still need encouragement to engage in this inner quest? Aren't there times when people run into dead ends in their search for spirituality and need to talk about it with others? Isn't the connection between spirituality and basic human needs likely to be closer when intimacy and caring are part of a person's experience? And isn't it likely that his or her spirituality will be enriched by the chance to express it in public or to see it acted out and reaffirmed by trusted loved ones?

Certainly it is unnecessary to look far to find strong statements about the inherent connections between a commitment to healthy, caring communities and spirituality. Philosopher Robert Fuller, reviewing the recent literature in a number of academic disciplines, concludes: "Wholeness or fulfillment is . . . necessarily a collective rather than a personal issue. In the complex web of life, individuality is important, but never final."[15] In a similar vein, Gordon Kaufman asserts, "Life itself has a structure of interdependence, and unless human living and thinking and working can become increasingly oriented accordingly, and we learn to subordinate our particular interests and desires as individuals and communities . . . to this wider loyalty to on-going life—both human and other—we shall certainly all perish."[16]

The possibility that spirituality is becoming a victim of the loss of community was suggested some years ago in Thomas Luckmann's book *The Invisible Religion.*[17] Luckmann argued that fundamental religious convictions and world views in modern societies are increasingly separated from our dominant institutions—namely, the political and economic institutions that govern so much of our lives. As a result, spirituality is becoming more a matter of personal choice and private belief. But, he asked, can these choices ever carry the weight once associated with the God of heaven whose existence was independent of ours? Don't we need to live in community with others in order to see that the hand of God is not simply a figment of our imaginations?[18]

In a more recent book, some anecdotal evidence of how much religious faith may have retreated into the inner life is provided by Robert N. Bellah and his coauthors in their widely read volume *Habits of the Heart*.[19] They interviewed a woman named Sheila who had invented her own religion and named it after herself (Sheilaism). This woman, they argued, represents only the latest of a long history of pietists in our society who have looked inside themselves to find evidence of the divine. What is different, they suggest, is that this woman's faith is contained entirely inside herself. It is not an inner light planted in her conscience by a transcendent God, but an inner strength that comes from knowing herself and resolving to be good. Faith of this kind, said Bellah and his coauthors, "involves a kind of radical individualism that tends to elevate the self to a cosmic principle."[20]

Certainly a person's faith must be personal, a matter of conviction, a belief that is part of that person's fundamental outlook on life. When we say that religious beliefs are personal and private, though, we may ignore the importance of their public dimension. Throughout history, men and women of faith have declared their convictions in public, taken a stand on what they believed to be right, and sometimes given their lives for those convictions. In our society, it has become much more common to believe that people should keep their religious convictions to themselves lest they offend someone by speaking out. Even among devout believers, a norm of polite civility that turns every absolute truth into a matter of personal opinion seems to prevail.[21]

It is also partially correct to say that personal spirituality does not depend on being involved in any religious organization. The prevalence of this view first became evident in a 1978 survey in which 78 percent of the American public agreed that "a person can be a good Christian or Jew if he or she doesn't attend church or synagogue." Ten years later, a follow-up study found that an equally high proportion (76 percent) still held this view.[22]

For the last few years of his life, my grandfather lived in a nursing home in a different town from the one where he had gone to church all his life. He was a man of deep faith, and this faith remained central to his life until his death, even though he was unable to be part of a religious community. He was living proof of the validity of the statement asked about in the poll. Some of the men who were held as hostages in the Middle East during the 1980s kept themselves going through the long days and nights of their captivity by cultivating their relationship with God. They were able to do so despite being thousands of miles away from the religious organizations with which they were formally affiliated. Our culture, however, has taken this partial truth and extended it. Millions of Americans claim to believe in God and say spirituality is important among their values, but they do not belong to any religious community and do not participate in the services of any religious organization. In the survey just cited, 80 percent of the public agreed that "an individual should arrive at his or her own religious beliefs independent of any churches or synagogues."

Many people in our society have turned inward to find God because they have become disillusioned with the clergy and the churches. People of faith have always recognized the dangers of pledging too much unthinking loyalty to religious authorities. The Protestant Reformation, for example, asserted explicitly that people should be their own priests rather than thinking that the clergy had more direct access to God than they did. It also criticized the established church for being badly out of step with the times, if not morally and spiritually corrupt. These attitudes have reappeared in new guise in our own culture in recent decades. At an earlier time, clergy were regarded with respect for having heard a special call from God and having devoted their lives to that calling, including gaining extensive knowledge of the scriptures and of theology. In our time, though, many clergy are uncertain of their calling, and their authority seems fairly ordinary compared with the vast knowledge commanded by other professionals, such as scientists and physicians.[23] The church has become but one among many ways in which people can pursue their spirituality. If they disagree with the church's position on issue X, they can merely stay home, watch a religious program on television, read an inspirational book, or meditate to their favorite devotional tape.

Observers of American religion also believe the turn inward has been encouraged by the pluralism and relativism so widely evident in our culture. With a thousand and one different denominations to choose from, it has been easy for many people to conclude that all churches must be alike. Just going to one that you like is the important criterion. But it is an easy step from there, once you become dissatisfied at that church, to say that it doesn't make much difference whether you attend at all. The important goal is to believe something firmly and to behave yourself when you are around other people whose views are different. As evidence, one survey found that more than half the American public (57 percent) agreed that "it doesn't matter what church a person attends—one church is as good as another."[24]

For all these reasons, the communal dimension of spirituality has suffered. Many people in our society are so withdrawn into themselves that they find it difficult to seek help from others when their convictions start to unravel. They may find it equally difficult to give support when other people seek answers. The result is a privatized faith that may leave the individual feeling alone and alienated. Even if such faith remains strong for the individual, it may prove difficult to transmit to one's children, and it may do little to address the wider ills that beset our society.

SMALL GROUPS

The small-group movement has emerged as a serious effort to combat the forces of fragmentation and anonymity in our society and to reunite spirituality with its roots in human community. The movement developed on a national scale in the 1960s as a result of a wide variety of local efforts that proved to have increasing value to those involved in them. Training or "T-groups," as they were called, emerged in business settings to give people experience in discussing personal and work-related problems with their peers. Encounter groups grew out of the more specialized group therapy sessions that began in the 1950s and then spread quickly, especially on college campuses and among young professionals who found that these groups offered ways to overcome their isolation in large urban settings.[25] Religious organizations soon realized that small groups could play a vital role in their programs. Retreat centers found that small groups were an effective way of encouraging spiritual renewal. Youth ministries adopted the small group as a favorite style of teaching and fellowship, and new religious movements among young people often followed suit. But it was in the established churches and synagogues that small groups became especially prominent.[26]

A Long History

In many respects, the use of small groups in religious settings has a long history. The ancient Israelites gave expression to their faith in family and tribal units that were always closely bonded as a people of God. During their sojourn in the wilderness, when they became too numerous to gather easily in small units, Moses and Aaron divided the Israelites into family groups approximately equal in size for administrative and religious purposes. Jesus formed the core of his ministry around a group of twelve men who spent much of their time together. The first Christians met in homes for mutual support and to affirm their common faith.[27]

Throughout the next millennium of church history, small groups provided the basis of most of the religious orders that were established. The seeds of Reformation in the sixteenth century often grew in small gatherings that met in private homes. When the first settlers came to America, they did so as self-styled "colonies," often consisting of relatively few members, and modeled their interaction on the close-knit cells of religious dissenters from which they had come in England and Scotland. Subsequent waves of immigrants often came as small groups as well, sometimes all related to one another or from the same village, and in many cases they settled in neighborhoods and in farming communities where they could share a common faith.

As the population grew and became more ethnically diverse and more geographically scattered, these tight-knit communities often diminished in importance, thus leaving large numbers of individuals without close bonds of religious support. But the denominations that grew most rapidly during the nineteenth century were ones that made effective use of small groups. Methodists, for example, employed the class meeting as a way of encouraging unity among small groups of believers. Baptists accomplished the same purpose through their widespread use of midweek prayer meetings. Later in the century, new organizations such as the Salvation Army and the Young Men's Christian Association found that small groups also served well as a means of incorporating immigrants into their ministries and spreading these missions to new populations in the cities.[28]

At the beginning of the twentieth century, most churches were still small enough that the need to divide their members into smaller groups often was not particularly acute. The typical Protestant church generally had no more than eighty to a hundred adult members: a single worship service brought everyone together, mingling could happen after the service, and if there were Sunday school classes for adults, a single gathering could easily accommodate those who wished to attend. Protestant church members often cultivated spirituality through weekly prayer meetings and in their homes, as well, by reading the Bible to their children and praying aloud at meals. Catholics also practiced many of the same forms of public piety. Neighborhoods, ethnic and family ties, attendance as children at parochial schools and catechism classes, and regular participation in the mass provided a strong communal basis for their faith.

Twentieth-Century Developments

As the twentieth century unfolded, religious participation among Protestants and Catholics increased both numerically and as a percentage of the larger population, so that many religious organizations grew substantially. While churches in rural areas might have had relatively small congregations, urban and suburban parishes grew to an average size of around three hundred by midcentury, with Catholic parishes often considerably larger than Protestant churches. Size alone forced religious leaders to think harder about how to orchestrate their programs for maximum effectiveness, and the rising competition among the churches in many communities enhanced their interest in cultivating such programs.

To this end, the Sunday school program often became the principal means of dividing congregants into smaller, more homogeneous units. Following the idea of age-grading that had been implemented in children's Sunday school programs before the Civil War, churches applied the same logic to adults. Young adults generally could be separated on the basis of a common interest in the activities of their children, middle-aged adults might need different social activities and have an interest in different kinds of lessons, and older adults sometimes wanted classes of their own. Increasingly, separate classes for women and men became popular, sometimes as an outgrowth of ladies' auxiliary and missionary societies that met during the week and sometimes as all-male gatherings of deacons, elders, or trustees.[29]

These age- and gender-based classes continued to be the primary small-group activities in churches through the 1950s and 1960s. Probably the most common format for these classes was the teacher–student model in which a single individual led the group, gave didactic instruction, and often followed one of the popular standardized "international" lesson plans that provided members with something to read beforehand and a short list of questions for discussion. Other than the adult classes, the most common group offerings in churches were the prayer meetings, ladies' missionary society meetings, youth organizations, and an occasional task-oriented gathering, such as choir practices or meetings of elders and deacons.

Distinctive Features

The small-group movement that emerged in the late 1960s and 1970s built on the precedents long established by these classes and other specialized meetings, but it also differed from these more traditional gatherings in significant ways:

- Small groups were initiated deliberately as additions to the more traditional classes and church meetings, often by clergy and lay leaders who were convinced that these traditional gatherings were not entirely effective in meeting their own needs or the needs of others in their congregations.
- As a supplement to the instructional, administrative, or task-oriented activities of the established classes and meetings (which were often retained, especially in the form of Bible lessons and prayer sessions), the new small groups were often consciously oriented toward the cultivation of community, support, and relationships; activities such as eating together, playing games, sharing problems, and having time for informal conversation were specifically encouraged.
- The new groups often drew explicitly on ideas from the 1960s about group dynamics and group process, and they paid special attention to mutual interaction rather than following the earlier didactic models. They often borrowed heavily from the emerging literature on expressiveness, thus taking as an end in itself the goal of giving members a chance to express themselves and discover new insights through group discussions. Medical and therapeutic models increasingly influenced the thinking of group leaders and members and encouraged them to believe that greater self-awareness, healing, and the realization of deeper life goals could be nurtured by talking about themselves. There was thus a new epistemology: knowledge was not something that already existed, needing to be transmitted to an audience of learners by someone in authority; it was something to be generated by the group itself though discussing the personal views of its individual members.

- The basis for forming specific groups generally expanded beyond gender and age-grading as well, often taking into account the centrifugal social forces affecting contemporary urban and suburban congregations. Thus groups were created on the basis of members' geographic location, lifestyle attributes (such as singles, young marrieds, and parents-without-partners groups), and more specialized concerns, such as racial integration, experimental worship, in-depth spiritual knowledge, or social action. Small groups thus became a way for established churches and synagogues to respond to the growing cultural diversity of the society. They also focused increasingly on specific personal needs, such as recovery from addictions.

Continuing Growth

During the 1980s, the small-group movement grew rapidly, especially as religious leaders began to recognize its potential as a way of revitalizing declining congregations and of achieving rapid growth in new congregations. The movement spread widely in other settings as well, particularly as therapists began to recommend group participation as a way in which individuals who could not afford high-priced fees for professional counseling or psychotherapy could at least help one another in small ways, and as alcoholism and other forms of drug addiction forced growing numbers of people to seek group support as a means of recovery.[30]

In the 1990s this growth has, if anything, accelerated. Increasing numbers of religious congregations are experimenting with small groups of ever-widening variety. Catholic parishes that were involved in the Renew movement have often turned to small groups as a way of maintaining some of their momentum. Jewish communities are experimenting with *havurot* and other small, informal, gatherings in homes.[31] Protestant pastors are encouraging small groups as a way of securing church growth. Therapy groups and various support groups modeled after the twelve steps of recovery developed by Alcoholics Anonymous appear to be increasingly popular. Many small, supportive groups have sprung up in the workplace and in volunteer organizations. Some of these groups gather simply to discuss issues of common interest; others meet primarily to accomplish specific tasks, but in the process give emotional and spiritual support as well. In addition, countless varieties of self-help groups have been formed to meet more specialized interests in the population. From job-seekers groups, to weight-control groups, to support groups for the dying and the bereaved, the small-group movement shows signs of enormous and continuing vitality.

THE EXTENT OF INVOLVEMENT

Many estimates of the scope of the small-group movement have been made, generally drawing on whatever means happened to be available: mailing lists, numbers of study guides distributed, telephone directories, leaders' impressions. But such estimates are notoriously unreliable. While there is a widespread impression that the small-group movement has grown, therefore, it has been difficult for anyone to say with certainty whether the movement was indeed pervasive or whether it was limited to a very small proportion of the total American population.

To find out how many people are actually involved, we commissioned a nationally representative survey of adults age 18 and over living in the continental United States (see Appendix A, Methodology). According to this survey, exactly 40 percent of the adult population of the United States claims to be involved in "a small group that meets regularly and provides caring and support for those who participate in it." This is an extraordinary figure. It does not include all the children and teenagers who are also in groups. It means that approximately 75 million adult Americans are meeting regularly for some kind of small-group interaction and support.

We discuss what kinds of groups these are and how they function in later chapters, but here we need to pause briefly to consider just how many groups this might be in order to appreciate fully the magnitude of this phenomenon in our society. Let us make two very conservative assumptions: (1) that every person who is involved in at least one group is involved in only one group (actually, 38 percent of those involved in at least one group are involved in two or three), and (2) that groups have 25 regular members on the average, even though this number is at the upper end of what most people mean by a small group.[32] With these assumptions, we can estimate the total number of small groups currently in the United States at approximately 3 million groups. Again, this figure does not include all the groups that children and teenagers attend.

This number is worth pondering for a moment. It suggests what a fundamental feature of our society these groups have become. We often think of the church as the most common of all voluntary associations in our society. But if church means an established local congregation with some kind of building, then there are only 300,000 of those in operation.[33] By comparison, small groups—many, of course, meet in churches—are far more numerous.

If small groups were distributed evenly throughout the United States, there would be one group for approximately every 80 people—men, women, and children. There would be one group of 25 adults for about every 60 adults in the population. Thus we can see how influential these groups might be, even for those not involved in them. Of that number, quite a few might be former members of groups, interested seekers who maybe attend some group once in awhile, or the spouses, girlfriends, boyfriends, or business associates of people in groups.

Without exaggerating their importance, we can also gain an initial sense of the impact these groups could have—and maybe already do have—on their host communities. In an average-to-small-sized town (such as the one in which this book is being written) with a population of 50,000 people, there would probably be at least 600 small groups operating at any given time. In a city of 2 million people, there would more than likely be at least 25,000 such groups. It is interesting to imagine, even from this information alone, the effort that goes into these groups and the great extent to which they may glue our society together.

WHO JOINS?

We might look at these figures another way, however. If only 40 percent of the population belongs to a small group, this figure leaves 60 percent who do not. Perhaps the group members are all from one corner of the society—having groups with each other—leaving vast segments of our world uninterested, alienated from such activities, and still living the anonymous lives of the proverbial isolated, apathetic couch potato. Or vast segments may simply feel no need for small groups. Perhaps, for example, the group participants are mostly middle-class women living in the South and Midwest who join such groups as part of their suburban way of life. Or perhaps they are mostly young people in big cities who join groups because they hope it will increase their chances of finding friends or a suitable mate.

The best way to see if small groups are mostly reaching a certain segment of the population and not others is by comparing the social characteristics of people who are involved in groups with those of people who are not involved. Table 2.1 presents this comparison. As the table shows, some segments of the population are more likely to be involved in small groups than others. Women, for example, are somewhat more likely to be involved than men. People in their fifties or older are the most likely to be involved; people younger than 35 are

Table 2.1

MEMBERSHIP IN SMALL GROUPS

Percentage of Each Category That Is Currently in a Small Group That Meets Regularly and Provides Caring and Support for Its Members

National	40
Women	44
Men	36
Age 18–34	35
Age 35–49	42
Age 50 and over	45
High school or less	37
Some college	43
College graduates	48
Income less than $20,000 a year	39
Income $20,000–$39,000 a year	42
Income $40,000 or more per year	43
White Anglo	40
Black	41
Hispanic	46
South	39
Midwest	39
Northeast	41
West	45
In large cities	41
In medium cities	42
In towns or rural area	40

least likely to be involved. The better educated are more likely than those with lower levels of education to be members. But all these differences, it should be observed, are relatively small. In no case is the proportion who are involved in groups lower than a third.

On the whole, the various segments of American society are remarkably similar in the extent to which people are members of small groups. Blacks, white Anglos, and Hispanics, for example, are all about equally likely to be in small groups, a significant fact given the many other ways in which racial and ethnic populations differ. The same is true for different regions of the country, people living in different-sized cities, and people in different income categories. Overall, this broad appeal means that the small-group movement is also quite diverse, reaching people of virtually all ages, socioeconomic groups, and geographical locations. No major demographic category seems to be excluded from this phenomenon.

Suspicion that small groups may be prevalent only among some peculiar segment of American society is also allayed by the fact that many of the 60 percent who are currently uninvolved were involved in the recent past. Of this 60 percent, to be exact, 39 percent at some time in their lives had been involved in a small group that met regularly and provided support or caring for those who participated in it. In addition to the 75 million Americans currently involved in small groups, then, as many as 40 million have been involved in the past. Of this 40 million, moreover, 88 percent say their involvement has been during their adulthood, a quarter have been involved in two small groups, and another quarter have been involved in three or more groups. A fifth of all these people—approximately 8 million—have been involved in a small group within the past three years. And two-thirds of that number were in their groups for a year or longer. These former group participants, it is worth noting, are also distributed widely across all the social, economic, and geographic categories of American society.

The importance of small groups in our society is also underscored by the fact that more people seem likely to be attracted to them in the future. Of those not presently involved in a group, a quarter say they would like to be involved in one. And of this number, more than half (54 percent) say it is very likely or fairly likely that they will join a small group within the next year. Almost as many (44 percent) say they have a specific group in mind that they would like to join.

How widespread, then, are small support groups? It would not be unreasonable, on the basis of these figures, to suggest that they involve one out of every two people: 40 percent of the American public who are currently involved, another 5 percent who have been involved within the past three years, and approximately 7 percent who are likely to become involved within the next year.[34]

THE LEVEL OF ACTIVITY

But numbers alone do not begin to capture the significance of the movement. Anyone familiar with organizations of any kind knows that many people may profess membership, but seldom show up for anything. Is this also true of small groups? Perhaps they only seem widespread, drawing more nominal interest than actual participation. There are several ways to examine this possibility. Let us consider some of the more jaundiced stereotypes of small groups that may come to mind as a context in which to understand the actual level of involvement.

One of these perceptions is that small groups are too ephemeral to be very important. What is a small group, after all, but a gathering of people that meets for a short span of time to discuss some issue, deal with a set of personal problems, or accomplish some task? Once it has served its purpose, it quickly sends its members their separate ways. If this image is correct, it means that 75 million people may be involved at a given moment, but the same people would not be active if they were contacted again in a few months.

Another criticism sometimes voiced about small groups is that when they do meet, they meet for such a short time (perhaps an hour at most) that people scarcely get settled before they pick up and leave again. This image resonates with people talking about how many meetings they have to attend. Clearly a meeting isn't likely to make a very significant impact on people's lives. Yet another impression of small groups is that they consist mainly of a few faithfuls, while a large number of hangers-on may be nominally affiliated with the group but inactive. If so, 75 million group members might quickly vanish into a core of a tenth that many. The same image suggests that many group members would admit that their involvement is fairly unimportant.

Some of the characteristics of small groups that can be gleaned from the thousand group members we surveyed are shown in table 2.2. It is worth spending a few moments looking at this table because it contains several surprises.

Table 2.2

THE NATURE OF INVOLVEMENT IN SMALL GROUPS

*Percentage of Current Group Members Who Gave
These Responses About Their Group*

How long the person has been involved	
Five years or more	48
Three or four years	16
One or two years	21
Less than one year	14
How long the group has been in existence	
Five years or more	76
Three or four years	5
One or two years	10
Less than one year	3
How often the group usually meets	
Weekly	57
Biweekly	11
Monthly	27
Other	4
How often the person usually attends	
Weekly	50
Biweekly	13
Monthly	27
Other	11
Length of an average meeting	
Two or more hours	41
One and a half hours	25
One hour	30
Less than one hour	3

First, consider how long people are typically involved in their groups. Half say they have been involved five years or longer. Only one person in seven has been in his or her group for less than a year. If groups were really as ephemeral as popular mythology sometimes suggests, this longevity of involvement would be impossible. But the table also shows that most groups have existed as groups even longer than their current members have been involved in them. Three-quarters of all group members say their group has been in existence for at least five years.

Second, consider the question of how long the average group meeting is? It is true that some groups meet for only an hour or less at a time. But only a third of group members say that this is true of their group. Another fourth say their group usually meets for about an hour and a half. The largest category—four people in ten—say their group usually meets for two hours or more.

Third, the question of attendance can also be answered. If groups seldom meet, then their members, of course, have no chance to participate. The majority of groups, though, meet at least once a week. Virtually all the rest meet at least once a month. Group members do admit that getting people to attend is sometimes a problem, but perhaps not as much of a problem as one would think. Two people in three say almost everyone in their group attends every time, while only a third say a lot of the members of their group do not attend. As for themselves, about half say they attend every week, while virtually everyone else attends at least once a month. In other words, attendance patterns pretty much reflect how often the group actually meets. Indeed, 78 percent of all group members attend as frequently as their group meets: 82 percent of those whose groups meet weekly attend that often, 73 percent of those whose groups meet biweekly attend biweekly, and 86 percent of those whose groups meet monthly attend that often.

On balance, these figures suggest that small groups command a very serious level of commitment from their members. Most members attend faithfully and often, the norm being several hours each week. They do so over extended periods of time in groups that somehow enjoy a great deal of stability. The subjective assessments people give also suggest a high level of commitment to their groups. Nearly three-quarters say their group is very important to them (30 percent say it is extremely important). Almost everyone else says the group is fairly important. Scarcely anyone admits it is not very important.

By comparison, this level of commitment is, of course, in no way equal to the time people dedicate to their jobs or to their families. It doesn't even stack up well against the amount of time most people spend watching television. As far as voluntary activities that take people out of their homes are concerned, it nevertheless represents a significant commitment. Certainly it would compare favorably with the amount of time most people spend at meetings of the various professional organizations or fraternal societies to which they might belong. It would compare favorably with the amount of time they spend voting and attending political rallies. Even church attendance, which elicits at least half-eyed wakefulness from some 80 million Americans for an hour each Sunday, does not outdistance the time people spend in small groups by very much.

SMALL GROUPS AND COMMUNITY

With this information in mind, we can now return to the question of community. This question will merit closer attention in a later chapter, but we can gain an initial sense of why small groups have become so important in our society by considering the movement's relationship to people's desire for community. In the survey, members of small groups were posed with some questions about such needs as having neighbors with whom one can interact freely and comfortably and being able to share one's deepest feelings with people (see table 2.3).

Virtually everyone who is currently in a small group has experienced these needs at one time or another. The figures range from 98 percent who say they have felt the need for friends who value the same things in life that they do and who have felt the need for people who can give them deep emotional support to 83 percent who say they have felt the need for people who are never critical of them. It is not surprising that so many people have experienced these needs. The fact that these needs are so widespread, though, is clearly one of the bases from which the current interest in small groups has sprung. It is, of course, not the only one. People who are not in small groups probably experience these needs as well. But the desire for intimacy, support, sharing, and other forms of community involvement is certainly an essential precondition of the small-group movement.

The table also shows how many group members say these needs have been fully met. Three tentative conclusions warrant consideration. First, it appears that many small group members are in some way meeting a significant number of their needs for community, either through their groups or in other ways. Two-thirds, for example, say their need for people in their lives who give them deep emotional support has been fully met, and about the same number say this about having friends they can count on when they are in a jam. At least half say they have fully met their needs for friends who value the same

Table 2.3

MEETING THE NEED FOR COMMUNITY

*Percentage of Group Members Who Have (A) Felt Each Need
and (B) Met Each Need Fully*

	A	B
Having neighbors with whom you can interact freely and comfortably	93	43
Being able to share deepest feelings with someone	94	57
Having friends who value the same things in life you do	98	58
Having people in your life who give you deep emotional support	98	66
Being in a group where you can discuss your most basic beliefs and values	90	50
Having friends you can always count on when you're in a jam	97	64
Having people in your life who are never critical of you	83	29
Being part of a group that helps you grow spiritually	90	53
Having cooperation rather than competition with people at work	85	31
Having people you can turn to when you feel depressed or lonely	96	62
Knowing more people in your community	95	32

things in life by having a group where they can discuss their basic beliefs, being in a group that helps them grow spiritually, and having people they can turn to when they are depressed or lonely. The role of groups in helping people meet these needs is suggested by the fact that active members are more likely than marginal members on nearly all these items to say their needs have been fully met. Second, certain needs seem to be fully met for a considerably larger number of people than other needs. Having neighbors with whom one can interact freely and comfortably, having cooperative coworkers, and knowing more people in one's community are needs that a majority of people seem to have trouble meeting, either in their groups or in other contexts. And third, large numbers of people in small groups are probably there because their needs for community are only partially met. This possibility is suggested by the fact that between a third and two-thirds of group members do not believe their needs for community have been fully met.

What do all these facts tell us about small groups and community? They suggest that nearly everyone in our society desperately wants community, but that most people have trouble finding it in all the ways they would like it to be present in their lives. Neighborhoods and the workplace provide opportunities for interaction, but for most people these arenas do not yield the sharing and caring they desire. Small groups are an alternative. They do not necessarily tie people in better with their neighbors and coworkers. These groups do, however, give other chances for people to become acquainted and to share their basic values. Enough of those who participate in small groups receive enough fulfillment there to keep going back. Quite a number keep going back, too, because their needs for community are still in the process of being met.

Another indication of the relationship between small groups and the quest for community comes from examining the relationships between group membership and having friends in one's community. If small groups are a way of fulfilling the quest for community, we would expect group members to be more likely to say they have friends in their immediate community than nonmembers. This is the case: of those currently involved in a small group, for example, 46 percent say they have more than five close friends in their present community, compared with only 33 percent of those who are not currently involved in a small group. We might also expect that having been in a small group in the past would continue to make some difference. It does: 39 percent of former small-group members have more than five friends in their community, compared with only 31 percent of those who have never been in a small group. Finally, we might also expect that among nonmembers there would be a relationship between having fewer friends and wanting to be in a group. Again, this is the case: among those who would like to be in a small group, only 30 percent have more than five friends in their community, compared with 35 percent of those who say they would not like to be in a group (apparently more of the latter feel they already have enough ties to their community). At present, we must regard these conclusions as tentative. We consider how small groups foster community and provide support in later chapters.

SMALL GROUPS AND SPIRITUALITY

Before going any further, we must now turn directly to the question that probably already has emerged in many readers' minds. Maybe what people were thinking about when they said they belonged to a small group was their Tuesday night bowling team, or their Wednesday lunch with fellow used-car dealers, or their Friday evening bridge club. Maybe there is very little connection between these kinds of groups and spirituality.

We consider this connection in detail in later chapters, but here it suffices to say that the majority of these groups, whatever their make-up or auspices, are perceived by their members as having contributed to their spiritual development. Specifically, 61 percent of all group members say their "faith or spirituality" has been influenced by being involved in their group. And more than half of these people (57 percent) say their faith has been "deepened a lot" by their involvement. These proportions are also higher among persons who say their group is very important to them: 73 percent say their faith has been influenced; of these, 63 percent say it has deepened a great deal.

Several other preliminary indications of the extent to which small groups and the quest for spirituality go together are worth considering as well. One is that among people who have been involved in any kind of small group in the past, 63 percent say they were in a group that focused on religious or spiritual matters. Another sign is that among current group members, 65 percent say their interest in spiritual matters has increased in the past five years; only 4 percent say it has decreased. And still another indication is that approximately half of all group members (46 percent) say "wanting to become more disciplined in my spiritual life" was a reason why they became involved. We also saw in table 2.3 that 53 percent of all group members say they have fully met their need to be in a group that helps them grow spiritually; another 35 percent say they have partially met this need; only 10 percent say they have never experienced it.

So, even if some of what we are tapping consists of nothing more than a bowling team or a bridge club, we are for the most part dealing with something that is of major significance to the spiritual lives of many Americans. Indeed, what else in our society might we think of that is influencing the spirituality of so many of those who participate in it?

Certainly it is their potential contribution to spiritual development—and, indeed, to the redefinition of spirituality—that makes small groups especially interesting. Were we just interested in how small groups work, we could read the vast literature that social psychologists have written on this topic. The groups we are interested in here are not ends in themselves. They are the settings in which millions of Americans are currently trying to find themselves and to discover what it means to be more fully human and more fully in tune with their own spirituality and with God.

We considered earlier the question of whether spirituality has become such a private matter in our society that its communal dimension needs to be rediscovered. We suggested that a number of characteristics of our culture have worked together to drive spirituality inward and to erode the authority of established religious institutions. We can now ask what the relationship of small groups is to these cultural trends. Do people involved in small groups regard spirituality as a private matter and do they have misgivings about large religious organizations? Is that why they are turning to small groups? Or is their involvement in small groups a countertrend, turning spirituality once again into a more communal enterprise?

These are complex questions and demand closer examination in a later chapter, but we can suggest their importance by considering briefly how small-group members nationally respond to some statements about the nature of spirituality and the role of churches. These responses are shown in table 2.4. Two patterns are particularly worthy of emphasis. First, small-group members are by no means devoid of privatized views of spirituality and critical views of the churches. A majority, for example, say their own religious beliefs are personal and private, agree that their spirituality does not depend on being involved in a religious organization, and assert that it makes no difference what you believe as long as you are a good person. Their views of the churches are mixed: only one in five believe all churches are alike, but two in five think that churches are badly out of date. Second, the responses of group members who say their group is very important in their lives differ systematically from those of members whose groups are less important. The former appear to be less privatized in their view of spirituality, somewhat less relativistic, and somewhat less critical of the churches. To this extent, small groups may be stemming the

Table 2.4

VIEWS OF SPIRITUALITY AND THE CHURCHES

*Percent of Group Members Who Mostly Agree with Each Statement
Among Those Saying the Importance of Their Group Is High or Low*

	High	Low
My religious beliefs are very personal and private	57	63
My spirituality does not depend on being involved in a religious organization	55	71
The clergy are generally no more spiritual than other people	46	17
A lot of churches are out of date	37	47
All churches are pretty much alike	19	24
It doesn't matter what you believe, as long as you are a good person	47	68

tide of privatization in American religion for at least some of their members. And yet, the differences are not great, and there are other ways in which small groups are influencing spirituality as well. While they draw people back to the churches, they also do so, as we shall see, by making spirituality more palatable. Their members are often faced with the dilemma of wanting a more solid, communal form of religious commitment and at the same time picking up the privatized, relativistic messages that infuse their groups from the wider culture. Indeed, this conflict is why the small-group movement is now at a critical juncture in its development.

In subsequent chapters we sort out the meaning of these responses by looking at people in different kinds of groups, by examining other attitudes and beliefs, and by listening to them talk about their faith in their own words. For now, the important point is that small groups are clearly a phenomenon in our society to be reckoned with if we want to understand better how spirituality is nurtured—an aim that millions of Americans share, whether they are in groups or not. The small-group movement is clearly linked to a long tradition of collective quests for the sacred. It is not at all unusual for Americans to band together as they pursue their interests in the sacred. That they are banding together is nevertheless important to realize, especially in view of the fact that so much emphasis has been placed on the ways in which faith is becoming more private. With the changes that have been taking place in traditional forms of community, it is also not surprising that new forms of banding together have had to be invented. Why these forms have become so widespread in our society is the question to which we must now turn.

3

EXPLORING THE OPTIONS

Varieties of Small Groups and
Their Constituencies

Donna, age 30, the mother of two small children, still lives in the white, two-story farm house in which she grew up. She even attends the same church her parents did—where her father was a deacon, and the pastor is the same one who baptized her. If anyone defies the stereotype of a mobile, anonymous, rootless suburbanite, she does. She has lived in the same small community all her life. This is where her friends are. Yet she is a vivid case of how much even people in stable communities have been undergoing change.

As a child she did all the usual things, like Girl Scouts and Sunday school, but in her teens she became very rebellious. Her adopted brother, seven years older, became a drug addict and took up so much of her parents' energy that she always felt starved for attention. She quit going to church; indeed, she dropped out of almost everything. Intelligent but never very motivated in school, she attended the local community college for a year and a half after high school. After her parents moved to another state and left the house to her, Donna suddenly found herself very much alone. For the next three years she worked her way up the ladder in various office assistant jobs at local companies. Between a close friend from high school and occasional phone calls to her parents, she kept herself secure and happy. Soon after she married, she quit her job and had her first baby.

Then, despite all the stability she had been used to, everything started to change. Her husband, a successful stockbroker, loved her dearly and provided a good income, but he was also a recovering alcoholic and she felt the need to protect him from friends who might get him drinking again. Motherhood was a completely new experience. She also found herself in constant conflict with her husband's family. They belonged to a different faith and were deeply upset when she started taking the baby to the church in which she had grown up. She felt they were increasingly mean to her and didn't know how to respond.

Through the church she heard about a "study and support" group for young mothers. The word support especially attracted her. She also hoped the group would "have some good answers for me on some of the problems I was having at the time." For the past four years she has attended the group faithfully every week for an hour and a half. Usually there are about ten women. They gather at a convenient hour each week in the fellowship hall of an old-line, white brick church several miles from her home. At each meeting they have coffee and danish pastries, stand around and talk informally for a while, have a brief time of prayer together, and then discuss a passage from the Bible or a chapter of some religious or inspirational book. The meeting does not last long, but it is one of the high points of the week for most of its members.

Donna has enjoyed the new insights about herself that she has gained from the Bible studies and book discussions, and she has gotten to know other women in the community she can use as a sounding board. They have been a constant source of advice, helping her to face the challenges in her life. What she has found most appealing of all is just their honesty. "I had kind of never seen anything like that before," she remarked. "At first I just sat there kind of quietly because I didn't know anybody; I just tried to absorb what was going on. And then it hit me: there is really a truthfulness and an honesty here that I'd like to share."

If Donna illustrates how the quest for community can lead from rebellion and isolation to warmth and support, at least for a couple of hours a week, John's journey took an entirely different path. Husband, father of three, and a doctor who practices medicine at a large suburban hospital on the edge of one of the nation's largest cities, John could be the stereotypical busy professional who has no time for anything but his work and his family. But he isn't. He could also be the sort of person who joined a supportive group in order to hold the anonymity of suburban life at bay. That image comes closer, but doesn't quite fit either.

John comes from a line of people who date their distinctive interest in spirituality to the sixteenth century. Always on the fringe of established religious traditions with political clout, they banded together in small groups, sometimes hiding from persecution, other times just praying and experiencing the joy of worshipping and singing and eating together. John's grandfather, a farmer, carried on this tradition, serving as a lay pastor for his community, and John's father and four of his uncles became ministers.

Growing up as the second of three children, John was enfolded in an intensely loving community that included not only his immediate family but droves of cousins and other relatives and all the members of the church where his father was the pastor. As he reflects on his childhood, two things stand out: spirituality touched every part of his life (his mother taught him to pray about everything, even his Little League team), and the most meaningful parts of his life were spent in groups (Little League, YMCA, Boys Brigade, and the church youth group, among others). From earliest times, there was never a question in his mind about the connection between spirituality and community.

When John went away to college (he didn't go far), he was suddenly uprooted from family and church. It was the late 1960s and campuses everywhere were in turmoil. But John found an enclave that protected him from all the upheaval. This was also the time when small groups were spreading across college campuses and, given his background, John inevitably joined one that forged an even closer connection between his sense of community and his thirst for spirituality. The group sustained him for four years.

Then came medical school. Living for the first time in the inner city and having to study twenty-five hours a day, John easily could have broken his life-long religious habits. But he didn't. Feeling lonelier than he'd ever felt before, he soon found a couple of friends who shared his beliefs and formed a group. They hung out, went to coffee-houses together, and talked a lot about their religious values.

In residency in another city, and working even harder than before, John again found several people who shared his religious views and started a group. This time the group met weekly for Bible study and prayer, and before long it had grown to twenty people. This was how John met his wife, Sara.

John and Sara have been in small groups ever since. In one town, before they had children, they became leaders of a small youth group at a church. In another they attended a weekly Bible study group with seven other couples their age. This custom went on for about four years. Everyone was starting to have children and the group provided a great deal of support to those enduring the long nights of colic and the long days of diapers. More recently, John and Sara have joined a group called Matrix at a large nondenominational church in the area. The group is for couples with established families who want to go deeper in their faith and focus on how to apply it to all the important decisions in their lives. For seven years John also has been in a small support group for business and professional men. They meet regularly, listen to each other talk about their problems, and give encouragement, but they also get tough with each other sometimes: "This is what you say you believe," John reports that one of the guys will say to him, "but look how you're living your life!"

John's story illustrates, in a way that Donna's does not, how small groups can function over a long period of time. In a society like ours, no single group can provide a cradle-to-grave community like the one John's ancestors lived in during the sixteenth century. But having been conditioned as a child to think of community and spirituality in unison, a person like John can move from one group to another as situations and needs require. His journey—from YMCA and Boys Brigade to college group, to medical society, to young singles group, to young married group, to discipleship group, to men's group—illustrates the range of contexts in which people can explore their needs for community and for spirituality. In his case, there was considerable continuity in the groups he attended over the years. All of them focused on common Christian values. They kept him interested in his faith, even though he was moving from community to community. At the same time, none of these groups tied him down or got in the way of his career. Indeed, they made it easier for him to leave one place and move on to another.

Donna and John also illustrate that the small-group movement encompasses an enormous variety of support groups. Diversity, as I have already indicated, is much more the hallmark of the movement than is uniformity. Some readers thinking about support groups are likely to have in mind a women's Bible study group such as Donna's. Others may have in mind a men's group such as John's. But different readers perhaps would think about an Alcoholics Anonymous group, a book discussion group whose members have drawn close together, the

Sunday school classes that provided them with support when a family member was ill, or perhaps a civic group that provided caring and fellowship.

Its diversity is one of the reasons why the small-group movement has been the subject of debate and misunderstanding, even by those involved in leading the movement. While I was conducting the research, for example, clergy sometimes asked me questions about my findings that presumed the entire movement was like the Bible studies they were sponsoring in their churches. Leaders of self-help groups, in contrast, would phone to ask about the study and register surprise that Bible studies were part of the picture at all. Others who were interested, say, in singing groups or book discussion clubs were anxious to know if they were being included. Each was looking at the small-group movement from his or her own perspective and therefore making different assumptions about it. Thus, the most basic contribution that this kind of research can make is to answer the simple questions of what the main varieties of groups are and how they compare in terms of membership and other characteristics.

Any of these groups can legitimately be considered a support group because they meet regularly and provide caring and support for their members. But, clearly, they function in different ways, and their structure, members, and activities are likely to differ as well. To be sure, common features characterize most small groups and many members of small groups. The small-group movement is, in this sense, a distinctive phenomenon in our society. We can speak of it in the same way that we speak of churches, families, or voluntary organizations. But just as there are many different kinds of churches, families, or voluntary organizations, so there are many varieties of small groups. It is, therefore, important for us to understand what the main types of groups are so we can determine which ones are most prevalent in our society and see how they differ from one another. Group leaders will be interested in knowing how typical or atypical their particular kind of group is. Members and prospective members are likely to be interested in what kinds of groups are available and how they may differ from each other. And persons wanting to understand how this movement fits into American society can do so better by knowing in greater detail how it is composed. Once we have considered these matters, we will also be in a better position to evaluate the social implications of this diversity—particularly what it means to have so many different options available to us.

THE VARIETIES OF SUPPORT GROUPS

One of the main reasons why so many Americans can be involved in support groups is that these groups come in all shapes, colors, and sizes. They are much like breakfast cereals: Big boxes of all-purpose cereal are there for the whole family, but smaller boxes are available for people eating alone. Some may prefer nutritious cereal that takes time to prepare. Others may want something "lite." Support groups can be found to meet virtually everyone's taste.[1]

The analogy between support groups and breakfast cereals also points to a very important feature of American society. Community is no longer something we are born into. It is now something we must *choose*. And because people have diverse needs and interests, the range of communities competing for their attention has become equally diverse. Some support groups, like Donna's and John's, are deeply rooted in religious traditions and appeal to people from those traditions. Other support groups have developed for people with specialized needs in their personal lives, such as an addiction to alcohol or a longing for comfort after bereavement. Support groups exist as part of a market. They compete with one another to attract members by finding niches in the market that have not yet been filled, by providing more attractive "merchandise" than their competitors, and by helping potential customers become more aware of their needs. The support-group movement thrives on this competition and on the variety that results from it. The great value of the movement is that is provides something for everybody. But the potential danger of the movement stems from this same variety. If we can find a group that fits perfectly with our individual needs at the moment, then we may not be challenged by that group to become anything different from what we might be anyway, we may move on to another group when our interests change, and we may find it more difficult to stay with other commitments that demand more of us.

The variety of small groups in our society is so great that labels, names, and other descriptions often can be quite misleading. Two people may belong to the same group, but one calls it a Bible study and the other calls it a discussion group. Or the same person may refer to the group he or she attends as a therapy group in one context and a self-help group in a different context. One way to gain at least a partial sense of the variety of small groups, therefore, is to ask people what labels apply to their groups—but let them apply more than one label if they choose.

Table 3.1 shows the labels that members of small groups use to

Table 3.1

THE VARIETIES OF SMALL GROUPS

*Most Common Types of Groups According to Descriptions
Members Said Applied to Their Group*

	Percentage of All Group Members Who Said Each Description Applied to Their Current Group
Discussion group	60
Support group	52
Special interest group	45
Prayer fellowship	44
Bible study group	44
Sunday school class	29
Women's group	28
Self-help group	26
Youth group	20
Men's group	18
Couple's group	17
House church	12
Therapy group	12
Singles' group	11
Anonymous group	9
Covenant group	9

describe their groups. Not surprisingly, labels such as "discussion group" and "support group" head the list. These labels can apply to a wide variety of groups. After these general categories, however, groups with specific religious labels, such as "Bible study," "prayer fellowship," and "Sunday School class," are among the most commonly used descriptions. The widespread term "self-help group" is used by approximately a quarter of all group members. Then come labels referring to groups oriented toward the interests of particular age categories, men, women, singles, and couples. And low on the list are labels such as "therapy," "anonymous," or "covenant" group.

Even with this limited information, then, we can begin to understand some of the diversity in the small-group movement. It is not limited to just a few kinds of familiar groups (such as Bible studies or

Alcoholics Anonymous); it includes a much wider variety of offerings. Yet all of these small groups meet regularly and provide some kind of caring and support for their members.

Sunday School Classes

Because these labels can overlap considerably, a better sense of the main varieties of small groups can be obtained by classifying them into several broad types. By doing this, we find that the most common kind of support group is still the adult Sunday school class—possibly the oldest of all such groups. At present, slightly more than a quarter of everyone claiming to be in any kind of support group (29 percent) describes it as a Sunday school class. Thus, between 18 and 22 million people, perhaps as many as a tenth of the adult population (one church-goer in four), belong to this kind of group. Sunday school classes tend to be bigger than many other kinds of support groups, averaging around 25 members each. It would not be unreasonable, therefore, to estimate the number of groups that can be described as Sunday schools at approximately 800,000. Indeed, this estimate may be too low. Statistics published each year in the *Yearbook of American and Canadian Churches*, for example, reveal that approximately 140,000 of 200,000 Protestant congregations operate Sunday school programs, so their combined enrollment may range as high as 28 million.[2] As many as two-thirds of this number may be children. But virtually all churches that offer any kind of Sunday school program do so at both adult and children's levels and most adult programs involve multiple classes, so these churches alone might well account for at least 400,000 such groups. Add in Roman Catholic, Jewish, and the numerous Protestant denominations not included, and the total would probably exceed 800,000. Because Sunday school classes generally meet regularly (86 percent meet every week), they also account for more individual meetings per year than any other kind of small group.

According to the people surveyed, moreover, most of these classes are support groups. Sixty percent of the members of Sunday school classes, for example, say the term "support group" is a good description of their group; 94 percent say the class provides them with emotional support, and 87 percent say it is a place where they can share their problems. Most Sunday school classes employ the traditional format of studying and discussing the Bible (95 percent of members say they do this) and praying together (according to 98 percent of their members).

Nearly all of them have a formally designated leader, and three-quarters include a lesson that people are expected to study in advance. Rather than the didactic academic or lecture format, though, most of these classes include personal sharing, singing, collective prayer, informal socializing before and after, parties, and eating together.

The fact that Sunday school classes were mentioned so often in our survey is significant. For religious leaders, such classes have long been regarded as a central feature of any comprehensive program of religious education.[3] In recent years, the field of religious education has been ripe with interest. New models have been proposed, much rethinking about the relationship between grass-roots programs and formal theology has taken place, and the meaning of education has been broadened and deepened. Much of this attention has been pitched at the professional and academic level and has involved highly abstract discussions. Yet several important strands of these discussions have converged around the idea of community. Religious education, according to these arguments, occurs best when it takes place within some kind of supportive faith community.[4] Sunday school classes that regularly provide caring and support for their members appear to be an important example of how religious education and community might be combined.

The couples group that John and Sara belong to typifies the kind of Sunday school class that doubles as a support group. Sandwiched between two worship services on Sunday mornings, it meets at a convenient hour. Couples with young children find this Sunday school especially convenient because classes are available for children at the same time. With some 1,900 people attending John and Sara's church, getting people involved in the class has not been a problem. Rather, the difficulty has been keeping the number down to a reasonable size. Right now, about 40 people attend regularly. Over the past five years, the figure has ranged between 20 and 100. Usually when attendance starts getting too high, people drift away to some of the other (more than a dozen) classes available at the same time. To make sure that the class functions as a support group, the clergy has designated it as a subdivision of the congregation (one of several "small churches") and a coordinator is assigned to keep things running smoothly. The room where the group meets is attractive, well-lit, and close to the sanctuary in which worship services are held. Couples about the same age as John and Sara wander down the corridor, enter the room, and get a cup of coffee before the meeting officially begins. Each Sunday the group starts with singing, shares prayer requests and prays, listens to a brief presentation on some topic of mutual interest, and spends the rest of the time sharing their thoughts on that issue. There is a leader, but a majority of the group participates in the discussion. At least once every three months, the group has a party, usually at one of the members' home, and during a typical week people in the group see each other informally or spend evenings together at someone's house.

Bible Study Groups

The next most common type of support group is what people describe variously as Bible studies, prayer fellowships, house churches, or covenant groups.[5] Each of these phrases has emerged within the small-group movement to describe a specific kind of group. According to one report, Bible study groups focus on biblical truth and aim to help members learn what the scriptures say by discussing books of the Bible, specific biblical passages or themes, or books on Christian living. Prayer fellowships bring people together primarily to pray, to focus more directly on God and communication with God rather than on the study of God's word as such, and generally expect that God will answer the prayers of those in the group. A house church generally tries to include all or most of the functions of a religious service (worship, education, prayer, ministry, and growth) but in a smaller, more informal, and more intimate atmosphere than in a traditional church service. Covenant groups combine many of the functions of the other groups but are especially concerned with obedience to Christ.[6]

Not counting people who may use one of these terms to describe their Sunday school class, Bible study groups comprise a quarter of the membership of all support groups in the United States. In round numbers, as many as 15 to 20 million people—one adult in ten—are involved in these kinds of groups. Because these groups tend to be somewhat smaller than Sunday school classes (averaging around 20 members), there are more of them, perhaps as many as 900,000 altogether. Because they meet somewhat less often (only 58 percent meet every week), they account for fewer individual meetings per year than Sunday schools. But they do tend to meet for more time each week than the typical Sunday school class (66 percent meet for an hour and a half or longer, compared with only 53 percent of Sunday school classes that meet that long). So, by some indications, Bible study groups are the most important kind of support group.

Support is a very important function of Bible study groups, just as it is of Sunday school classes. More than half of all Bible study members describe their group as a support group, 95 percent say it provides them with emotional support, and 90 percent say it is a place where they can share their problems. But these groups focus heavily on explicitly religious activities as well: 95 percent include prayer, 85 percent study the Bible, and 91 percent discuss religious topics. The most common terms used to describe these groups are "prayer fellowship" (used by 81 percent of their members), "Bible study" (71 percent), "discussion group" (71 percent), "house church" (24 percent), and "covenant group" (15 percent). Approximately 10 percent of these groups may be part of the so-called charismatic movement, judging from the proportion of members who say their groups practice "speaking in tongues."[7]

Donna's "study and support group" illustrates many of the characteristics of Bible study and prayer fellowships. They meet at all hours of the week (hers gathers on Tuesday mornings) to accommodate their members' schedules. Many meet in private homes, but a majority (like Donna's) make use of church facilities that would otherwise be standing empty during the week. They usually devote some of the time to sharing prayer requests and then praying collectively (verbally or silently) about these needs. Usually the Bible is studied, but long periods of time may focus on other religious or inspirational books. Donna's group, for example, has worked its way through several short devotional guides for women and has recently spent time on a book about children. These groups also have started to specialize around particular interests and needs. Donna's attraction to this particular group owed much to its focus on women with young children. Another group at her church focuses on the interests of professional women whose children are generally older. It meets on Thursday evenings to better accommodate their schedules. Other Bible studies (as John's story illustrates) may be geared toward college students, young single professionals, young married couples, men in mid life, women in mid life, or retirees, or the basis of coming together simply may be living in the same neighborhood or wanting to discuss a particular topic. Usually the supportive element in these groups is enhanced by their informality and by the socializing that occurs before and after each meeting (perhaps over dessert) and between meetings.[8]

Later chapters consider whether Bible study groups differ significantly from Sunday school classes, because they are the two kinds of support groups most directly concerned with spirituality. The published literature certainly gives the impression that they are different. Bible study groups have not exactly been described as a replacement for Sunday school classes, but they clearly have generated more enthusiasm in recent years as potential spark plugs for dynamic congregations and ministries. Church-growth proponent John Ellas, for example, writes: "A large growing church will often use a combination of Sunday schools, specialized ministries, and small home groups. However, the most consistent characteristic of a large growing church today is small home groups."[9] Another writer asserts bluntly, "Small groups are the key to effective mission and ministry . . . the missing ingredient in the overall strategy for the ministry of all of God's people."[10] In comparison, Sunday school classes may seem dry and ineffective, yielding the kind of embarrassing results that Mark Twain satirized when Tom Sawyer, after much prodding from his Sunday school teacher to recite the names of the first two disciples, blurted out "David and Goliath!"[11]

For now, it will suffice to say that Bible study groups and Sunday school classes resemble each other quite closely in terms of their activities. The main differences are that members of Bible study groups are more likely to say that they study the Bible and that they hold each other accountable; members of Sunday school classes are more likely to say their groups provide child care, have a leader, and have parties. As already noted, Sunday school classes meet more often on average than Bible study groups and tend to be larger, but Bible study groups' meetings generally last longer. Perhaps the most significant difference between the two is that Sunday school members tend to be older and more established in their communities, while Bible study members are younger and newer to their communities—meaning that Bible studies may, indeed, be more effective than Sunday school classes in attracting new members to local churches. Sunday school members also say they joined because they were in a previous group, whereas Bible study members are more likely to say they were invited and joined looking for emotional support.

Self-Help Groups

After Sunday school classes and Bible studies, the most common type of support group is what has come to be known as the self-help group. Approximately one-eighth of all small group members belong to this kind of group. In the adult population as a whole, this figure includes between 8 and 10 million people. At an average of about 20 people per group, the number of groups totals at least 500,000. According to their members, four people in ten in any kind of self-help group participate in one that focuses on an addiction, approximately a third (31 percent) of all self-help groups follow the twelve steps to recovery developed by Alcoholics Anonymous (AA), and about the same proportion (30 percent) describe their group as an anonymous gathering of one kind or another (most of the non-twelve-step groups are described by their members as therapy groups). The members of these groups are very likely to emphasize support: 87 percent describe their groups as support groups, 88 percent say they share their problems in these groups, and 89 percent say they receive emotional support.

What qualifies as a self-help group is, of course, subject to debate. The term has become so widely known that we were able to use it in our survey to let people tell us what kinds of groups they were in. From the other data collected in the survey from these people, we can safely infer that most of them were using the term in a way consistent with published definitions. For example, *The Self-Help Sourcebook* explains that self-help groups generally provide mutual aid or mutual support to their members, are composed of peers who share common experiences or situations, are run by and for their members, and operate on a voluntary, nonprofit basis.[12]

The contemporary self-help movement is only the latest development in a long history of cooperative and mutual-aid ventures. Its roots can be found in late medieval and early modern guilds, trade unions, and religious orders. During the eighteenth and nineteenth centuries, industrialization posed new challenges and resulted in the creation of many more such organizations. By 1800, for example, nearly 200 "friendly societies" had been founded in England, most with the purpose of providing poor relief and workmen's compensation to their members. As the labor union movement built on this legacy for the working classes, middle-class citizens founded reading clubs, self-improvement associations, salons, and civic organizations in profusion. Many of these groups were transplanted intact into American soil by immigrant groups, while others were founded in new ethnic neighborhoods to replace family ties left behind.[13]

The greatest surge of self-help activity, however, has come since World War II. The mental health movement stimulated some of this activity in the 1950s. National foundations established to care for the needs of polio victims or for other needs, such as cerebral palsy, encouraged members and their families to start mutual support groups. The campaign to bring alcoholism treatment more into the open helped promote Alcoholics Anonymous (AA) groups. And, especially after 1960, government programs of all kinds began to stimulate special purpose groups that combined activism and lobbying at the national level with self-help groups at the community level.

Self-help groups in recent years have become increasingly specialized. In addition to AA, self-help groups have emerged to help people cope with a myriad of other addictions and dysfunctions. Examples include Al-Anon (for the family members of alcoholics), Adult Children of Alcoholics (ACOA), Narcotics Anonymous (NA), Overeaters Anonymous (OA), and Co-Dependents Anonymous (CODA), for people who compulsively take responsibility for others, as well as numerous specialty groups for people recovering from addictions to gambling, smoking, marijuana use, shoplifting, and sexual abuse, among others, as well as support groups for parents, grandparents, homosexuals, widows, sufferers of emphysema, divorcees, chronic workaholics, and former fundamentalists. AA networks in many large metropolitan areas frequently include even such highly specialized groups as Anorexic Bulimics Anonymous, Families of Sex Offenders Anonymous, and Victims Anonymous. Secondary levels of specialization have also become increasingly noteworthy as self-help groups have been started for subgroups of the addictive population (such as Alateen and Gamateen, for teenagers) and for people with multiple addictions (such as Dual Disorders Anonymous).[14]

The Saturday morning CODA meeting at Central Valley Community Church illustrates why self-help groups have become so popular. As the meeting comes to order, about 35 people are already seated in a large circle in the church fellowship hall. All of them are white, and women outnumber men by a ratio of three to one, but the group includes people of all ages. Dress is casual, but (with the exception of an unspoken norm in favor of wearing sandals) there is more variety than similarity. The leader opens the meeting by asking the members to say their first names, starting with the person on her left. After this, she invites any who would like a smaller group to "hive off" to an adjacent room, and a few do. The remainder listen as she reads a brief statement explaining how widespread codependency is in our society and how damaging it can be to personal relationships. Once the meeting opens up, people share what they have been struggling with in recent days. One man, recently divorced, is struggling with having to confront his "ex" about some financial issues. A young woman tells how hard it is to reenter mainstream life after being institutionalized for six months at a psychiatric clinic. A middle-aged woman says her son hasn't been seen for three days and she fears he's on drugs again. For the next hour, one issue after another is shared. As the meeting ends, everyone clasps hands and repeats the Lord's Prayer. Afterward, those who linger for hugs and brief conversations with one or two others far outnumber the ones who slip quietly away.

Self-help groups differ from Bible study groups in some obvious ways (for example, they are more likely to focus on addictions and less likely to study the Bible). When other differences are taken into account, however, prayer is about as common in one as in the other (although the prayers in self-help groups may be shorter or more perfunctory). Other differences are: self-help groups are somewhat more likely to be described as singles' groups or men's groups, while Bible studies are more likely to be described as women's groups; self-help groups are more likely to include members who say they joined because of personal problems or an emotional crisis; self-help groups typically have been in existence longer than the average Bible study group, but their members have been participating over a shorter period of time; self-help group members are more likely than Bible study members to describe themselves as "free spirits" and "loners," and they are more likely to say they worry about loneliness, guilt, trying to figure out what's important in life, and problems at work.

Special Interest Groups

The remaining third or so of small group members divides about equally into three categories of special interest groups: members of discussion groups that focus on political issues and other current events, members of book discussion groups, and members of sports or hobby groups. In each case somewhere between 5 million and 10 million adult Americans probably are involved, and each kind of group may number around 250,000. It is, however, difficult to separate these groups into distinct categories because what one person calls a book discussion another may call a hobby group and another may call a current events group. Overall, about three-quarters of the members of special interest groups say they work on special projects, nearly two-thirds say they discuss social and political issues, an equal number do things to help people in their communities, nearly half engage in sports or hobbies together, and about a third read and discuss books.

These groups stand apart from those previously described in several important ways. While some of them (about a third) include prayers, religious content is notably absent from most. Only one in five involves discussions of religious topics, and fewer than one in eight ever study or discuss the Bible. Special interest groups also tend to meet somewhat less often, sometimes as infrequently as once a month, although about a third meet weekly. However, these groups do provide support, rather than merely accomplishing instrumental tasks. Their members cherish the sense of belonging that develops, the chance to share their thoughts and experiences with kindred spirits, and the caring they receive. About two-thirds of their members, for example, say they receive emotional support from their group and have a chance to share personal problems. These members are, however, less likely than those of self-help groups to say they joined because of addictions, personal problems, emotional crises, or a desire for personal growth. A few of these groups, while avoiding biblical or religious topics as such, raise spiritual issues in the course of other discussions, and some intentionally promote meditation, introspection, and development oriented toward the soul as well as the mind or body.

The enormous variety of these special interest groups is evident in the journey that Terry, age 30, an only child of wealthy New England parents, has taken during the past two decades. At age 10, Terry started taking classes in Tae Kwon Do (the Korean martial arts). These classes provided the group experience, camaraderie, and mentoring that he lacked at home (his parents recently had been divorced). Drawing most of his identity from the rigors of this training, he increasingly lost interest in school. Five years later, in ninth grade, he managed to cause so many problems at school that his father, with whom he was living, agreed to let him drop out. Devoting all of his time to Tae Kwon Do, he earned a black belt and began traveling with a demonstration fighting team. At 19, faced with a choice between earning his living teaching the martial arts or returning to school, he opted for the latter. Rapidly overcoming what he had missed in high school, he eventually earned a joint degree in philosophy and psychology from Boston College and enrolled at Harvard for a graduate degree in neurolinguistics.

During the past five years, since finishing his studies at Harvard,

Terry became increasingly interested in his relationship with God. But he is not the kind of person who seeks Gods through the church. Raised by religiously mixed parents (Jewish father, Catholic mother), he has attended both church and synagogue periodically all his life. He doesn't appreciate the dogma or the liturgical practices, though, and sees them as "man-made rules and regulations." He feels he has direct access to God. When he feels the urge, he attends whatever church or synagogue happens to be closest. He's sure God will be there! What has nurtured Terry's spiritual life most is an offshoot of his training in graduate school. For nearly a decade he has experimented with various special interest groups. Tae Kwon Do awakened his thirst to know God better. For a while, he was a devotee of Werner Erhardt's E.S.T. training and was part of small groups in that movement. He underwent hypnosis. He participated actively in gestalt therapy groups. He also experimented with meditation, the New Age movement, and various human potential organizations, such as Forum and Lifespring. Many of these activities provided him with a sense of family that he desperately needed. Much of what he found, however, seemed to be only "fluff" in terms of spirituality. The groups fulfilled his needs temporarily, when there was a trained leader present, but left him feeling he had no skills to carry with him into the remainder of his life.

In comparison, his training in neurolinguistic programming (NLP) proved far more helpful. NLP is a method of programming the brain to more effectively understand the meaning of particular events. NLP assumes that people have the resources they need to do this, but are generally unable to get in touch with these resources. Terry considers himself a "10" in terms of active involvement in NLP. He takes classes, attends seminars, participates in small training groups, and attends intensive two- to four-day retreats. He regards NLP largely as a tool for gaining greater control over his thoughts and feelings. As such, it also aids his spiritual life. It helps him transcend the "models of the world" that he has always taken for granted. It helps him to focus on courage when he needs it and to find power and hope for his life. It also helps him to feel that he is in direct contact with God. He does not see NLP as a replacement for church (for example, he still loves the experience of worshipping collectively), but he feels that NLP groups have enriched his spirituality.

Table 3.2 summarizes the estimates of members and numbers of groups in each of the categories just considered. The categories suggest some of the variety that makes small support groups so appealing

Table 3.2

ESTIMATES OF VARIOUS TYPES OF GROUPS

	Estimated Number of	
	Members	*Groups*
Sunday school classes	18–22 million	800,000
Bible study groups	15–20 million	900,000
Self-help groups	8–10 million	500,000
Special interest groups		
Political/current events	5–10 million	250,000
Book/discussion groups	5–10 million	250,000
Sports/hobby groups	5–10 million	250,000

to the American public. Even more impressive, however, is the enormous variety that exists within each of these broad categories.

VARIETY WITHIN VARIETY

Whether it be Sunday school classes, Bible study groups, self-help groups, or other special interest groups, leaders have tried hard to "differentiate the product" in order to reach the widest number of people with the widest array of possible needs. The idea is to have something for everybody. Downsizing is the secret. Because most groups are small, there can be an almost infinite variety of them.

Variety thus has become the watchword of the small-group movement. The pastor of a Presbyterian church in North Carolina, for example, remarks, "Variety is a key to our small-group ministry. The groups are formed according to what the people want. When new members come into the group, we give them a card with a variety of questions on it to determine which small group they should join." A United Church of Christ minister in suburban Chicago enumerates the offerings currently available at his church: a Wednesday morning men's Bible breakfast, several women's support groups, a feminist-theology discussion group, half a dozen midweek fellowship groups, seven Sunday-morning coffee groups, a support group for unemployed men, and several that deal with social issues. "Variety," he says, "is what we want." At a large Baptist church in Houston, the number of such groups has grown so much in recent years that a special phone number has been added. Callers are directed by prerecorded messages to information about the times and meeting places of more than a hundred different groups.

By emphasizing variety, pastors try to ensure that everyone with every conceivable need or interest can find a place in their church. But is this the case? Isn't it still likely that some people will have a much richer array of offerings or at least a greater chance of finding like-minded people than others? And what about like-mindedness? Do small groups separate people into such tiny lots that they seldom interact with anyone different from themselves? Or do they bring diverse people together within the same groups?

In the past, gender, age, and marital status were among the most popular ways of dividing people into activity groups. The support-group movement is no exception. Individuals seeking kindred spirits can find groups composed of people of the same gender, age, or marital status whether they happen to be oriented toward Sunday school classes, Bible studies, self-help groups, or other special interest groups. But it is somewhat easier for women to find groups that cater especially to the needs of women, it appears from the survey, than for men to locate groups that offer the company of other men. Couples groups and singles groups are available for people interested in any of the main kinds of support groups. The numbers, however, also suggest that a majority of groups are open to men or women, to married or unmarried people, and to married people who wish to attend with their spouse or by themselves. On average, about one group in five is geared to young adults; most groups are nonspecific with respect to age.[15]

Even though most support groups develop explicit norms about how often to meet, how long to meet, and perhaps even how many people they can comfortably accommodate, there is also great diversity in all these norms. Someone interested in finding a Bible study group, for example, that meets only once a month would have a relatively good chance of doing so (28 percent of Bible studies meet that often), even though most Bible studies meet more often. Most Sunday school classes meet for less than an hour and a half each week, but someone interested in meeting longer would have no trouble finding one (about a quarter meet two hours or more). A person wanting to be in a self-help group would have the best chances of finding one with about 20 members, but should that size seem too large, many have fewer than ten members (about 30 percent). These variations again reveal how diverse the small-group movement is.

You can also find groups of virtually any kind that include activities in which you might be interested. If you are interested in singing, at least some singing could be found in 82 percent of all Sunday school classes, 70 percent of all Bible studies, 25 percent of all self-help groups, and 33 percent of all special interest groups. If, however, you are interested in participating in a group that includes physical exercise, this activity is available in 19 percent of all Sunday school groups, 13 percent of all Bible studies, 28 percent of all self-help groups, and 21 percent of all special interest groups.

Probably the most intimidating feature of small groups for the average newcomer, of course, is the fact that so many of them have been in existence for a long time. Prospective members might wonder whether they could break into an established group, let alone shape it to meet their interests. The cold fact is that more than four groups out of five—Sunday school classes, Bible studies, self-help groups, and special interest groups alike—have been in existence for more than five years. What tempers this reality, however, is that many people have not been involved in their group for that long. In the average Sunday school class, one out of every six people joined only within the past year. In the average Bible study group, one out of eight did so. And in the average self-help group, the figure is nearly one person in four.

BIRDS OF A FEATHER?

With so many different kinds of groups available, the question that increasingly has plagued group leaders and members alike is how to meet specialized needs and yet ensure some diversity within the group. There have been two opposing views on this question. In the 1960s, when the small-group movement first picked up momentum, the slogan everywhere seemed to be "let's get together now," as one popular song expressed it. Small groups became one of the main cures for social ills that grew out of the 1950s.[16] If the society was racist, let people of different races join together. If the Organization Man, as William Whyte dubbed him, was experiencing too much specialization in his work, let him meet different kinds of people at an encounter session.[17] The important thing was to promote communication. The ideal self could only be cultivated in small groups that brought diverse people together.[18] In the late 1980s, when small groups again began to attract attention, the logic was different. The new emphasis was on specialization. Addictions could only be dealt with effectively if people got together with others like themselves. Religious leaders saw the need to market their groups more effectively. The way to do that was to identify new niches and fill them with specialized groups.

From the beginning, some small groups have been more internally diverse than others. The AA meetings, ladies' aid societies, and church youth groups that flourished in the 1950s, for example, reflected as much specialization as many of the groups that were founded in the 1980s. But the two philosophies reflect radically different diagnoses of what is wrong with American society and what should be done to fix it. The view that champions internal diversity still harks back to the ideals (if not the practice) of the 1960s counterculture. The trouble with modern society, in this view, is that everything has become too large, too bureaucratic, too technocratic, too specialized.[19] The center holds, but does so at the price of alienating everybody. The remedy is to downscale in size. Small is beautiful becomes the slogan for a new era. Cultural differences, gender biases, racism can all be overcome as people learn to trust and support one another. Encounter groups, intentionally bringing diverse individuals together to "encounter" one another, were perhaps the epitome of this orientation. As one writer observes in retrospect, "The encounter group was one of the social innovations of the time which claimed to have the key to a fundamental transformation of society—the dawn of a new era—from the Greening of Society to the Age of Aquarius."[20] The other view is less optimistic about overcoming differences. It is, however, more optimistic about the positive benefits of specialization. Rather than perceiving modern society as an alien, faceless crowd, it relishes the diversity of contemporary life. The city, as symbol, is not a fearsome place, strange because of its anonymity, but wonderfully rich because of its differences, because of the opportunities that its strangeness creates.[21] In this view, communication of a different sort is the main problem. People simply need to learn what their opportunities may be. Effective marketing becomes the way to enrich group life.

It is understandable that these two views emerged when they did. For those who began small groups in the 1960s, there was as yet very little competition. AA groups, for example, often found themselves unable to specialize too narrowly because people with interests of all sorts flocked to them. By the time the second generation of group founders came along, the environment was much more competitive.

One church could scarcely succeed just by starting home fellowships if three other churches on the same block already had them; a support group for unemployed single professionals seemed like a better idea. And yet both kinds of groups coexist at present, adding even further diversity to the overall menu of available options.

How homogeneous or heterogeneous small groups are can be assessed in several different ways. We have already suggested that some groups appeal mainly to people of a certain age or gender, while others are more diverse. We can see more clearly how small groups stack up in terms of certain kinds of diversity from the data presented in table 3.3. In terms of age, for example, small groups appear to be divided about equally between those that aspire for diversity and those that specialize. Slightly more than half of all group members say they belong to a group composed of all different ages. Fewer than a third say they belong to a group of people mostly their own age. But most of the remainder (about one in five) locate the majority of the group as being either older or younger than themselves. These patterns, it might be noted, generally hold true when the responses of younger, middle-aged, and older persons are examined separately.

Gender diversity also seems to be built into about half of all groups, insofar as these are composed of about equal numbers of men and women. Of the remainder, about half are gender exclusive and the rest are tilted heavily in one direction or the other—usually toward women. More than a third of all group members belong to groups that are entirely or mostly composed of women, whereas only one person in six is in a group composed exclusively or almost exclusively of men. This pattern also means, of course, that women are more likely to belong to gender-homogeneous groups than are men. Specifically, more than half of all women in groups belong to groups made up mostly or totally of women; only a third of men belong to groups consisting mostly or totally of men.

Diversity is least present in the racial composition of groups. While only about half of all members belong to groups that are entirely of one race, fewer than one person in eight is in a group that is about evenly mixed racially. This pattern is much more the case among whites, though, than it is among persons of other races. Among the latter, three in ten belong to a group that is about evenly mixed racially, and another tenth are in groups that are mostly white. These kinds of homogeneity, of course, may not be as significant as the more subtle, ideological lines that sometimes divide people.

Table 3.3

PERCEPTIONS OF VARIETY IN GROUPS

Percentage of Small Group Members Who Say
People in Their Group Have These Characteristics

Age composition	
Mostly their own age	28
Mostly younger than them	9
Mostly older than them	9
Of all different ages	54
Gender composition	
All women	18
Mostly women	19
About equal numbers of men and women	47
Mostly men	10
All men	6
Racial composition	
All white	44
Mostly white	32
About evenly mixed	12
Mostly nonwhite	3
All nonwhite	7
Religious views	
Mostly conservative	27
Mostly middle of the road	18
Mostly liberal	5
A mixture of liberal and conservative	32
Don't know	18
Political views	
Mostly conservative	22
Mostly middle of the road	17
Mostly liberal	7
A mixture of liberal and conservative	26
Don't know	29

When people are asked about the religious ideology of their group, only about a third say it is a blend of liberals and conservatives. When asked the same question about political ideology, an even smaller proportion (about a fourth) indicate being in a group with a good liberal-conservative mixture. Some of the reason is that a substantial minority of people do not know what others in their group think about religious or political issues. But this response is also attributable to the fact that more groups are religiously conservative than religiously liberal and to the fact that conservatives seem to stick together to a greater extent than liberals. For example, 57 percent of the people who describe themselves as religious conservatives say their group is mostly conservative, whereas only 15 percent of the liberals say their group is mostly liberal. Moderates, as might be expected, are most likely to be in groups that combine a mixture of liberals and conservatives, followed by liberals, and then conservatives.

There are also some interesting differences in the tendencies of the various types of groups to be homogeneous or heterogeneous. Sunday school classes tend to be relatively homogeneous in racial composition, but vary on most of the other dimensions. On age, for example, about half of all Sunday school classes combine a mixture of all age groups, while the other half tend to be grouped into homogeneous age categories. On gender, nearly two-thirds of all Sunday school classes include nearly equal proportions of men and women; a third are composed almost entirely of women, while only 5 percent are composed almost totally of men.

Bible study groups are the most likely of any type of group to include people of diverse ages. But they are also most likely to be composed only or mostly of women (42 percent). Bible study groups, along with Sunday school classes, contain a higher than average proportion of religious conservatives (42 percent) and are least likely to include a mixture of religious liberals and conservatives (29 percent).

Self-help groups on the whole exhibit the greatest amount of diversity on these characteristics. They are fairly likely to include people of different ages, score highest of all types of groups in bringing together people with different religious views and different political views, and include more racial diversity than most other kinds of groups. They are, however, relatively homogeneous in terms of gender, with more than a third consisting mostly of women and a fifth made up mostly of men. The fact that most of these groups have norms against discussing religious and political issues also means that their internal diversity on these matters may not actually lead to greater understanding of different points of view.

Special interest groups, finally, show about the same mix of religious and political diversity as self-help groups, but are even more likely to involve gender divisions: four in ten are made up mostly of women, and nearly a third are composed mainly of men, while only a third include men and women in equal numbers.

On the whole, it seems clear that neither the model of narrow specialization nor that of striving for internal diversity has been entirely successful. Or, perhaps it would be more accurate to say that both have been successful, with each kind of group drawing a substantial number of participants. Because both kinds are available, people can flock together with kindred spirits if they wish or branch out when the spirit moves. (We say more about this issue in a later chapter.) But it also appears that many small groups have the potential to build bridges among people from different segments of the society rather than simply isolating them further among their own kind. Whether these groups can do so effectively is one of the challenges their leaders are now having to face. Especially for those who have been advocating a pyramidal structure, in which different groups focus on different social strata, the idea of forming cross-strata groups represents a significant new development for the years ahead. Says one leader, "To deal more effectively with heterogeneity will be a sign of the movement's maturity."

THE MULTIPLICITY OF MOTIVES

What matters to many people as they explore the options available to them is not that a group consists of men or women, or even that it calls itself a Bible study or a self-help group, but why people are there. Have they been drawn to the group because of certain values? Certain desires? Certain problems or issues they want to address? Are they in the group because of being in the same circuit of friends and neighbors? Or are they there simply by accident? Most people want to feel they are joining a group in which people, however diverse, will at least be like themselves on these fundamental questions.

The characteristics of groups that we have already considered provide one answer to these questions. Because Sunday school classes, for example, do study the Bible, pray, and discuss religious topics, a person can be pretty certain that people in those groups are there because they are interested in these activities. But, of course, there may be hidden agendas as well. And sometimes these hidden agendas are more important than what meets the eye. Were people candid about their motives, they might admit that the real attraction to the group was something else.

Few of us ever do anything for just one reason; usually it takes a push from several directions to get us off the dime. And joining small groups is no exception. What, then, are the main reasons people join these groups? And do these reasons differ among the various types of groups?

The main reason most people give for becoming involved in a small group is the desire to grow as a person. This reason is listed by about three-quarters of all group members (see table 3.4). Much less commonly mentioned—indeed, at the bottom of a list of nine reasons—is feeling isolated in their community. Taken together, these two responses suggest some interesting questions that deserve further examination in later chapters. For instance, is it really the search for community that leads people to be interested in small groups? Do people seek community in groups mostly as a way to find themselves? And if they find community in small groups, what (if anything) does this have to do with the communities in which they live?

Table 3.4

REASONS FOR BECOMING INVOLVED

Percentage of All Group Members Who Say Each of the Following Was a Reason for Becoming Involved in Their Group

The desire to grow as a person	73
Being invited by someone you know	60
Wanting to become more disciplined in your spiritual life	46
Hearing about it through your church or synagogue	43
Being in another group like it previously	33
Needing emotional support	28
Having problems in your personal life	18
Experiencing a crisis in your life	17
Feeling like you didn't know anyone in your community	11

The fact that a high proportion of people list personal growth as their reason for being in groups does suggest, of course, that there may be substantial like-mindedness among group members, whatever kind of group they may join. The desire for personal growth is mentioned as a reason for their involvement by 88 percent of all Sunday school members, by 79 percent of all Bible study members, and by 77 percent of all self-help group members. Only among special interest groups is this figure substantially lower (54 percent). This emphasis on growth, incidentally, is one of the important reasons why the idea of a journey seems so appropriate in discussing small groups.

The reason mentioned next most often by group members—being invited by someone they know—also reveals how people sort themselves into various groups. Despite all the ways in which communities are breaking down in our society, most people still have friends. And these friends provide the impetus for them to become involved in groups. Indeed, this response helps us understand better why so few people say they become involved in groups because they don't know anyone in their community. The truth is, they do know people in their community. They just want to get to know them better.

There are few differences among the various types of groups in the likelihood of people joining because someone invites them. Bible study group members are most likely to say they joined for this reason (65 percent), followed by special interest group members (63 percent). Self-help group members are a little less likely to give this response (58 percent), perhaps because they are more motivated by personal needs. Sunday school class members are the least likely to say they joined because of being invited (55 percent), perhaps because they hear about groups more easily through their churches. One implication of the fact that so many people join groups because they are invited, of course, is that they are more likely to find kindred spirits there than if they walked into a group at random.

The motive that sorts people into different kinds of groups better than any other is wanting to become more disciplined in one's spiritual life. This reason is a very strong unifying force among the members of most Sunday school classes (75 percent mention it) and only slightly less so among members of Bible study groups (67 percent mention it). Not surprisingly, it is much less often cited among the members of self-help groups (21 percent) or of special interest groups (10 percent). Hearing about the group through a church or synagogue also varies considerably from one type of group to another, but is important enough to cause us to pay special attention to the role of religious organizations in the next chapter.

What is perhaps most surprising about the reasons people give for joining groups is that relatively few say they are there because of personal needs or problems. Only about a quarter, for example, say they joined because they needed emotional support, and fewer than one in five lists personal problems or crises as a reason for joining. As might be expected, members of self-help groups are somewhat more likely to mention these reasons than members of other groups. But even here, the proportions are not high. For example, 47 percent include personal problems among their reasons, 46 percent mention needing emotional support, and 41 percent say they have experienced a crisis. Members of special interest groups are least likely to mention any of these reasons, followed by Sunday school members. Bible study members resemble Sunday school members on these items more than they do self-help members.

It is premature to speculate much about the implications of this finding. In later chapters, we consider in greater detail the kinds of support, sharing, and caring that takes place in groups. We have already seen that most members say their group gives them a chance to discuss their problems and provides them with emotional support. But the fact that people deny they are there for these reasons is also significant. It means, for example, that a person who feels an overwhelming need to be in a group because of some crisis or personal problem may not feel entirely comfortable with the other members of the group. This may be one reason, of course, why self-help groups have been flourishing in recent years, compared with Sunday school classes, Bible studies, and special interest groups.

It is also worth noting that the process of finding a group in which a person feels comfortable is indeed a process. Often it involves exploring one group and then another. Among all current members of small groups, six in ten have been involved in some kind of group before, yet only three in ten list being in a previous group like their present one as a reason for joining their present group. In other words, a lot of people have shopped around and tried out different kinds of groups. With so many options available, it is little wonder that people explore several before settling on any one.

The huge variety that characterizes the small-group movement is thus one of its most important features. Understanding this variety helps us see why the movement has become so widespread in American society. People with different interests and motives can find a group suited to their taste. The chances are also high that they can identify a group that will meet at the right time and bring together like-minded people. In a mobile society populated by people with changing needs, small groups are, therefore, a highly convenient way of meeting these needs.

Such a diverse array of groups is possible in our society because relatively few costs are involved in starting and operating these groups. They are not like AT&T or the Catholic Church, requiring such huge investments that only competitors with major funding are able to enter the arena. Nevertheless, small groups do depend heavily on social institutions, networks, and other resources. Their success cannot be explained simply in terms of demand; the supply side of the equation must be considered as well. We turn to this issue in the next chapter.

Sunday School Class

Bible Study
      prayers
      house church
      Covenant (spiritual discipline)
Self-help groups

Special interest groups
      discussion - politics, current events
      book discussion grps
      sports/hobby

4

A GOOD PLACE TO BEGIN

Institutional Underpinnings, Networks, and Resources

E mmanual Alliance Church is one of the fastest-growing congregations in the country. Its head pastor recently won a national award
for his leadership. Just to drive by, however, one would scarcely imagine anything exciting was going on. Still in a rented building, the
church has put all its emphasis on informal fellowship groups that
meet in people's homes.

At present, the congregation consists of 40 "prayer circles" made up
primarily of professional men and women, 20 "care circles" that meet
anywhere from weekly to monthly on the basis of geographic location,
scattered Bible study classes that usually meet at the church, several
singles' groups, one group especially for newcomers, and a few "2:7"
groups (taking their theme from Colossians 2:7, a verse about discipleship) that require intense commitment to Bible study and memorization. About 50 percent of the congregants are members of at least one
of these groups.

Pastor Ingram believes that his church would continue to flourish
through the work of these groups even if they had no building at all.
"Ultimately," he says, "the goal is that the church could operate apart
from the building. You can think, 'What if there was a fire and the
building burned down?' or 'What if one of the pastors were to leave?'
In most cases, whew, that would probably be it, or your attendance
drops to next to nothing until you are rebuilt. But we want our parish-

ioners not to be aligned to any one person or to the beauty of the building."

His goal is to get at least 80 percent of the membership involved in a small support group. He thinks this can be done by offering groups expressing a wide variety of interests and necessitating varied levels of commitment. He has a systematic plan for developing these groups and is in the process of training laypeople to lead them. He believes the future of his church and of his own ministry depend on his success in starting small groups and encouraging people to share their most intimate thoughts and feelings in these groups. If someone were interested in finding a group to join, a church like his would be a good place to look.

THE RELIGIOUS CONNECTION

Churches, synagogues, and religious organizations of all kinds have played a vital role in the founding and nurturing of small support groups. A wide variety of other organizations, ranging from hospitals and businesses to civic organizations, foundations, and community centers, are currently involved in sponsoring these groups as well. If one institution had to be singled out as being vital to the small-group movement, however, it would have to be the church. This is where any interested person would need to start, whether that person wanted to learn what it takes to run a group, was interested in finding out about most of the groups available in the local community, or simply wanted to understand the movement better.

No movement can be successful unless it secures resources. It needs facilities, funds, and leadership. It needs a way to identify potential participants. It needs models, slogans, and ideas that are already somewhat familiar to potential participants. Religious organizations provide all these resources for the support-group movement. Perhaps it is a symptom of malaise in established religious organizations, as some observers suggest, that the movement has developed at all. But, equally, the movement's strength depends on the fact that religious organizations have remained enormously powerful in American society. They have the facilities for meeting space, the leaders, the models, and the appeals necessary to sponsor support groups and to organize them into a significant national movement. Support groups do not exist simply because millions of individuals feel a private need for them. They exist because hundreds of thousands of churches and synagogues have devoted time and energy to bringing them into being.

There is a saying, however, that "who pays the piper calls the tune." The fact that religious organizations provide most of the resources for support groups has had serious implications for the shape and direction of the movement. It has helped these groups to grow, assisted them in meeting the needs of their members, and encouraged members in their spiritual journeys. As we shall see, the involvement of churches has been one of the important reasons why the new quest for community has also focused so clearly on spirituality. But religious leaders have also tried to turn the movement into a vehicle of growth for their own organizations. Like Pastor Ingram, they have encouraged groups to develop, to seek new members, to split, and to multiply in hope that the results would be larger congregations and more abundant offerings. And the two objectives have not always been compatible. What has been good for members has not always been good for the clergy who have promoted groups as instruments of church growth. Clergy, for example, have often tried to develop systematic goals, plans, and guidelines, and to control what went on in groups; members, in contrast, generally favor informality and being able to do what they want. Group participants like their groups because the clergy are absent and do not appreciate it when clergy try to manipulate their groups.

Other conflicts are also evident. Clergy express concern about the quality of what goes on in Bible study groups and worry, for example, that these groups can be seed beds of heresy if left untended; group members generally prefer to downplay rigorous definitions of theological correctness and accept all views that are expressed with sincerity. Clergy sometimes view groups as training grounds for lay leaders, who then can be deployed in other groups; members want their leaders to stay with them. In many churches, AA and other self-help groups have emerged, largely without clergy supervision, attracting members who find them more vibrant than traditional church programs; clergy, in turn, have sometimes felt threatened by these programs. One of the quandaries facing the movement at present, therefore, is how much it should continue to depend on religious organizations for resources, and, if it does, whether it should be guided more by the programmatic interests of religious leaders or by the desires and interests of its participants. The question is one that movement leaders must face, but it is also one that members, potential members, and interested observers of American culture must understand more broadly.

At present, between half and two-thirds of all small-group members in the United States have connections of one kind or another with religious organizations or with religious teachings and practices through their groups (see table 4.1). Two-thirds include prayer as part of the regular practices of their group, and nearly this many discuss religious topics. A majority include discussions or studies of the Bible. More than half hold their meetings at a church or synagogue. Even more belong to groups that are formally a part of the regular activities of a church or synagogue. Two-thirds are members of congregations that encourage people to become involved in small fellowship groups. And more than half are members of congregations that regard small fellowship groups as part of their plan to grow.

We saw in the last chapter that nearly half of all group members say that they first heard about the group through their church or synagogue and that they joined because they desired to become more disciplined in their spiritual life. More than half said they joined because a friend invited them, possibly a friend from their church. We know, for example, that 81 percent of all group members are also members of religious congregations, and of these, that more than two-thirds say three or more of their closest friends belong to the same congregation.

Table 4.1

CONNECTIONS BETWEEN SMALL GROUPS
AND RELIGIOUS ORGANIZATIONS

*Percentage of Group Members Who Say Their Current Group
Has Each Kind of Connection*

Group is part of the regular activities of a church or synagogue	57
Group usually meets at a church or synagogue	51
Group meetings include praying together	69
Group meetings include discussion of religious topics	63
Group meetings include study or discussion of the Bible	56
Member is part of a congregation that encourages people to become involved in small fellowship groups	71
Member is part of a congregation in which small fellowship groups are part of its plan to grow	59
Member is part of a congregation in which at least half of the people are involved in small fellowship groups	38

Among members of groups formally connected to a church or synagogue, this proportion is even higher.

The question that must be asked, then, is what small groups gain from having so many connections to religious organizations? Is it merely accidental that small groups so often have a religious focus? Is it simply because people have a longing for spirituality that small groups so often seem to spring up in soil cultivated by religious leaders? Or do religious organizations provide many of the resources needed to make small groups grow? And, if so, what are these resources, and what advantages and disadvantages are associated with them?

PHYSICAL RESOURCES

A place to meet, the most basic requirement of any group, is often overlooked until someone raises the question, "Where can we meet?" In some societies, this question is very challenging: private homes are too small for social gatherings, and larger facilities are either lacking or closely controlled by government authorities. Such was the case in Eastern Europe until quite recently. In American society, public space always has been relatively plentiful; and yet in recent decades it, too, has declined in some important ways. For example, neighborhoods that used to have their own meeting rooms in town halls or at the local volunteer fire station now find there is no space that does not belong to someone (developers sell increasing amounts of land to private buyers, and stores are located in privately owned shopping malls instead of around the town square). Like seventeenth-century enclosure laws in England that turned public lands into private pastures (when "sheep ate men," as it was said), zoning laws and profit motives again threaten to eat up communal space.

Churches and other religious organizations are thus one of the significant places where small groups can meet. Many of these groups are sponsored by religious organizations, so it is not unusual to find them meeting in classroom buildings on Sunday mornings or in church basements on weekday evenings. Altogether, 80 percent of the small groups that are part of the regular activities of a religious congregation meet in the facilities of that congregation. With more room than their parishioners can use, many churches have also opened their facilities to other small groups. Scouting programs for children have long made use of the generosity of churches and synagogues. Increasingly, Alcoholics Anonymous and other twelve-step programs also have been making use of this generosity. Some churches, strapped for financial resources because of declining memberships, have turned to renting space to small groups. Overall, about one group in eight that is not sponsored by a church or synagogue uses the facilities of some congregation for its meetings.

Moreover, many of the spaces provided in private dwellings for small groups also owe their availability to religious organizations. The time when householders could be convinced to open their homes for social-cum-pecuniary gatherings by the prospect of free TupperWare has long since passed. But hundreds of thousands of private homes are made available each week for home Bible studies, house churches, and prayer meetings. The teachings of religious organizations help legitimate these practices. Hospitality is considered as much a Christian virtue today as it was in the Middle Ages. The common identity of members in religious organizations helps ease fears about personal security and privacy that are so common in the anonymous communities in which we live. Even more importantly, religious organizations have bulletin boards, phone lists, and personal networks that can be used to identify available homes.

Of groups sponsored by churches or synagogues, about one in eight meet in private homes, and this number is divided about equally between those that meet at one member's home and those that rotate among several members' homes. In view of all the attention that "house churches" and "home Bible studies" have received in recent years, it is perhaps significant that this proportion is so low.[1] Yet, when groups that meet in church buildings are set aside, this figure amounts to more than half of all the remaining groups. By comparison, only one church-sponsored group in twenty meets in a community hall or some other public building.

The other physical resource that religious organizations often provide—a key factor in making it possible for many people to attend small groups—is child care. This, as we saw in the last chapter, is one of the advantages of Sunday school classes. A longstanding commitment to families and to children has made churches and synagogues mindful of the need for child care at other times as well, and the fact that so many groups meet in church buildings means that the space for child care may be readily available. "I started coming to the group and leaving my one child with . . . we provide child care here during the group time, an hour and a half," explained Donna, the young mother who has been attending a Bible study group at her church for the past four years, ever since her baby was six months old. The fact that the church offered child care really made the difference: "It was a nice way for me to get out and really be separated from my baby for the first time comfortably."

Comfortably is the key word here. Obviously, many other ways of obtaining child care are available in today's society. But religious organizations, perhaps more than any other place in the community, have a long history of providing such services, generally free of charge, and of doing so in a way that makes parents feel that their children are in good hands. Overall, 26 percent of all group members say their group provides child care (this figure is 32 percent for group members who have children living at home). Among members of groups sponsored by churches, 35 percent belong to groups that provide child care, compared to only 14 percent of the members of groups not sponsored by churches.[2]

For those who thought American society was a nation of individualists and who marvel at the extent to which people are rediscovering community in small groups, then, one of the significant reasons for this development is the vast infrastructure of physical resources available through the nation's churches and synagogues. For clergy interested in fostering community, an enormous asset is already at their disposal. They probably have meeting rooms standing empty that could easily be made available to people interested in initiating small groups. And the churches may be a place where secular groups can meet as well.

PLANNING

It has sometimes been suggested—only half in jest—that the most efficient, rationally organized business operations in the Middle Ages were the monasteries.[3] Monks employed elaborate accounting schemes that, despite the heavenly orientation of their orders, made some of the monasteries very profitable ventures. The same can be said of many of today's religious organizations. Although some undoubtedly squander their resources, many, says management consultant Peter F. Drucker, would put the corporate boards of IBM and similar blue-chip companies to shame.[4]

The same planning that lies behind the carefully orchestrated worship services is frequently employed to organize small groups as well. To the casual participant these groups may seem as friendly and informal as the comfortable living rooms in which they are held. What appears on the surface to be "just people getting together with people," however, is probably the result of an elaborate planning process. We saw earlier that more than half of all group members say they are part of a congregation that considers small groups as part of its plan to grow. Nearly this many say their own group is part of such a plan. Among members of groups formally sponsored by churches, this figure rises to an astonishing 82 percent (see table 4.2).

A Baptist pastor described what he believed to be a fairly common practice in his denomination. Each year the pastor sets a goal for the small-group program to reach by the following year. For example, it might be to increase the proportion of the church's membership involved in small groups from 35 percent to 50 percent; it might be to expand the number of active groups by 20 percent; or it might include offering a wider variety of groups. To help reach these goals, each current group in his church has a trusted person who has been designated an "enlistment director." This person's assignment is to identify persons in his or her group who might make good group leaders and to recommend them to the pastor. The pastor then invites these prospective leaders to attend a course in which they receive special instruction in the basic doctrines of the church and criteria for membership. Those who pass the class go on to be group leaders.

If such procedures sound similar to the way in which the Communist Party established "cell groups" in its heyday, the analogy is not entirely coincidental. Some pastors speak of small groups as disciplined cells through which the work of the church is to be spread. Those who use this language often cite Dr. Paul Cho's Full Gospel Yoido Church in Seoul, South Korea, as proof of its validity. By drawing congregants into tight-knit cells, Dr. Cho was able to build the membership of his church to the point that it is now thought to be the largest in the world, totaling as many as 500,000 members.[5]

"The cell group is where the *real* action is in our church," says Pastor Bill Harkins, head of a 300-member congregation in Michigan. "I'm completely sold on them." His voice becomes animated as he tells about hearing Dr. Cho describe his program. "These groups are the future of the church. It's been proven in Korea. It can work in all denominations here too." Just the week before, one of his members had told him, "I've been going to this church all my life, but the small groups have grown me spiritually more than anything else has ever done." Pastor Harkins has about six such groups going right now. His plan is to get all of his congregants involved in them as soon as he can.

Table 4.2

RESOURCES SUPPLIED BY RELIGIOUS ORGANIZATIONS

Percentage of Group Members Who Say
Each of the Following Is True of Their Group

	Among All Group Members	Groups Connected to a Church or Synagogue Only
Composed mostly of members of this church or synagogue	54	94
One of a number of such groups at this church or synagogue	48	83
Part of the church's or synagogue's plan to grow	47	82
Using plans, lessons, or other materials provided by a church or synagogue	45	79
Under the supervision of one of the clergy	37	65
Something one of the clergy helped to start	32	56

Father Patrick J. Brennan is another member of the clergy who has become sold on Dr. Cho's cell group model. As president of the National Center for Evangelization and Renewal and director of the Archdiocesan Office for Chicago Evangelization, he finds that priests and laity are desperately seeking ways to revitalize their parishes. All too often, however, they have no plan and no knowledge of where to find a solution. Father Brennan recognizes that different plans are likely to be needed for different situations. Nevertheless, he believes the cell group model is rooted firmly both in biblical wisdom and in common sense. Small groups, he says, "are vital for anyone interested in evangelization."[6]

Other clergy increasingly have begun to take their cues for organizing small groups from the sales organization manuals of business people in their churches. A member of an independent evangelical church, for example, told how a regional sales manager for a large computer products company was chosen to head the church's burgeoning small-groups program. With some fancy time-sharing on the company's computers, the church's membership was divided into geographically homogeneous strata of approximately similar sizes, a leader and a leader-in-training were identified for each area, and a suitable "host facility" was selected on the basis of seating capacity, location, and other criteria, such as absence of "disruptive entities" (small children). A common stock of study materials was ordered, forms were printed, and a single reporting point was established so that group leaders could provide a weekly summary of attendance, prayer requests, and any other information deemed relevant.

Another example of advanced planning that turned up in several of the churches studied was a scheme that makes election to prestigious church leadership positions contingent on satisfactory apprenticeship in attending and directing small groups. Elders, deacons, and members of other highly visible lay boards are defined as those who primarily serve as "shepherds." Those who attain these ranks have climbed successfully up ladders that started in small groups. The first step is regular attendance as a participant, then come various quasileadership functions such as hosting or supplying food, leader-in-training roles such as serving as substitute group facilitators, and finally the formal title of group leader. This system ensures that anyone hoping for power or prestige in the church has to serve faithfully in the small-group process at least three to five years. Besides ensuring some continuity and stability (or expansion) in the planning process, this system also guarantees one of the other key resources on which small groups depend.[7]

Planning of this kind is, however, a resource that can have negative implications for groups. To be sure, some planning is necessary. People who feel lonely and isolated do not just happen to gravitate to the same church basement at seven o'clock on a Wednesday evening. Someone has to have planned the event. But planning can be carried too far. It can stifle the informality, spontaneity, and creativity that must be present for groups truly to develop close interpersonal bonds of caring and support. If lesson plans are orchestrated by the clergy, and if prayer requests are channeled back to the clergy, the members of small groups may take less initiative to care for each other. Even if strings are being manipulated behind the scenes, members must develop a sense of ownership for their group. As one pastor, who has watched the small-group movement in various settings for more than 30 years, explained:

"Churches with a heavy clergy-driven agenda typically do not do well with small groups; the laity has to be at the center."

LEADERSHIP

Emmanual Alliance Church is also a vivid example of the leadership that religious organizations often provide. Although both the head pastor and the associate pastor are keenly interested in small groups, they have delegated primary responsibility for these groups to a third member of their team. Assistant Pastor Strom devotes more than half his time to coordinating the numerous groups that the church sponsors. As established groups mature, some of the more effective lay leaders are also pressed into service in initiating new groups. The 2:7 groups are designed explicitly to give members the requisite biblical knowledge they need to become effective group leaders.

A progressive evangelical Presbyterian church in South Carolina provides further evidence that small groups do not come about simply because people want them, but because somebody went to the trouble of organizing them and providing them with trained leaders. With a membership of 1,300, 30 percent of whom are already involved in groups, the church is still waging a vigorous campaign to make even more groups available. "Just last week," the pastor notes, "we identified 30 new leaders to start their own groups to supplement those already in existence."

A more specific example of how leadership works comes from the Reverend Jim Stone, a pastor in Colorado who has been on the forefront of the small-group movement for more than a decade. Recently, he held a marriage enrichment seminar at his church. To advertise it, he printed a small brochure and had all the couples in the church give it to their friends. The stated theme was "The Enduring Marriage." But there was an underlying theme as well. Pastor Stone explains: "Lots of people out there don't know anything about God. They may have a bad experience with the church. But you know what? They really agree with our value. They'd like their marriage to last a lifetime. They've got no problem with that. And so I set up an environment, there's a trained master's level counselor who's going to give a workshop for three Friday evenings for two or three hours and just talk about the major issues that go on in marriage and how we deal with those. He's a Christian, and along the way he'll be incorporating his faith where he thinks it's appropriate."

What did this seminar have to do with small groups? After it was over, Pastor Stone observed that 41 percent of the people who came had never been in the church before. The seminar got them into the building, and once there, drew them into some short-term, small-group discussions. The pitch came at the end of the three Friday evenings: "We say, 'You know, some of you would really like to follow this up and do six to eight weeks on just building your marriage with a small group of people.' And so a certain percentage of people signed up to do that. And some of them even ask, 'What does the Bible have to say to us about good principles for lasting marriages?'" Pastor Stone thinks that people feel more comfortable when they can see that the church is "starting with my needs rather than their gospel." What gets people into small groups, he believes, is feeling that "they take *me* seriously." That feeling may be subtle, almost intangible, but it doesn't just happen. It emanates from Pastor Stone's leadership.

Clergy in other churches where small groups are less abundant frequently acknowledge that a lack of leadership is one of the main reasons. One Episcopal priest, for example, indicated that there was a very strong demand for small groups in his parish but that the clergy had a policy of letting lay leadership emerge to meet such needs. Up to this point, none had come forward: "Even though small groups may be able to spin out on their own, they need nurturing and support from the center of the parish. You let people do what they want to do, but don't put them in a boat without a sail. This support from the center just is not there right now."

The importance of leadership is clearly highlighted by our survey. Among all group members, 90 percent say their group has a leader; among members of church-sponsored groups, this figure is even higher (94 percent), a fact we consider more closely in the next chapter. The role of clergy leadership is also in dramatic evidence. Although only a third of all group members say their group is under the supervision of a member of the clergy, this proportion rises to nearly two thirds among members of church-sponsored groups. It also appears that some member of the clergy helps to start more than half of all church-sponsored small groups (table 4.2).

As the small-group movement grows, seminaries, lay institutes, para-church groups, and other religious organizations are paying more attention to the training of small-group leaders. At the Institute for Small Group Development in Chicago, for example, laity and clergy can enroll in a two-year program of intensive study that includes everything from basic biblical knowledge to personality assessment, group dynamics, evaluation, spiritual formation, and marketing. Through a wide network of abbeys, convents, and Catholic retreat centers, growing numbers of people are also receiving training in spiritual direction and its application in group settings.

This evidence is of practical significance for people who may be interested in starting small groups. Although sharing and mutual encouragement may be the goal, some leadership structure must be put into place. Churches have an advantage in this respect because clergy are already available to fill this role. For those trying to understand the larger social significance of the small-group movement, the main implication is that the movement is succeeding because American churches are putting vast resources into it: the time and energy devoted to it by paid religious professionals is a very significant investment. Clearly, the churches feel this investment is worth it. They could, for example, devote that energy to foreign missionary activity, to pastoral counseling, or to running soup kitchens and shelters for the homeless. But most of the clergy we talked with thought that it was important to devote at least some of their own time, or that of their staff, to planning and leading small groups. Only if people feel cared for, and only if they learn to care for each other, these clergy explained, can people be encouraged to give time and money to support other church programs.

By investing clergy time, therefore, the churches are making a statement about the importance of community to the health of American society. They are saying, just as de Tocqueville did a century and a half ago, that the society is stronger if people band together and learn how to take responsibility for themselves. Churches also are gambling that this strategy will be beneficial to their survival. Grass-roots movements involving millions of people can easily get out of hand. They can draw people's interest away from established religious institutions. Clergy have always worried about faith healers, tarot readers, fortune tellers, and cult leaders for this reason. But the small-group movement appears to be firmly in the clergy's hands. Whatever direction it takes in the future, the clergy have the capacity to guide it.

Readers interested in the character of American religion should also be aware that the small-group movement has already begun to alter the thinking of clergy—and, indeed, has been changing the role of the clergy. The leadership that clergy provide for small groups is quite different from that associated with traditional tasks, such as preaching, administering the sacraments, and teaching Sunday school classes. In those roles, the pastor represents the sacred, serving as an instrument of the divine and having divine authority for interpreting scripture, performing sacred rites, and communicating church teachings. As a planner and leader of small groups, the pastor's role is more that of an administrator. Someone with management skills could perform the task just as well. Moreover, the pastor generally is not physically present when the groups meet. Absence may make the heart grow fonder, but it also means that group members serve much more directly as their own priests rather than looking to the clergy for authoritative answers. As one pastor explained, "I give no directives, no commands, no imperatives. My job is to support you in looking at how Jesus is moving in your life." Thus group members must take more responsibility for their own spiritual journeys—a shift that most of the clergy we talked to viewed positively. It can also put faith on a slippery slope, however. Group members can attribute authority to anything that fits readily with their own experience, including the affirming words of friends in their group. This new focus, as we see in later chapters, can significantly trivialize the nature of divine wisdom and authority.

MODELS

Some churches have tried to combat this tendency for small groups to become their own arbiters of divine authority by providing instructional materials and other examples for groups to follow. Models are extremely important for getting anything started. When Karl Marx and Friedrich Engels, early in their careers, tried to fan the flames of revolution that were beginning to sweep across Europe in the 1840s, they looked carefully at the successes and failures of the great French Revolution of 1789. When Billy Sunday began his revival meetings early in this century, he modeled his methods on those of Dwight L. Moody. Small groups are no exception. Successful ones often grow because they follow a well-conceived model. Churches, synagogues, and other religious organizations play an important role in providing these models.

The pastor of a large Presbyterian church in the South told us he presents a ten-week course at least once a year to train new group leaders because there is always a greater demand in his congregation for small groups than there are people to lead these groups. In his course he presents two models: one is a study of the life of Timothy, so that people who are young in the Christian faith can grow into the kind of maturity that made Timothy a good leader; the other focuses more specifically on how to be a small-group facilitator and generally follows a model worked out by Christian writer Lyman Coleman.

This latter model, known as the Serendipity approach, is one that Coleman has been refining for more than three decades. Many churches and para-church organizations invite him personally to lead seminars on how to organize small groups; last year, for example, Coleman conducted nearly a hundred of these seminars nationwide, with a total attendance of more than 10,000 people. Other churches simply obtain his published material, most of it in booklet form. Among the most widely used of these are booklets on how to begin a small group, on small groups to cover basic biblical teachings, and on small groups especially for professionals, men, women, and couples. Coleman is currently developing materials for advanced courses and has recently completed a series of study guides for groups concerned with addiction or codependency.[8]

The value of materials such as Coleman's was driven home in a conversation with the pastor of a small Methodist church in Indiana. Although the membership of his church had dropped to about fifty, he was trying to promote new vitality and a sense of community by starting some small Bible study groups. He knew he needed some ready-to-use materials because none of his parishioners felt comfortable leading in the way that he taught classes or chaired committees. So he ordered Coleman's materials and started a couple of Serendipity groups. When asked why, he explained, "Well, I would have used the small-groups package put out by my denomination, but they require someone going through a training course that costs $600. We just couldn't afford it."

Coleman's model is but one of many on which churches are drawing for their small-group programs. At an Episcopal church in New Jersey, for example, about 40 "covenant groups" have been started in the past two years in a setting where people had virtually no training or experience with Bible study and prayer groups. Apart from the pastor, the most active role in starting these groups was played by a businessman who had been converted to Christianity while working at a Wall Street brokerage firm. Recognizing the need for workable models, he borrowed heavily from the prayer group he had become involved in on Wall Street, then had fellow leaders study a book on small-group Bible studies by Roberta Hestenes, president of Eastern College in Philadelphia and one of the pioneers of the small-group movement.[9] He also visited other churches in several neighboring states to find out what was working best.

In talking with other clergy and going through the literature on small groups, we found that religious organizations are able to play a very central role in initiating small groups because they have accumulated a great deal of wisdom in this area and have the channels in place to disseminate this information. The three main channels are: (1) Clergy and laity talking to people they know who already have been in groups to see what worked and what did not work. About 60 percent of all group members, as we have seen, have been in some kind of group before, and among members of church-sponsored groups, about four in ten have been in a similar group previously. (2) Religious bookstores, magazines, and book catalogues that contain information about books and study guides written for small groups as well as articles on problems associated with leading groups. (3) Denominational agencies and para-church organizations, such as youth ministries, that put out handbooks and study guides. For example, the Presbyterian church has a published guide for small group leaders, the Southern Baptist Convention has for years provided a planned curriculum and literature for its thousands of women's missionary societies, and campus organizations such as InterVarsity, Navigators, and Campus Crusade for Christ offer a wide range of Bible study booklets and leaders' manuals.[10] Among all group members, 45 percent say their group is using plans, lessons, or other materials provided by a church or synagogue; 79 percent of members of church-sponsored groups say this (table 4.2).

The value of such models must, of course, be considered critically. On the one hand, models are one of the reasons why the small-group movement has been so successful. Churches do not just enlist leaders and then send them out to start groups. They provide these leaders with very clear models, often in the form of how-to books, that tell them everything from how to arrange the furniture in their living rooms to what to do if one member talks too much. On the other hand, many of these models fall short because they deal with structure at the expense of content. Or, if they do focus on content, the guidelines are so simplistic that members may not be challenged to think very deeply. For example, these models take the form of "look up the verse" or "share something that happened yesterday" rather than attempting to convey deeper understandings. As a result, group meet-

ings may contribute only to a superficial understanding of the teachings and doctrines that have always been central to churches' traditions.

KINDRED SPIRITS

Some of the other resources that churches supply to the small-group
movement depend less on conscious planning or organization and
more on the fact that church members constitute one of the major
sources of recruitment for the movement. The simple fact that so
many members of small groups belong to churches—often the same
congregation—is terribly important. Virtually everyone who belongs to
a church-sponsored group says that most of the members of their
group are from the same church; more than half the members of all
kinds of groups say this. Almost the same proportions say that their
group is but one of a number that exist at their church or synagogue
(table 4.2). What do these numbers mean?

The findings mean that religious organizations also provide a kind
of screening function. Congregations help ensure the success of small
groups because people feel they have something in common with
other members and can feel safe and secure enough to open up their
hearts to them. If you walk into a group that you've seen advertised in
the newspaper, you have no idea whether you are among kindred spirits or not. Nor do you know whether the leaders have any special training, whether the group is part of some organization you'd rather not
associate with, or whether current members are happy with the group
or not. All these questions, say experts on secular groups, need to be
checked carefully. But if you see a group announced in the church bulletin, you figure that you probably have something in common with its
members by virtue of being at the same church. At least you will probably all have the same religious faith and will all know the minister;
perhaps you already have met some of the other people in the group.
In smaller churches this likelihood is very high. You can check with
these people to see who the leader is, how well the group functions,
and whether or not they are happy with it.

The pastor of a Baptist church noted that people found it fairly easy
to get involved in small groups in his church because many of them
were loosely related to one another. Others were able to talk about
their problems because they were similar to those of other people in
the group: "The church is comprised of extended families—aunts,

uncles, and so on—that have been here for years. There is a certain closeness that develops over the years that allows people to trust one another with their problems—these are problems that are probably shared by others in the group."

Other clergy often remark that people in their churches gravitate toward small groups on the basis of similar interests or lifestyles, such as people of the same age group, the same marital status, or from the same geographic area. Again, the church provides a screening function. How would someone know that there are other people of the same age and marital status who are interested in being in a group? The church is, among other things, a pool of information (often collected in membership surveys) about such characteristics and interests. Some churches keep such information on their computer and can generate lists of people with common interests whenever a new activity or program is being planned. In other cases, church people simply are able to gravitate toward "birds of a feather," as we saw in the last chapter, because they already have a sense of who the conservatives are in their congregations or whether a particular group is likely to be dominated by moderates or liberals.

The value of this screening function is that people can more easily find a small group in which they will feel comfortable. Feeling secure is an important human need. People need some place where they can feel safe enough to open up, share their doubts and anxieties, and just be themselves. Small groups are enormously beneficial because they provide a secure place of this kind. But there is also a cost. Small groups—especially ones that are prescreened on the basis of church membership—are unlikely to be places where people have to confront others who are quite different from themselves. In consequence, the group may be a place where preconceptions are reinforced rather than challenged. People can nod and smile and tacitly agree that Volvos are good cars, that the Bible is fundamentally true, or that abortion is inexcusable, all because nobody in the group holds a different view.

A COMMON LANGUAGE

The same costs and benefits derive from the language that groups employ. Every subculture develops its own distinctive language: people who understand it feel a common bond with other insiders; those who do not know the jargon are destined to feel like outsiders. Religious organizations are, among other things, settings for a common language. Some of this language—the idea of fellowship, for example—is so widely diffused that anyone can feel comfortable using it. Other language is more specialized. These are the words and meanings that play a very significant role as common ground for the formation of small groups.

Take the idea of "discipleship." Many of the pastors we talked to used the term as if it were part of anyone's vocabulary. Of course it is—and it isn't. Discipleship to the uninitiated can mean something like discipline, perhaps the sort of discipline one learns in boot camp. Or it can mean brushing up on some relevant skills, like one might at a summer tennis camp. It might even be understood by the thoughtful outsider as having something to do specifically with Christianity, since nearly everyone knows that Jesus' followers were called disciples. But pastors usually mean much more when they use the term. To them, it conjures up certain scriptural passages—like Colossians 2:7, to which the pastor who mentioned 2:7 groups was referring—and even certain study guides or religious periodicals.

Just as religious organizations help screen potential group members on the basis of common interests, they screen for a common language as well, and this selectivity contributes greatly to a group's success. After all, how can members engage in group discussion unless they share a common language? Twelve-step groups have been successful because over the years they have developed a common language (based on the concepts of the twelve steps). This language has become so widespread that traditional church groups are beginning to incorporate it into their own language.[11] The important point is that they have some common vocabulary from which to speak. The same is true of Jewish groups. Havurot is part of a broader set of concepts that describe fellowship and group responsibility.

Having a common language helps people in a group communicate better with each other, but the added feature of religious language is that it also points the conversation toward basic values and the deeper issues of life. This understanding is what forges stronger ties among group members than those normally found at business meetings and civic gatherings. It also distinguishes recreational or interest groups, even ones that might be sponsored by religious organizations, from those that focus on spirituality itself.

Donna, the young mother we met in chapter 3, drew the contrast between a social gathering she attended and her support group in precisely these terms. "In the social group there's not much emphasis on

Christianity. It is a group of people who are basically all in the same boat, in that we all have young children and we all like to get out and away from those children and just strictly socialize without a two-year-old hanging on your pants or a four-year-old asking you for a cup of apple juice." She said the support group she attends at the same church is much more important to her because "it has more the religious underpinning." When the group studies a book, for example, "we might tie in the Christian overview or the outlook that a Christian might have on this book, even though it has nothing to do in the book with Christianity, we'll bring that into it. And we'll bring our own lives, very personal things about our own lives into it. Like I said, the truthfulness and the honesty and the sharing in that group is just much more important to me than having a night out."

The cost of relying on a common language is that the deep assumptions built into taken-for-granted words may never be questioned and, therefore, never fully understood. People may, for example, say that they "believe" in the Bible and yet never pause to consider what this word may mean in contemporary culture. The common language also makes it harder for strangers to assimilate into groups. Even though the group wants to include newcomers, it may exclude them by talking in ways that make them feel like outsiders. The diversity of small groups, of course, means that newcomers can move on until they find another group in which they feel more comfortable. But the growth of the small-group movement also is likely to be limited because of the insider language that develops in all such groups.

MOTIVATION

Underlying all the other resources that religious organizations can provide is the most important of all: motivation. At the grass-roots level, people join small groups not only because they have some intrinsic need for community but because community is a value instilled by religious tradition. This value is also an important factor in religious organizations' willingness to devote resources to the small-group movement. Religious leaders, clergy and lay, are motivated to take an active part in developing small groups for three reasons.

The first reason is that small groups have a vital theological basis in the Judeo-Christian tradition. Most religious leaders believe that God made each person to be a communal creature, not to live as an isolated individualist. Indeed, the scriptures argue that God is a relational being and that humans are made in God's image. They command believers to show love toward others, to care for them, and to learn how to love themselves by witnessing God's love through the actions of other people. The scriptures also give ample evidence of the practical value of small groups—from Jesus' disciples as a small group to the apostle Paul's emphasis on sharing and community among believers in the early church. Small groups are thus understood as a vehicle for realizing the depth of human relations, despite the fragmentation of our society, and in this way, they become a means of rediscovering the reality and power of God's presence.[12]

The second reason is that small groups are widely regarded among religious leaders as a reliable source of spiritual conversion, discovery, and renewal. In addition to providing the sort of caring community that religious leaders may see as an end in itself, small groups serve as a means to the higher end of most religious organizations, which is to encourage individual members in their spiritual journeys. In part, small groups serve this purpose well because they are a safe haven in which to talk about members' spiritual journeys. Among small groups of fellow believers, people can talk about God without embarrassment. With trusted acquaintances in such groups, people know they will be accepted. They feel safe enough to admit their need for God, safe enough to voice their prayers, perhaps even safe enough to scream at God and express their anger.

The third reason why religious leaders are motivated to sponsor small groups is that these groups serve important organizational ends. Faced with tight budgets, with the growing appeal of secular attractions, and with an increasingly privatized or mobile population, religious leaders have come to see small groups as an answer to their problems. The pastor of one church in a highly transient section of the country, for example, described small groups as an almost desperate effort to keep up with the centrifugal forces scattering people to the four winds. "You've got to foster that sense of community fast in the church among the new members," he observed. "If you can't get them into a small group in the first three weeks, then you've likely lost them." Religious leaders also recognize that large, imposing structures are often the last thing people want when they are seeking spirituality, especially when they work in impersonal bureaucratic structures all week. Said an Episcopal priest, most newcomers see us as "closed and bureaucratic." People need to find that there are small groups where people really will care about them. Many pastors are also quite explicit in their understanding of small groups as a way to revitalize or expand their churches. As Pastor Stone puts it, "This is one of the major conduits for Americans to come back into the church in the future; it's being used all over the place to attract people back."[13]

At present, all three of these reasons are being reinforced by the small-group movement. Early in its development, movement leaders had to draw on traditional church teachings to make these arguments. For example, they often pointed to Jesus' disciples as an example of a small group. But now, given the success it has experienced, the small-group movement is able largely to legitimate itself pragmatically. It can point to its own successes in fostering spirituality or in encouraging churches to grow larger, and it can use those successes as reasons for others to join the movement. But there is also a danger. As the movement generates its own ideology, it can obscure the fact that its view of the world is not the only view that has ever existed. To say that God is a communal being, for example, may now connote that God the father, God the son, and God the holy spirit are sitting around having a small group among themselves. Such an idea would have been quite foreign to the early church teachers who expounded the idea of the trinity. Or, examples of churches that have grown to several thousand members because of an active small-group program can be held forth as models for all churches to emulate. But it is not clear that store-front churches with fifty members should jump on the bandwagon. Nor is it clear that a vibrant small-group program would save a church whose members are all moving away to find better jobs in new communities.

VARIATIONS AMONG RELIGIOUS ORGANIZATIONS

Thus far, we have emphasized the connections between small groups and religious organizations in general. But American religion has long been divided confessionally and denominationally. Readers can legitimately question, therefore, whether our points apply equally, say, to Catholics and to Protestants and whether the movement is being fostered by some denominations more than others. Our image of the movement, for example, would be quite different if it were largely sponsored by theologically conservative denominations, causing them to grow larger, than if it were being fostered by liberal denominations and helping them to revitalize.

Anecdotal evidence certainly suggests that small groups are flour-

Table 4.3

RELIGIOUS PREFERENCES OF SMALL GROUP MEMBERS

Percentage Who Say Their Religious Preference Is:

	Small Group Members	General U.S. Population
Protestant		
Southern Baptist	11	10
Other Baptist	10	10
Methodist	8	9
Lutheran	5	4
Presbyterian	4	2
United Church of Christ	3	2
Episcopalian	2	2
Other Protestant	17	19
Total Protestant	60	58
Catholic	28	27
Jewish	2	2
Other	6	4
None	4	9

ishing in virtually all Protestant denominations, among Catholics, and among Jews. Certainly there are differences in the styles of groups peopled by the various faiths. And yet, the best evidence indicates that people in small groups do not differ substantially from the total U.S. population in their religious preferences. About the same proportion of group members, for example, are Southern Baptists as in the general population, and the same is true for other kinds of Baptists, Methodists, Lutherans, Presbyterians, Episcopalians, Catholics, and Jews (see table 4.3). Indeed, the only significant difference is in the proportion claiming to have no religious preference (more of the general population than among group members).[14] It is also the case, as we consider more fully in chapter 11, that religious conservatives are more likely to be involved in small groups than are religious liberals. Yet many of these self-proclaimed conservatives are members of mainline Protestant churches or of Catholic parishes.

These findings suggest that the resources religious organizations provide for small groups are by no means limited just to a certain, perhaps narrow, segment of the population. Judging from the evidence we have already considered, it seems likely that people are finding their groups from within their own congregations. Those who do not seem to be able to find small groups somewhere in their communities, whether they are Protestants, Catholics, or Jews. This conclusion can be pinned down more solidly by comparisons between the Protestants and Catholics in our survey (too few Jews were included to compare them). Virtually all members of both faiths said that their congregations encourage people to become involved in small groups and believed that these groups were part of their church's plan to grow. Protestants were more likely than Catholics to say their group was formally sponsored by their church. Among those who belonged to church-sponsored groups, though, there were few differences between Protestants and Catholics in the kinds of resources their churches provided: most used materials provided by their church, were under the supervision of one of the clergy, and belonged to groups that the clergy had helped to start. The biggest difference between Protestants and Catholics was that more of the former belonged to Sunday school classes or to Bible study groups, whereas more of the latter belonged to special interest groups. As a result, Protestants tended to be in groups that were somewhat smaller, met more often, and prayed more regularly, whereas Catholics tended to be in groups that worked on projects together, focused on specific needs, and provided support (see table 4.4).

It is worth underscoring, too, that religious organizations supply resources for a wide variety of support groups, not just those geared toward promulgating the doctrines of a particular church or bolstering its membership. Increasingly, religious leaders are recognizing the value of making their physical facilities, accumulated wisdom, time, and training available to nonsectarian support groups as well. At Shomrei Torah Congregation in Wayne, New Jersey, for example, Rabbi Richard Eisenberg recognized the need to develop a broader base of support for the growing number of unemployed people in his community. Working with several members of his congregation, he was able to help create a support group for out-of-work executives. He agreed to host meetings of the group at the synagogue if churches in the area would publicize them in their bulletins. At Trinity Episcopal Church in Princeton, New Jersey, a similar group emerged, largely through the efforts of a prominent lay leader in the congregation. The time he was willing to volunteer to the group as a professional man-

Table 4.4

PROTESTANT/CATHOLIC COMPARISONS

Percentage of Protestant and Catholic Group Members
Who Say Each of the Following

	Protestant	Catholic
Congregation encourages small group involvement (don't knows deleted)	94	88
Small groups are part of church's plan to grow (don't knows deleted)	85	81
In a church-sponsored group	69	43
If yes:		
Group uses church materials	80	73
Clergy supervise group	63	66
Clergy helped start group	53	65
Group studies Bible together	69	38
Is a special interest group	42	51
Meets at least once a week	63	49

agement consultant was multiplied by the fact that the church made available its staff of switchboard operators. Before long, the church was receiving more calls about its job-seekers group than all other queries combined.[15]

Self-help groups focusing on addictions have received perhaps the warmest encouragement from religious organizations.[16] Alcoholics Anonymous, founded in 1935, was deeply influenced by religious teachings, having its roots in a movement called the Oxford Group, a post-World War I Christian renewal initiative.[17] Dependence on a "higher power" remains very much a part of AA teaching and practice, as do quasireligious rituals such as reciting the "serenity prayer" or the Lord's prayer.[18] As AA has spread, and as hundreds of other twelve-step and anonymous groups have formed, many have either emerged directly in conjunction with religious organizations or have made use of churches and synagogues as meeting sites.[19] According to a study of more than 3,000 self-help groups conducted by the New Jersey Self-

Help Clearinghouse, for example, 44 percent of these groups were meeting in church or synagogue facilities. By their names, many of these groups appeared to have been started especially for members of particular faiths; for example, Jewish Widowed Persons, Divorced and Separated Catholics, and Presbyterian Stepfamily groups. Most, however, appeared to cater to a more religiously diverse constituency and to unite people primarily around common problems or life experiences, such as miscarriages or stillborn deliveries, caring for an aging parent, or recovering from sexual abuse.[20] The New Jersey study appears to be fairly typical. Nationwide, according to our survey, four of every ten people who describe their group as a self-help group say it meets at a church.

There is much to be gained in these arrangements for all parties involved. "For decades Alcoholics Anonymous groups routinely met in church basements, but not much except their cigarette smoke seeped upstairs to the congregations," says Peter Steinfels, religion writer for *The New York Times*. But that situation is beginning to change, Steinfels believes: "Religious leaders have begun suspecting that more lives are being transformed in the basements than in the pews."[21] As a result, growing numbers of clergy are becoming members of twelve-step groups. They can be themselves better there—perhaps finding it possible to work on their own addictions and dysfunctions—than in Sunday school classes and Bible study groups where parishioners may look to them for spiritual leadership. Other clergy are turning to self-help groups to learn how intimate sharing can lead to emotional—and sometimes spiritual—healing.

Research also indicates that religious organizations currently facilitate, directly and indirectly, a wide range of other social, volunteer, and community-service projects, many of which may include small support groups or lead to the founding of such groups. According to *From Belief to Commitment*, a national study conducted by Independent Sector, 79 percent of all congregations provide family counseling; 45 percent are engaged in community development or community service projects; 44 percent are involved in programs assisting the mentally retarded and physically disabled or have crisis counseling options; 42 percent sponsor musical, dance, or other artistic groups; 29 percent provide programs concerned with teenage pregnancy; and 25 percent offer programs for battered women. Overall, nine out of ten congregations reported making their facilities available to groups within the congregation, and six out of ten reported that their facilities were available to other organizations in their communities. Concludes Brian O'Connell, president of Independent Sector, "A very large part of the nonprofit sector's service to society is performed by religious institutions."[22]

On balance, these findings suggest that churches are supporting the small-group movement mostly in ways that are beneficial to the churches: Bible studies, prayer fellowships, and Sunday school classes are the kinds of groups most likely to receive support from religious organizations. These groups are largely under the supervision of clergy and provide church members with activities likely (as we shall see) to reinforce their involvement in other church programs. Churches are, however, expending some of their resources on other kinds of small groups. The cost of providing facilities for twelve-step groups or support groups for people with special needs may, of course, be quite low, and may be justified as part of the churches' ministry to the wider community. Sponsoring such groups is also a way for the churches to keep a hand in efforts that might flourish under other auspices. To round out the picture, then, we need to briefly consider these other programs.

OTHER PLACES TO LOOK

Although religious settings might be the best place for people interested in joining small groups to look, other contexts provide rich environments in which to find small groups. Many self-help groups and special interest groups meet in other settings and under other auspices. They, too, depend on organizations, planning, leaders, and various kinds of models in order to succeed.

First, we need to mention again that many resources are available for persons with interests in spiritual exploration, Bible study, or religious topics who are not connected with local churches or synagogues. At least one group out of ten that is not sponsored by any religious organization is a Bible study group or prayer fellowship. Such groups are able to draw easily from the materials published by Lyman Coleman, Roberta Hestenes, and others, or simply purchase Bible study booklets at their local religious bookstore.[23] Another resource that has played an important role in the founding of many such groups is an organization called Neighborhood Bible Studies. Since its inception in the 1950s, it has supplied hundreds of thousands of study guides to people all over the world.[24] Local, regional, and national conferences, training sessions, and other resources for such groups are made available through various institutes and newsletters.[25]

Second, many of the groups that were classified in the last chapter as self-help groups have been facilitated in recent years by a vast array of physical, material, human, and even electronic resources. The twelve steps are an important resource that should not be overlooked. These steps not only guide individuals in the recovery process but create a common language, a set of rules, and even an agenda for many small-group meetings. In recent years, so many publications classified as self-help or recovery literature have proliferated that most commercial bookstores stock entire sections with these books. Another important resource has been the development of self-help clearinghouses. Often operated through local and regional mental health associations, there are presently more than 50 clearinghouses in 20 states and the District of Columbia. Their functions include keeping track of the many self-help and mutual aid support groups available in their state, region, or municipality. Many maintain toll-free numbers staffed around the clock to provide callers with information about how to contact specific kinds of groups. Some also publish source books with self-help groups listed by subject, information about how to start a group, and special resources for the homeless, those with mental health concerns, or people with rare or genetic disorders.[26] Many local newspapers and telephone directories also contain lists of self-help groups. Legitimation is also essential for any kind of movement, and just as Bible studies gain legitimation from religious teachings, the self-help movement has acquired a great deal of legitimacy in recent years from the testimonials of members, from therapists, and even from the medical community. Research studies demonstrating the positive effects of group involvement on health, happiness, and longevity figure prominently in the subculture of the self-help movement.[27]

Third, small groups that represent various special interests, such as sports, hobbies, meditation, physical exercise, political activities, and discussions of current affairs, have been nurtured in recent years, especially by the growth of nonprofit organizations and the so-called voluntary sector more generally.[28] One way in which the voluntary sector has contributed to the growth of support groups is by starting such groups for the training and emotional nurturing of volunteers. Rescue squad workers and volunteer firefighters, for example, frequently rely on support groups to talk out their feelings after dealing with particularly traumatic incidents. Another way in which nonprofit organizations facilitate small groups is by supplying paid professionals to lead these groups. Just as clergy do in religious settings, other professionals play an important role in planning, organizing, and moderating small-group meetings in mental health centers, hospitals, and civic associations. Other contributions include making space available, referring clients to groups, and disseminating models, common languages, and motivational appeals that encourage participation in small groups. Listener-supported public television stations, for example, have played an important role in publicizing the ideas of John Bradshaw, Anne Wilson Schaef, Melodie Beattie, Robert Bly, and other proponents of small group participation.

The relationship between the nonprofit sector and self-help groups has been especially close. National administrative structures provide guidance and coordination for small groups at the grass-roots level, and these in turn serve on the front lines to provide services, financial resources, or even pools of activists for the various causes these nonprofit organizations are attempting to promote. The list of nonprofit organizations that have been instrumental in starting small groups, providing information about them, and encouraging members to join them is enormous. The Association for Retarded Citizens is but one example. Founded in 1950, it now includes more than 1,300 local chapters that sponsor support groups and other activities for people with mental retardation and their families. Other examples include the Immune Deficiency Foundation, the American Hepatitis Association, Parents Without Partners, and the National Federation of the Blind, all with chapters nationwide, and more specialized or geographically limited organizations such as Eye Openers, Y-Me, Chapter Nine Group of Hollywood, the Philadelphia Unemployment Project, and W.A.T.C.H. (Women and Their Cheating Husbands).

Finally, support groups have been facilitated significantly in recent years by resources provided directly or indirectly by business and government. The fact that one small group member in five belongs to a group that uses a community building or town hall for its meetings attests to one kind of resource provided by government. Many of these groups may pay rent, yet the fact that the space is available should not be overlooked. Among young people in high school and college, meeting space for Bible study and prayer groups has been declared constitutional, and campus facilities are increasingly being used to host therapy groups, rape counseling support groups, twelve-step groups, and special interest groups of all kinds. Tax laws that allow deductions for mental health expenses are another way in which the government supports the small-group movement, at least indirectly, because therapists often encourage clients to become involved in group counseling or in self-help groups. Employer contributions to health plans that cover mental health costs constitute a similar means of indirect support. One indication from our survey of how significant the mental health industry may be in encouraging the small-group movement is that one group member out of every eight is currently involved in some kind of counseling or therapy. This figure compares with one person out of every 25 among people not in groups. Much more direct is the role of management-sponsored support groups for employees needing to reduce stress or improve communication skills. Of importance, too, are business organizations that encourage small groups as a means of providing a public service, thereby enhancing their visibility in the community or even selling specific products. In her study of book discussion groups in Houston, for example, Elizabeth Long discovered that local bookstores were playing a key role in supplying advice and encouragement to these groups.[29] Commercial publishers, such as Harper/Hazelden, Health Communications, and Prentice-Hall, have also been extensively involved in the small-group movement through the vast numbers of study guides and recovery books included in their offerings.[30] It is estimated that at least 300 bookstores nationwide are devoted entirely to recovery and self-help titles.[31] Bulletin boards listing meeting times and places of a variety of support groups can often be found at these bookstores, as is the case at countless Christian, New Age, seminary, and religious bookstores.

The small-group movement is flourishing in our society, therefore, not simply because of the resources being devoted to it by religious organizations but also because of resources from a wide variety of secular agencies. The significance of the latter is that groups are being initiated that probably would not exist if it were up to religious organizations alone. Such groups can meet specialized needs and provide community without raising issues of faith or spirituality. For people who prefer to regard their spirituality as a strictly private matter, such groups may be an attractive option. For people who claim to have no religious faith, of whom there is an increasing number, such groups may also be an appealing alternative. It is important, however, to recognize that secular support groups are likely to have more difficulty in securing resources than are religious groups. Churches, of course, operate with tight budgets, and they may face cutbacks when the economy falters. But, to a greater extent, secular groups depend on uncertain government initiatives and have to struggle harder to maintain national agencies or statewide clearinghouses. The huge sums earned by a few popular self-help advocates probably do not spread very widely throughout the population. Thus, it may be important for secular groups to cultivate alliances with the churches rather than viewing themselves strictly as alternatives.

MAKING CHOICES

In the final analysis, no one can deny that small groups sponsored by religious organizations are likely to appeal to a different clientele than those that develop under other auspices. Leaving aside all the differences that distinguish special types of groups from one another, a simple comparison of church-based and non-church-based groups establishes this point beyond question. Members of church-sponsored groups are far more likely to say they joined because they wanted more discipline in their spiritual life or because they heard about the group through their congregation. They are also far more likely to say that they are on a spiritual journey, believe themselves to be deeply religious, have experienced God's presence in their group, and have had their faith influenced by the group (see table 4.5). For those who yearn for spiritual growth, groups sponsored by religious organizations are clearly the place to begin.

But other kinds of small groups deserve consideration as well. While the proportions of members who report changes in their spiritual lives may not be as high, these proportions are still considerable. At least half the members of these groups claim to be deeply religious, more than a third say they are on a spiritual journey, and about this many report having their faith influenced and experiencing God's presence in their groups.

Important, too, is the fact that both kinds of groups seem to be populated by people struggling with many of the same issues in their personal lives (table 4.6). More than half the people in church-sponsored and in non-church-sponsored groups alike, for example, say they have been bothered lately by trying to figure out what is really important in life. Almost as many in both kinds of groups have been troubled by concerns about their health. A quarter in both kinds of groups are there because of some need for emotional support. At least this many say they are currently bothered by problems with their spouse or

Table 4.5

CHURCH-BASED AND OTHER GROUPS

Percentages of The Members of Each Kind of Group
Who Say the Following

	Church-Based Groups	Other Groups
Joined to become more disciplined in spiritual life	68	15
Heard about it through church	76	7
Think of self as deeply religious	87	53
Are on a spiritual journey	60	37
Group has influenced faith	81	31
Felt God's presence in the group	86	38

family and that they are feeling lonely, anxious, sad, or depressed. In nonchurch settings, group members are even more likely than in church settings to say they are troubled by their work, guilt, or other problems in their personal lives.

The chances for people to find others struggling with the same issues are high in any kind of group. The great variety of small groups available makes it possible to make choices. For the individual, the challenge is to make the most informed choice possible. Most religious organizations can provide valuable information. Many other networks, hotlines, and referral systems are available as well. For religious organizations, the main challenge is to meet the needs of individuals who come seeking. If these organizations do not rise to the challenge, other groups increasingly may emerge to fill the gap.

Two concluding observations are especially worth highlighting because they set the context for some of the most important issues we consider in subsequent chapters. The first is that small groups depend on leadership, planning, and connections with other social institutions. The second is that many of these connections have a religious focus. The first point is important because, as we shall see, people are attracted to small groups, not because of institutional structures, but because the groups are warm, friendly, and informal. There is thus an

Table 4.6

COMMON ISSUES OF GROUP MEMBERS

Percentages of the Members of Each Kind of Group
Who Say the Following

	Church-Based Groups	Other Groups
Trying to figure out what's important in life	51	56
Bothered worrying about health	47	52
Having problems with spouse/family	27	41
Feeling lonely	21	28
Feeling anxious	30	27
Having problems at work	20	31
Feeling sad or depressed	25	23
Feeling guilty	19	26
Joined to get emotional support	29	26
Joined because of personal problems	14	17
Joined because of a personal crisis	16	17

inherent tension between those who may wish to control these groups for institutional purposes and those who may attend them to get away from rigid organizational structures. The fact that so many groups are connected with religious organizations is important because these groups find it natural to emphasize spirituality. But in doing so, there is again an inherent tension. The gods people worship in their groups may not be the same gods that smile on established religious organizations. The former may be pragmatic gods that help the individual get along in daily life; the latter may be the gods of theological tradition, of creeds and liturgy, of the clergy, and of church-growth programs.

Up to this point we have considered the small-group movement mainly from the outside. We have placed it in a historical context, demonstrated how widespread it is in American society, painted a social profile of its members, examined its main varieties, and discussed the institutional resources on which it depends. All this analysis lends clear support to the view that the movement is a major phenomenon in our society. It is major not only in terms of numbers, but because it builds on historical precedents, adds new elements, adapts to a diverse social environment, and draws strength from established institutions. Having considered its significance in these ways, we are now in a position to look more closely at the interior of small groups and to ask why they work, how much caring takes place, and how individuals balance their own needs with those of their groups.

PART TWO

HOW SMALL GROUPS FUNCTION

5

MAKING IT WORK

Group Structure, Activities, and Member Satisfaction

Begun nine years ago, Logos Fellowship is a survivor. It was born when Pastor Ken, four years into his ministry in a sprawling suburban community, realized that his church was growing faster than he could keep up with. "The bigger we became," he recalls, "the smaller we needed to become." Convinced that the key to Jesus' ministry was reaching the masses by working with a small group of committed disciples, Pastor Ken decided to try the same strategy. Praying and meeting individually over lunch with several of the men he trusted most in his congregation, he soon identified several who were willing to become leaders of home fellowship groups. This was how Logos got its start.

In the years since, Logos has seen several different leaders. Many of its members have moved away and new people have joined. But its current leader feels it is still carrying out its fundamental mission of discipleship. About 15 people attend faithfully every other Sunday evening. Most are from the same geographic area, some thirty miles from the church. The group consists mainly of couples in their thirties and forties. The men work mainly in blue-collar jobs, and their wives are employed, too, as secretaries, office assistants, and sales clerks. They generally meet in the leader's home, an older, two-story house that resembles most of the other homes in the neighborhood; it seems less confusing to meet at the same place each time.

125

Usually people arrive at 7:30, although Fred, a man in his late thirties who has been leading the group for the past three years, never
plans to start until 7:45. He wants everyone to have a chance to mill
around, drink coffee, and loosen up for a while. And people do just
that. As they arrive, they greet each other casually, discussing the
weather, ball games, illnesses in the family, and other matters of common interest. The couches and easy chairs fill up first; late-comers
take folding chairs or sit cross-legged on the floor. The first order of
business is always prayer. In sequence, Fred goes around the circle,
asking each person to mention one or more prayer requests, sometimes pausing briefly to offer a word of advice or encouragement. One
person asks the group to give thanks because the bake-sale she organized went so well. Another reminds the group that her uncle is suffering from high blood pressure. "Just pray for his health," she says.
Another repeats her weekly request that "my sister comes to know the
Lord." Another asks God to give their pastor wisdom as he prepares his
sermon for the following week. As each request is mentioned, Fred
writes it down so that he can call on volunteers to pray for specific
items but also to have a record of what people are "wrestling with." All
heads bow and everyone in the group prays, after which Fred gives a
closing prayer. Sometimes, just to loosen things up, he leads the group
in singing a few choruses. The lyrics are printed on photocopied
sheets, but many of the group know them by heart. As they sing, some
of the members also mumble "praise you, Lord" or "thank you, Jesus."
   Fred then asks them to open their Bibles. By custom, the group
turns to the Bible passage on which Pastor Ken has preached earlier in
the day. Fred's job is to draw out their thoughts, and he has prepared a
long list of questions to help do that. He mentions some of Pastor
Ken's main points, based on notes he took that morning. "Do you
think he's right about that?" he asks. Heads nod. "Well, why is he
right?" The discussion continues through each of the sermon's main
points, and members often stop to ponder some story or anecdote that
Pastor Ken had included. Several of the members bring notes they
have taken on the sermon, but most do not, and several have not
heard the sermon at all. Occasionally someone in the group raises a
question and Fred tries to provide an answer. If everyone seems to
understand the main idea, Fred asks them how they can apply it in
their lives. "Is this really going to work?" That, he says, is the crucial
issue. Although he tries to keep the comments focused, they often
wander. The implicit norm of the group is to accept anything that

people say. Thus, one person reports an experience that seems to fit the verse; that anecdote reminds another person of a similar experience; and so on.

At about nine o'clock Fred draws the discussion to a close, usually with five or ten minutes of "teaching," a time in which he summarizes the main points of the evening and "charges" the group with some things to think about and do in the coming week. He tells them, for example, to be steadfast in their faith and not to be tempted by the wiles of the devil. He reminds the group that it is a blessing to have each other's company and encourages them to pray for one another during the week. His wife then brings out the refreshments—cake, cookies, chips, popcorn, and soda—and everyone mingles for another half hour or longer.

THE WEDNESDAY WOMEN'S GROUP

In another suburban community, much like the one in which Fred lives, a modern red-brick building with a plain white steeple sits prominently by the road. It is surrounded on every side by condominium and single-family housing developments that have sprung up in the past ten years. At exactly 9:20 this Wednesday morning, Penelope Brown pulls up in her tan station wagon. As leader of the women's group, it is her job to arrive first, unlock the building if nobody else is there, turn on the lights and heat, and get the coffee started. Within minutes, several other cars arrive, and by 9:30 the group—approximately 20 women—has assembled. Mothers of small children rush down the hall to the nursery to get their offspring settled as quickly as possible. Others exchange friendly greetings while they warm up their cold metal chairs. By 9:45 Penelope is able to call the group to order.

After welcoming a couple of visitors, she asks if there are any prayer requests. "I have something for praise," interjects one of the group. "They're not going to foreclose on our house! We're not going into bankruptcy!" Everyone applauds. "Yes," she continues, "the Lord caused someone at the mortgage company to have compassion on us." After listening to a lengthier rendition of what happened, Penelope, the leader, exclaims, "I'm all full of goosebumps! That's wonderful! What else do we have?" "Well," says another woman, "pray for my mother. She's sitting all day on Saturday with Lizzy (a friend who is sick), and she's never done that before." Another woman requests prayer for a sick neighbor. Another says that her mother, whom the group has been praying about for several weeks, is thankful to be out of the hospital. Somebody else asks the group to remember her this week because her husband is going to be away on business for several days. Soon the requests die down and Penelope calls for several volunteers to pray and mentions that she will close.

The sharing and prayer conclude at about 10:15, and the group members habitually reach for their study guides. They are in the middle of a three-month series on "the Christian woman," using a booklet by the same title that provides brief introductions to the subject each week, suggests Bible verses to read, and includes some questions to consider in advance. Its purpose is to help women live their daily lives in a way that is not only consistent with God's rules but also more conducive to personal happiness. Penelope's copy is a little longer than the rest because it includes questions for discussion.

She introduces the topic of the day, raises some of the questions she thinks might be interesting to discuss, and then opens the discussion by telling a story about something that happened to her recently. From that point, the discussion flows freely with Penelope intervening only occasionally to call on someone who has been trying to get into the conversation or to move the discussion to another item in the study guide. For example, several of the members had seen a program on television the night before about child abuse that they wanted to discuss for a few moments, after which Penelope broke in, "Okay, the next question says, 'Give examples of well-organized relaxation in your personal life.'"

One woman chuckles, "It's very hard to be well-organized, isn't it?" Another responds, "Yeah, every time I try to schedule something, there's an interruption." "But, you know," Penelope intervenes, "this question reminds me of when I was younger and had a horse. I knew I had to feed it and exercise it every morning. That was a routine, and so it was kind of relaxing, too." "I know," interjects another, "it's like when I really get engrossed in a good book. I know when I'm sort of getting addicted to it and shouldn't be reading so much. One day my husband came home and said, 'Fran, that sure must be a good book!' And I felt so guilty!" "What book was it?" someone else wanted to know. "Oh yes, I've read that one, too."

From there, the discussion goes on to include comments about finding time to do needlework projects to generalizations about differences in temperament. A number of the women register minor complaints about how their husbands relax. "Yeah," says one, "Vinnie just sits and sleeps all evening." "I guess it's different," says another, "having your schedule organized for you all day at work." Several offer comparisons between themselves and their mothers-in-law as well.

Again, Penelope breaks in, asking the group to look up some of the Bible verses listed in their study guides. One verse reads, "I will lay me down and sleep." "What does that tell us?" Penelope asks. "That we have a need for sleep," someone responds. Another verse says, "He makes me to lie down." One of the women comments that God has slowed her down lately. She was having to tell people no on the phone and sometimes those refusals made her cry. But then she realized it was okay because God wanted her to slow down. Several of the other verses also talk about the importance of relaxing, giving other members of the group opportunities to tell stories about how they have been working too hard.

At eleven o'clock sharp, Penelope indicates that time has run out. She says they will continue the discussion next week, announces a few upcoming events, and adjourns the meeting. By 11:15, with children collected and casual conversation over, everyone has departed to their homes.

THE SILVER CHASE MEETING

They call it the Silver Chase Meeting because it gathers every week in a small, semirural village with this name. Each Sunday evening, anywhere from 10 to 25 people gather at the oldest of the four churches nestled near the main intersection of town (the other three are dark). The participants are not members of this church; most are not members of any church. They meet here because the church lets them use the fellowship hall free of charge. Like so many other such groups, this one follows the twelve steps. It attracts a wide assortment of people, all of whom are recovering from some form of dysfunction in their family.

A typical meeting begins at 8 P.M. Different members rotate the leadership of the meeting. Usually this involves preparing a few thoughts beforehand and arriving early to unlock the building and turn on the lights. The meeting opens with a reading of the twelve steps, sometimes in unison, sometimes in sequence, each person taking a particular step. Then the leader recites a few basic rules for the discussion and introduces the theme of the week, usually one of the steps. The leader may share something of what's been happening during the week. Other participants take the conversation from there. Some relate their comments to the theme of the evening, but there is no pressure to do so. Nobody speaks very long at a time, but people commonly speak more than once. A woman explains that she is getting in touch with her feelings of anger toward her father, who abused her repeatedly as a child. "I just never knew I could feel so awful. This week I've really done well trying just to accept myself." A young man with long hair starts to say something and then buries his face in his hands and sobs.

Others talk about loneliness, depression, and anger at God. Many express anger at their parents, recalling conversations and experiences from their childhoods. "I just remember how my father would always walk away," one says, for example. "He'd shout 'that's ridiculous,' but then he wouldn't stay and talk it out." Others nod. They know the feeling. Promptly at 9:15 the leader calls the meeting to a close by initiating a unison recital of the Lord's prayer. A few people leave immediately; several linger in subgroups of two or three; a few go off together to a local restaurant for a snack and further conversation.

All three of these groups have been fairly successful. Logos Fellowship has been meeting continuously, except in the summers, for nine years. The Wednesday Women's Group has been meeting formally nine months of the year and informally during the summers for five years. The Silver Chase Meeting has been going on for at least six years. They are very different. And yet their current members all express deep commitment to them and believe they generally work well.

Why? What is the secret of these groups' success? Why do their members keep coming back week after week? What can be learned from these groups that may be generalizable to groups in other settings?

The support-group movement is, as we have seen, successful on the whole because of sweeping forces in American society—the tradition of interest in spirituality, the erosion of more established forms of community, and the availability of facilities, leaders, models, and other resources through churches, synagogues, and secular organizations. But some support groups are more successful than others. The reasons have less to do with large features of the society and more to do with what goes on inside the group.

A large literature has developed to instruct group leaders how to run effective groups. The advice offered in this literature reflects the kind of society in which we live. We not only must seek groups, rather than being born into them; we also must run these groups like little businesses. Everything should be planned ahead of time. There should be a precise schedule, goals for the group to achieve within a specified period of time, an agenda for each meeting, a study plan, and a set of elected officers. Especially when groups are part of a religious organization's master plan for growth, such ingredients receive great emphasis. And yet, it must be questioned whether this organization is the only thing that makes groups effective. Certainly, people in the past would have never thought to arrange their personal lives in this way. Warmth and intimacy were the opposites of bureaucratic efficiency, not something that could be furthered by a formally organized group.

The evidence gained from groups such as Logos Fellowship, the Wednesday Women's Group, and the Silver Chase Meeting suggests that groups succeed largely because they provide an informal atmosphere in which intimate sharing and caring can take place, not because bureaucratic rules and regulations have been properly followed. Indeed, the bureaucratic view of small groups may conflict with the open discussions and interpersonal relationships that members desire. How we understand the movement, therefore, depends greatly on whom we listen to. If we listen to the leadership manuals, we would understand it as an extension of rational, bureaucratic planning into the inner crevices of our personal lives. But if we listen to group members, we realize that something quite different is happening. The movement is thoroughly populist and democratic. It exists, not because of strong leaders and agendas, but despite them. Yet, both views contain some of the truth.

Again, we perhaps can understand the movement best by realizing that it has combined two features of contemporary society. It has utilized the methods of organization found in American business, thus ensuring that someone will be there to lead, that someone will have made the coffee, and that all members will have studied the same lesson. It is a highly rational enterprise, in this respect, operating like dinner parties, salons, and arranged marriages did in the past—all quite carefully orchestrated for the purpose of fostering interpersonal relationships. At the same time, small groups create space within these rational structures for highly personal and informal interactions to take place. A small group presents itself as family, as a substitute for neighbors and kin. The significance of this juxtaposition, in a sense, is that the movement has found a way of bringing together the best of both worlds. It should not be understood, therefore, simply as a reaction against the rationally organized features of contemporary life. It has, rather, used those features to its advantage. But the movement also has had to temper them, succeeding best by keeping them in the background. We find support groups to our liking because we have been trained to fit into a well-organized society, but also because we have learned to make small places for ourselves within that society.

By combining these features, small groups have been able to grow. But structure, on the one hand, and informality, on the other hand, do not always combine easily. For example, the Wednesday Women's Group flourishes because the members feel they can say and do pretty much what they please. Its leader is respected because she is "one of us" and because she accepts virtually all points of view. If the pastor decided to impose a rigid structure on the group (like some of the pastors quoted in chapter 4), he would probably have a small-scale rebellion on his hands. Even the Silver Chase Meeting illustrates some of the tensions between structure and informality. It has an occasional business meeting to discuss procedures and at least tacitly accepts the rules that twelve-step meetings are supposed to follow. Yet it has been small enough and in existence for long enough that its members have developed their own informal ways of doing things. Some weeks, its discussions are hardly recognizable as an example of a twelve-step meeting.

In this chapter, we consider how these characteristics—structure and informality—come together and how they contribute to member satisfaction and to the effectiveness of groups. This is information that group leaders need to understand. Most of the guidelines that have been developed for group leaders are based on the personal experiences of a few leaders rather than on systematic research involving large numbers of support groups. The evidence here requires rethinking some of that literature. But I am also interested in the broader significance of small groups. How they combine structure and informality is, again, a way of understanding how small groups are changing our relationships to each other. They are like informal gatherings of friends, but because they are formally organized they also give us a different sense of community than we have had in the past. In the process of participating in small groups, we are able to meet with kindred spirits on a regular basis, but we may also sacrifice the uncertainty that is always part of more naturally occurring relationships. We can cultivate some kinds of bonds, for example, telling others we accept them and would like to encourage them for a couple of hours a week. But we are less likely to care for each other physically, economically, or over long periods of time. Whether to have more structure or more informality is also a critical question that group leaders and members need to consider. There are forces pulling the movement in both directions. What has worked for the movement thus far may, therefore, need to be reconsidered in the future.

WHAT THE EXPERTS SAY

It should be obvious from the three examples presented at the beginning of this chapter that small groups vary enormously in style and structure. What makes one work effectively may not be applicable in the case of another. Nevertheless, the enormous literature on the subject suggests that small groups do not just happen. Because they are intentional, rather than spontaneous, they require some degree of planning, organization, and coordination. The following list summarizes what some experts have identified as key ingredients to the successful functioning of any small group:

- A well thought-out, explicitly formulated statement of purpose for the larger organization (church, synagogue, social service agency, self-help clearinghouse) into which the small-group program is to fit.
- A clear, well-organized strategy for meeting this objective that shows the place of small groups in relation to other activities and programs.
- A research and planning phase that involves gathering information from other small-group programs and adapting this information to one's immediate situation.
- An intensive period of training for potential group leaders and a rational plan for selecting leaders.
- A pilot phase in which several "test model" groups are initiated in order to work out unforeseen problems.
- A review system for group leaders to use in evaluating their meetings so that, in consultation with one another, they can maintain quality control.
- A coordinated plan for initiating new groups and adding new members.[1]

Before proceeding further, we should acknowledge that a list like this would probably make the eyes of many group members glaze over and prompt others to say "I'd rather die than be in a small group." From members' own remarks, what they like about small groups is their warmth, not the fact that they have been organized as carefully as a branch office of UPS. The value in pitting these two images against each other, however, is to point out one of the ironies of small groups. Many people view them as reactions to the impersonality of modern life. They are supposed to provide the intimacy that people cannot find in their places of work. As cold bureaucratic efficiency takes over more of the world, small groups are said to be pockets of resistance, or at least enclaves in which people can find shelter from the storm. But a list like this suggests that small groups may be a product of the rational, bureaucratic planning that dominates other sectors of contemporary life. Indeed, small groups may be extending such planning into an area of life that formerly depended on nothing but the goodwill of neighbors and friends.

The main question this juxtaposition of UPS-style rationality and warm informality raises is whether a well-organized structure is really vital to the effective functioning of small groups. Perhaps organization is largely irrelevant, something that clergy, saddled with the mission of making their churches successful enterprises, worry about in their spare moments. Perhaps such structure is not really that important to the success of small groups. It might even have negative consequences, given the possibility that people join small groups in order to escape such bureaucratized modes of thinking. Or, perhaps, groups vary, with some kinds relying more on advanced planning and heavy-handed leadership than others.[2] If bureaucratic organization is not essential, then group leaders should at least realize this fact so that their energies could be directed more toward cultivating what really counts.

Logos Fellowship is an example of the more highly structured, pre-planned groups. It was started as part of the church's overall plan for the community. The groups are divided geographically and at least twice a year all the members of the church are encouraged to become involved in the group closest to where they live. Every group follows the same agenda. Leaders are selected by the head pastor, undergo training, meet with him at least once a month, and play an active role in the group's discussions. The Silver Chase Meeting, in contrast, functions with a minimum of structure. Its members and leaders represent no other organization, so there are no worries about whether the group is fulfilling that organization's mission or not. Members participate only because they are getting something important from being there. The Wednesday Women's Group falls in the middle. Although it is part of the formal activities of a church, it was started by the women. The pastor is glad that the group exists, but he plays no role in selecting its leaders or setting its agenda.

Which of these styles is adopted depends on a wide variety of circumstances. If the group is part of a church's plan for ministry, for example, then it may be important to impose more structure on the group than if it has sprung up spontaneously. The starting place for understanding why small groups work, though, is to recognize that there are certain common elements, even among groups that differ vastly in purpose and style. We can see more clearly what a small group is by considering some of these common elements.

Leadership is one of these elements. Its role is certainly evident in Logos Fellowship and in the Wednesday Women's Group, but even at the Silver Chase Meeting leadership is crucial. There have been times when the leader failed to show up and the meeting still went on (its members sitting on the grass near the church's graveyard), but this could not have happened consistently without the group falling apart. Among people in small groups nationally, nine out of ten say their group has a leader (table 5.1).

People who have observed the dynamics of social gatherings recognize that leadership emerges in almost any kind of group. Families, for

Table 5.1

TYPICAL CHARACTERISTICS OF SMALL GROUPS

Percentage of All Group Members Who Say Their
Current Group Has Each of the Following

A leader	90
A stated purpose or goal	84
A name	76
An agenda or schedule	75
Elected officers	57
Business meetings	53
Something to study in advance	49
A membership fee	26
Child care	26
A contract that people have to agree to	18
A term after which it disbands	13

example, usually depend on one or more persons taking responsibility to see that household jobs are assigned and that important financial decisions are made responsibly. But even in an informal gathering, say, of neighbors drinking coffee together, one person may emerge as the informal leader by virtue of talking more, knowing the other participants better, or having initiated the gathering in the first place. The leadership role in small support groups, however, is even more important than in these natural or informal gatherings. The reason is precisely because small groups are neither natural nor informal. In a family, where people live together and interact daily, leadership of some kind generally emerges because decisions have to be made. In a small group, people have to make a choice about being there. If there were no leadership, the group probably would cease to exist. Unlike an informal gathering, moreover, the group also takes more effort to keep going on a regular basis. Some friends might stand together and chat after church occasionally, but it would take leadership to mold them into a group that met regularly and provided each other with support.[3]

The experts also have a point when they argue that small groups need to be clear about their purpose or goal. The fact that they are voluntary, intentional, means that people must have a reason to be there. Otherwise, it is easier just to sit at home and watch television. To be sure, each person's reasons may be unique to that person, but it helps enormously if people know in advance that the group is formally oriented toward a particular goal. With this knowledge, people know what to expect, can choose among various options with some chance of getting into the right group, and can exclude activities that do not seem appropriate. Nationally, five out of six group members say their group has a stated purpose or goal.

Does this statistic mean that the goal has been written down so that members can read it or memorize it or recite it when asked? Usually not.[4] Asked if Logos Fellowship has a goal, for example, Fred immediately responded "yes." He thought he could talk at length about it. But when he tried, he found much of the group's goal could be summed up in the word fellowship. Besides that, he said, the main goal is just to help people live what they read in the Bible. At the Silver Chase Meeting, most of the members knew there was no formal charter with the group's purpose stated in so many words. But they did have ways to describe the group in purposeful terms. Some said it was a place to express their pain, others to receive encouragement, others to work on their dysfunctions. The important thing, here as in all groups, is that members believe there is a goal. Believing this, they have a reason to attend. They feel that people are there for a reason. And this belief is why the question of whether groups work is important. People would not necessarily raise a pragmatic question like this about their friends or neighbors, but they do feel it is a legitimate question to pose about their support group.

Even something as simple as having a name is a very important feature of small groups. Three out of four people in the survey said their group has a name. It may be something as informal as the Home Fellowship or the Wednesday Women's Group, but groups without a name usually get one before long. The Silver Chase Meeting is an example. Many of its members attend other twelve-step groups in the area, so calling this one by its location helps them identify which group they are talking about. A name helps give the group an identity as a group, something corporate, rather than just the individuals who participate in it. All the better, therefore, if the name emerges naturally from the group's members.

The other structure that most small groups have—three-fourths according to the survey—is an agenda or schedule. It can be a well thought-out agenda like the one Fred has in mind for Logos Fellowship. He feels unhappy if the group strays too far afield of his prepared questions and tries to bring the discussion back to what he considers are the important issues. Or it can be the sort of agenda that the Wednesday Women's Group and the Silver Chase Meeting follow: a framework from which they are willing to depart. Even the loosest, most spontaneous groups, however, rely on some kind of schedule. Knowing when and where to meet and having some idea of the topic is essential.

While it may seem obvious that small groups should have a leader, a purpose, a name, and an agenda, many of the other structures that group leaders and planners feel are important seem to be more optional. Elected officers and business meetings, for example, are found in only about half of all small groups—a proportion that may still seem surprisingly high to those who believe that small groups operate without any structure. Usually it is the larger groups, or those (such as Sunday school classes) founded in an era when the voluntary association was the model, that employ these structures. There are exceptions, however. The Silver Chase Meeting, for example, occasionally has a formal business meeting to air any grievances that have been accumulating and to talk about mid-course corrections. Something to study in advance is also a feature of only about half of all groups, according to the survey. The Wednesday Women's Group finds it helpful to use study guides because these materials encourage participants to relate their experiences to ideas in the Bible or in the works of popular writers. The Silver Chase Meeting, in a sense, has something to study in advance because members know the discussion is going to take a particular step as its theme; but most members pay little attention to the theme and focus more on issues from their own lives.

Other structures that some experts have argued for appear to be relatively uncommon in small groups. Child care, for example, is available in about a quarter of all groups, but is irrelevant to the needs of many group members. A membership fee of some kind is also required by about a quarter of all groups. Some experts believe charging a fee is a good idea because it makes people value their group more highly and take its meetings more seriously. But most groups accomplish the same thing with donations in kind, such as a rotating schedule for hosting the group, making the coffee, or bringing dessert. In some quarters, a formal contract is thought to be important to the effectiveness of groups. But fewer than one group member in five claims to belong to a group that has one. As we shall see, establishing an informal contract may be more important. It also has been suggested in some of the literature on small groups that limiting their duration to a specified term is a good idea; thus, people can bow out gracefully and do something else if the group isn't meeting their needs. As yet, though, only about one group in eight appears to have adopted this strategy. The fact that so many members have been in their groups for several years or longer suggests that people may be less eager to make a polite exit than planners have thought.[5]

This evidence appears to at least partially vindicate the claims of experts who say that careful planning, leadership, and organization are essential to the functioning of small groups. We consider later whether these structures make groups function better. But at least we now know that most groups include some structure. They are not simply informal gatherings of people who happen to know each other. The new quest for community involves a high degree of planning and organization.

WHAT PARTICIPANTS SAY

Structures such as leadership, goals, names, schedules, business meetings, and the like may be important features of small groups, but these kinds of features probably serve best by remaining in the background. Even an effective leader may function best as a facilitator rather than as a loud, intrusive voice in discussions. What participants say about groups usually bears little connection to these formal structures. To be sure, people sometimes complain because their leader is too active or because there has been confusion over the agenda. But what participants talk about most are the less tangible dimensions of the group.

Feeling at home is one of the most important factors in whether participants think their group functions well or not. Because so many groups are available in any given community, or even in many churches, most participants can shop around, trying on various groups to see how well they fit. People come to the Wednesday Women's Group, for example, because they feel comfortable interacting with other young mothers from the same community. In some cases, this feeling comes almost instantly because the group is good at welcoming newcomers. In other cases, the group may have become so ingrown that a newcomer feels comfortable only because some individual in the group makes a special effort.

Even subtle factors may make it easier or harder for people to assimilate into the group. At the Wednesday Women's Group, for example, several of the women found it hard to assimilate because several of the others were related to each other. At Logos, Fred recognizes that discussing the sermon makes it almost impossible for people who are not already active in the church to feel comfortable in his group. Those who do come, though, feel very much at home, in part just because Fred's house is a comfortable place to meet. Ambience is important to most of the people who attend the Silver Chase Meeting as well. "I liked the casual atmosphere," one participant explained. "I liked the physical setting of it. It's a nice pretty room, and I liked the town. It's a neat thing to drive into that pretty little town, go into the nice room." This, of course, wasn't the main reason she settled into the group; she had tried several others and when she heard about this group she figured that the people probably had experiences similar to hers. But the physical setting was also important.

The following list gives some of the most frequently mentioned characteristics of small groups that members say they like and in a few other cases express dissatisfaction about.

Making newcomers feel welcome.
Having well-prepared leaders.
Having people who trust each other.

Addressing important issues.
Respecting all different points of view.
Drawing everyone into the discussion.
Making me personally feel appreciated.
Helping other people outside the group.
Having members faithfully attend.
Having everything working smoothly and efficiently.
Meeting emotional needs.
Having members hold each other accountable.

When participants are asked to say what they like about their groups, the more intangible items on this list usually are mentioned most frequently. "I liked the feeling" is how one woman expressed it. She had been in groups most of her adult life, but had never lasted very long in any of them. In one, she liked the people, but they seemed to be there for different reasons than she was. In another, she wasn't able to assert herself enough to get what she needed from the group. In still another, everyone seemed to be struggling with such serious issues that she didn't feel legitimate. She's stayed in her present group four years, though, mostly because she feels she can be herself and the group will accept her.

This sort of Goldilocks syndrome has been the experience of many of the people we talked to. They couldn't quite put their feelings into words, but they knew one bowl of porridge had been too hot, another too cold, and another just right. First impressions were often lasting impressions. They enjoyed being welcomed warmly. They felt good if the group seemed to be interested in the same issues they wanted to explore. They didn't enjoy groups where they couldn't get a word in edgewise, but often appreciated groups in which they had the freedom to sit quietly too. Being appreciated—for what they had to contribute, but even more, for who they were—was perhaps the most important feeling of all.

Of course, it makes sense that people shop around until they find a group in which they feel comfortable. But the fact that people can shop around tells us something very important about the small-group movement and about the way in which it is changing the character of American society. Although it is very much in the American tradition to choose our friends, neighbors, jobs, and churches, the ability to make such choices always has been somewhat limited. Circumstances limited us. For example, having bought a house in a certain neighborhood, we were limited by our circumstances as far as who our neighbors were. And the same was true of our jobs. But the greatest restriction on our choices was our understanding of commitment. Friendship meant that we were committed to a relationship, often for a lifetime. Being a church member meant being involved in only one church and participating in it because we respected its traditions and wanted to contribute to its future. But small groups encourage a different view of commitment. Because there are so many, we are seldom limited by circumstances. We can, indeed, shop around. There may be fifty different groups from which to choose within five miles of our home. And the logic of shopping emphasizes satisfaction rather than long-term commitment. The idea is to try it out. Groups are supposed to be open to newcomers. A person who happens to like the group may stay, perhaps for six months until the group disbands or even for five years, if the group is more enduring. But, always, the contract is tenuous. It depends on whether the individual member remains satisfied.

Most members are quite satisfied with their groups, our research shows. On the whole, five group members out of six in the survey (84 percent) said they were at least very satisfied with their group (33 percent were extremely satisfied); only 1 percent said they were currently dissatisfied. These responses suggest, of course, that people who become dissatisfied pretty quickly drop out of their group, join a different one that they like better, or stay unaffiliated. High rates of satisfaction, in other words, do not mean that small groups are necessarily doing everything right. But these findings do mean that the people who participate in small groups are by and large a loyal, contented lot who find enough about the group likable to keep going back.

Group leaders naturally want to know even more precisely what the nature and extent of this satisfaction is. On what aspects do participants rate their groups highest? And on what aspects are there indications that things may not be entirely satisfactory? Coming back momentarily to our list, respondents in the survey generally gave high marks to their groups on almost all these items. Perhaps surprisingly, the highest mark of all was given for making newcomers feel welcome (see table 5.2). In much of the literature on small groups, special attention is given to techniques for welcoming newcomers because there is a widespread belief that small groups can become too inwardly focused to do so naturally. Many of the group leaders we talked to were personally concerned about this issue, too. But apparently their concern is translated into action that does make newcomers feel welcome. Of course, we should be cautious in interpreting this response in the survey. We do not, for example, know what newcomers might have said, especially those who attended but did not come back. Yet there is also reason to believe that people in small groups appreciate having newcomers in their midst.

Group members also give very high marks to their leaders. They appreciate it when leaders are well prepared, even though specific leadership styles may vary widely. Some leaders were respected for their depth of knowledge, say, in understanding the Bible. But more common were comments about leaders who were in tune with the needs of individual members in their group. People liked leaders who could sense that someone was shy and needed to be drawn out or who could sense that the discussion was wandering off on a tangent and bring it back to the main issue. These findings are interesting because they suggest that members do not regard leaders simply as a necessary evil. Although the small-group movement, on the whole, is quite devoted to principles of equality and mutual help, most members respect their leaders and value their presence. The reason, though, is that leaders try to fit into their groups and behave as equals, rather than posing as authorities who know more than everyone else.

Most groups receive high ratings, too, for various attributes of the discussions that make up the core of their time together. Members want to feel that they can trust each other, that the issues they discuss are important, that everyone has an opportunity to contribute to the discussion, and that different points of view will be respected. On all these attributes, better than 80 percent of group members say their group does at least a good job; more than a third rate their groups as excellent on these items. So, for leaders hoping to foster successful groups, open discussions, activities that engender trust among group members, and tolerance toward diverse views appear to be vital considerations.

Other characteristics are rated somewhat lower, although positive ratings still outweigh negative ones by an overwhelming margin. If anything, these aspects are somewhat less highly rated because they are less highly valued or are considered irrelevant to the functioning of some groups. Holding each other accountable, for example, is given low ratings by more people than any other item on the list, despite the fact that it is emphasized strongly in some groups. Other groups regard accountability as a form of intrusion into individuals' lives. In

Table 5.2

MEMBERS' EVALUATIONS OF THEIR GROUP

*Percentage of All Group Members Who Rate Their Own
Group on Each Characteristic*

	Excellent	Good	Fair	Poor
Making newcomers feel welcome	51	41	6	0
Well prepared leaders	43	44	8	1
Having people who trust each other	41	49	6	1
Addressing important issues	38	44	11	2
Respect different points of view	38	51	8	1
Drawing everyone into the discussion	37	47	11	1
Making me personally feel appreciated	35	49	13	0
Helping other people outside the group	29	37	19	5
Having members faithfully attend	28	47	22	2
Having everything working smoothly and efficiently	27	54	16	1
Meeting emotional needs	24	43	21	3
Having members hold each other accountable	13	34	24	9

this view, people should be accountable to themselves, but should not try to take responsibility for each other.

Some of the items on the list also suggest worrisome situations. The fact that meeting emotional needs ranks near the bottom of the list in terms of positive ratings may mean that small groups have only begun to tap the surface of the vast need for emotional support that exists in our society. The fact that a quarter of all group members say their group does only a fair or poor job of helping people outside the group is also a worrisome sign. We consider both of these issues in later chapters.[6] For now, it is enough to say that the small-group movement, on the whole, does a reasonably good job of helping members with emotional needs and encouraging them to reach out to the needs of people beyond their groups as well; but a substantial minority of small-group members also worry that not enough is being done.

WHAT INFLUENCES GROUP FUNCTIONING?

Having considered some of the characteristics of groups, we can now return to the question of whether these attributes contribute positively to the functioning of groups. It may be, for example, that groups with a clearly stated goal function better than those without. Or it may be that the presence or absence of a goal makes no difference. These are matters with which group leaders need to be concerned. They also help us understand more clearly what Americans find so appealing about small groups.

To raise these questions is to imply that group functioning can somehow be measured. But how? Our survey data provide two possibilities. The first is to see what factors influence member satisfaction. As we have seen, about a third of all members are extremely satisfied with their groups, another half say they are very satisfied, and the rest express only weak satisfaction or dissatisfaction. It is thus possible to compare these members to see why some are more satisfied than others. Satisfaction is, of course, a purely subjective measure, but its intangibility does not make it unimportant. Satisfied members are more likely to keep coming back and more likely to devote energy to their groups. If they are satisfied, they also may gain more from their group and help to cultivate an atmosphere that encourages other members as well.[7] The other possibility is to measure group functioning by aggregating members' ratings of their group on the more specific attributes we have considered. These ratings are still subjective, but they go beyond mere satisfaction. They focus on specific functions, such as cultivating trust, making newcomers feel welcome, and addressing important issues. This second measure, then, is a composite of the twelve attributes shown in table 5.2.

To see what influences member satisfaction and member evaluations, we should consider the relative importance of the various organizational structures that have already been discussed. We also should consider the effects of other group activities that were discussed in chapter 3—activities such as eating together, singing, following a twelve-step program, or engaging in physical exercise. What we want to know is whether groups that include some of these structures and activities seem to function better than groups that do not. Because some members seem to express satisfaction or give high ratings no matter what, we must take some of these predisposing differences into account. We should, for example, take into account differences associated with gender, age, frequency of church attendance, and frequency of participation in the group. Because the various kinds of groups have different expectations and aims, we should consider results separately for each of the four major kinds of groups. Having the results organized in this way makes it possible for readers who may be members of one or another of these kinds of groups to see, on the basis of responses from hundreds of people in similar groups, what generally makes some of these groups work better than others.

Sunday School Classes

Judging from both member satisfaction and overall member evaluations, Sunday school classes seem to function best with a relatively high amount of structure. Taking into account gender, age, frequency of church attendance, and frequency of participation in the group, members who express higher-than-average levels of satisfaction tend to be in groups with the following characteristics: elected officers, an agenda or schedule, a name, and child care. Using the composite evaluations, members who give above-average evaluations of their Sunday school classes are in groups that have: business meetings, elected officers, a stated goal or purpose, a name, and child care. It is important to note that these are the specific characteristics that make a difference. High levels of structure in general are not the issue. For instance, neither satisfaction nor composite evaluations is significantly influenced by membership fees, fixed terms, or contracts.

The activities that contribute significantly to both satisfaction and high composite evaluations in Sunday school classes are: singing together, eating together, doing things for the community, meditating, and speaking in tongues. This list suggests that Sunday school classes work better when they involve members in a wide range of activities, rather than simply meeting together to discuss the Bible or some other lesson. Indeed, the characteristic that seems to make the most difference runs contrary to stereotypical notions of Sunday school classes. Those notions emphasize the fact that these groups are classes and, for this reason, assume that they function best by presenting solid intellectual learning experiences. If such notions were correct, our data would have shown significant results for activities such as studying the Bible, praying together, discussing religious topics, considering social issues, studying books, and having something to study in advance. But none of these aspects made a significant difference to member satisfaction or composite evaluations. What did make a difference were the nonintellectual experiences provided by some Sunday school classes. As we see in later chapters, though, the factors that influence spirituality are not entirely the same as those influencing member satisfaction.

From these findings, we can also draw some tentative conclusions about the ways in which Sunday school classes are being modified by the logic of the broader support-group movement. The traditional Sunday school class involved a teacher who lectured on a topic or who moderated a carefully guided discussion of some specific religious teaching. Didactic instruction, borrowed from secular education, was the model. Sunday school classes also were centrally organized, usually following a curriculum specified by the denomination or by the local church. The fact that Sunday school classes still depend heavily on structures such as stated goals, formal names, business meetings, and elected officers suggests that this model is still what many people expect when they attend such classes. However, classes that only provide didactic instruction have had to compete with other kinds of groups that promote sharing and caring to a greater degree. Thus, the satisfied Sunday school member now expects to become more fully integrated into the class. Singing, eating, and other activities must be present to enrich the experience. Having fellowship has come to be more important than learning religious ideas.

Bible Study Groups

We saw earlier that Bible study groups resemble Sunday school classes in many respects. The two, for instance, are virtually indistinguishable in terms of how likely they are to include discussions of the Bible, prayer, and sharing of personal problems. They are also similar in terms of the proportions that have a set agenda, a name, a fixed term, a leader, and something to study in advance. The two even resemble each other closely in their capacity to draw members into the discussion, make newcomers feel welcome, cultivate trust, and make members feel appreciated. And yet, the profile of what makes a difference is quite dissimilar.

Whereas certain kinds of formal structure have a positive effect on Sunday schools, they make no difference in Bible study groups. Indeed, child care was the only structure that definitely contributed to satisfaction. The only other structure that contributed to higher composite evaluations was having business meetings. On both measures, groups that placed their members under a contract scored lower than average.

The activities that make a difference in Bible study groups also differ from those that matter in Sunday school classes. Eating together is the one activity that contributes to higher satisfaction in Sunday school classes and Bible study groups alike, but it is not related to higher composite ratings in Bible study groups. Otherwise, what matters most in Bible study groups is sharing problems, praying together, and engaging in hobbies or sports together. Doing things for the community is a negative factor as far as satisfaction and composite evaluations are concerned. Again, certain kinds of Bible studies seem to generate higher levels of satisfaction, no matter what; for example, Bible studies that include speaking in tongues or that focus on an addiction. But these groups are a small minority of all Bible studies.

We also learn from looking closely at the data that satisfaction and composite ratings seem to depend on somewhat different things in Bible study groups. If a group were interested simply in making its members extremely satisfied, the best things to do would be to eat together, have parties, and engage in hobbies and sports. Our composite evaluations, however, turn our attention to how well the group is doing on a wide range of functions (trust, attendance, meeting needs, etc.). This broader context seems to require Bible study groups to sponsor a wider range of activities for their members. Thus, engaging in sports and working on hobbies contribute positively, but so do discussing books and meditating.

On balance, the comparison between Bible study groups and Sunday school classes seems particularly interesting in light of the emphasis that has been given to the one, relative to the other, in recent years. A century ago, Sunday schools were advanced by church leaders for many of the same reasons that Bible study groups are being championed today: they would revitalize the church, draw in slack attenders (especially men), encourage deeper faith, and reach out to the needs of the community. Many religious leaders still recognize the value of Sunday school programs, but the enthusiasm has shifted decidedly toward small-group Bible studies in recent years. And yet, our data show that the two are not that different in many respects.

Where the two differ is perhaps especially revealing. Whereas Sunday schools seem to thrive on conventional structures and activities, such as having elected officers and singing and eating together, Bible study groups seem to function better when formal structure is lacking—or at least they function well whether it is present or not. Bible study groups may require the advance planning that the experts suggest, but that sort of structure probably is best when it stays in the background. Indeed, Bible studies may have been successful, compared with Sunday school classes, precisely because they have done a better job of keeping administrative structures out of sight. Bible studies are also, in a sense, more voluntaristic than Sunday schools. People may come to church and then stay for Sunday school because there is a well-organized program. They are less likely to venture out on Wednesday mornings unless there is genuine sharing of problems and a wide range of shared interests to draw them together.

To the extent that Bible study groups may be replacing the traditional Sunday school class (or at least attracting more attention), then, we again have a valuable clue to the ways in which the small-group movement is changing American society. Bible study groups do encourage studying the Bible. But the name is also somewhat misleading. What most of these groups also do—and what contributes most to member satisfaction and effectiveness—is eating together, singing together, working on projects, meditating, and even participating in sports and hobbies. They are essentially fellowship groups. What counts is less the studying of specific lessons (and certainly not religious worship), but activities that people enjoy, that allow them to interact informally with a few other people, and that, in many ways, are not decidedly different from the activities that other people who are not in such groups do in their leisure time. Bible studies are thus accommodating more traditional religious patterns to the needs and interests of contemporary society. They are a new format that allows people to gain some exposure to religion while pursuing their need for community.

Self-Help Groups

If Bible study groups provide an alternative for people who like less structure than is common in Sunday school groups, self-help groups provide an even clearer alternative. Touted by advocates for their informality and fluidity, they are often described as an alternative to bureaucracy, professionalism, and hierarchy. They sacrifice efficiency for maximum participation, keep authoritative structure to a minimum, and try to cultivate consensus. This, at least, is how they are described in the literature.[8]

Curiously, however, these groups do not lack structure. For the most part, they are just as likely as other groups (if not more likely) to have business meetings, elected officers, stated goals, agendas, names, and the like. But most of these structures do not consistently increase member satisfaction and composite evaluations. The data show that having business meetings is the only structure that improves satisfaction. Composite evaluations, in contrast, are not influenced by business meetings, but they show that members are more satisfied when their groups have an agenda, a goal, and something to study in advance. Like other kinds of groups, self-help groups are positively influenced by child care.

Satisfaction and higher composite evaluations result from sharing problems, focusing on special needs, following a twelve-step program, meditating, and helping members overcome addictions. Praying and discussing of books also make a positive difference. Negative factors include working on projects, discussing social or political issues, and doing things for the community—all of which are formally discouraged in many self-help groups in order to keep their attention on their own needs.

The overall pattern here is quite clear. Self-help groups in our society are enormously diverse. Many of them exist to help their members accomplish some specific task, like learning how to cook healthier food, breast feed a child, or cope with unemployment. About a third of these groups are concerned with heavy personal and emotional issues, such as an addiction, and about this many follow a twelve-step program. These groups earn the highest ratings from their members. By design, they exist with minimal structure or, if they have formal structure, they minimize its importance, regarding it as a means to successful group functioning rather than as a way of showcasing leaders or of rewarding faithful members. Their members come because of some special need and they go away feeling satisfied if they have had a chance to share their problems. Indeed, as evidence in chapter 6 suggests, members who come to self-help groups because of some emotional crisis express the highest levels of satisfaction.

These findings help put the larger phenomenon of self-help groups into a clearer perspective. The reason the groups have gained so much attention in recent years is not entirely that they are structured in radically different ways from, say, Sunday school classes or Bible study groups (although their absence of formal ties with religious organizations is significant). It isn't even that their members, on the whole, are so much better satisfied than the members of these other groups. It is rather that some self-help groups are meeting very special needs and, as a result, generating very high levels of satisfaction from their members. As we see in later chapters, these groups also make a difference to the spiritual lives of their members, but do so in ways that contrast sharply with Sunday school classes and Bible study groups.

I want to venture a tentative conclusion about the role of self-help groups within the larger small-group movement. Their contribution is enormously important. They are providing support and encouragement for people experiencing emotional crises or facing other serious personal needs. Judging from the high levels of satisfaction that their members express, they are doing a good job of meeting these needs. Of the various kinds of groups, they are the most democratic, the least dependent on formal organization, and the most capable of functioning without strong leaders. For these reasons, they have influenced public perceptions of the small-group movement very widely and currently are being emulated even by leaders of Sunday school classes and Bible study groups. Yet their limitations should also be recognized. In numeric terms, they represent only a fraction of the small-group movement—perhaps (as suggested in chapter 3) as few as an eighth of its members. And the self-help groups dealing with serious emotional crises or addictions make up an even smaller percentage. Thus the small-group movement more broadly should not be equated with support groups that are following self-help or twelve-step models to address deep personal crises. Most are providing some kind of significant emotional support. But most are also devoted to the more ordinary desires for community that the average American faces routinely. And most are attempting to fulfill these desires through activities that are quite commonplace, such as eating together, singing, praying, and talking. It is not so much the activities that are changing American culture as the way in which these activities are organized. The shopping around, the emphasis on fitting in, and the fact that these activities may be substituting for more traditional expressions of family and spirituality are having the greatest impact on society.

Special Interest Groups

Finally, special interest groups are the most diverse category of all. As we suggested in chapter 3, they are composed of people who may be interested primarily in discussing books together, engaging in sports, pursuing other hobbies, focusing on current events, or engaging in politics. They are a little more likely than other kinds of groups to have formal structures, such as business meetings, and elected officers, perhaps because they are, on the whole, larger than other kinds of groups and oriented toward accomplishing specific tasks.

It is therefore interesting that these groups seem to function better, according to member evaluations, as a result of having formal structure, but this structure does not seem to contribute positively to member satisfaction. Specifically, on the composite measure, higher ratings were given to groups with business meetings, elected officers, a contract, an agenda, child care, leadership, something to study in advance, a stated goal, a fixed term, a membership fee, and a name. In contrast, satisfaction was rated lower for groups with business meetings, elected officers, child care, a leader, and something to study in advance.

The activities that influence satisfaction and composite ratings are more consistent. Both ratings rose for groups that discuss books and religious topics, provide emotional support, follow the twelve steps, and focus on an addiction.

These results suggest that formal structure is essential to the functioning of special interest groups, but that member satisfaction probably depends more on the specific type of special interest group than anything else. Special interest groups that help with addictions or use twelve-step programs seem to generate the highest levels of satisfaction. In this sense, these special interest groups are quite like self-help groups. Their members just used different labels in the survey to describe them.

It is also important to observe that effectiveness and member satisfaction seem to differ more from each other in special interest groups than in most other small groups. This is probably because special interest groups are more likely to focus on tasks than on the emotional needs of members. These groups can sometimes accomplish their tasks whether individual members receive good feelings or not. The support that members experience is a byproduct of other activities, not the goal of the group. This, it seems, is a valuable component of the small-group movement that should not be ignored. While many small groups seem to be depend almost entirely on making their members happy, some have retained the capacity to address wider social, political, and intellectual concerns and still provide community for their members.

The Diversity of Groups

What, then, makes small groups work? Groups leaders would like to know the magic formula, as would prospective members who want to find the ideal group. But, based on these results, it is clear that no single formula can facilitate the functioning of groups of all kinds. What makes a Sunday school class work well probably will not benefit a self-help group. Nevertheless, with the few exceptions that have been noted, organizational structure certainly does not emerge as a decisive factor. This conclusion does not mean that groups could survive without any kind of planning or leadership, but it does suggest that structure is not key to how satisfied members may be or how well they consider that the group functions.

The activities we have considered fall mainly into three categories. For Sunday school classes, they include singing, eating, meditating, and doing things for the community. For Bible study groups, the activities that make the most difference are added features that expand the interests and interaction of members, such as sharing personal problems and working together on sports or hobbies. And for self-help and special interest groups, they are mostly activities concerned with addictions, meeting deep personal needs, or following a twelve-step program.

However, many of the other activities in which small groups engage do not have a statistically significant impact on member satisfaction. When everything is taken into account, working together on projects, for example, does not seem to make much difference. Nor does discussing social issues. But none of these results mean that groups should quit doing what their members enjoy. They only mean that what works in small groups is generally less a function of programs and structure than it is a reflection of the informal interaction that develops among group members.

These results also suggest an important point about member expectations. The structures and activities that lead to member satisfaction and higher composite evaluations are, with few exceptions, those that define the nature of the different types of groups.[9] Singing, parties, and potluck dinners have been part of the Sunday school tradition for decades. Bible study groups, as anyone reading the literature on them could immediately discern, are expected to pray together, discuss books, and encourage their members to share problems. Self-help groups are in business to provide emotional support and to address special needs. Special interest groups, diverse as they may be, are probably associated in many people's minds with having such formal structures as business meetings, agendas, goals, and fees.

At this stage in its development, therefore, the small-group movement has established certain identifiable genres. Like literature, small groups fall into certain identifiable types because of the rules they follow or the structures around which they are built. Not every group has to follow the same rules. But the presence of particular patterns helps members identify what kind of group it is and develop certain expectations about it. Member satisfaction is thus influenced by the fulfillment of these expectations. Just as an audience will be disappointed if they go to the theater expecting Shakespeare and hear a musical, so the members of small groups will be disappointed unless their Sunday school class, Bible study group, self-help group, or special interest group does some of the things we associate with those kinds of groups. It is important for group leaders to be aware of this fact. The success of the small group movement depends not only on the fact that there is variety, but also on the appearance of variety. Group leaders can improvise, but they must do so within certain recognizable categories. Their constituents want to know ahead of time what they are getting into.

This point emphasizes the diversity of groups, but there is a point to be made about the similarities among groups as well. To generalize about some of the more specific items on which members rated their groups, we would concentrate primarily on their evaluations of trust among group members, faithful attendance, and making newcomers feel welcome. Of all the factors members rated, these related most closely with overall levels of satisfaction. Trust has a lot to do with how willing members may be to learn from the group and to receive support from it. Faithful attendance is a condition for trust, but it is clearly a desirable characteristic in its own right. And making newcomers feel welcome is a challenge that all small groups face. Trust, attendance, and openness to newcomers are issues that small group leaders and members alike struggle with because these groups are subject to the fragmenting forces of our society. In a world of strangers, cultivating trust is not easy. Nor is faithful attendance, especially when people increasingly take their commitments lightly. And, because turnover in most communities is now considerable, small groups must constantly recruit new members in order to keep going. Before concluding, therefore, let us consider each of these factors briefly.

TRUST: THE NORM OF RECIPROCITY

We saw earlier that about four group members in ten, on average, rate their group as excellent in terms of "having people who trust each other." Members of self-help groups are most likely to rate their groups highly on this characteristic. Bible study members also tend to rate their groups above average on trust. Sunday school classes, in contrast, are generally rated below average by their members. And special interest groups are rated in the middle.

The main factor that generates trust, however, is whether or not members feel they have a chance to share their problems with one another in the group. In addition, groups that meet every week seem to cultivate trust better than those that meet less often, and trust is higher in groups where nearly everyone attends faithfully than in groups where many of the members do not come every time. The data also show that smaller groups score higher on trust than larger groups. This finding confirms something that group leaders have long suspected: heart-to-heart sharing becomes much more difficult when a group becomes larger than fifteen or twenty people.[10] It is perhaps worth noting, too, that some of the group characteristics that experts sometimes focus on do not seem to enhance trust. The data do not indicate that groups in existence for a longer period of time do better at cultivating trust, that individuals who have been in their groups for a longer period of time rate their groups higher on trust, or that homogeneous groups, church-sponsored groups, or groups rooted in personal friendship networks do better.

Sharing certainly appears to be the key to cultivating trust.[11] The reason can easily be illustrated by the comments of group members. The Matrix group that John, the physician, and his wife attend every

Sunday morning is a good example. In a church of 1,900 members it has been difficult to keep the group small enough to provide close support. At present, attendance averages around 40, and with dozens of these groups running at once, a full-time member of the church staff is needed to coordinate them. But this person stays entirely behind the scenes. From week to week, the leadership of the group rotates among its more active members. There is also plenty of time for socializing, praying together, and discussing selected topics of study. John makes an insightful observation about how this pattern affects the way he and his wife feel about the group: "We don't leave it like we do a concert, saying 'Oh, did you hear how they played?' We aren't in the critiquing mode anymore. We're a part of it. And so things could go poorly and we still have a fulfilling experience because we aren't going there only for the program or what we get out of it. It's what we get in relationship."

In other words, sharing cultivates trust of the group as a whole. John and Sara do not trust the group simply because they know the intimate details of the lives of particular individuals in the group. They trust it because they identify closely with it. They are no longer detached from it, but feel a sense of ownership. Sharing is what makes them feel that it is truly their group.

For a contrasting example, we need only to consider how Donna described her feelings when the study and support group she attends was unable to share because one person in the group started to dominate it. "We had a woman who moved into the area who was very, very needy and really had a bad problem with alcohol. She would come into the group and totally dominate the entire dialogue for an hour and a half without letting anybody get a word in edgewise. And for a while you can be supportive and say this person really needs us and let's just grit our teeth and just bear it for a while. And then after a while, it wasn't the same group that it was because nobody else was getting a chance to talk. And I would try to lead the dialogue away from her to someone else who was trying to speak. And she would just interrupt them totally and not let them finish a sentence. And it would go back to her. So it became almost like a really bad situation. She ended up not coming over the summer and not coming back this year. But I think it was because some people confronted her about smelling alcohol on her breath at nine o'clock in the morning. And she hasn't come back this year, so it hasn't been a problem. But that was a very awkward position to be put in because it's a support group. You're supposed to support people who come there. But on the other hand, do you let one person totally dominate? So it was a very awkward position to be in."

This remark can be interpreted in a way that puts church groups, like Donna's, in a bad light compared with twelve-step, anonymous, or other self-help groups. The important point is that groups develop implicit norms about reciprocity. People come expecting to support each other, but also expecting to be supported themselves.[12] Trust may require some preliminary assumptions about the honesty, integrity, and sincerity of the other members. But even more than that, it involves assumptions about the norm of reciprocity. Members trust others in the group to honor their expectations. If the norm is to discuss alcoholism, then trust requires the group to listen as members share their problems with this addiction. If the norm is to share thoughts about the Bible, trust necessitates structuring the discussion in a way that allows most members a chance to speak.

FAITHFUL ATTENDANCE: AN IMPLICIT CONTRACT

Because most peoples' lives are so pressured, there has to be more than simply a "come if I please" attitude if a small group is going to function effectively. Even the idea that people will come as long as the group meets their needs is too fragile: how well would a business work if people only showed up when they felt like it?

A woman who had struggled over a long period of time to make her once-a-month church fellowship group work expressed clearly the problem that many other group leaders also acknowledged. "I've been running it or helping to run it for four and a half years. And my opinion of it is that, that lifestyle, the pace that people keep nowadays or the working long hours and commuting and—I don't know, that somehow people don't find the time for it. They'd rather stay home or they'd rather, if something better came along, like to go out to dinner, they'd rather do that. There's not a real firm commitment there in that group. And I don't know, we've been trying to work on it and maybe change things around and it just has not come together."

She was frustrated because people did not attend faithfully. As we have seen from the survey results, faithful attendance is one of the most important correlates of group satisfaction. Why? One reason, of course, may be that dissatisfaction (from whatever sources) is the cause of flagging attendance. The fact that attendance remained a critical factor in our statistical analyses when everything else was taken into consideration, however, suggests that there may be more to it than this. What we learned from talking individually with members was that attendance, or its absence, is contagious. Even faithful participants feel something is not quite right if others do not take the group seriously. Members are sincere when they say in meetings that they miss certain people who are not there.

An implicit contract to attend faithfully is thus a minimum requirement for making small groups work well. As it turns out, faithful attendance is not easy to manipulate, however. According to our survey, attendance does not vary much by type of group: self-help group members rate their groups a little above average, but that is the only noticeable difference. Church-based groups do not differ significantly from groups not connected to churches. Homogenous groups do no better than more diverse groups. Nor are large groups any better, or worse, than small groups. One thing that does make a difference is how long the group has been in existence: newer groups do better than older groups. Perhaps this variation is because members of newer groups are more likely to feel ownership of their groups or because they still know why they are there. It is also interesting to note that groups receive higher faithful attendance ratings when they meet less often than when they meet more often. As we have seen, meeting more often is conducive to trust but, with the hectic lives most people lead, less frequent meetings may be the key to better attendance. Certainly, many of the group members we talked to said their groups had found it better to meet biweekly than weekly, and the weekly groups often met with a number of their members missing.

NEWCOMERS: GROUP NORMS AND OPENNESS

As the examples in this chapter suggest, every group establishes its implicit operating rules. Sometimes these are discussed and agreed upon at some point; more often they are customs that rather quickly become established and are then followed by most of the group's members. In one home Bible study group, for example, the custom was for everyone to put their own coat in the closet; in another, the host took coats and laid them on one of the beds. Unspoken norms as simple as this can be difficult for newcomers to absorb. When the group has in-jokes or prays for Sam in ways that only old-timers can understand ("Lord, you know what he's been going through"), the difficulties newcomers face are even more severe.[13]

Among the various kinds of groups we have considered, the survey data show that Sunday school classes appear to have the hardest time making newcomers feel welcome. Self-help groups seem to do best. Contrary to what many people probably believe, groups that have been in existence for a long time seem to do as well as newer groups. Of course, groups unable to make newcomers feel welcome may die out before they become well established.[14] Groups that meet often do better than those that meet less frequently, perhaps because the problems they face in getting their own members to attend faithfully encourage them to be more open toward outsiders. Homogeneous groups seem to do a little better than more diverse groups. So do larger groups—lending some credence to the view that small groups can become so ingrown that it is hard for new members to feel at home. The other factor that contributes positively is being invited to the group by a friend. Apparently, invitations of this kind are a sign of openness toward new members.

THE SMALL-GROUPS PARADOX

To tie together what we have learned in this chapter and to relate it back to the themes outlined in the opening chapter, let me suggest that small groups can best be understood by thinking about their internal structure as a paradox. This structure involves a relatively high degree of formal organization—leaders, goals, and agendas in most groups; lessons to study, business meetings, and elected officers in many others. It also involves a relatively high degree of informality— warmth, encouragement, acceptance, and the privilege of talking openly about one's personal problems and interests. The paradox, moreover, is genuine: the informality of small groups depends on having formal structure, and the formal structure is tolerated only because of the informality it encourages. Groups vary, of course, but the paradox of structured informality applies pretty much across the board.

The reasons why structured informality is conducive to successful group functioning should be readily apparent by this point. Because small groups are intentional, rather than spontaneous, they require leaders, goals, and agendas to define what is or is not appropriate. These structures solve some of the ordinary housekeeping tasks that all groups face: knowing when to meet, having a place, welcoming newcomers. They also resolve more difficult issues that may arise, such as telling a disruptive member to keep quiet or healing a conflict in the group. But they work best when they are understood to be means rather than ends—that is, when their purpose is to foster informal interaction. Formal structures create a space, as it were, for people to get to know each other. Trust can develop more easily because people do not have to worry much about group goals.

I do not wish to give the impression that small groups are the only phenomenon in our society that depends on this paradoxical combination of formality and informality. If we think about it for a moment, we recognize that families do, too. Spouses take for granted that they are married and will be for a while, and thus they are free to behave more openly and spontaneously with each other. Some implicit understanding between parents and children about who will cook and pay the bills is also conducive to focusing on other, more personal needs and interests. If we take a somewhat less obvious example—corporations—it may be evident that some of the same dynamics are at work. Here, leadership, goals, and agendas are likely to be much more heavily structured, but informal caring relationships, trust, and chit-chat at the coffee machine may contribute importantly to a successful corporate environment. Small groups are similar to other features of modern society in these respects.

Nevertheless, small groups differ from these examples in at least one very significant way. Although they are intentional organizations, their fundamental reason for existence is quite often to provide deep, intimate interpersonal support—period. This is not true of families. Intimacy and support have, of course, become much more important in the modern family, but children, rearing children, passing on values, and gaining a sense of intergenerational immortality still remain the stated ideals of most people, and sexual pleasure, maintaining a material household, and providing for mutual physical care would rank high among family goals as well. Certainly the goals of corporations would be different. Perhaps those that provide recreational activities would come closer to small groups. But here again, profitability or corporate survival would have to take precedence over the sheer joys of interaction.

The small-group movement thus is adding an important new element to the way in which modern life is organized. It is extending the principles of formal organization into an arena of interpersonal life that was largely spontaneous and unorganized until very recently. At an earlier time, Sunday school classes helped people adapt their needs for religious instruction to the tighter schedules of industrial society. Then, in the twentieth century, special interest groups became popular as ways to pursue family and neighborhood objectives in a more organized way. Now, Bible study groups, prayer fellowships, twelve-step groups, and other self-help groups are extending these practices. Rather than caring and emotional support depending on family, friends, and neighbors, it is now subject to advance planning. One does not have to put up with long hours of listening to the neighborhood gossip to make sure someone will be available when emotional support is needed. One simply devotes an hour each Sunday evening to a group set up for this purpose. For busy people, this arrangement is enormously attractive. It helps fit the need for personal support into the highly organized, structured ways in which we lead our lives. The fact that informal interaction takes place in small groups makes the degree to which they are formally organized less obvious. They provide genuine support. Yet they also help us adjust to the demands of our society.

This arrangement is all to the good, of course. We are too busy to cultivate friendships with our neighbors. Living so close to them, we worry that they may interrupt our schedules or drop by to visit at awkward times. Having a group that meets for two hours on Tuesday evenings is easier to manage. We know the group will accept whatever we say. If it does not, we know we can move on to a different group. Especially if it is an anonymous group, we may be able to shield ourselves from having to interact with members at any other time. But the weaknesses of this sort of arrangement should be evident as well. When things are too carefully orchestrated, we wonder if true caring can really take place. We wonder, for example, if our experience will be like that of one of the members of the Silver Chase Meeting, a man who said he had suddenly dropped out of the weekly meetings and, after six months, not a single member of the group had bothered to try to contact him.

Small groups have to encourage informality, sharing, acceptance, and trust; otherwise, members begin to feel manipulated. But this focus also means that such groups may not be very effective at accomplishing other tasks, such as delving deeply into a topic or formulating a new policy, at least if these tasks require strong, intrusive leadership. Traditionally, churches and other community organizations relied on small groups mostly to perform specific tasks. The task force or management committee was the familiar model. But now, as one leader noted, "the small-group movement has blown that model wide open." Increasingly, small groups are being asked not only to provide interpersonal support but also to take up administrative tasks. The inherent danger, therefore, is that support groups may be viewed as the answer to everything. They probably can provide certain kinds of support reasonably well when that is their primary aim, but they may falter on all counts if they are expected to provide support and at the same time fulfill such aims as planning new church programs or solving community problems.

6

GETTING AND
GIVING SUPPORT

*The Role of Small Groups in Nurturing
Individual Needs*

Karen's father and step mother split up, got divorced, reconciled, and married each other again while she was in high school. They also moved three times, making it difficult for her to make friends and keep them. She seldom received emotional support from her parents. When she left for college, she was more than happy to get away. But after a year at college she felt she was just drifting. She dropped out, moved in with a family she'd met in the area, and got a job. A year later she transferred to another college, took a part-time load and worked on the side to support herself. Soon she had a boyfriend, got engaged, and after a year of sustaining a long-distance relationship, got married. He went to college full time until he graduated. She continued to attend part time, now working to support both of them.

When her husband graduated and got a job, Karen was able to quit work and return to college full time. He was commuting an hour in one direction; she, an hour in the opposite direction. There was no time to make friends in the community. Two years later they moved again. Both were now employed and they looked forward to being able to pay off their loans, live a little more comfortably, save some money, and buy a house. Five months later, Karen was pregnant. Suffering from extreme nausea, she had to quit her job. The next year was one of the worst in her life. Weeks went by when she hardly felt like raising her head from her pillow. She tried working as a door-to-door saleswoman, but couldn't make a go of it. They tried living with her husband's father, but the tensions became so severe they had to move out. A few months later, they were forced to move again after a run-in with the landlord. Meanwhile, Karen's best friend committed suicide, leaving Karen emotionally devastated.

It took another three years for Karen and her husband to get on their feet. Less than two years after the first baby was born, a second one arrived. By this time, they had purchased a modest house. But about the same time, her husband lost his job and had to spend several months finding another one. Karen got a clerical job to tide them over, but had to quit when babysitting arrangements fell through. Then she found another job, but it required her to work every evening. Months went by, it seemed, when she never saw her husband. She liked the job because it gave her a sense of identity, but after a year, she decided it was time to quit. At age 26, she now devotes herself full time to being a mother.

To someone who did not know her, Karen could appear to be the traditional American success story: sheltered housewife and mother, living comfortably in the suburbs, married to a devoted husband who brings in a steady income. But knowing her story, we realize how turbulent her life has been. Like so many young people in America today, she found that getting established was harder than she ever expected.

What sustained Karen through most of this time was her church. But even that was a difficult commitment to maintain. As a child, she seldom had been taken to church. Then, as a teenager, she started attending a Seventh-Day Adventist church that her mother had become interested in. Karen became intrigued with the idea that there were answers in the Bible to her questions about how to live her life, but she wasn't making much headway reading the Bible on her own. She had an aunt, though, who was actively involved in a large independent Protestant church some 45 minutes away. And through this aunt, Karen became involved too.

She remembers that she was suffering from extreme depression at the time. Her father had asked her and her brother to move out in an effort to win her stepmother back. This was why Karen was living temporarily with her mother. Neither parent was interested in driving her that far to attend church, so she was forced to rely on aunts and uncles, cousins, and church people for transportation. Still, she got there regularly enough to find some support in its youth group. It was also about this time that her natural mother became reconciled with her second husband, whom she had divorced, and remarried him, too.

Karen felt like she was living on an emotional roller coaster. "It was all very bizarre," she admits. Even her sibling relationships were constantly changing. Having one natural brother, a half-brother on her father's side, and a half-sister on her mother's side, she never quite knew whether to think of herself as the oldest or the youngest, and she always felt like an intruder wherever she went.

The youth group, she says in retrospect, "just held my life together at that point." It was also where she met the young man who a few years later became her husband. And later, when they moved back to the area after college, they found support at the same church again, only now in a Bible study for couples. More than anything else, this group made the church a community for her. Because the church was so large, she says, "You could run into thousands of people every week and not know who they were, so this small group was very vital to the church." She also liked the fact that most of the people in the group were young married couples. "We formed a lot of close friendships," she recalls, "so that was very special for us." Had everything else been going smoothly, Karen and her husband might have settled into this group for a long time. But then she became pregnant; they dropped out of the group and soon moved away from the community as well. Thus, it has only been in the last couple of years that Karen has again found a support group she likes.

This group is a women's Bible study group at a local Protestant church. Karen attends every week—"faithfully." What she likes most about the group is that it meets both of the needs she feels most acutely in her life: her need to know God and her need for support. "I was looking for the Bible study part of it," she says, "because that was really lacking in my life." But, she admits, "I was also looking for a break." Her first pregnancy had not been planned, so she has struggled a lot during the last three years with resentment. With another baby in the house now, it helps a great deal when she can get away for an hour without a crying baby on her hands. At the Bible study, she can get away and tell her problems to God. It feels good, too, to have some other women to whom she can talk. "I really need the support of some young mothers," she says. "I just need some friendships."

FRANK'S STORY

"In 1980," says Frank, a man now in his early fifties, "my marriage ended. I was drinking. My drinking was out of control. It's not that I was drinking a lot, but my drinking was out of control. So I had an affair, because my life was filled with pain. Just pain. I didn't understand it. I moved to Boston to live happily ever after with this girlfriend. But that relationship soon ended. As I got sober and she got sober, it ended.

"I began a spiritual journey at that point. I knew at that point that God was doing something. I wouldn't have said it that way at the time. I just said, 'There's somebody messin' with my life.' Events were occurring that were clearly out of my control."

What Frank began to realize in 1980 was that events in his life had always been out of control. He just hadn't faced the truth before. When he was five, his mother had a nervous breakdown, but nobody talked about it. He remembers walking the long road to the school bus stop by himself each fall feeling completely alone and abandoned. But for years he never fully realized why September made him so sad. All through high school he felt like he didn't fit in. The high school he attended was in one of the wealthiest districts in the state, but Frank lived in a feeder area composed of families too poor to have their own high school. He felt like a square peg in a round hole. But nobody talked about it.

"I had all kinds of insecurities and inadequacies. But I was told not to feel them. I remember very distinctly being given two lessons: don't upset your mother and there's nothing to be afraid of. But I was afraid and I didn't know what to do about it."

The problem continued when Frank went away to college. Because of a lingering illness, he arrived on campus several weeks after all the other freshmen. Missing the orientation meetings caused him to feel like an outsider. "I felt like I didn't belong and I didn't fit and there was somethin' wrong and there was all that kind of stuff that was still not resolved."

During his junior year Frank finally found a place for himself. He was on academic probation, close to being thrown out of school, but he had met some buddies, a group of Korean War veterans, older guys who knew how to have a good time. "I was havin' a ball. All of a sudden I had some identity—something I'd never had. Partying, raising hell, I mean, God, it was wonderful!"

After college Frank had no idea what to do with his life. His parents had always told him that the church was the one place where people really belonged. Frank didn't think so. But his parents began pressuring him to go to seminary, so Frank followed the path of least resistance and went. Being in this atmosphere stimulated all his earlier fears. "All my insecurities came roaring back. 'I don't belong here' and 'I don't fit in,' blah-blah-blah—all that stuff was right back in the forefront." Frank remembers walking down the hall one day in his first week there. All he could think about was "I'm outta here."

But then a strange thing happened. "I heard a noise behind a doorway across the hall. I went in and there were four guys sittin' there playin' cards and drinkin' beer." It was just like the old days in college. "I knew I was home!"

These companions helped Frank make it through seminary. They weren't terribly interested in religion, but it was the sixties—other things were more important. Having felt like an outsider all his life, Frank found himself drawn toward the protest movements being launched in the name of the downtrodden. "I wanted to deal with the underdog; I wanted to be needed," he recalls. He took part in the civil rights march in Hattiesburg, Mississippi. Soon he was involved deeply in other civil rights activities and, after that, the peace movement.

For the next ten years, Frank championed one cause after another. He worked with the poor. He became a counselor and tried to help people with alcoholism and other addictions. He remembers the coworkers at one of his jobs, a youth agency, beating on him to try to get him to open up and talk about himself. But he was too defensive. All the while he felt like a black sheep. And all the while his own drinking problem was getting increasingly out of control.

Out of work, unable to find a new job, divorced, and in deep pain from his affair, Frank hit bottom in 1980. Alcoholics Anonymous (AA) saved him. He began attending at the suggestion of the woman with whom he was having the affair. When their relationship ended, he continued. For more than a decade now he has attended AA meetings at least three times a week. This experience has given him the support he needed to look honestly at himself.

"AA has given me a sense of peace and understanding and spirituality." One of the first realizations Frank came to in AA was that he needed to get in touch with his own emotions. "I had no emotional component to my life. I mean, I couldn't identify a feeling if I had to." AA taught him that he had always been trying to make other people happy, trying to fulfill their expectations, but had denied that they could do anything for him. He discovered his own vulnerability, his emotional need to be close to other people.

Once he knew how much he needed other people, Frank found himself getting involved in all sorts of small groups. AA led him into other "step groups," such as ACOA (Adult Children of Alcoholics), Al-Anon, and CODA (Co-Dependents Anonymous). His awakening sense of God working in his life also led him into a group called Spiritual Seekers that has met regularly for the past two years to explore mystical traditions, how to meditate, and the life of spirituality in general. But AA has continued to provide the bedrock of his existence.

The main reason Frank takes AA so seriously is that he regards the group as a life-and-death commitment. "If you don't do the work of recovery, you will die. You're going to drink and you'll die." It has the kind of urgency that a prayer group does for someone who is desperately seeking communion with God. The other reason AA is so appealing is that Frank can see the changed lives of those who participate. "I see people who had been involved for 10, 15, 20 years and they are happy and their lives are working and they are content. I assume that if it works for them, it will work for me."

But what Frank appreciates most about AA is the caring that develops among the people who participate. "It's the place where I can share all the pain in my life," he says. "My abandonment and loneliness—I mean, it's where I go to cry and to hurt." The people at AA allow him to express these feelings. They understand what these feelings are like. They have experienced them too. They don't tell him he shouldn't have them, or even try to make them go away. They just share the journey, whether it is one of triumph or of trial. This solidarity, more than anything else, was the reason Frank became involved.

WHAT THE SURVEY SHOWS

Karen and Frank have experienced what millions of other Americans are finding out: shattered, fragmented lives can only be rebuilt in the company of others. The small groups in which they participate function in a much deeper way than simply helping them to accomplish some task, such as gaining up-to-date information about parenting, or to pursue some specialized interest, such as recreational swimming. What they experienced sounds a great deal like the functioning of "primary groups," so named almost a century ago by sociologist Charles Horton Cooley because he believed them to be the basic building blocks of society. Unlike the task group, primary groups are valued in their own right. They involve their members as whole persons and generally do so over a long period of time. They become an important source of the individual's personal identity and provide emotional support, standards of personal behavior to live up to, and significant others to emulate.[1]

Throughout most of history, the support necessary to create a stable, secure personal identity has come from the family. But the traditional pattern of growing up in a nuclear family with one mother and one father, getting married, staying in that marriage, and having children is now increasingly atypical in our society. As family sociologist Judith Stacey observes, "The 'modern' family of sociological theory and historical convention designates a form no longer prevalent in the United States—an intact nuclear household unit composed of a male breadwinner, his full-time homemaker wife, and their dependent children."[2] Even within nuclear families, changing understandings of gender have forced many men and women to renegotiate their roles—a process that is often painful and necessitates feedback, acceptance, and new role models. Karen and Frank turned to small groups as a substitute for stable relationships with parents and spouses. In their cases, the group became an important source of self-identity. They were able to lead more productive lives as a result of being in a group.

But how well do groups generally function? Do they help most of their members? And, if so, how? What kinds of support do people receive? Are Karen and Frank typical or atypical? The answers to these questions are crucial to how we understand and evaluate the small-group movement. If small groups claim to provide people with care and encouragement but do not, then we must think harder about what their appeal is. But if they do help their members, then we must understand this contribution to our society. We must also perceive it correctly, not allowing ourselves to expect more of the small-group movement than it can deliver. If it generally supplies temporary encouragement, for example, but not long-term or truly intimate support, that is a limitation we need to understand.

The global term to describe what people receive from groups is "support." But support means many different things. Some of what it means can be gauged by the results of the survey (see table 6.1). The most common type of support experienced by small-group members appears to be the feeling that they are not alone. More than four group members in five say they have received this kind of support from their group. It is what Karen is talking about when she says she needs to be with other young mothers or what Frank experiences when he is with other recovering alcoholics.

Table 6.1

SUPPORT RECEIVED FROM GROUPS

*Percentage of Group Members Who Say They Have Received
Each of These Kinds of Support from Their Group*

Made you feel like you weren't alone	82
Gave you encouragement when you were feeling down	72
Helped you celebrate something	51
Helped you through an emotional crisis	43
Helped you make a difficult decision	38
Helped you out when someone was sick	38
Brought meals for your family	23
Provided you with physical care or support	21
Provided you with babysitting or child care	12
Helped you overcome an addiction	7
Loaned you money	4

Emotional support comes in as a close second. Nearly three-quarters of all group members say they receive encouragement from their group when they are feeling down. Sometimes this encouragement comes simply from seeing that one is not alone. It often depends on the normal interaction involved in any group—for example, on having to focus attention on something else for a while or on being greeted by someone you know. This sort of routine encouragement can be especially vital when there is a more acute need for emotional support as well. Nearly half of all members say their group has helped them through an emotional crisis. And, of course, not all emotional support is associated with negative experiences. Half of all group members say their group has helped them celebrate something. More than a third say they have been helped in making decisions.

Physical support is somewhat less common, perhaps because there are other ways of obtaining such services in our society, or perhaps because these are not the needs that drive people to join small groups. But many group members say they have received some kind of tangible assistance from their groups. More than a third, for example, say their group helped them when they or someone close to them was sick. About a fourth say their group has brought meals for their family. About a fifth have received physical care and support from their group. Twelve percent receive child care or babysitting. Seven percent have received help in overcoming an addiction. And four percent have been loaned money by their group.

On the whole, the survey results indicate that support is, indeed, one of the significant features of small groups. In all, 92 percent of the people surveyed said they had received at least one of the kinds of support listed in table 6.1. Eighty-two percent said they had received two or more of these kinds of support. Two persons in three had received at least three kinds of support. And more than half (54 percent) had received four or more of them. In short, small groups are filling a definite need. People are joining, not simply because they are bored or have a free evening, but because groups are a source of encouragement, advice, and camaraderie.

The survey also reveals that people with special needs who join small groups generally feel that they have received support for these particular needs. Of those who say they joined a small group because of personal problems, for example, 95 percent say they have received encouragement from their group. Of those who say they joined a small group because of a personal crisis, 85 percent say their group has helped them through a crisis. A similar pattern is evident among people who joined a group in order to find community. Of those who said they joined a group because they did not know anyone in their community, 89 percent say their group has made them feel less alone. And of those who say they are bothered a lot by loneliness, 84 percent say they feel less alone as a result of their group.[3]

The survey does suggest, however, that small groups may meet certain kinds of needs better than others. It is difficult to draw decisive conclusions from survey data because people in groups were not studied before they became involved, as well as after, to determine what changes may have taken place. Compared to the high percentages just reported, however, people who were experiencing other kinds of problems were generally less likely to receive concrete support from their groups. Of those who said they were worrying a lot about money, for example, only 6 percent had been loaned money by their group. And of those who were worrying a lot about health problems, only 38 percent had received help from their group with illness itself, and even fewer had received physical care (24 percent) or meals (21 percent).

It may be objected, of course, that small groups are not in business to loan money or care for the sick. Friends and family probably would have done so in the past. But increasingly we do not feel comfortable loaning money even to our best friends. And we send the sick to health care professionals. So, in this sense, small groups reflect the sentiment in American culture that people should take care of themselves. What small groups do best, the survey suggests, is provide encouragement. But do they provide encouragement uniformly to everyone? Or do people with certain concerns find more help than people with other concerns?

The survey provides some partial evidence on these questions. The most revealing evidence comes from comparisons among people who say they are worried a lot, a fair amount, or only a little by particular concerns. In virtually every case, those who are worried a lot are more likely to say they have received encouragement from their group than those who say they are worried only a little. These responses, of course, make sense. Small groups don't prevent people from having problems or from worrying about these problems. But if the concern is acute, and if the small group is doing its job, people should feel they are receiving encouragement. The point I wish to emphasize, however, is that small groups seem to do a better job of providing this encouragement for people with certain kinds of worries than for people with other kinds of worries.

Which worries in particular? Loneliness and depression. On both of these, there is a reasonably high statistical relationship between the extent of the concern and the likelihood of feeling support from one's group. Several other concerns elicit at least modest levels of support: worries about one's health, guilt, anxiety, and family problems. On each of these issues there is a weak but statistically significant relationship between the extent of the concern and the likelihood of receiving encouragement. The issues that small groups seem to be less responsive to are worries about money and problems with one's work. On both of these concerns, there is no relationship between the extent of concern and the likelihood of receiving encouragement. Again, then, the support that small groups provide is restricted. They provide companionship and cheer people up, but probably do not attempt to forge a wider variety of links that might involve such needs as medical assistance, care for the elderly, financial help, or job counseling.

It is worth noting, too, that different kinds of small groups provide different kinds of support. Groups associated with churches, as we noted in a previous chapter, are more likely than nonchurch groups to provide child care. They are also more likely to provide meals and to give help when someone is sick. These services are simply part of the expectations that churches have tried to live up to over the centuries. Nonchurch groups, however, are more likely to deal with problems of addiction. Otherwise, the various kinds of groups are remarkably similar. Encouragement and help with emotional crises are the stock-in-trade of nearly all kinds of small groups.

Having received support during an emotional crisis is, according to the survey, the best single predictor of being highly satisfied with one's group. In comparison, receiving advice or physical support does not seem to affect levels of satisfaction very much. This is true among both church-based and nonchurch groups.

For a better understanding of the various kinds of support—both emotional and physical—and of the ways in which small groups provide them, we need to consider other kinds of evidence. From the personal statements of people in groups, we can see better why certain kinds of support are so badly needed in our society and how significant support can be to those who receive it. We must recognize that even though support is common in small groups not all members experience this support equally. Understanding the support people receive helps us know why people become involved in groups in the first place and why some are more likely to stay involved than others. It also reveals the importance of giving support to others in the context of small groups.

EMOTIONAL SUPPORT

At Emmanual Alliance Church, the goal of small groups is explicitly stated to be providing emotional support. The leaders of these groups recognize, however, that emotional support doesn't just happen. It is part of a process that requires careful planning and orchestration. Says Pastor Ingram: "The small groups are a vehicle for people to break down [social barriers], then to find support for problems among friends . . . [they're] not a social gathering—the idea is 'let's get down to reality.' Then you start to really have something going."

The process at Emmanual involves getting people to know one another informally and to trust one another, then gradually increasing the amount of time devoted to worship and Bible study. Ironically, the need for fellowship will decline as people get to know each other. This is because people can cut through the pretenses usually involved in dealing with strangers or casual acquaintances and get right to the heart of what their needs really are. "As the group matures, we get them away from saying a prayer for Aunt Mildred. Its an easy way to start off and it certainly serves a purpose, saying 'Hey, I've got this friend who has got some problems,' but we try to get them to the point to say 'Pray for me.'" Pastor Ingram believes this transformation from external foci to internal foci is the real objective of the small groups in his church.

The most common variety of emotional support that people find in small groups is what we might call *empathic support*. Someone who shares a personal problem in a group setting often receives little more than "yes, I've experienced that too," but this can provide an enormous sense of relief. Suddenly you realize you are not the only person in the world with problems. Others at least understand what you are going through because they have experienced it, too. In our observations of groups, we noticed frequently that nothing needed to be said at all for empathy to be communicated. Many times people would be telling stories about themselves when it became obvious from a smile or a small nod of the head that someone else in the room was feeling cared for. The reason was that they had found themselves in the same boat. Empathy, then, is a relatively easy form of support to provide. Group members have to do little to provide it other than show up at group meetings, disclose some of their own problems, and behave sympathetically when others disclose theirs.

A second form of emotional support involves a more active response from group members. We can use the term that groups often employ—*encouragement*—to describe it. Encouragement literally means to instill with courage. It strengthens the person, often through simple affirmations like "hang in there" or "keep up the good work." It also becomes contagious, helping those who give encouragement to become more interested in the lives of those they are supporting, more intrigued with these individuals' concerns or dreams, and perhaps more positive about their own lives as well. "All the imagination, hope, and boldness that are so often blocked when it comes to your own dreams," write therapists Barbara Sher and Annie Gottlieb, "come rushing out when you're thinking for a friend. And they flow out of your friends whenever they think for you."[4]

Although it is easy to think of encouragement as a brief slap on the back, it is sometimes much more than this. Living as we do in a complex society that constantly demands new things of us, many people suffer from an abiding lack of confidence. They may not need the courage it took their ancestors to conquer the wide-open prairies, but they need to be instilled with courage to face the uncertainties of everyday life. They fear they are doing the wrong things or that they will not be able to rise to a new set of challenges because they have never done these things before. They need feedback, but all too often the only feedback they receive from supervisors, teachers, or even close friends is negative. Encouragement, then, is a need that many of us feel. It stems from conditions in our society that make us feel unsure of ourselves.

No news, presumably, is good news. But positive reinforcement generally feels a lot better. One member of a self-help group, for example, recalls that her group was especially beneficial just because she joined it about the same time she was starting full time into her career. Being in the group did not help her make specific professional decisions, but it did help her have more confidence about how to make decisions in general and how to view her new identity as a professional. "I remember just sort of saying, sharing, that I've always been a person to run away from things when I had a problem." She says learning the Serenity Prayer has been especially helpful for her. It reminds her to accept the things she can't change, to change the things she can, and to think hard about the difference. Being in a professional career has made it harder for her to do this. Often she is called upon to make judgments with insufficient information. Sometimes she feels pressured to decide things the way her peers would decide them. She doesn't look to her support group to make these decisions for her. She does, however, find that sharing her anxieties there is reassuring. The group has also affirmed her confidence in her own conscience. She feels she can trust it. "I just realize that morally I feel a certain way and I don't need to change my moral views in order to fit in with some things. I've made a lot of hard decisions that way."

Like most self-help groups, this woman's group has explicit rules against members giving each other advice in the context of the group.[5] Even telling a story about one's own experiences that is too obviously geared toward providing someone else in the group with a hint about what to do is frowned upon. Encouragement is thus one of the byproducts of group interaction that results mainly from the process of self-discovery. In other groups, however, advice, criticism, and other proactive forms of encouragement are more a part of the acknowledged tasks of the group. People don't wait passively for someone to share a problem and then give an affirming response. They build into their understanding of the group's functions some explicit probing into each other's lives and an expectation that this probing will also occasion encouragement and advice. That way the norms of everyday life, where people implicitly operate on a "mind your own business" policy, are explicitly contravened. They are replaced with a norm of accountability involving a dual obligation—an obligation to share one's personal life with the group and an obligation to accept graciously the group's comments, criticism, and advice.

John, the physician we met in chapter 3, experiences this kind of accountability norm in the men's group he attends each week. "Almost every time we're together," he says, "we go over five questions: How are you doing with God? How are you doing with your wife? How are you doing with the kids? How are you doing at work? And how are you doing with friends? So there's an encouragement process."

In John's case, this process lies at the core of his individuality. It makes him feel stronger. And his wife benefits enough, too, that she encourages him to do it. "It's one of the only things I do," he explains. "Like if I said to her 'I'm going to go out and play golf,' she may or may not like that because it takes time away. One of the only things I do that is away from family, that she *truly* encourages me to do is to go to be with that group of men, because when I'm with them, they build me back to her, they encourage me. I come home a more loving husband and father, and so she encourages that. It's the kind of group that's individually at the heart of my being."

On the surface, it is easy to see why emotional support is often so badly needed in our society. People are lonely, suffering the loss of a loved one, trying to overcome an addiction, or facing death. In times past there would have been an extended family, a kin group, or a neighborhood to provide support. But, as we discussed in chapter 2, the increasing transience and fragmentation of modern life has undermined the presence of such naturally occurring support systems.

We miss seeing the broader picture, however, if we focus entirely on the physical breakdown of more traditional forms of community. An important cultural element also must be taken into consideration. Some have described it as utilitarian individualism; others as a kind of relativistic or extremely libertarian ethic that is summed up well in the phrase "do your own thing." This ethic suggests that we are ultimately responsible to pursue our self-interest and that each person, independently of others, must decide how best to do that. Even if people have families, friends, and neighbors, therefore, they may not receive the support they need—or feel too uncomfortable to ask for it. The social norm tells them that they should not get involved in their friends' and neighbors' business. It says that people should figure out their own lives, make their own choices, and suffer their own mistakes. This form of malaise is much harder to combat. People in groups may be attracted to the warm interdependence that seems lacking in the rest of society, sensing that people in the group do at least care for others besides themselves. Yet, as we consider more fully in the next chapter, the groups may be fostering utilitarian individualism and cultural relativism, for example, by encouraging people to solve their own problems or by giving equal weight to all points of view. While the movement, therefore, may be mirroring and even reinforcing, larger cultural trends, it nevertheless provides some comfort for the individuals who have experienced these trends.

Donna, the woman who attends a study and support group at her church, says that she was a victim of this cultural ethos while she was growing up. "I think I needed a direction in my life, but nobody was giving me a direction. My parents are very easy-going people, so they never kind of sat down with me and said 'Donna, we'd really like you to go to school. We'd really like you to become this.' It's real important for parents to say to their children, 'this is what we hope for you, this is what we see you as being.' But my parents never did that. And because they didn't do that, I think I kind of wandered aimlessly for awhile. I wish they would have said, 'Gee, we really want you to go to college, we really want you to do this, or to do that.' They never did that. And I think as a result, I didn't think it was important. Because my parents weren't pushing me. They were like too easy-going, almost, like, 'Oh well, if she goes . . .' It would have been nice to be in a group, I think." She still suffers from this sense of parental neglect. For the time being at least, her group seems to make her feel more secure.

GETTING AND GIVING HELP

Small groups that provide nonemotional types of support, such as health care, transportation, meals, lodging, education, information, and financial donations, tend to be distinguished from the kinds of groups we have just considered. This is not to say that emotional support is any less real than, or that it can be given in isolation from, other kinds of support. But the basic dynamics, and even the memberships, of the two kinds of group tend to be different.

The assistant pastor at a large Southern Baptist church illustrated the distinction between the two kinds of groups in contrasting the ladies' missionary societies in his church with the groups that had emerged in more recent years among young single people. The former, he said, were mostly service oriented, keeping the rest of the church aware of missionaries' needs by making announcements and having special fund-raising drives. Their members were mostly married middle-class women who had supportive families and friends and who would not have felt it appropriate to exhibit vulnerability or ask explicitly for emotional support from their missionary societies. The singles groups, in contrast, were composed of people who were involved mainly because they needed support. "They are hurting for a lot of different reasons. It could be abusive situations, family problems, or simply that they thought they had found the right person and it turned out not to be so."

Although women's missionary societies are an example of groups that function mainly to help others in a tangible way, it also appears that women tend to be somewhat more inclined toward groups that provide emotional support, while men gravitate toward groups engaged in more instrumental tasks or else shy away from groups entirely. We noted in chapter 2, for example, that on the whole women are somewhat more likely to report small-group involvement than men. By a margin of 48 to 36 percent, women are also more likely than men to say that being "helped through an emotional crisis" is one of the important consequences of their group involvement.

One pastor who said that he had observed these differences between men and women in his church explained them this way: "[Men] usually get together for one project such as working on somebody's house or building something for the church. . . . I hadn't really thought about why, but I guess it has something to do with traditional gender roles. It's not that [men] have to get all vulnerable and open up their personal secrets in the group. I think it is just more that men want to be able to have something concrete to show for their work and time. They want to be able to complete something and then point at it and say 'I built that' or 'I painted that.' Plus, they often just say 'I'm not much for meetings.' And that is just a function of moving into adulthood, taking on responsibility, having a busier life style, and, hey, you've got to be in meetings all day so it is not something that you want to do during your free time."

The fact that groups providing physical support are often different from groups giving emotional support does not mean, of course, that the two cannot overlap. Physical help, which may require a greater expenditure of time or money than emotional support, can be facilitated by the emotional ties that have already developed among a group of people. For example, the couples group that John and his wife attend meets formally for prayer and discussion only on Sunday mornings, but a norm has developed that whenever some couple in the group is having a baby, group members will provide meals and child care for a week or more. The men's group John has been in for the past five years is smaller and more intimate. Thus far, nothing tragic has happened that might require them to help each other in a major way, but they know they could count on each other if something did happen. John emphasizes, "Those guys would die for me. And I mean that literally. If I were to die tomorrow, I would not worry at all about my family. Because I know my wife would have three husbands."

Many groups, however, seem to function in just the opposite way. Formed initially to provide physical services to their members, they eventually expand their functions as people get to know each other better. Linda, a 40-year-old mother of two who lives in a suburb of Philadelphia, for example, belongs to a group that she describes in these terms: "We are part of a group of four families that schedules what we call 'work days' every two or three months, and the men help each other with big jobs like painting or, in our case, raking leaves in the fall. We have a lot of trees. It's really nice, because we make a social event out of it and have a potluck supper, and the kids all play together." She says that the members of this group have also come to mean a lot to each other emotionally and socially.

As we see in chapter 10, the stories that groups tell about their caring for each other are sometimes an indication that they have ceased functioning merely as individuals and have adopted an identity as a corporate entity. Often these stories are generated by instances of clear physical need to which the group responds in a particularly helpful way. A secretary, age 54, who lives in San Diego described how some of the people from the group she and her husband belong to at their church pitched in on one such occasion: "I have wonderful friends from church. When you're in need, they'll be here in a minute. For example, we were in Hawaii two years ago and our house was broken into and one of the guys came and changed all our locks and fixed our windows. They stole our car keys. And he took the wheels off our cars and jockeyed them so no one could get inside to drive and he really went to a lot of trouble for us. A couple of other people are just like that. They would just do anything for you. We really have absolute friends that would do anything for you. We have thought several times about moving out of this area for one reason or another, and we just can't do it because we wouldn't see these friends that we like so much. We might lose touch with them. Friends that we travel with, we cry with and we just share each other's burdens. They've had a lot of children problems. Some pretty serious ones, and, boy, we just all stick together, no matter what. You can tell anybody anything. Yeah. You get through it. It's most unusual."

In Frank's case, being in physical and material need was also the key to realizing how much the group cared for him. They didn't solve his financial needs or pull strings to get him a job. But their acceptance and support, when he had nothing else, showed him they really cared for him as a person. "I had no money, I had nothing," he recalls. "All my identity and all that identity that comes from family, job, paycheck, bomp-bomp-bomp, well it was *gone*. Those people showed me a love and acceptance and they included me when I had nothing worthy of inclusion but me. They began the lesson of teaching me that I was fine with nothing. I remember lots of Saturday nights when I had no way of getting to the meeting because I didn't have the money to buy gasoline. And they would take me to the meeting, they would take me to dessert and take me home. And just include me. That's the best example I can give you of genuine support."

JUST SHARING

Then there are groups that do not provide much emotional or physical support but still perform an important function in giving people an opportunity to share common interests. The same Southern Baptist minister described the small groups he provides for teenagers in these terms. "For teens," he observed, "the small groups are as much social as anything else. Even though they are for discipleship training and building Christian character, teens mainly just want to be around other teens. They want to see what they are wearing and maybe even get dates."

People can interact with others on many occasions: a business transaction, working together, seeing a friend at the mall. But it is important to understand that sharing is a special word. It points to something seemingly ordinary that requires the kind of social space that may not ordinarily be present in our lives were it not for small groups. We can understand better the meaning of sharing if we listen to what Donna has to say about her group for young mothers. What she likes most about the group is, in her words, "the honesty and the being able to share personal things with one another and trusting that it stays in the room and that you know you can count on these people."

The confidentiality quotient ("it stays in the room") is important, but the key to sharing is elsewhere. It involves two rather simple conditions, neither of which is very often available in everyday life: *opportunity* and *acceptance*. The opportunity to share involves bracketing out intrusions so that one is able to make a full disclosure of something important. The acceptance is a norm that legitimates making certain kinds of personal disclosures.

Here is what Donna says about opportunity. She observes that the group sharing is especially valuable to her "because I don't think you [normally] do that. I don't think unless you—I personally, I mean, I would with my best friend who lives down at the shore now. That's my very best friend. But I think in everyday life, when we walk around and we see our neighbors and we have our kids on our leg, you're not going to share something real personal with somebody when you know you're going to be interrupted in two seconds because somebody's going to want apple juice or somebody needs to go to the bathroom or somebody just got hit with something. So at least in my life and the life that I see going on around me, the people who live around me—I don't see that real sharing because there's just no time put aside for it."

Her remarks are equally lucid about acceptance. She observes that in our everyday lives we normally do not share honestly and truthfully with other people: "We don't come out and be perfectly honest with people that we might see on the street or in our neighborhood or, you know, if somebody asks you how you're doing and you're fine, you know. [laughs] You're always 'fine.' 'Cause that's just the automatic answer. You're not going to tell that person, 'Oh, gee, I just had a terrible . . .' Whereas in here, if you weren't fine, you could say it and not feel badly about it. So I think that's kind of nice to have a group of people that you can say, 'Gee, I'm not fine today. I really had a rough morning. And this is what happened to me. And does anybody have anything to say about that?' And they can all kind of relate."

Opportunity and acceptance must be part of the group's implicit norms. In groups that encourage casual sharing these norms may simply open the door so that people can walk through if they feel so inclined. More intensive sharing and caring comes about when these norms are supplemented by a sense of urgency. In such groups sharing does not occur because it helps to build community; it occurs because life depends on it.

Frank's AA group clearly takes sharing and caring to this extreme level of seriousness. That's why he attends three times a week. He believes he would die if he didn't. "The traditions of AA have established a format which allows people freedom to share without judgment and to be open without judgment," he explains. "But the other thing is, everybody knows that this is very serious. This is not something— I mean, I learned a long time ago that, um, the primary purpose is for me to stay sober and not have a discussion or a debate with somebody about what they think and I think. Now there's a line in the Second Step about resigning from the debating society. The last line of the Preamble says that our primary purpose is to stay sober and help other alcoholics to achieve sobriety. So the meetings run smoothly because I don't really care whether you're right or wrong. I don't care whether your comment is dumb or not. I'm not there to change your mind. I'm not there to make you right. Or to make you wrong. So I think that's a lot of it. We understand that this is a life or death issue and so it's important to just let it flow."

UNINTENDED BLESSINGS

Nonetheless, many small groups come into being, not for the purpose of giving their members support, but to accomplish other tasks, such as political agendas, business, or administration. These groups often generate very significant amounts of support for their members, too. Marilyn, a woman in her early forties who lives in Minneapolis, for example, noted how much her work with an organization called Feminists for Life has become a source of personal support. "A lot of my friends are members of Feminists for Life, and they're always into helping each other, or other people." She mentions a garage sale she and her friends had recently sponsored. They donated the money to an organization for unwed mothers and sent some left-over clothing to Appalachia. But projects like this also build ties that lead to support within the group. "We provide a lot of support and encouragement," she says. "I always try to, you know, check on the [other members], asking how are they doing in their personal lives without getting snoopy . . . just showing an interest in them."

SUPPORT WITHOUT GROUPS

Thus far we have focused on the support people receive from one another in small groups. But, as we saw in chapter 2, only about four people in ten in our society are in any kind of small group. Does this mean the remainder are suffering from unmet needs for support? Or is their lack of involvement in small groups explained by the fact that they have other means from which to obtain support?

For the majority of those not involved in small groups, the answer is that they already have support in more naturally occurring settings. In the survey, 55 percent of those who were not involved in a small group said they were "part of a circle of friends who sometimes do things to help each other out."

The data show that informal circles of friends are, indeed, important sources of emotional support (see table 6.2). Of those who have such circles, only about one person in twelve claims not to receive emotional support as a result. The proportions who receive other kinds of support from these circles also compare favorably with the proportion who receive such support from small groups. For example, about four in ten share child care and an equal proportion help each other financially.

Judging from the survey results, members of informal social circles get together with one another and for the most part do things, such as give gifts or work on projects together, that become a basis for deeper friendship, sharing, and encouragement. A substantial number of these relationships may be long term given the fact that nearly half were formed in high school or college. Neighborhoods provide the physical setting in which about half of these relationships are formed. But clearly it has become necessary for many people to keep up their circles of friends by traveling to other neighborhoods and by using the telephone.

We may take a cynical view of the television advertisements that lead us to think that emotional support depends on having a "reach out" plan sponsored by one of the major telephone companies. Yet there is a great deal of truth to the claim that communications technology can, to a degree, substitute for more immediate forms of community. Shana, a single woman in her late twenties who lives in

Table 6.2

ACTIVITIES OF INFORMAL GROUPS

Proportions Who Say Their Circles of Friends Do Each of the Following

See each other socially	95
Support each other emotionally	92
Give each other gifts	71
Work on projects together	67
Live in the same neighborhood	51
Know each other from high school or college	44
Help each other financially	40
Provide child care for each other	39
Have any regular meetings	18

Boston, is quite typical in the way she obtains emotional support despite the geographic mobility that often undermines the stability of friendship networks. "I have a group of friends," she begins. But then she has to backtrack in order to explain what she means by this. "We used to be together when we were undergraduates, and then we sort of all moved to the four corners of the world. And so we keep in contact, but it's not the day to day stuff, except for one couple who live near where I do, but I'm lucky if I see them once a month." The others, nevertheless, are still there when Shana needs them. "For emotional support," she says, "it's a great group, even if we are separated."

Despite the fact that social forces in our society largely work to undermine traditional forms of community, these forces also leave many segments of our society relatively intact. Millions of people do not move every three to five years: they stay for long periods in the same neighborhoods. Millions more find ways to make and retain friends despite the hurried pace of their lives. Mixing with many different kinds of people, such as our workplaces and communities provide, helps them over a period of years to pick and sort among their acquaintances until they find a few who become truly good friends. With these few a bond of trust develops. Unlike the members of a small group, these friends do not need to meet regularly. There is simply a longstanding contract. It can be renewed periodically. And it is sufficiently strong that if someone happens to need serious emotional or physical support, the network is there.

D.J., a man in his early forties, has lived in Minneapolis all his life. He has gotten to know lots of people because of jobs he has held in sales and real estate. Many of his friends have moved away or he has outgrown them, but a few are all he needs to feel he is part of a caring community. "I'm sure I could get 20 people in here tomorrow if I needed it for help with a major project or something like that," he ventures. Asked what sorts of things he and his friends do to help each other, he cited a long list of activities. "I've helped put up a garage. Helped pour a concrete floor. I've helped build barns. I've helped cut wood. A friend of mine's got some acreage up north and I've gone with him once a year for quite a few years just to go up and cut some lumber, so he could burn wood in his fireplace/wood burning stove, just for fun, to help him out." Over the years, he says, these kinds of outings have established a permanent bond.

Increasingly, too, people are making conscious decisions to leave the anonymity of urban life in search of the more traditional communities of support that exist in rural areas and small towns. In those settings, old-fashioned neighborliness is still alive. Often the contrast with urban life is extreme. Listen to what Sam, a 45-year-old Oregonian who commutes to his job in Portland, says about life in the village of fewer than a thousand people in which he lives: "[There's] just a bunch of people that we've met over the years that basically help each other out when they see a need, or you can call them up if you're in need, like your car broke down or anything like that. They're real tight out there in that community because they live according to norms that have faded away in cities. Going out there and living is like going back to 1900. They're a real tight community. Everybody knows everybody there on a face-to-face basis. In the city, you don't. You go around the corner and you don't even know who that person is. So they're really tight and close-knit."

It is important, however, to keep in mind that a substantial minority of the American population has no circle of friends on whom they can depend, and many of these people yearn for the kind of support that others are finding in small groups. Judging from the survey, at least one American in four (27 percent) has neither an informal nor a formal group to turn to for support. Of this number, about 20 percent admit they would like to join a small group.

Even for those who are not a part of any support group, however, the standard picture of anonymity, of people not knowing anyone, that some observers of our society have painted fails to capture precisely the nature of the problem. People do know one another. They can often name dozens of people whose names and phone numbers are on their Rolodex because of business relations or because they are clients or because they provide services of some kind. The problem is that these relationships stand in the way of forming deeper friendships. A therapist, for example, may spend all day listening to clients tell about their deepest problems, but the therapist cannot in turn reveal any such problems to these clients. People who sell widgets to each other may be equally reluctant to reveal any of their inner selves because the information might work against their business dealings.

A dentist who had moved into a suburban community three years before offered this observation when asked if he had made any friends: "Well, that's been a real sticky point for us right now. We've been living here for three years and yet the number of friends we've been able to make has been relatively small. Part of the problem is I meet a lot of people through my profession, but to become socially involved with them is tricky. You can't mix business and pleasure. In the neighborhood itself, we tend to be on the younger side. This is an older development and there are just not a lot of young families. I guess we are living in a different world than a lot of these other people. Their kids are either older or in college and we just don't fit in."

For people like this, small groups can be an effective solution because these groups stand outside their normal work-related or neighborhood contacts. To be sure, small groups may seem artificial because they do not grow naturally from the relationships a person experiences in day-to-day life. But the support they provide is no less real. Over a period of time, the small group becomes a supportive community. It does not become the only community in which people choose to live their lives. It nevertheless provides the psychological and emotional support that cannot be found in the workplace, in the neighborhood, or for many people, even among kin.

THE SIGNIFICANCE OF SUPPORT

The other reason why support is so vital is that we all are desperate for self-esteem. Community: perhaps we have enough of it already or don't have time for it. But self-esteem? We are bottomless pits! Why? Because we are taught to struggle and achieve in order to be good enough. Because our parents kept us in line by telling us how bad we were. Because we live in a competitive world where everyone else is too needy to pass on an affirming word. And, frankly, because support groups, the broader mental health movement, and many of the churches have popularized the importance of self-esteem in recent years.

The quest for self-esteem can, of course, be blown out of proportion. Critics suggest that this quest is just another indication of our obsession with ourselves. They worry that we are spending all of our time seeking reassurance and looking for ways of making ourselves feel good, rather than helping the needy, staffing soup kitchens, staging protests, and lobbying for public policies that will make our society a better place. And these are legitimate concerns. People also need to hear tough, critical advice and to be called to follow high moral principles, rather than taking the course that simply makes them feel good. But there is also a need for balance in our lives. For a woman like Karen, who has been jerked from one community to another most of her life, it certainly does not hurt to have some place where she can turn for encouragement. And for a man like Frank, whose alcoholism was deeply rooted in a barrage of negative messages about himself, positive support—coupled with a clear dose of reality—is sorely needed.

Small groups nurture our self-esteem, at least in small ways, because the other people in the group take us seriously. They listen, they accept, they empathize, they support. They give us all the things we never find in everyday life. Why? Because they are not everyday life. They are not the source of our employment. We don't share bank accounts. We don't bear mutual responsibility for the welfare of our children. We don't go to bed with them at night. But the people we share with in groups are nevertheless significant enough that we value what they say. Their caring means a lot.

John, the physician, says he gets "intravenous injections of self-esteem" from his men's group. Even little things are sometimes enormously important. For example, John recalls one time when the group was evaluating a retreat they had sponsored. "One man said to me, 'John, give me your comments on what we did.' And I shared. This is a person I esteem highly. And he said, 'John, what you think means so much to me.' I mean, when you're with people who value your thoughts and opinions, who don't always agree, but *value* them, it can't help but do something for your self esteem."

This kind of encouragement, simple as it is, means a lot because it runs against the norm of many places of employment and may not occur naturally in neighborhoods, either. Their separation from the everyday structures of society allows small groups to provide encouragement, but it is also their limitation. A kind word is important, but it does not pay the rent. A pat on the back at a weekly meeting will not help someone recover from alcoholism, either. If small groups are to go beyond mere encouragement, they may have to foster deeper levels of commitment than they have to date. As is already happening in some groups, members may need to chip in monetarily to help fellow members who are in economic difficulty. And the deeper, life-and-death commitments that have developed in many twelve-step groups may need to be extended to other settings as well.

The support that most small groups currently provide, we must admit, is very much for ourselves (our "selves"). Even though we are in a group setting, much of what happens is deeply personal, psychological, emotional, inward. Leaders of the small-group movement have often contributed to this quest for self-gratification. Recognizing how deeply ingrained the desire for good feelings has become in American society, they have advocated that small groups cater to this desire. The consequences may be wonderful for individual participants. But this focus on the self can also be a serious limitation of the small-group movement. Some of the leaders and members we spoke to expressed concern about it. For example, John worried that many groups, including his Sunday school class, were making people feel better about themselves but were not necessarily motivating them to be better people. Similarly, Frank was concerned that people in some of the twelve-step groups he attended were there just to talk about themselves and to receive pats on the back, but were unwilling to struggle with the pain and sacrifice that genuine recovery involves. The kind of encouragement that support groups provide is, then, a source of tension at this juncture in the movement's development—tension between the individual and the group, tension between self-interest and spirituality, and tension between the group and the wider community. We must turn our attention to each of these issues.

7

BALANCING SELF AND OTHERS

Compatibility, Conflict, and Compromise Between Individualism and Group Commitments

> To be present to another, to be a true friend, means to be forever on call, forever open, forever willing to be involved in the friend's troubles.
>
> —Douglas V. Steere[1]

Most of us want the emotional, physical, and social support that small groups provide, but these benefits do not come free. There is a cost, sometimes a very high cost. We want our freedom, our independence to do what we want and have what we want when we want it. Groups tie us down. If we can afford it, we may prefer to pay a therapist to give us emotional support because we owe nothing else to the therapist. Group members may be there for life, calling us in the middle of the night with their own emergencies. There is thus a tension in any group between the needs and interests of the individual members and the needs and interests of other members or of the group as a whole.[2] How do support groups deal with this tension? Do they encourage people to temper their own interests in order to help others? Or do they somehow manage to promote the self-interest of each individual?

These questions are important because much concern has been

189

raised in recent years about the direction of American society. Many observers argue that the pursuit of self-interest has gotten out of hand. They argue that only a willingness to give up our individual self-interest and pay more attention to the needs of others can redeem our society. If this argument is true, then the support-group movement may be the answer—but only if it encourages putting the needs of others ahead of our own. If the support-group movement is composed only of individuals getting together to further each person's obsession with his or her personal needs, then the movement may be the wrong place to look for part of the answer. Of course, critics of the movement have raised this issue, but it is increasingly one that some leaders within the movement also have begun to consider. "If it's narcissistic, self-centered, and introverted," complained one, for example, "I don't want to be part of it. You can be that in any context. [Small groups] need to have a deeper sense of mission."

Close consideration of what goes on in small groups suggests that they are attractive to many Americans because they do, indeed, provide a comfortable balance between the needs of the individual and the needs of the group—but the balance is comfortable because it is often tipped decisively in the direction of the individual. To be sure, caring, encouragement, and acceptance, as we have seen, are very much a part of most groups. Many individuals are guided subtly by their groups to be at least somewhat different, perhaps more caring, than they might have been otherwise, and in a few cases groups gain a great deal of influence over the lives of their members. In these ways, it can be said that the group's power is greater than the individual member's. Yet, it is striking that most group members feel they compromise nothing to be part of their group; they do not even feel that the group nudges them in one direction or another. They like being in their group because it allows them to express their individuality. They relish the fact that other members are all different from themselves. And they seldom witness any serious conflicts, except for minor irritations, and even these are more likely to smolder in private rather than being confronted and resolved by the group. The secret of the small-group movement's success is thus that it provides some sense of caring and community but does so without greatly curtailing the freedom of its members. This is no small accomplishment. We need to consider some of its pitfalls as well. The place to begin, however, is to consider briefly the extent to which self-interested individualism pervades American culture.

THE QUESTION OF INDIVIDUALISM

In many ways, the logic of small groups seems to run counter to the American way of life. Study after study has described us as a nation of individualists.[3] For many of us, something of the pioneer spirit remains. We want to be free to come and go as we please. Even the thought of car pooling or riding public transportation seems like an infringement on our freedom. Compared with people in many other societies, we value our privacy. We feel uncomfortable if somebody asks too many questions about our personal finances or our sexual behavior. After working all day, we want to escape and spend time by ourselves.

Given these images of our society, it almost seems paradoxical that some 40 percent of the American public is involved in small groups. Surely there is a contradiction here. Perhaps we are not a society of rugged individualists after all. Or perhaps we have not fathomed what small groups are all about: maybe our individualism colors them deeply with its hues.

We could, of course, avoid these possibilities if we could establish that there are really two Americas: the rugged individualists and loners, on the one hand, and the community-seeking, people-loving small-group members, on the other hand. We cannot address this possibility directly because most of our survey was conducted only among small-group members. Even with partial information, however, it seems doubtful that the idea of two Americas really holds water.

Table 7.1 lists the percentages of all small-group members who indicated that various phrases describe them personally either "very well" or "fairly well." For present purposes, there are two important things to note about the figures shown in this table. First, there is plenty of support here for the idea that small-group members are out-going and oriented toward other people. Indeed, nine out of ten describe themselves as "a people person." An even higher proportion (95 percent) say they are good neighbors. And a substantial majority (61 percent) say they are extroverts. Second, these findings notwithstanding, there is also plenty of evidence that small groups contain a large number of individualists as well. One out of two says the term "rugged individualist" is a fitting label. Two out of three accept other individualistic labels, such as "free spirit" (67 percent) and "highly ambitious" (71 percent), and nearly this many (58 percent) describe themselves as "a very private person." Nearly half say they need a lot of time alone.

Table 7.1

SELF IDENTITIES OF GROUP MEMBERS

*Percentages Who Say Each of These Phrases Describes Them
Very Well or Fairly Well*

A good neighbor	95
A people person	89
Deeply religious	72
Highly ambitious	71
A free spirit	67
A leader	66
An extrovert	61
A very private person	58
Career oriented	55
On a spiritual journey	50
A rugged individualist	48
Someone who needs a lot of time alone	45
An introvert	25
A loner	22

And, despite the apparent pejorative connotations, about a quarter describe themselves as introverts and loners.

Well, someone might say, perhaps the "people persons" are really the active core of any small group, while the individualists are on the fringes somewhere. But this is not the case, according to the survey. When members who attend their group at least once a week are compared with those who attend less than once a month, exactly the same proportions say they are "people persons." This is true even for those who say this description fits them very well. Other people-oriented descriptions, such as "good neighbor" and "extrovert" are also selected just as often by the infrequent attenders as by the frequent attenders. More to the point, there are few differences on the statements about individualism either. Only slightly more of the infrequent attenders (51 percent) say they are rugged individualists than among the frequent attenders (44 percent). Exactly the same proportions of each say they need a lot of time alone and describe themselves as "very private persons." Nor are there any differences in the proportions who say they are introverts or loners.

If we assume, incidentally, that the small minority of group members who attend once a month or less (about 10 percent) are only marginally involved in their groups and thus more like the rest of the population who are not involved, then these findings are all the more interesting. They suggest that small-group members are probably just as individualistic, private, and introverted as any cross-section of the American public.

Or, if we suspect that this 10 percent in some way may not be the marginal members we are seeking, the same conclusion can be drawn from looking at other divisions among group members. For example, comparing those who attend every week with those who attend once or twice a month reveals no differences, either. Nor are the group members who say their groups are not very important to them (about a quarter of all members) much different from those who say their groups are very important to them. On this measure, the marginal members do appear to be slightly more likely to be individualists than the core members, but the differences are quite small. For example, 51 percent of the marginal members say they are rugged individualists, compared with 47 percent of the core members. Exactly the same proportions of each (58 percent) describe themselves as "very private persons."

"I spend a lot of time alone. It's part of what nature is for me. I mean being out there and just watching, observing. Whatever comes into my head, because I need that." This is how one of the women who described herself as a very private person explained what she meant by that phrase. She added: "If I find myself in a constant people situation, I just get squirrelly. I need to get out for a walk, and to do something." Yet she is a faithful member of a small group. Even though being with people makes her feel stressed out, she participates in her group because, as she says, "I can't be a hermit either. I know that about myself, because I also need people because they bring me out of myself. I see other views of things that I don't see." Her comments were shared by many of the other people we studied. They described themselves as loners, insisted they needed to spend a lot of time by themselves, and yet they found it necessary to balance those needs by interacting with other people in small groups.

The main observation is that small groups in our society are peopled by large numbers of private, individualistic people who say they need lots of time alone. These people are probably no more common in small groups than in the wider society (judging from our comparisons between core and marginal members). Thus, it would be inaccurate to conclude that small groups attract a disproportionate share of people who are, say, seeking their own gratification or who are such loners that they cannot find community in other settings. But we can say that small groups are colored by the same shades of individualism that pervade the rest of our society. Members are not people who are disproportionately oriented toward community or toward fitting in, helping others, or bending their interests toward the will of the group. They are strong individualists who bring their individual needs and interests to their groups. This fact certainly must have some important implications for how small groups in our society operate. We should consider both the problems that arise and how some of these problems are resolved.

NEGATIVE EXPERIENCES IN GROUPS

Although (as we saw in chapters 5 and 6) most group members express satisfaction with their groups and claim to receive a great deal of support from them, no group is perfect. Many members acknowledge that there have been problems. About half say they have had disagreements with other members. A third say they have felt shy or reluctant to share their feelings. An equal number say they have found it hard to make time for the group. One person in five admits to feeling uncomfortable in the group. One in six claims to have felt pressured by the group. And a few people say they haven't quite fit in, felt the group was expecting too much of them, found it hard to be open and honest, felt the group didn't understand them, felt they were being criticized, did not feel appreciated, or felt the group was invading their privacy (see table 7.2).

Readers should be clear about one thing. These problems are not felt mainly by the loners and individualists who participate in small groups. Nor are they attributable to the presence of strong-willed free thinkers in groups. Such problems are to be expected in a society like ours that places a high premium on individuality. Indeed, it might be surprising that more group members do not report strains between themselves and other members or between their own needs and the dynamics of the group. That is, it would be surprising were it not for the fact that few groups demand much from their members. Thus, it

Table 7.2

NEGATIVE EXPERIENCES IN GROUPS

*Percentage of Group Members Who Say They Have
Experienced Each of the Following*

Disagreeing with other members of the group	53
Feeling shy or reluctant to share your feelings	35
Finding it hard to make time for the group	34
Feeling uncomfortable	22
Feeling pressure from the group to do something	17
Feeling like you didn't quite fit in	15
People in the group expecting too much from you	13
Feeling like you couldn't be open and honest with the group	12
Feeling like the group didn't understand you	11
Feeling that people in the group were criticizing you	8
Not feeling appreciated by the group	7
Feeling the group was invading your privacy	3

is possible for most group members to be strong individualists without experiencing conflict with other strong-willed people in their groups. As Donna says about her group, for example: "You can be a strong individualist. People will express very different points of view, but then someone else will say, 'Oh, yes, I guess that makes sense, too.'"

It is also important to note that most groups seem to find ways to work out the problems that do arise. To some extent, of course, there is a built-in problem-reducing mechanism: disgruntled members exit the group. Because there are so many other groups, they simply can leave and look for a group more to their liking. But member satisfaction is relatively immune to the effects of these problems. A statistical examination of the joint effects of all these problems on levels of member satisfaction, for example, found that only two of them made any significant difference at all: disagreements with other members and feeling that one's privacy was being invaded. The data also showed that some of these problems diminish with time. Being shy or reluctant to share, for example, is understandably much less of a problem for people who have been in their group for two or three years than it is for newcomers. The same is true for people who find it hard to be open and honest with the group or who feel that the group doesn't understand them.

Were we interested only in the question of whether or not small groups run smoothly, therefore, it would be easy to say, "yes, for the most part" and turn our attention to other matters. The larger, and more puzzling, question of individualism remains, however. How is it that so many people in a nation of individualists are able to maintain such an active commitment to small groups? What more can we learn about groups, knowing that they are peopled by individualists? What is the dynamic of fitting into a group and yet retaining a strong sense of one's own identity? And what are the pitfalls?

The quote at the head of this chapter about being involved in friends' troubles helps put the question in a clearer perspective. Some readers undoubtedly will assert that there is nothing contradictory about being a rugged individualist and participating in a small group. But would they be willing to undertake a deep, long-lasting involvement with the troubles of people in their group? Would they be willing to sacrifice a great deal of their time, energy, money, and personal freedom to help fellow group members? For that matter, would they want fellow members intervening that much in their own lives? Or, perhaps at a much more mundane level, how is it possible for people with such diverse lifestyles and interests to function comfortably together as a group? What sorts of compromises are involved to form a group? And to what extent does the group function as a whole, a body, rather than simply servicing the needs of its individual members?

These questions are difficult to think about. In other contexts social scientists have tried to address similar questions for more than a century. It is clear from the many volumes on community, for example, that we no longer live in the traditional villages or neighborhoods that once, allegedly, solved all these problems for us. In those settings, our personal identity and the identity of our tribe were virtually the same. People had no choice but to be what the group taught them to be. It is also clear that none of us is a pure individualist, the type of person who is completely self-sufficient and who decides everything without reference to anyone else. The vast majority of us derive our personal identity from the groups in which we participate. But we exercise a great deal of choice in this matter, too. It is no small feat that we are able to participate extensively in small groups, feel comfortable in them, and yet retain our own sense of individuality. Most of us may be able to maintain that delicate balance, but it is nevertheless delicate. Too much attention to ourselves, and the group fails to function as a group. Too little attention to ourselves, and we subject ourselves to dangerous, manipulative group practices.

Thus, we need to consider some of the characteristics of the contemporary small-group movement that allows it to fit in so well with the prevailing individualism in American culture. I do not deny that small groups provide community; as we saw in the last chapter, many people receive emotional support, encouragement, and reassurance, and a substantial minority receive physical help as well. Small groups certainly provide an occasion for getting to know other people and for discussing values and concerns with one's friends and neighbors. But they do not fundamentally challenge our individualism. They allow us not only to retain our individuality but also to focus deeply on our own personal interests and needs and, for the most part, to limit the time we spend with other people or the levels of obligation we are willing to incur toward them. Small groups adapt us to the individualistic norms in our culture more than we generally realize. They do so because of selective perception, by encouraging us to express our individuality, and by protecting our private space. Each of these mechanisms merits consideration.

SELECTIVE PERCEPTION

One of the most obvious reasons why small groups fit easily with our individualism is that these groups can be so specialized that everyone in them is basically like us. Were we forced to participate in certain groups, we might throw up our hands and say, "Let me out of here!" But a sorting process works to ensure that we will feel comfortable. Out of a community of 50,000 people, for example, only 10 people may be Presbyterian, female, age 28 to 35, married to professionals, mothers of preschool children, and residents of houses that cost approximately $200,000. If you are lucky enough to find the other nine who fit this description, you may be able to form a group that feels very comfortable.

But even this kind of sorting works only because people engage in selective perception. Among these ten, some may be much better educated or more intelligent than others, some may work outside the home and others may work at home, some may be alcoholics, some may love gardening, some may take the Bible more seriously than others. Indeed, as we saw in chapter 3, diversity of one kind or another is the norm in most groups. Age, racial and ethnic background, religious orientations, and political views may be quite varied within the same group. How is it that such diverse people are able to get along?

Essentially, they manage by denying the importance of all these other characteristics. As Donna put it, "We get along well because of our Christianity, our children, our families. I see the things we have in common. I don't see the differences as much." She is not saying everybody should be—or is—alike. She is proud of the diversity that exists within her group. She is, however, asserting the very profound observation that it is possible for people to get along by emphasizing what they have in common, rather than the differences that might pull them apart.

Selective perception is, of course, one of the coping mechanisms we use in all areas of our lives, but small groups encourage it in a significant way.[4] No matter how important they may be to those who participate in them, small groups are almost always based on some single overriding concern. It may be a commitment to the truth of the Bible or knowing that staying sober is essential to staying alive, but this concern binds the group together. Small groups are, in this respect, like single-issue movements in politics. They are devoted to a particular principle or cause. Consequently, small-group members can overlook or devalue many of the differences within their group. These differences are unimportant.

Frank, the man who was involved in an AA group, illustrated how agreement on one basic concern can cause all other differences to pale in comparison. Asked what the differences were among people in his group, he was caught short and had to reflect for a moment. Starting slowly, he mentioned personality differences and financial differences, then added: "People are married, people are single, people are gay, people are straight, people are old, people are young." Suddenly he realized the differences far outweighed the similarities: "My God, everything. I'm trying to think what are the similarities? The only thing that's similar is a bunch of drunks trying to stay sober."

This kind of selective perception is perhaps the key to being in a small group at all. The individual does not have to become like other group members in all respects. The individual must, however, be willing to acknowledge the fundamental importance of whatever has brought the group into existence. For the brief time that the group meets (if not longer), participating in the group is thus a means of ordering one's priorities in life. Commitment to a group is a statement to the effect that studying the Bible, for example, is more important than associating with people your own age, or having fun with your neighbors, or spending time with your spouse. The individual already may have decided on the importance of that priority. But participating in the group exercises a genuine influence as well. If nothing else, it bends individual wills in a common direction. And yet, for many people, this bending is possible because the group takes only a small portion of their time; for example, they can make the Bible a priority on Tuesday evenings, but not have to worry about it while at work.

Of course, the concerns of their small group are not marginal for everyone. For Frank, staying sober is, indeed, a fundamental, life-orienting principle. In the case of John, the doctor, his devotion to the Bible has also been a guiding, life-time commitment. But many of the group members we talked to could overlook their individual differences and focus on the group's core issue because the group met for only an hour a week and because it did not require them to alter their lifestyles in any significant way. They could study the Bible for a few minutes, nod in agreement, and then the next day say to themselves, no, I don't think that was the point at all. And they could listen to the leader tell them to "pray without ceasing," knowing that it would not be difficult to utter a brief prayer ("God, help me through the day") from time to time and that nobody would check on whether they did or not.

EXPRESSING INDIVIDUALITY

Because small groups do focus attention on one set of priorities rather than another, we may think of them as ways of finding community, of getting back some of the solidarity with other people that has been lost in our society, and of combating some of the rampant individualism that has become so evident in our culture. Bending our wills in a common direction becomes a way of finding community through the pursuit of shared values. But, ironically, small groups are also a way to adapt our religious faith or other shared values to the individualism prevailing in our culture.

Let us compare the small group with a more traditional way in which religious faith was made public—namely, through preaching and teaching. In the standard sermon format, a single voice speaks and all others listen in silence. You look around, others seem interested and intent, so you assume they agree with what is being said; those who do not, you are aware, probably voice their dissent by not being there in the first place. So your sense of community involves agreeing with an official point of view or else feeling uncomfortable and leaving. The same situation obtains in the standard teaching setting, where a single voice expounds on the truth and everyone else listens. The small group, in contrast, usually encourages give and take. You may basically agree with what others are saying, but it is okay if you do not. Indeed, one way of showing your individuality is by disagreeing politely, offering a different point of view. The group, in this sense, provides a forum in which spiritual individualism can be legitimated.

Listen to the way one woman in a middle-class suburban setting explained how it was possible to be a strong individualist and a good member of her spiritual direction study group at the same time: "We all have different points of view and someone may give their different point of view and someone else may say, 'Oh, that's a good point.' So I think that they encourage that, more than discourage it." She added that in her group outright disagreement was fairly common. "Somebody may read a statement and say, 'Oh, that was good.' And somebody else may say, 'That was garbage.' So there's a lot of debate like that. I think that's good."

What some have called "privatized" values or "individualistic" spirituality is institutionalized in the norms of many small groups. We tell ourselves that faith is essentially a matter of personal discovery and that values are not absolute, universal standards, but discretionary matters about which we can have our own opinions. We then carry these views into our groups as well. A written text of some kind may provide a common framework, but the values it embodies are so general that everyone can read something different into it.

At the women's Bible study group that Karen, whom we met in the last chapter, attends, the norm of tolerance and acceptance that Karen found so supportive also proved to be a way in which religious truths were often turned into matters of personal interpretation. In a study of I Timothy, for example, the leader tried to offer some strong statements about how rich Christians should behave. She referred to the biblical injunctions as "commands." She summarized some of them as imperatives: "Avoid arrogance." "Don't put your hope in wealth." "Be generous, willing to share." She also made a special point of drawing a connection between these imperatives and her listeners: "You may not consider yourself rich, but relative to the rest of the world, you have quite an abundance of things!" But then the group interrupted, offering personal applications, and in the process significantly weakened the force of what the leader had been trying to say. "Boy, you wouldn't believe how much I'm paying to send my kids to camp," one member volunteered. Another complained that her husband was accusing her of spending too much money on clothes. "It just isn't true," she asserted. "Stand up for yourself," someone advised. "Yeah, tell him to quit playing golf," suggested another member. Before long, each member of the group was feeling better. Imperatives had been transformed into personal opinions. The biblical imperatives were not only palatable; they were downright comforting.

Self-help groups have also elevated the acceptance of individual opinion to a high art. At the Silver Chase Meeting, for instance, the twelve steps provide a reference point, but group norms encourage each person to interpret and apply them as he or she sees fit. Because each individual's experience and situation is unique, there can be no right or wrong interpretations. Taboos on what is called "cross-talk" also prevent different opinions from being challenged. Person A and person B can each express opinions, but neither can directly challenge what the other has said. As a member of another group explained, "I can read a paragraph and make a comment about how I think this paragraph applies, and you can make a comment absolutely contradictory to me and nobody's going to say either one of us is wrong." The result is an exceptional level of tolerance for diversity, which of course is one reason why people are attracted to these groups. Their opinion is respected, perhaps even affirmed. The group also functions more smoothly, especially when 30 people are vying to vent their feelings about what an awful week they have had. The difficulty is that an insight from another member of the group that might have been helpful cannot be offered. Another difficulty is that every view enjoys equal authority, no matter how unhelpful or unrealistic it may be.

This way of championing diversity is perhaps more common in mainstream religious settings or in the wider community than it is among believers who have a stricter sense of what divine truth should be. But even in those contexts there is a language that quickly legitimates a great deal of individual diversity. In theological terms, this is the language of "calling," suggesting that God calls people to live in different ways. In sociological terms, it is the language of "organic solidarity"—true community comes about when people play different roles and thus become interdependent. Both are implied in the following remark by a member of a deeply evangelical religious group: "We want you to be what God has called *you* to be. I'm not going to tell you that you have to be a, b, c and d. We're going to try to build a community of faith that is responding to God. So there has to be diversity." What sort of diversity? Not Muslims and Buddhists and atheists, to be sure. But the speaker talked at great length, illustrating his point by showing how valuable it was to have single and married people in his group, older people and younger people, men and women, people with different occupations, and people with diverse personalities. In small groups, it is but a small step further to assume implicitly that the unique perspectives, opinions, and assertions of each member are all equally valid because each member is simply expressing his or her "gifts."

KEEPING PRIVATE SPACE

Another way in which group participation and the needs of the self are reconciled is through norms that restrict what can happen when the group gathers. Groups function because people come wanting to share, but most groups have a strong sense of members' private space as well. People can thus participate without sharing very much of themselves. Many people feel uncomfortable about having to share, for example. Having to pray out loud is also an important issue. In a society where, as we saw in chapter 2, the vast majority feel more comfortable praying in private—and define this as part of their basic spirituality—it can sometimes become very awkward, or at best superficial, when people have to pray out loud.

Donna, in reflecting on her group, said that praying out loud was the one thing that always made her uncomfortable: "The one thing I'm not comfortable with is praying out loud. I guess 'cause I was raised Presbyterian and to me that was always something private. Your prayers were something you kind of, I don't know, it was a very private thing. And they like to, at certain times, do what they call a round-robin prayer. Which wouldn't even be too bad, if it was a smaller group. But if you have ten or twelve people in a group, I feel personally it's real hard to sit there and go around. Each person says part of the prayer. What it is, is I might pray for something. And then it goes to the next person. And they may add something to the prayer. Then it goes to the next person." For her, part of the problem is feeling that the group is nudging her to do something she does not quite understand. She also feels she is having to share a part of herself that she would rather not disclose.

Understanding the tension between private space and public disclosure takes us back to the point in chapter 5 about the importance of acceptance norms in groups. Contrary to what some observers of our culture have suggested, the problem is not that we are so private about our lives that we are unwilling ever to divulge any of our secrets. Nor, unlike the claim of other observers, is the problem that we are so confused about what should be private or public that we run around expressing our inner lives in public all the time. Like anything else, we may be quite willing (even eager) to reveal our deepest feelings, but only when the situation is right. Norms govern situations, telling us when it is appropriate to do this and when it is not.

In everyday life, as Donna's comment reveals, our norms usually prevail against divulging much of ourselves. This prevents personal issues from intruding on the routine efficiency of the workaday world. In more intimate settings, norms are more tolerant of self-disclosure, but the variability of life in these settings can still generate a great deal of uncertainty. Telling your spouse that you are suffering from acute depression may not be exactly what he or she most wants to hear when rushing out the door to attend an important meeting. Small groups are thus a protected place in which norms can deliberately be established about when, for how long, and what kinds of self-disclosures are appropriate.

But these norms cannot be manipulated in a completely arbitrary fashion. Some group could decide officially that everyone would now take off their clothes, but few people would feel comfortable doing so. By the same token, it takes a while for informal norms about sharing to catch up with the formal norms. People must interact with one another long enough to see self-disclosure modeled, learn how the group is going to respond, and know enough about the behavior and expectations of other people to feel assured that nothing terribly shocking is likely to happen. Once that level of understanding is established, people can move with greater confidence across the boundary between their private space and self-disclosure.

How this understanding of group norms reduces the tension between individuals and the group is clearly shown in the statement of John, the physician, talking about the group he and his wife attend: "How much of yourself do you expose? I think it all depends on the comfort level you have with the group. Our group has changed somewhat over the last year, just by people coming and going, and it takes some time to adjust. I mean, you don't sit down with someone you've never seen before and begin to share deep intimate secrets of your life. And I think we've seen in the last, say, month, a much more openness to exposing yourself because there's a level of trust." John is saying, then, that a fairly extensive and intimate level of involvement may be required for people in groups to share their most basic concerns; otherwise, the sharing is likely to remain at a superficial level that, in effect, protects the private space of the individual.

Group leaders recognize the same tension, but view it from the standpoint of what may be dysfunctional for the overall purposes of the group. Even though the group may be concerned with the personal problems of individuals, there may be strong norms against people becoming too open about these problems. The pastor of an Assemblies of God church, for example, reflected this attitude in describing the main goals of small groups at his church: "The home fellowship groups have a four-fold thrust. First, there is encouragement. This is I guess what would be called in the secular community the psychological aspect. Second, it is an evangelistic set up—we are trying to bring people into the ministry and to God. Third is a teaching aspect. Much of the time in the fellowship groups is spent going over basic biblical doctrines and teachings—exploring it in depth and thinking about how it applies to their personal lives. Finally, there is the interpersonal part. It helps people communicate with one another, and that makes them better Christians—better people for that matter." Given these purposes, the groups that this pastor has started have been discouraged from sharing personal problems too deeply.

As he explains, "Personal divulging of problems does not occur in the home fellowship groups all that much. People come in and ask the group to pray for them, sure, but they are not really coming in and leaving themselves vulnerable. If there is a problem, the leader of the fellowship group reports it to the pastors and we try to work one-on-one with the person to correct the problem. The fellowship group is more centered on the Bible and the time is always set aside for worship rather than any sort of therapy for the individual. Whether prayer is centered on persons inside the group or for those outside the group depends totally on the lesson. If the pastor talks of being introverted and exploring an inner self, then the group will likely be focused internally, but sometimes it is a general message about exploring the world around you."

These remarks illustrate clearly the importance of group norms and expectations. People attending self-help groups would find it odd to be told they couldn't share their deepest problems, but were expected to talk about the Bible and seek guidance from the pastor for anything else. But even self-help groups have norms that draw sharp distinctions between what can be shared in the group and some part of the person that must remain private. Most groups, for example, respect the privacy of the physical body of the person, although in many groups hugging by mutual consent is accepted. Many self-help groups that encourage open disclosures of private feelings nevertheless discourage judgmental or disparaging statements directed toward other members of the group.

The frequency with which group members talked about "judgmentalism," suggests that this is an important concept that somehow helps individuals protect their private space while participating in their groups. One woman, for example, went into some detail to explain why criticism from several people in her Bible study group greatly annoys her. "There's two women in particular that I think have strong opinions and think that that's the right way. And it causes what I feel to be a judgmental type of attitude. We have a woman who just does everything perfect. She *hates* it when people are late. And she had even said it one time, 'I *hate* people who are late.' Now I know she didn't mean 'I hate the people who are late,' she hates their lateness. But it reflects in her attitude toward the person. And it's a pet peeve of mine. Legalisticness is a pet peeve of mine. Some people think that legalism is the way to go because it's organized and that's the way it should be. I just disagree. I don't think that's the way Christ was and I don't think any church-related group should function that way."

This sort of comment comes up so frequently that it begins to seem like part of the deep code by which small groups in our society operate. Seeing social norms clearly is often easiest when they are violated. Everything can be going smoothly at a Sunday morning church service, for example, until a homeless person wanders in, walks down the aisle, and asks the pastor for some spare change. How uneasy people become and how they handle their uneasiness is a good barometer of where their true values lie. So it is with tolerance in small groups. The fact that members feel uneasy to hear rules enforced too rigidly or to hear criticisms being expressed of absent members (or to express them themselves in interviews) suggests that people come desperately wanting to be accepted just the way they are. Probably they have been criticized all their lives. Perhaps they have internalized these criticisms to the point that "critical voices" interrupt their serenity from within their own heads. They want their groups to provide a break from those voices.

There is, however, a curious side to this desire for acceptance. If people want so badly to be tolerant, how do they express the things that annoy them about the group? Telling someone, for example, that you are annoyed because he or she wants everyone to get to the group on time may make you seem as intolerant as that person is. Rousseau identified this same problem years ago when he suggested that there is one thing a tolerant society cannot tolerate: intolerance.

Some groups have suggestion boxes for members' anonymous complaints. Others have gripe sessions or business meetings where problems can be hammered out. But our research leads me to believe that most groups handle annoyances with silence. The reason is, in the first place, a strong desire on the part of members to believe that everything about their group is going swimmingly. Otherwise, the obvious question is, why don't you drop out? But our society also values individual differences and opinions so much that it is hard to imagine any 25 people thinking exactly alike on all relevant issues. In short, there is bound to be disagreement and, if candor were permitted, annoyance. And yet, to express these annoyances openly is to fly in the face of the norm of tolerance and the belief that "everything is okay here." So people are likely to remain silent, letting unstated group norms hold sway. If they become annoyed enough, they drop out. And instead of confronting others who hold differing opinions, they simply let those people come to the gradual realization that they don't belong. Rather than voicing their opinions very long, they will likely move on to a group in which they feel more comfortable.

An example that supports this argument comes from a Bible study and prayer fellowship at a church in a middle-class, white suburb. Like most such churches, college education and professional training had made most of its members deeply respectful of individual differences. But they also believed firmly that everything should be done in an orderly (predictable) manner. It was the kind of church, one member explained, in which everyone prayed at eight o'clock in the morning and ate their breakfasts at nine. The problem came when a new member who had different views of prayer joined one of the small groups at the church. Upon learning that a person in the church was seriously ill, she proposed holding an around-the-clock prayer vigil in hopes of convincing God to effect a miracle. When she passed around a sign-up sheet, only 4 people out of 25 signed their names.

Nothing was said. There was never a discussion of differences in views of prayer. Just silence. "She wasn't accepted," one member recalls. "It wasn't a verbal thing where someone went up to her and said, 'Look, your views are too far out of reach for us.' But just each week when something would come up, you just got the feeling that she didn't belong in the group." Before long, the woman left and went to a different church.

As we gained the trust of people in the groups we studied, we discovered all sorts of minor annoyances and personal grievances simmering just beneath the surface. Child care was a frequent source of discontent. Some members, for example, felt that only parents should be expected to perform child care duties; others thought these responsibilities should be shared by all members. Duties in general were often a source of unspoken resentments. "I always have to make the coffee" or "they never take a turn having the group at their house" were typical remarks. Rules governing group meetings were another source of disagreement. Some wanted rigidly enforced rules about when the meetings should begin, what topics would be covered, and how long it was appropriate for each individual to speak; others wanted flexibility. Many of these concerns were expressed privately with such vehemence that they seemed to be more than minor irritations. Yet few people had ever confronted the group as a whole or even others individually about these concerns. They simmered in silence, vowing to leave before they ever spoke up, and in the meantime trying hard to deny that there were any significant problems.

Thus, not talking about certain things, such as petty annoyances and irritations, may be a way to protect the private space of individuals (tolerating their right to be themselves), but it is also a norm encouraged by the group. In the short term at least, this norm allows groups to go on with their business as if everything is okay. Dissatisfied members find it easier to drop out than to express their dissatisfaction openly. The norm of silence is but one way in which tensions between the individual and the group can be avoided. And yet it also illustrates that small groups may need to learn more effective ways to reveal, confront, and resolve internal grievances if they are to promote community at a deeper level.

ESCAPING THE TENSIONS

The tensions we have been considering are built into the different needs we are likely to feel as individuals and the needs we encounter in the presence of others. These tensions are thus natural, inevitable, and to some extent unresolvable. Yet many of the people in our study seemed oblivious to them. Asked if they ever found it hard to fit into the group, or felt pressured, they said no. How is this possible?

Some years ago, at a time when the totalitarianism of Nazi Germany and Stalinist Russia were very much in the public mind, psychologist Erich Fromm wrote a widely acclaimed book called *Escape from Freedom*.[5] Fromm's thesis was that people find individual freedom so frightening that they often flee from it and seek refuge in authoritarian social structures. In subtle ways, small groups can also become an escape from the terrifying freedom that comes from truly being ourselves.

In the first place, small groups can shield us from having to make decisions for ourselves. They provide security—security in numbers, security in consensus, security in the figure of a leader who tells us what to do.[6] Various authors have identified four ways in which group members may fall prey to this lust for security: (a) always doing what the group wants you to do; (b) doing everything instrumentally—to achieve a desired outcome; (c) doing what is reasonable and logical; and (d) doing what will satisfy some authority figure who claims to understand true spirituality. In the groups we studied, these pitfalls generally were not obvious enough to be matters of concern. Most group members remained detached enough from their groups that they were not about to do everything the group told them to do. However, in some cases members indirectly betrayed greater dependence on the group than they may have been willing to acknowledge. For example, one person said it would be difficult for him to live without attending his group every week. Another said she had come to think of herself very much in the terms that other group members used to define her. Still another tried hard to follow the steps for a successful life that his group leader encouraged the group to pursue.

Secondly, individuals may experience no tension between themselves and the group because group members tell them only what they want to hear. This is the danger point where support and acceptance become too much. In the extreme, the person who uses the group as a mirror turns out to be nothing more than what he or she sees reflected in the mirror. At this point, the group functions only as a hall of mirrors, distorting reality in an unhelpful way, just so that members can get along with each other and to keep peace.[7] There may be times, however, when genuine differences of opinion need to be expressed, no matter how painful. Group members may need to confront their own negative feelings about themselves rather than having them plastered over with smiles and pats on the back. Openness and honesty cannot be completely genuine without some pain. Frank, for example, said he would still be a drinking alcoholic had it not been for some people in AA who encouraged him to face the hard truth about himself. The pastor of a church that was currently sponsoring a large number of small groups expressed a similar concern. He likened these groups to his role as chaplain. "I go to the hospital to see Pete, and Pete says, 'Boy, I just had an hour of physical therapy, and it about killed me.' And I pat him on the arm and say, 'I feel for you, Pete.' That's what small groups usually do. But I also know that if hospitals were just a bunch of chaplains, nobody would ever get well. You do have to have that physical therapy to get better. And it's going to be painful!"

Thirdly, every group member has probably encountered someone who, no matter how bluntly the criticism was given, failed to hear it. This is the problem of wearing masks, as some groups call it, or of playing roles rather than being authentic. Groups invite this problem, especially for people who are unused to being in intimate settings with other people. Every group encourages people to behave a certain way and live up to certain standards. For a while, an individual member may play along, feeling good about the accolades the group gives for good behavior. But at some point this behavior may begin to feel phony. Part of the reason is that we are all complex creatures. If the group allows us to express only one side of ourselves, we will eventually feel cheated and dehumanized, and yet we may be able to deny those feelings for a long time.

Finally, the denial of feelings can allow individuals to fit too easily into a group. It may seem strange that this should be a problem, especially when small groups so often focus on feelings. Yet group norms also govern what type of feelings legitimately can be expressed. In some groups it may be that only happy feelings, such as rejoicing, giving praise, and living the victorious Christian life, can be expressed. Donna, for example, said it was often harder to express doubts in her Bible study group than to tell what the Lord had done for her during the preceding week. In other groups just the opposite may be the case: unless you can say how bad you are feeling and what a rotten week you've had, something is wrong. For example, Frank admits that some of the twelve-step groups he attends seem to be populated by people who really don't have that much to complain about, but who always complain anyway. Either way, people need to be able to probe the full range of feelings likely to be elicited by the group. If they do not, they are likely to think everything is going well until some unexpected event shows them they were living in denial.

RESOLVING THE TENSIONS

Thus far we have considered ways in which people draw the boundaries between themselves and their groups, thus protecting their individuality from being effaced by the group. Yet this portrayal is in many ways too simple, because we are not only individuals some of the time and group members some of the time. Our individuality is not fully realized apart from our group identity. Or, to put it differently, being in a community should also be an integral part of what makes us more human as individuals. But what does this mean? And how does it happen?

One common way in which group participation contributes to the self is by giving individuals feedback about who they are. Interaction with others in a group, in this sense, provides people with a mirror in which to reflect upon their lives and reaffirm their self-definition. The cases of Karen and Frank in the last chapter both provide examples of this process. In each instance, the individual self was able to grow because of the interaction and support found in small groups. The metaphor of growth is quite prominent in the language of many group members.

When people say they grow as a result of being in a group, they do not mean simply that their self has become more distinct, autonomous, or differentiated. Personal growth in some cases can mean that people are focusing on themselves at the expense of others. But what often has been regarded by social critics as a disturbing form of selfishness in our society should not be equated automatically with individuals' concern for personal growth. Quite often what personal growth means is a better capacity to fulfill the vital roles one is expected to play. Personal growth can, for example, mean being a better mother. In this sense, it is scarcely any different from, say, learning how to be a better chemist. The main difference is that what is defined as better may in one case be more closely associated with personal attributes and in the other with specialized knowledge and skills. Thus, being a better mother might be regarded as a form of personal growth if the point was learning patience and responsibility; it would be called something different if the point were learning at what age to feed infants strained vegetables.

But if personal growth means learning new roles, or more accurately, developing personal traits that are conducive to new roles, then the contribution of the group becomes obvious. Most children do not learn to ride bicycles by themselves. Even if their intention in learning this skill is to ride off into the sunset by themselves, they learn in the first place by watching other children, by letting their parents help them, and by practicing with their friends. The same is true in learning how to be a mother. The ultimate goal may be selfish (taking care of one's own children), but the means to that goal involves other people. Personal growth is, in this sense, a matter of learning roles by interacting with people who already know those roles.

The example of learning to be a mother suggests another important point about small groups. In all societies, people have banded together with others of the same age group to learn certain developmental skills. Young hunters, for example, practiced hunting together with their peers. The reason is that people often learn more effectively by watching others in the process of learning rather than seeing someone who has already mastered the tasks. Watching people in a similar situation try, fail, and succeed also provides encouragement. In our society, learning to be a mother is a developmental task of this kind. By the same token, exploring one's feelings about different career options, thinking about how to choose a mate, dealing with midcareer crises and the empty-nest syndrome, and experiencing declining health are all developmental tasks that can be learned better by interacting with groups of one's peers. Our society heightens the importance of such learning. Living in fluid situations, we have to learn multiple roles, and we have to learn new roles throughout our lives. Our society also makes it less likely, however, that the groups of peers who can teach us these roles will form naturally. Except for schools and colleges, few institutions are age-graded. People work and live in communities with people of all different ages. But they may not have close relationships with the mentors who could teach them most. New mothers may be distant from their own mothers, for example, or feel that they do not wish to raise their children the way they were raised. Thus, it becomes necessary to learn mothering in small, intentional groups.

Karen, for example, was quite candid in admitting that her group perhaps had helped most by giving her examples of what it means to be a wife and mother. "I've grown as a wife. I'd have to say the area that's been touched the most in my life, though, is being a young mother. Maybe more because it's the area that I needed the growth in. I needed to mature and to accept the responsibility that the Lord had given me. And to accept it joyfully. The group has really helped me to do that. Along, of course, with maturing physically, spiritually the group has really been there for me."

Another way in which small groups facilitate self-identity is by giving members an opportunity to compare themselves with each other. A member of a twelve-step group gave the following example: "Just from hearing the things that people contribute, you realize that people are at very different stages and working with quite different things in different ways." What made these differences meaningful for her was that the people were otherwise similar enough that she could identify with them. "There seems to be a fair similarity in background in the sense that you rarely hear anybody—I think there are definitely people in the group who have had their own alcohol abuse problems. I've never heard anyone mention substance abuse other than alcohol. Most of the people appear to have come from middle-class backgrounds rather than upper or blue-collar or poor backgrounds. So those are similarities. But I think the diversity is more in personality and in stages of where people are." Just hearing other people talk about their problems helped her to see more clearly what stage she was at in her own journey.

In a society such as ours in which we are forced to play many different roles in a wide variety of settings, small groups may also contribute to the integration of a person's self. They do so by bringing together the various elements of an individual's life. These elements are not brought together literally in most cases, as they might have been in smaller communities; for instance, when a man who was a banker, father, and church member was asked to be the treasurer for his daughter's youth group at church. But they are brought together now by the self-disclosures that people are asked to make in their groups. In having to talk about how things are going at work, our hypothetical banker may now be confronted with his own feelings, for example, and have to reconcile these feelings with his religious views or his worries about his family.

The fact that self-definitions are constantly being reshaped in groups means, incidentally, that when there is deep support and caring in a group, people also must come to accept a certain level of discomfort. We might even say that this tolerance of discomfort is a sign that the group has moved to a level of intimacy that transcends the usual group norms and becomes much more like those operating in a family. You can handle people telling you what to do because you know they genuinely care. You also know that this is part of life. Stage managing how much or how little of yourself to divulge is moot because people now know you so well you cannot hide.

John, for example, gave a very clear illustration of this kind of discomfort: "When you're sitting with people who *know* you, you can't B.S. You can't. And they know. I've canceled a lunch with people in my group because I knew I didn't want to have to face them. You know? That's where the level of discomfort comes, 'cause you know you can't be dishonest. It's like your spouse. You can sit there and say something, but they *know*. The level of discomfort isn't one of who are these people, but really living out honestly in front of them at a deep level."

Probably the most basic of all the ways in which groups can contribute to the discovery and fulfillment of the individual self is by providing occasions to do things and be things that the person cannot do or be alone. The range of things that fall into this category is enormous: you cannot be a son, daughter, sibling, father, mother, or grandparent without being part of a family group; you cannot be a lover or a sexual being entirely alone; it is impossible to be a friend or companion or helper by yourself; it is probably not even possible to experience the full range of human emotions except in the community of others.

Laughing is a good example because it is commonplace. Nothing could be more human—indeed, it is often said that humans are the only animals that laugh. Yet laughter is also something we generally experience most richly in groups. Of course it is possible to chuckle to ourselves about some joke we heard or read in a magazine. Often, though, those occasions are funny because we have a mental picture of some social relationship. The live event sparks true laughter—which is why comedy must be performed live and why it depends on adjusting the timing to the social interaction involved. So if we are never in groups, or never in groups that encourage laughter, our humanness as individuals is never fully realized.

John had been thinking a lot about laughter when we talked with him. His work had its lighter moments, of course, and he laughed and played with his children. But, he said, being part of a group of other married couples really brought out this dimension of his life. "If you would ask me who in my life do I laugh with? It's the people in this group. And I think that says a lot."

Frank made a similar discovery in AA, except in his case it was learning how to cry. On his own, he had always denied his feelings, but at AA meetings he saw other people expressing their pain by crying. For a whole year Frank attended AA meetings and let the tears flow freely. Today he says he feels more fully human, more "real." He believes there is more to him now or that more of him is available, so he can relate more fully to other people and enjoy intimacy with them at a deeper level.

THE INEVITABLE TENSION

For all the ways in which people can reconcile their individuality with their involvement in small groups, it must also be recognized that genuine group life, at many levels, does run against the grain of the rugged, go-it-alone, individualistic ethos in American society. This ethos may not prevent us from having friends and families, but it does work against establishing intimate, caring ties with the fellow members of churches or other groups. We find it difficult to ask others for help because we have been taught to be self-sufficient. The same training may make it difficult for us to respond positively when others ask for help. We tell ourselves that they should be taking care of themselves. We may even recognize that our religious beliefs call us to a life of caring, and yet we concentrate more on cultivating a direct line to God than a party line that includes our neighbors. One final example illustrates this point.

Don and Betty, both age 42, are deeply involved in an evangelical church in Tennessee. They know the people in the church, which calls itself a "fellowship," very well. But they frankly admit that they find it hard to become involved in active caring and sharing relationships with these people. Don thinks some people in the church ask for help too often. This is something, he says, that "we have to overcome." He also recognizes, however, that sometimes people should ask for help, but do not. "I don't know if it is a pride thing or not. I don't think people ask as much as they should." Betty recognizes that there is a problem, too, but explains it more in terms of the size and impersonality of the larger culture in which they live. "When you live in a large environment, people tend to take care of their own business and neglect everybody else's. You just become very involved in your own affairs."

She admits that this is a selfish way to live. "But it's kind of hard to get involved in other people's lives."

Don adds the important point that the churches he has attended during his lifetime have often trained him to avoid relating to people who are really in need or even to think about them as close, fellow human beings. He says the church sometimes encourages people to work at church activities and to participate casually with other Christians, where it is safe, but fails to encourage reaching out to one's neighbors. "As a matter of fact," he admits, "I have great difficulty generating enthusiasm for social activities because to me they are relatively unimportant. For instance, some people are very neighborly and they want to go and just help all their neighbors and be involved in their neighbors' affairs." He says he and his wife grew up thinking just the opposite. "We believed it was not good to be very friendly with your neighbors because it could create problems. So as a result of that we haven't had that much to do with our neighbors, immediate neighbors where we live. We try to hold our standards high as far as living for the Lord, but as far as getting involved with their lives we just don't do that."

Support groups can have some impact on this kind of self-sufficiency. They may be composed largely of people concerned about their own suffering, their own crises, their own personal needs, more than the needs of others, but these groups can encourage people to share their needs with others. They can encourage private anxieties to be made public in the presence of a few trusted others. As individuals share, they realize that they are not alone. Others have the same problems. It becomes possible to receive their expressions of concern. It may also become possible to give others support. These are small steps. But they can help temper the rugged individualism that has decayed the fabric of communal life in our society.

To help mitigate the ill-effects of individualism, however, the small-group movement must become more aware of the ways in which it also promotes individualism. Just because people are joining support groups, we should not conclude that they have made the needs of others a priority in their lives. They may be seeking community but only finding themselves. They like the group because it gives them a chance to display their opinions and receive affirmation for whatever they happen to think is right. Such kudos will make them feel good. But they will have to work harder for genuine growth to occur.

PART THREE

SMALL GROUPS AND
THE SACRED

8

THE SPIRITUAL DIMENSION

Personal Faith in Small Groups

"They press me hard. It's uncomfortable, and sometimes I don't want to be there. But I want to grow, so that's why I continue doing it." That was the way John summarized what he has experienced in the couples group he and his wife attend.

"The group is geared to looking at our lives and to say 'what does the Bible teach us about the kind of people we should be? What does that mean in terms of living it out?' So on occasion in our discussion time we'll talk about, 'Well, what are we doing?' And there is always that tension of living out what we say we believe. And because this group says the Bible is the basis of what we believe, then that tension of looking and saying 'No, we're not doing that.' So there's a constant encouragement to push and change and be more the kinds of people that we want. Sometimes you walk away, convicted and uncomfortable, in fact, with where you are in your living of life, to say, 'Yeah, I need to change, I need to do things differently.' That's pretty much the orientation of the group: consider material that says, 'This is the kind of people that God has called you to be. Are you being that?'

"You know, when we get on topical issues, like parenting and exploring those issues, there have been times where I've seen areas of my life that need to be personally changed. Or in relational issues, say with my wife, that I have struggled with, trying to bring into congruity with what is being laid out, what the Bible says. So there's that constant

219

tension, actually, but for me, that's why I'm there. I want to grow. I don't want to be a static kind of person.

"Two weeks ago we looked at *very* personal issues. We were looking at how God wanted to change our lives in terms of our relationship to him. And people actually filled out questionnaires that were put together and put in an envelope and closed and sealed and are going to be sent back in several months to say 'Are you doing those kinds of things?' I mean, they're kind of fun exercises we do together, but are constantly pushing us to say 'Are you being what God has called you to be?'"

SEEKING TO BE MORE SPIRITUAL

To understand why many people are involved in small groups that have spirituality as their central aim, it is not enough to point to the loss of community in our society or even to the clever ways in which people manipulate their involvement in groups to assert their own individuality. Many people are there because they want to be spiritual. Otherwise, they could just as well join the local bowling league. It is not sufficient, however, to suggest, as some religious writers do, that people have a natural thirst for spirituality that is quenched when they become active in a religious group. Nor can we assume that this is the same spirituality that people have longed for in the past. To be sure, many people say they join small groups because they want to become more spiritual. Indeed, 46 percent of all small-group members listed "wanting to become more disciplined in your spiritual life" as an important reason for being in their group, and this figure rose to 76 percent among members of Bible study groups. But what exactly does spiritual discipline mean in this context?

Thirst would be a good metaphor if it meant the body-wracking thirst that comes from being without water for too long in the desert. Most people in the United States have never experienced that sort of thirst in spiritual terms. They haven't had to survive for days on end with no access to life-sustaining refreshment. Spiritual water fountains are on every street corner and in every bookstore and on every television. Americans have plenty of ways of gaining quick, easy exposure to the sacred. But having experienced the sacred in these other contexts, many people want more of it.[1] The sacred fulfills them. Many take seriously the idea that God is too important to be visited only on Sundays. They want to know more about God, experience God's presence more deeply, and orient their lives to the principles they find in scripture.

A man like John has taken the concept of spiritual thirst a step further than most people. A better metaphor for someone like him, although still in the same mode, would be to say that he is sincerely engaged in constructing something akin to the Hoover Dam. People like John just can't get enough water. Not only do they want to drink it; they want to go scuba diving in it. And while they are building the Hoover Dam, they are getting a joint Ph.D. in hydraulics and marine biology as well. Water fascinates them so much that they want to orient their whole life to learning more and more about it and becoming as close to it as they can.[2]

This longing for the sacred is why many people are in small groups seeking spirituality. They may not be as serious in their pursuit of it as John is, but they are somehow interested in the sacred. They see spirituality as the solution to their problems. They sense that people like John may have found something worth seeking. So they embark on their own quest for the sacred. The group helps them concentrate their energy. They pick up new ideas, see how others are pursuing the sacred, compare notes with them, and chastise themselves for not working harder. The spiritual journey on which they are engaged may be little more than a leisurely stroll through a meadow, taking time to nap and muse about the wildflowers. Or, for people like John, it may require planning, consistency, and hard work. It may involve chopping and hacking away at the underbrush, reading the blueprints, working early and late, bringing in reinforcements, getting that four-lane highway built to the promised land.

Here is John again. "I don't understand it fully, why an eternal God would care to know me and want to have a relationship with me. But it's one of the most cherished possession I own, it's my faith. And it's one that I, much as my relationship to my wife, is predicated on spending time and effort knowing that person, I spend a *significant* amount of my time wanting to know God."

For example?

"I have attempted to read through the Bible once a year for years and years. And I began to realize that even that had become a struggle, all form and not a part of a living, dynamic experience. (I feel that the problem with religion often is that you begin to do things which are *good*, but they become meaningless because of their repetitious nature.) And so here I am reading, doing lots of good things, but I began to realize that I wasn't getting *deep* enough.

"So two years ago I chose to take one small passage of the Bible. I took the Sermon on the Mount. And I studied it for a whole year. *Dra-*

matically affected how I began to look and relate to not only God but other people. And this past year I've been looking at people in the Bible and what happened to them when they met God, the change in their lives. And so, as you can sense, this isn't something I take casually. It's something that affects absolutely every area of my life. I mean, if you checked my date book, my checkbook, you would have a hard time not seeing that faith is an integral part of my life."

But that isn't all. "I have begun over the last two weeks, and I hope it becomes a lifetime thing—this is where I say my life, I hope, is constantly changing to meet God—to say 'what time do I need to get up?' Sometimes my schedule prevents it, you know, because I work nights in the emergency room. But when I'm sleeping at night, I say 'What time do I need to get up to accomplish the things of the day?' And then I set my alarm for 30 minutes before that. And I've begun to spend a half an hour just talking with God. It has been a *wonderful* experience to talk to God. And listen to God."

For John, then, being in several small groups is a way of pressing ahead with his intense spiritual quest. The couples group raises issues for him, shows him areas of his life that he needs to reexamine. The men's group "pushes me," "stretches me," it makes him look harder and explore deeper. This is the language he uses. It teems with vigor.

What is going on here? John is no meadowlark flitting from fence post to fence post hoping God will bless him. He pursues his faith like he did his studies in medical school. How does John explain this restless, ceaseless, energetic quest for God?

"I am much more contented, but not satisfied. Because I guess what I've come to see, a lot of the qualities I'm struggling to be are eternal qualities. I'll give you this illustration. Several years ago, Sara and I gave a two-day seminar down in Maryland on wholeness. And we've completely changed how we do that. Because we came to see that wholeness is an eternal quality that we can't achieve. We cannot achieve it in this lifetime. And where I came to know that was my father was a healthy man, played basketball in a college setting until his mid-fifties. I mean, he was a good athlete. But in his 65th year he started getting sick. And that summer of his 65th year, he had some cardiac dysrhythmias, was in the hospital, seemed to have been put under control, but I wanted him cardiac cathed and he didn't want one. Being a good physician, I said, 'You need a cardiac cath.' And I know he was praying to be healed. And I really struggled with that. I wanted it as a diagnostic tool and he knew the risks and he didn't feel that that was going to provide information. And in retrospect it may not, the risk potential may not have been—he may have been right, I don't know, we'll never know, because he died, like two months later, boom, sudden death. And about three years later, I was jogging and I was really wrestling with God. And I said, 'God, here was a man who loved you, why didn't you heal him?' It seemed like a simple enough thing. And a small voice said to me, 'But he is whole, now.' And see, I think that a lot of the—you may say I seem discontent. The fact of the matter is, I don't see things in a temporal light. I see them in an eternal light that says—I don't think I'm discontent, I think I'm not satisfied because that's what I want. I want a perfect relationship with an eternal God."

John recognizes that he will never achieve a perfect relationship with God in this life. But he insists that trying hard to achieve a better relationship with God brings joy to his life. It is the process that counts. Perhaps he tries harder than many people do. His achievement-oriented lifestyle pervades his spiritual life as much as it does his medical practice. But what he describes is, to a degree, common to many people in small groups. Unlike the stereotypical American who does nothing more serious than watch soap operas, these people are deeply committed to their spiritual lives. They believe that God is a reality and that knowing God is part of what it means to be a whole person. Knowing God, moreover, is not simply a matter of the mind, like knowing what time it is. Knowing God means being part of a relationship, like carrying on a romance. It matures, deepens, grows. Seeking spirituality is like being on a journey.

THE LONG JOURNEY

The extent to which small-group members are oriented toward spirituality is clearly evident in our survey results. Virtually all small-group members (90 percent) say "being part of a group that helps you grow spiritually" is a need they have experienced at some time in their lives. Among members of Bible study groups, 97 percent give this response. Two out of three small-group members say their interest in "spiritual matters" has increased in the past five years. Four out of five Bible study members say this. Half of all group members say the phrase "on a spiritual journey" describes them very well or fairly well. Two thirds of the members of Bible study groups give this response.

There are good reasons why so many people regard spirituality as a journey. The Bible, church history, and American culture all reinforce this view of spirituality. In the Hebrew scriptures, for example, Abraham's journey from Ur to Canaan provides a vivid image of the life of faith. So does the Israelites' journey out of Egypt to the promised land. Over the centuries, church history has reinforced these images. Mystical and monastic traditions, for example, emphasized contemplation, personal discipline, and other active modes of pursuing divine wisdom. After the Protestant Reformation, secular work increasingly came to be viewed as a calling in which rigorous, ethical activity became a way of pleasing God and spirituality became a kind of work. John Bunyan's allegorical depiction of the Christian's journey to the Celestial City in *Pilgrim's Progress* is perhaps the most familiar example in this tradition.[3] Contemporary pilgrims draw on these historic models. They discard other teachings that portray faith in static terms or that emphasize God's grace more than human activity.

In recent years, the idea that faith may be like a journey has also been reinforced by an extensive psychological literature on life stages and personal development.[4] Piaget and Erikson, for example, have been widely cited in discussions of spirituality, many of which draw on these theorists to suggest that faith must change over the course of the typical life cycle.[5] In young adulthood and again in midlife, individuals may find it necessary to confront doubts, rethink their childhood beliefs, and find a deeper relationship to God. Conceptions of moral responsibility and understandings of one's mortality and transcendence are said to undergo change as well.[6] Unlike Bunyan's Christian, therefore, the present-day seeker is much more responsible for mapping his or her own spiritual journey. The path is not fixed. Nor is the destination something that can be envisioned from afar. God does not lead pilgrims through the wilderness in order to prepare them for the promised land. Instead, pilgrims are guided by their sense that each person has a special destiny, that faith must be tailored to the individual's circumstances, and that spirituality must always be contingent on the needs, insights, and realities of the moment.

Advocates of small groups have drawn heavily on the language of journeys, using it as justification for placing high priority on group participation. "Christ has called us to a journey," states the opening sentence of one book on the subject, "a journey that can't be traveled alone. Pilgrims need other pilgrims."[7] Many advocates of Bible study groups focus especially on the importance of growth; some describe it as a process filled with pain, conflict, and setbacks, while others emphasize its joy and personal rewards.[8] The self-help movement also has contributed enormously to this language by emphasizing recovery from addictions and other dysfunctions as an ongoing journey. The logic is that people must pursue their own unique spiritual goals but can be helped by banding together with others. Implicit in much of this language is the assumption that there are no absolute truths that the individual can discover from personal experience, from reading scripture, or from studying sacred traditions. Instead, truth is sufficiently uncertain—at least the truth that really makes a difference in individuals' daily lives—that small-group members must share their insights with one another.

The secular culture in America, with its emphasis on individual responsibility, hard work, and achievement, has influenced our perception of spiritual journeys as well. Making a journey requires a goal, planning, and a map or guidebook, and it takes effort for the trip to be a pleasant experience. Although many of us believe our relationship with God is founded primarily on God's grace or on a particular moment of religious awakening or being "born again," these same traditions tell us that faith without works is dead.[9] So we work at our faith. Living in a dynamic social milieu, we expect our faith to be in constant flux. Likening it to a relationship, we expect it to change because we know how often our human relationships change. We believe it is necessary to grow in our understanding of God, to live our lives in a way that is consistent with God's desires, and to demonstrate our faith to those around us. Spirituality is thus hard work. It is not a matter of fitting into our natural environment and drawing whatever insights may emerge from our experience. Nor is it a matter of being enveloped in God's grace. It is, rather, a special pursuit, an added task, a set of skills to be mastered, like learning to play the piano.

How well we do this in practice is, of course, another story. Many studies suggest that people compartmentalize their lives, living one way on Sunday mornings and a different way during the week. Deeply committed religious people often pursue pretty much the same kinds of careers, use their money in the same ways, and vote similarly to those who claim no interest in religious faith. The fact that it is often difficult to know how to demonstrate spirituality in daily life is, however, one of the reasons why small groups are important. Realizing that their workplaces, television programs, or the supermarket are unlikely to help them very much in their spiritual pursuits, people flock to small groups to receive guidance and support. They feel better just knowing that they are making some effort to cultivate their spirituality.

One of the reasons why spiritual discipline seems like hard work in our society is that it often requires people to go against the grain. Colleges and universities seldom teach young people how to live spiritually disciplined lives.[10] Employers may be happy that their employees want to behave morally and ethically but are unlikely to feel comfortable giving advice on spirituality. Church services may provide inspiration and words of wisdom, but seldom go very far toward helping parishioners implement biblical ideals in their daily lives. Living in a nation of competing ethnic and religious traditions, we may also be confused about what we need to do to know God. Banding together in small groups is thus a way to hold the rest of the world temporarily at bay while we consider what it means to live a spiritual life.[11]

Consider the journey that Donna, the young woman we met in chapter 3, has taken in recent years. When Donna married into a Russian Orthodox family everything seemed easy at first. A Presbyterian, she figured she should try to fit in; after all, all faiths point to the same God, she told herself. But when her son was born, she knew that she wanted to raise him as a Protestant. Looking back on it, she considers this decision the starting point of a long journey that has been very difficult but has also forced her to strengthen her faith. "I prayed a lot about it and I really felt that if I chose this path of, you know, the Protestant path, that it would be hard. And it *has* been. It's been *terribly* hard for ten years, it's been—not ten years, eight years, it's been a real struggle for me. And I've been kind of like the black sheep and this—I mean, they've called me everything but the heathen woman who, you know, has taken their son away. So it has not been easy for me. But I really believe it was the right thing in my heart to do. And so I did it. And I think that since I've done it, like eight years to now, I've grown a lot spiritually."

Like so many other people in small groups, Donna insists that her participation in small groups has helped her to stick to her guns, to pursue her journey more successfully, to grow. Among all members of small groups, 61 percent say their faith or spirituality has been influenced as a result of being in their group. Thirty-five percent say their faith has deepened a lot, 24 percent say it has deepened a little, nobody says it has become less important, and 2 percent say it has changed in some other way. Not surprisingly, the figures for members of Bible study groups are considerably higher: 90 percent say their faith has changed, with 60 percent claiming it has deepened a lot and 30 percent stating it has deepened a little.

THE EFFECTS OF GROUP INVOLVEMENT

Words like faith and spirituality, of course, can mean many different things.[12] In a society like ours, where two-thirds of the population claims membership in a religious organization and more than nine in ten affirm belief in God, it would not be surprising to find that people in small groups also talk about spirituality. Indeed, the fact that more than half of all such groups are sponsored by religious organizations makes this possibility all the more likely. But broad terms can often be misleading. As we have seen, community means something quite different in small groups than it traditionally has meant in families and in neighborhoods. By the same token, faith may mean something different as well. If, as I suggested at the outset, support groups are changing our relationship to the sacred, then the ways in which people talk about their faith provide a valuable clue to understanding these changes.

To find out more specifically what people meant when they said their spirituality had deepened as a result of being in their group, we asked all group members to respond to a variety of statements describing various consequences that might have been experienced from participating in their group. Some of the statements emphasized consequences that probably would be associated with spirituality according to most conventional or traditional meanings of the term; for example, "feeling closer to God." Others employed language that is often associated with spirituality, although the same language might be used in other settings as well; for example, "a better ability to forgive others." Some of the other statements described changes that are often mentioned by people in small groups but are not always thought of as spirituality; for example, "more open and honest with yourself." We included a couple of consequences that might be thought of as negative as well; for example, "less interested in people outside your group."

Except for the negative consequences, almost all the other perceived effects were reported by a majority of group members (see table 8.1). At the top of the list were consequences that, for the time being, might be described best as personal or interpersonal growth. Eighty-four percent, for example, said they felt better about themselves as a result of being in their groups. At least three-quarters said they were more open and honest with themselves and in their dealings with others. Nearly this many said they had developed a deeper love for other people. These results are interesting because they suggest that personal and interpersonal growth define many of the most commonly shared faith experiences in small groups. Members did not argue that these experiences had nothing to do with faith; they overwhelming affirmed that these changes were among the ways in which their faith had changed.

Consequences framed in specifically religious language were experienced by slightly fewer people than those framed more generally, but were also selected by a majority of all group participants. Two out of three said they felt closer to God as a result of their group. Slightly more said they had improved in their ability to forgive others or to forgive themselves. About half said the Bible had become more meaningful for them, and about the same proportions said they understood people with different religious perspectives better, were more capable of sharing their faith with others, and had received answers to prayer. Although we cannot make too much of the differences, it is nevertheless significant that a substantially greater proportion had experienced closeness to God than had become more interested in the Bible. Perhaps small groups are encouraging an experiential form of spirituality more than one rooted in biblical tradition—despite the fact that so many of these groups claim to be Bible studies. This focus is at least a possibility, and we consider more fully in a later section.

The negative consequences (not shown in the table) were mentioned by relatively few group members. Only 11 percent said they had experienced conflict with people in their group, and only 5 percent said they had become less interested in people outside their group.

One way to understand what people in small groups mean by spirituality is to look more closely at these perceived consequences to see which ones are mentioned more often by people who think their spirituality has changed than by those whose spirituality has not changed. In other words, consequences that seem to go together with feeling that one's spirituality has changed give us some clues as to how people are defining spirituality.

The short answer is that all of these items are associated with spirituality. In every case, people who said their spirituality had changed were more likely to say they had experienced each of these consequences than were people whose spirituality had not changed. We

Table 8.1

PERCEIVED CONSEQUENCES OF GROUP INVOLVEMENT

*Percent Who Say They Have Experienced Each of the Following
as a Result of Participating*

Feeling better about yourself	84
More open and honest communication with others	79
More open and honest with yourself	78
A deeper love toward other people	73
A better ability to forgive others	71
Has helped me to serve people outside the group	69
A better ability to forgive yourself	69
Feeling closer to God	66
The Bible becoming more meaningful to you	57
More understanding of persons with different religious perspectives	55
Helping in sharing your faith with others outside the group	55
Answers to prayers	54
Healings of relationships	44

might conclude, then, that spirituality has a fairly broad meaning nowadays, one that encompasses things like feeling better about yourself as well as feeling closer to God. If so, the spirituality being cultivated in small groups is wide ranging, with ramifications along a variety of dimensions, rather than narrowly compartmentalized. Such spirituality should also have wide-ranging effects on personal behavior. At the same time, it may also have a more diffuse meaning than in the past. If spirituality means self-esteem and better social relationships, then its consequences may be little different from therapy or clinical psychology.

But some of the consequences included in the survey were more closely associated with perceived changes in spirituality than others. For instance, among those who said their spirituality had changed, 93 percent said they felt closer to God, while among those who said their spirituality had not changed, only 23 percent said they felt closer to God—a 70 percentage point spread. Other items that showed huge differences were: the Bible becoming more meaningful, answers to prayers, and help in sharing one's faith. In contrast, items that showed the weakest differences were: feeling better about oneself, more open in communicating with others, and more honest with oneself.

Our results, then, pretty much fit what common sense might tell us. Spirituality, for most people in small groups, retains its connection with specific religious concepts, such as feeling closer to God and understanding the Bible. Spirituality also connotes other behavioral consequences, such as being able to share one's faith, forgiving others, loving others, and forgiving oneself. It sometimes involves personal and interpersonal consequences, such as feeling better about oneself and communicating more openly and honestly, too, but these consequences quite often occur without people also thinking that their spirituality has changed.

Some readers will also be curious about the special effects of being in groups, such as Bible studies, that are particularly concerned with fostering spirituality, as opposed to the effects of being in any kind of small group. On the surface at least, the survey results should be very encouraging to advocates of Bible study groups. Among the members of Bible study groups, 95 percent say they feel closer to God as a result of their group, 92 percent say the Bible has become more meaningful to them, 91 percent say they are more able to forgive others, 89 percent say they have been enabled to forgive themselves, 83 percent have received answers to prayer, and 81 percent say they have learned better how to share their faith with others.

If these changes seem sensible, they are nevertheless a selective cut from what spirituality has meant throughout the centuries. Small groups seldom include worship. Their members are thus unlikely to come away with a sense of the power, majesty, authority, or transcendence of God. Instead, divine imagery tends to reflect the human relationships people experience in their groups. Indeed, relational language prevails. People feel closer to God, experience God as a parent or friend, feel loved, and believe that a kind of mutual understanding has emerged between themselves and this divine companion. God can be trusted to help, to make things work better, or at least to make you feel better, just as the members of your group can be trusted.

These views of God were very much in evidence in the groups we studied. At Logos Fellowship, for example, there was a vivid feeling among group members that talking to God was like confiding in a buddy. "Lord, we just thank you that we can pray to you," began Fred at one of the meetings, "and that you will help Sam's coworker recover from her surgery, and I just pray for Tom's gallstone." Others joined in.

"Lord, you know Ted's in the hospital, just give that family peace." "Lord, you're a true, walking, skin-on person; just put your arms around him." "Lord, thank you for caring for us at all times."

Undoubtedly it is comforting to have a divine friend of this kind. As some religious leaders have argued, it is refreshing to discover that God is a God of love, after centuries of religious teaching emphasizing a God of punishment, anger, and judgment. Yet there is also a danger if God becomes a being with the same characteristics as those experienced in one's support group. The danger is that God becomes an instrument used mainly to make ourselves feel better. If the group is the main model that helps us understand God, we also risk being let down by God—because the group at some point will surely let us down.

EXERCISING CAUTION

Before looking in greater detail at the ways in which small groups influence spirituality, it is important to add some caveats to what has just been said. In the case studies and in-depth interviews we conducted, we saw many examples of people being confronted by their groups to think more deeply about their faith. Like John, they discussed biblical principles, thought hard about their own behavior, and went home resolute in their desire to improve. For this reason, it is not surprising to find that many people in the survey also said they had grown spiritually and experienced specific consequences in their lives. But we must also recognize that information collected in surveys is imperfect. It does not track people over time to see how their lives may have been influenced. There are, however, some ways of examining the survey data to probe a little more deeply into the kinds of consequences that small groups may have.

One standard device for probing these consequences more deeply is to ask people to tell about something in the distant past and to use that information as a baseline. In the present case, we would like to rule out the possibility, for example, that people who say their faith has grown as a result of being in a group weren't deeply involved in religion even before they became involved in their group. To check this out, we asked people in the survey (before asking them any questions about their groups) how important religion had been in their families while they were growing up. We then asked how important religion was to them at present. What we found was reassuring. Among people who said their faith had not been influenced by their group, the percentage who said religion was very important to them now was 10 points lower than the percentage who said it was very important to their family while growing up. But among those who said their faith had been influenced by their group, the percentage who said religion was very important to them now was 21 points higher than the percentage who said it was very important while they were growing up.

We also asked a few questions to people who were not currently in groups to see how their answers might compare with those given by people in groups. For example, we asked people if they were currently involved in reading the Bible. As might be expected, virtually all members of Bible study groups (91 percent) said yes, and of all small-group members, 66 percent did so. In comparison, only 37 percent of the people who had never been in a small group gave this response. The percentage for people who had been in a group in the past, but who were not presently involved, was in between (53 percent). Most importantly, the figure for those who were not currently involved but who said they would "like to be" was also in between (54 percent). In other words, the data seem to suggest that people might join a small group because they are already involved in a religious activity such as reading the Bible; but being in the group increases the likelihood of engaging in an activity like reading the Bible.

Some other specific activities, such as reading religious or spiritual books, showed a similar pattern. It is interesting, however, that other activities, such as meditating and watching religious programs on television, show a different pattern. On the latter, people who say they would like to be in a group are just as likely to meditate or watch religious programs as are people in groups. I take this as additional evidence that respondents in the survey were telling the truth when they attributed certain consequences to their groups. Purely private activities such as meditating and watching religious television that can be performed apart from a group, and that are probably not encouraged by most groups, are no more likely to be practiced by group members than by aspiring members. Other activities, such as studying the Bible and reading religious books, are often part of the preparation for group discussions, and these activities are more likely among group members than among those who aspire to be in a group.

Perhaps the clearest support for the claim that group participation makes a difference to members' spirituality comes from comparing members who attend their groups every week with those who attend less often. Not only are frequent attenders more likely than infrequent attenders to say their faith has been influenced, they are also more likely to say it has been influenced in each of the specific ways we have been considering. For instance, 72 percent of those who attend every week say they have received answers to prayer as a result of being in their group; in comparison, only 41 percent of those who attend once or twice a month say this, as do only 30 percent of those who attend less than once a month. It is perhaps interesting as well that the strongest differences are on responses to items that have specific religious connotations: answers to prayer, feeling close to God, being enabled to share one's faith, and having the Bible become more meaningful.

Some other things can be learned from the survey as well. Before considering those results, however, we need to listen closely to what some of our individual respondents told us. Hearing in their own words how their faith has deepened will give us a better sense of the various dimensions of spirituality we have been discussing. It will also set the stage for considering how small groups effect changes in spirituality.

DEEPENING FAITH

For many people, small groups deepen their faith in some significant way. They may realize for the first time what faith is. It becomes possible for them to trust that things will work out, that life is still good no matter what happens, or that they don't need to be in control because something or someone greater than they is in charge. A deep faith, in this sense, needs little knowledge of the traditional attributes of God. Indeed, theology tends to be relatively unimportant. What matters is simply trust. There is a kind of detachment from anxiety, a sense of confidence that things will work out for the better. Frank, the man in AA, said he had always been terrified before he got involved in the group. "I lived my whole life terrified that there wasn't going to be enough money, that things weren't going to work. I always had to work harder and harder and harder, so that everything would be okay." But the people in AA have helped him see things differently. "I now realize that everything is okay, even if I don't do anything."

Faith like this can be nothing more than passive acceptance of life as it comes to us. But most people seem to have trouble with faith in such abstract terms. Believing that life can be trusted involves some notion of a God who is in control and, more than that, of a God who cares about each individual. The divine is thus personalized, turned into a trustworthy friend, colleague, supervisor, or mentor. Here is Frank again: "I remember [as a young man] believing that God led the Israelites out of Egypt and that God led people into and out of exile and that God was involved in the civil rights movement and the peace movement and with the confessing church in Germany during the Second World War. But God had no interest at all in me. I had no sense of a relationship, a personal relationship with God or any kind of spiritual light." That feeling has changed since Frank has become involved in AA. "I got sober and began to think maybe God is interested and does care. I have grown to realize that God absolutely cares about me and is absolutely involved in taking care of me. Has given me a job and a car and a wife and a relationship with my kids and money and on and on and on."

Frank has realized that he has to sit back and let God work things out. He is much less compulsive about his spiritual life than John is. Faith in Frank's life is more a matter of following the flow than of battling the rapids. Yet Frank illustrates that even following the flow requires effort. As he has learned that God cares for him, Frank has also become more interested in doing what he can to develop his relationship with God. Like most Americans, he learned at one time or another that a successful marriage or friendship requires work, so he feels it necessary to expend effort to make his relationship with God a success. "I have worked very hard and am trying to work—I was going to say I'm trying to work really hard, but I don't think that's true—I'm trying to work, [but] my fear is in the way. I'm working at trying to get my will and God's will into better alignment. And I'm aware that there are lots of spiritual disciplines that I know, that I don't do. I think I'm scared to find out what would really happen if I did them!" Being in small groups helps Frank feel like he is doing his part. Going to groups is itself an expenditure of effort. Being there helps him be more disciplined in his personal life as well.

Terry, the man we met in chapter 3 who is involved in neurolinguistic programming (NLP), approaches spirituality in much the same way as Frank. He is able to distinguish very clearly between NLP as a help to his spirituality and NLP as a hindrance. It helps him clear his mind and to question the meanings of events that he might otherwise take for granted. That clarity helps him become more attentive to deeper spiritual meanings and to the leading of God. Where NLP is a hindrance is its emphasis on control. Being a technique, it is goal oriented. But spirituality, in his view, should be thought of more as an experience. He describes it as an experience of surrendering to "my humanness, my 'non-ego,' just to God." In this experience of surrender, everything from NLP that has helped him also has to be surrendered, especially its emphasis on performance, effectiveness, understanding, and intelligence. "My regrets, my angers, my resentments towards people. Healing myself, letting go of resentments, letting go of the past. Healing my life, healing myself." Using the techniques to move beyond control and beyond the techniques themselves is the part he has found hardest.

If Terry had to choose a single word to describe how his group has influenced his faith, he would say "transformation." The group hasn't given him a specific recipe for living, but it has definitely reinvigorated his faith. "It's like a second shot at life for me at this point. What's next for me is the new life, minus the old strategies, minus the limiting beliefs. Or renegotiating. Not minus, but renegotiating. Some of the things I've been doing to myself, some of the ways I've been going at life, I don't need them anymore. They're limiting. They don't empower me to move on. I'm getting courage and strength about new goals that I think I've kept in the closet for a long time. My appreciation of each day has grown tremendously." In this sense, Terry is no different from most group members. The feeling that he is getting somewhere, that things are better today than they were yesterday, that he is experiencing progress is terribly important.

It is worth pausing here to note that—like John and Donna, whom we considered at the beginning of the chapter—Frank and Terry describe their faith as a journey. All four believe spirituality develops gradually. They also believe it requires work, discipline. But Frank and Terry take a somewhat different view of this work than John and Donna. Frank and Terry would probably liken their journey to flowing downstream in a huge river. It takes work, but the nature of that work is to learn better how to go with the flow. Life is better, in their view, when one becomes open to the natural rhythms of life. John and Donna would be more likely to describe their spiritual journey as one of swimming upstream. Just to go with the flow would seem too easy, too much like accommodating to the pressures of the world around them. The work required is not necessarily harder, but it is much more active, resistant. Rather than working hard at relaxing, one works hard to keep from relaxing. Instead of struggling to give up one's sense of control, one struggles to maintain control.

In the survey, both of these views of faith were evident. Among all group members, 42 percent said their view of faith was best captured by the statement "you have to work hard at developing your faith," 30 percent preferred the statement "you have to let faith unfold in its own way," 19 percent asserted that both statements needed to be kept together, and 6 percent said neither statement expressed their views. The survey also gave some support to the idea that working hard at one's faith is the view favored more by the churches than letting faith unfold and that working hard is indeed associated with experiencing spiritual growth in small groups. Church members, frequent church attenders, members of church-based small groups, and members of Bible studies were all more likely than other group members to say that working hard best described their idea of faith. Of those who chose this statement, 70 percent said their faith had changed as a result of being in a small group, compared to 53 percent of those who favored the idea of simply letting faith unfold in its own way.

Of course, churches benefit from the view that faith is something people must work hard at developing. If a spiritual journey is nothing more than learning to float down the river, there would be little reason for the churches to exist. But if spirituality is like learning to play the piano, then churches can perform a legitimate role by providing piano teachers, lesson books, and places to hold recitals. It is little wonder that churches have been playing such an active role in sponsoring the small-group movement.

CLOSENESS TO GOD

Most people in our society believe that God exists.[13] But they often find it hard to relate to this entity. Like Frank, they may agree intellectually that there is a God who at one time helped the Israelites through the wilderness, but they don't find God meaningful in the wilderness of their own lives. They have, to borrow the familiar language in which Alfred North Whitehead once expressed it, moved from "God the void" to "God the enemy," but they have not moved from "God the enemy" to "God the companion."[14] God remains the punitive figure they feared in childhood or the enigma who somehow allows suffering and death to happen despite the anguish it causes the individual.

The reason is often that the authority figures in people's lives taught them to fear God rather than depend on God or that these authority figures were themselves unapproachable. Having an alcoholic parent, for example, is often cited as a reason why people find it hard to believe that God loves them. As one woman explained, "A lot of people that are brought up in an alcoholic home will have trouble relating to God because they weren't able to relate to a father figure at home." In her own case, she needed someone in her life who was loving and caring. She thought God could probably be this someone. But she also found it hard to feel close to God because of what she learned in church. She never learned how to pray. She believed nobody but priests could talk directly to God. She was not disabused of this idea until she became involved in a small group.

Many people say they have grown closer to God as a result of their groups, not simply because they know God loves them, but because they now have a more detailed, better informed sense of who God is. God ceases to be a concept that only religious leaders understand. The deity is now much more like the good people one knows personally, possibly the good people in one's group. A woman who had come to believe in Jesus as a result of her group described the difference this way: "There wasn't a real understanding of what it was to be a Christian, what it was to have Christ in your life." The difference now, she says, is that "I have Christ in my heart. I accepted him as my personal savior, and I think now from there all I can do is grow. Grow spiritually, be convicted by things. Now that I have him and know he's there for me, he's helping me get through the tough times, making me deal with issues and just confront things and face things, and I know he's going to be there to get me through it."

A man who attends a self-help group makes much the same point: "Before this I knew God intellectually, at least I knew about God. Now a regular part of my life is spiritual experiences in which I feel that point which is between mental and physical, I feel the presence of God, I feel a part of God, of a higher power. I feel it in those glorious moments of silence, and not only moments of silence, I feel it in somebody's sharing in a way that communicates warmth."

What people generally mean when they talk about closeness to God is some kind of personal, experiential relationship. The person who feels the presence of God illustrates one way of understanding this relationship. For people like this, God is close in the same way a furnace is close: you know it because you can feel the warmth. For most of the people we talked to, though, getting close to God involved more than this feeling of warmth. Proximity to the sacred was like having a conversation. A furnace can warm you up, but another person can listen, respond, even tell you what to do. You can talk over your problems and receive advice in return. These people felt close to God for pragmatic reasons. They knew they were in the presence of God because God talked with them, consoled them, and perhaps even helped them with their lives.

The pastor of a church that sponsored a number of prayer fellowships provided a good example of this view of closeness to God. "People can listen to preaching for years and years and years," he noted, "and they have a nice little place in their brain where they can file that information and then walk out on a Sunday morning and potentially not have any impact at all on their life. When you sit down in a small group, it's a little harder to do that. You get to the point where you're asking people the real questions of life: What's going on in your marriage? What's going on with your children? What's happening in the workplace? That has a way of bringing the truth of where people really are in their lives out into the open. And that to me is where you apply the gospel. Does the gospel or does the Christian message work in the real stuff of life? That's what I mean by that. So getting down to the nitty gritty, it's what's going on with the relationship of your husband and wife, what's going on in your family, what's going on inside of you, what's the stress level? What are you wrestling with as an individual? And that obviously isn't the kind of stuff that happens in a large group meeting."

For this pastor, the key role that small groups can play in bringing people closer to God is in getting them to move beyond theology to real-life issues. "You can have all the theology down. You can have the smooth-running Sunday morning service, but if it doesn't help me deal and grapple with those things that we just talked about, then in a sense, it's not a real faith. The scripture says that 'Out of the abundance of the heart the mouth speaks.' In other words, what's really inside of me is going to come out eventually. Jesus talked a lot about finances. He said, 'If you want to know where a man's treasure is look to see how he spends his money.' So he was always, to me, indicating that the true test of a man or woman is what's deep in your heart, and the only way to find out what's really in your heart is to get to know people. And I think as you get into those levels, that's where character really gets shaped and tested."

For the God who is experienced in small groups to be real, therefore, it is not enough to have rational arguments about the nature of the universe. Such arguments seem hopelessly arcane to most members of small groups. Reality is now tantamount to being concerned with "real-life issues," especially the ones individuals experience in their everyday lives. God has to be a deity who cares about one's moods, finances, worries, and relationships. If spirituality makes some practical difference to these issues, then God exists. If God is simply a theological teaching, then it makes little difference whether the sacred exists or not.

The advantage of this conception of God, as most group leaders we talked to see it, is that God becomes more relevant in individuals' daily lives. The disadvantages are less apparent, but are nevertheless worth considering. One is that God ceases to be a supreme being who is in all respects superior to humans. Rather than being the inscrutable deity of the Reformation, for example, God is now a buddy. God no longer represents such awe-inspiring qualities as being infinite, all-powerful, all-knowing, and perfectly righteous. God is now on the same level as yourself, except perhaps a little warmer and friendlier. You can understand God pretty well because you have sensed what it is to lose a friend, hurt your finger, or enjoy the sunset. The other danger of the present conception is that a God of daily relevance can also become a God of triviality. The pastor who says people must go beyond theology to see the relevance of God in their daily lives may be correct—if they are going beyond theology. The more likely possibility (judging from national studies) is that they don't know the theology, either. Theology is too vague, boring, or abstract. What they do know is that God is present in their daily lives and that knowing God somehow works. But if the existence of God depends on whether or not God works, then it may be tempting to alter the criteria of what works to the point that minor victories are all that matter. God exists because people are struggling with the "nitty gritty"—which is conveniently left up to them to define. Or God exists because a person worried less the day before—not because God directed the person to pursue a different career, give up a lucrative deal, or blow the whistle on community injustices. It is, of course, comforting to feel that God is close, warm, caring, interested in our personal well-being, and so tangible that we can reach out and touch him. Yet, throughout the centuries, people of faith have also asserted the importance of believing in the existence of God even when God seemed to be distant, silent, or demanded obedience that went beyond human understanding.

ANSWERS TO PRAYER

Feeling close to God is, for many small group members, an important precondition for being able to pray and for believing that one's prayers are being answered. As Margaret Poloma and George Gallup suggest in their national study of prayer, "The most profound effects of prayer occur when a person goes beyond rote and ritualistic prayer and senses an intimacy with God."[15] None of the people we talked to felt they had to be in a group in order to pray. Most prayed in their daily lives, by themselves, as well as when they were in their groups. But they also stressed the importance of group prayer. Praying together was one of the things they liked best about their groups. And quite often they felt their prayers were answered. Prayer was thus an important component of their spirituality, and they felt it was being nurtured by their support groups.

One of the main reasons people felt their prayers were answered was that their groups helped them keep track of their requests and whether they were answered or not. Karen, the member of a Bible study group whom we met in chapter 6, said that what she liked most about her group was the prayer time. She described how this works in her group: "In the beginning we take prayer requests. I'm a very open person, so right away I just say prayer requests and things that are on my heart. And I have them praying for me. That is really the best part. And then I'll go a couple of weeks later and have things that had been prayed for moved over to the praise column and see how God answers our prayers." In short, successful prayer becomes a function of dual-entry bookkeeping. The group leader keeps a ledger, recording prayer requests on one side of the page and answers to prayer on the other. An example would be (prayer request), "I just want strength for the meeting I'm having on Wednesday"; (answer, the following week), "I just want to give thanks that I made it through the meeting without any trouble."

In other groups, recording answers to prayer is less formal. But members still like to report answers because they know the group will be interested. One man, for example, said he had passed the test he had been worrying about; a young woman had survived the recent visit from her in-laws; an elderly person asked her group to give thanks with her that she had a new grandson. In virtually every group where prayer was involved at all, the members uniformly asserted that they felt cared for and supported because other people were praying for them. They knew others were praying for them during the prayer time in the meetings, and they also believed that other members were praying for them at other times. Thus, when some problem was resolved, they felt compelled to tell the group. And, having told the group, they were more likely themselves to remember that their prayers had been answered.

Prayers generally focused on the specific needs of individual members: someone worrying about a sick relative, someone struggling with overeating, someone facing a tough career decision. Occasionally, prayer was also offered for the group itself. Sometimes it was perfunctory: "Lord help us to focus our attention as we study this lesson." In twelve-step groups it frequently provided a way of opening and closing meetings, often a recipe prayer that people could read or recite in unison. In a few cases, the group demonstrated its sense of "group-ness" by praying for some need that had arisen in conjunction with group activities. For example, the Wednesday Women's Group faced difficulties in providing the child care its members needed during the meeting time, so they decided to pray as a group. One of its members recalls: "This nursery need became such a great need. And the Lord just really laid it on our hearts that the way we were working the nursery, with three or four of us missing the lesson, is self-defeating. So we began to pray. It was really the first time we had prayed for the group as a whole." This was also an occasion on which the sheer act of praying became part of the answer. As the group prayed, more of the women realized the importance of the issue and, before long, everyone was taking turns sharing the nursery responsibilities.

Even groups that do not include prayer among their activities sometimes encourage prayer on the part of individual members. In some cases, prayer came up in the course of discussing other topics. Occasionally, members would say to each other after the meeting that they would be "praying for you." Some members were struggling with the notion of prayer. And yet, for them, just being quiet in the group, thinking about deeper issues, and realizing that they needed time in their lives to reflect, meditate, and perhaps draw closer to God in their own way was a step toward learning better how to pray. One woman recalls: "Keeping busy is a disease for me. What is that phrase the nuns always used? You know, the one 'Idle hands is the devil's workshop.' And I live that to the hilt, and I'll get five projects going at once. And I'll get them all done. I'm good at that. I heard something at a conference I went to, actually it was work related, but it was about somebody trying to write plays. And the person said, 'I just need time to look out the window.' And that phrase just hit it for me. Actually they say that's part of your job is that you look out the window, and I've been working on that in myself. I need time to look out the window and not just with my job but just in general. What the program has done is to let me recognize that that is legitimate, not only legitimate, it's essential!"

Of all the spiritual activities in which small groups engage, collectively and individually, prayer is thus the most distinctive. It gives spirituality a pragmatic flavor by focusing on specific needs and the resolution of those needs. It embeds spirituality in the relational character of the group. Prayer is no longer the preserve of an ordained member of the clergy who somehow has special access to God and who intercedes with God on behalf of the laity. Instead, each person in the group senses an intimate relationship with God and with each other. In short, prayer is democratized. But it is also collectivized. Its power is more evident because of the group. In the caring they experience from one another, members are convinced that their prayers have been heard.

BIBLICAL KNOWLEDGE

Another way in which small groups contribute to the deepening of faith is by heightening their members' interest in the Bible. A number of the people we talked to admitted they were starting almost from scratch in learning about the Bible. Many had attended church as children, but their churches had taught them arts and crafts rather than anything they could remember about the Bible. Some of them admitted, too, that they really weren't that interested in the Bible when they first joined their group. It was only later, after they studied the Bible a few weeks, that they discovered it was a valuable resource for their daily lives. As it became more meaningful, their interest in understanding it increased. "To begin with, I went just to meet other people," one woman recalled, "but then as the sessions went on and we learned to go through the Bible and different books of the Bible, that became a real stepping stone for me in helping me with my Christian walk. I was brought up Catholic. I had become a Christian when I met my husband, but I really still didn't know the Bible. Now if they say a book of the Bible, I can flip through the Bible and find it myself, where in the beginning I couldn't. So in the beginning it was to meet people, and then it just progressed, and now it's mostly I'm there to learn the Bible."

But just how well do people learn it? They do, as we have seen from the survey, become more interested in reading the Bible. There is also a significant difference between group members whose faith has been influenced and those whose faith has not been influenced by their groups in their views of the Bible. Significantly more of those whose faith has been influenced than of their counterparts say the Bible is the inspired word of God. They are also more likely to say that everything in the Bible should be taken literally, word for word, and to deny that the Bible may contain historical or scientific errors. Furthermore, they are a little more likely to say that the Bible is a detailed book of rules that Christians should try to follow.

It is difficult to know if these differences represent changes in attitude produced by group participation, however. A different process could be at work. For example, people who attend religiously conservative groups could hold these views of the Bible and say the group has influenced their faith, and yet undergo no changes in their views of the Bible as a result of this influence.

What we do know from the survey is that group members whose spirituality has been deepened by their participation were no more likely than other members to give the correct answer to a factual question that was included in the survey. This question asked respondents to say whether it was true or false that, according to the Bible, Jesus was born in Jerusalem. A surprisingly high 41 percent and 43 percent of group members whose faith had been deepened and of members whose faith had not been deepened, respectively, incorrectly said this statement was true. On another statement—"the book of Acts is in the Old Testament"—fewer of those whose faith had been deepened by their group incorrectly identified this as a true statement than those whose faith had not been deepened. The difference, however, was quite small (see table 8.2). Thus, we must question what kind of biblical understanding is being fostered in small groups. Certainly there were some members (John, for example) who had been encouraged by their groups to read and study the Bible on their own. But many of the people we talked to had been challenged only superficially by their groups. The weekly Bible study may have lasted for two hours, but only fifteen minutes of the time was devoted to studying the Bible. Moreover, the study often went verse by verse, so that members were left with little overall sense of larger themes in the Bible, or it quickly devolved into a discussion of members' experiences or what they thought a verse meant, rather than focusing on biblical knowledge.

Judging from the comments of group members, the most pervasive effect of participation on attitudes toward the Bible is that the Bible

Table 8.2
STATEMENTS ABOUT THE BIBLE

Percentage of group members who say each of the following among those who think their faith has or has not changed:

	Faith Influenced	
	Yes	*No*
Believe each is true:		
The Bible is the inspired word of God	93	77
Everything in the Bible should be taken literally, word for word	47	24
The Bible may contain historical or scientific errors	42	67
According to the Bible, Jesus was born in Jerusalem	41	43
The book of Acts is in the Old Testament	19	25
The Bible is a detailed book of rules that Christians should try to follow	71	63

becomes more meaningful as a guide for everyday behavior. Most Bible study groups are not oriented toward factual knowledge, memorization, getting the historical details of places and names correct, or learning how scholars throughout the centuries have interpreted the Bible; instead, they concentrate on applying some of the basic principles of Bible stories to ordinary life. We see in the next chapter how this process works. One example, however, can illustrate how most of the people we talked to approached the role of the Bible in their groups. A woman who had first started thinking deeply about God as a teenager and then entertained serious doubts about her faith in college said she had just felt the need to rediscover "the basics" in recent years. She said she needed God "as my strength, to get me through the stresses of being married and working and all that good stuff." Like many other people, she wanted a safe place in which to raise questions that puzzled her or even to express amazement about the spiritual dimension of life. "I was challenged again when I had the first baby to mature more, to learn more. I mean, here was the miracle of life in front of me. I never had to really deal with that before. Sure, I can deal with the miracle of a tree and gravity and how the whole universe works, but that's not day-to-day reality." She says she's learning the attributes of God all over again, not for a test, but for her. And she says, "It's really exciting."

It is also worth noting that a sizable segment of the American public has moved away from the Bible as a source of spiritual insight. They do not necessarily reject its truths, but they find it important to seek deeper meanings by considering how other people have interpreted and applied the Bible. Often small groups facilitate this process by giving people assigned readings to be discussed in the group. Small groups also become miniature information networks through which tips are passed about books that have been meaningful and helpful. For example, Frank reported that teaching him about the mystical tradition had been one of the ways in which a spiritual disciplines group had helped him. "Matthew Fox is a contemporary Roman Catholic mystic. Very spiritual. I heard a lecture of his, in which he said that there is in his mind this great underground stream of spirituality. We all have to find our own way to the stream, but once we find our way to the stream, we realize that we join hands with all of the other spiritual people in the world, and that's my experience. I have been reading to find out how other people have done it. And to raise my own level of spiritual consciousness."

Small groups, then, encourage many of their members to be interested in the Bible or other religious writings and to spend at least a few minutes each week thinking about spiritual truths. The Bible thus becomes more meaningful, especially as a way to find insights about how to live from day to day. The value of this trend is that sacred traditions that might otherwise be lost entirely in a secular society are being preserved. The danger is that what is being preserved may remain quite superficial. Group members may feel more comfortable interpreting the Bible in ways that reaffirm their own experiences rather than being challenged to live in ways that they might not otherwise have chosen.

SHARING ONE'S FAITH

When the idea of sharing one's faith is mentioned, it is easy to imagine televangelists trying to convert the masses or white missionaries in dark jungles preaching to the heathen. But this is not the way most people in small groups describe sharing their faith. Such methods are too abrasive and confrontational for most Americans. The spirituality being fostered in support groups, however, is even less oriented toward communicating religious truths to friends and neighbors than the leaders of these groups may realize. Group members do say they are sharing their faith, but they are not drawn to the formal programs of evangelism that many clergy advocate (knocking on neighbors' doors, inviting their friends to church, or perhaps eavesdropping to find poor troubled unbelievers they can help).[16] They are not trying to learn techniques for talking to the unconverted or even to gain logical arguments to use in defense of their faith. Rather, they are trying to incorporate some sense of spirituality into their lives so that it will shine through naturally. They worry, like all modern people seem to, about appearing unauthentic. They don't want their neighbors to consider them phonies. The group, perhaps more than anything else, gives them confidence that their spirituality is connected with the way they live. It does this by providing verbal connections between private piety and some community of significant others.[17] Thus, convinced that their faith is authentic, they feel that other people will be attracted to it naturally.

This idea was explained well by a young woman who had attended a Christian college and taken Bible classes there, but who was realizing that real life was a different matter. "Spiritually I am challenged once again to dig out the proof that God exists from college and make it a reality in my life. I feel challenged to do that because I can then share what the Bible says about God and his salvation plan to that person I work with, with fullest confidence, that what I'm speaking is the absolute truth, not just a truth, in a reality type way, not a lecture from school. I think of a girl in particular who is a young mother at work. I've become very friendly with her and we swapped babysitting when I worked full-time. I desperately want to share the gospel with her in a way that she'll understand as a young mother, and a person divorcing her husband."

Sometimes, the image group leaders have in mind—perhaps one that is even consistent with this example—is of a bubbly, smiling Christian with all the answers, a person who goes out from the group to tell the world how to live a more spiritual life. Usually what people themselves mean by sharing their faith is something both less and more than this—less, because the sharing generally comes more naturally and occurs among friends and family; more, because it may, if it occurs, have a deeper and more sustained impact.

Usually the sharing people have in mind means encouraging immediate family and closest friends to embark on their own spiritual journeys, not telling total strangers what they should believe religiously. Being able to share their faith with their children is the highest priority to many people. One man expressed this desire quite vividly: "It's always been a driving factor for me to instill the Lord into my children, if that's possible. I think God does that to a certain extent, but it's always been important to me to do everything *I* can do, everything that is humanly possible to make sure that they have a strong foundation and that they *know* what I want for them." He said that being in a Bible study group regularly since his children were little had assisted him in two ways: he was more knowledgeable about what he believed and he had learned how other parents communicated their beliefs to their children.

Another vivid example was given by a woman who described how her Bible study group had helped her see the need to communicate better to her children the meaning of Christmas: "Last Christmas [in the group] we read through the Christmas story in the Bible, and then we just spoke about what Christmas means to us and different things that we do at Christmas time. It was memorable because it made us as a family change our Christmas habits or customs. Now what we do is in the morning when we get up, we'll pray and we'll thank God for sending Jesus to us. And with the kids I have a birthday cake, and we blow out the candles, and we sing happy birthday to Jesus, and then we open up our presents. So that they too know what Christmas is all about, that it's not just getting presents."

In other cases, the group becomes a vehicle for spreading spirituality to others, but still the whole idea of the group is to spread the message in a more natural way than often has been done in the past. A young woman with a high school education who worked as a stock clerk in Boston, for example, remarked that her prayer group worked this way. "It helped foster and strengthen our belief in God. And we sang together, we prayed together, so it helped us keep strong in our faith. And then we would tell more people about this religious experience, and therefore, kind of spread the love of God without preaching. Not like the Baptists or the fundamentalists."

The value of sharing one's faith in this way is that people are not offended. They do not feel they are being lectured to by a fundamentalist who has all the answers. The danger is that the sharing is limited to family members or immediate friends, rather than including those in wider contexts who might also benefit. Small-group evangelism can be effective in its own way, but it is not, therefore, an effective substitute for the other programs of outreach that churches have traditionally sponsored.

FORGIVENESS

It is very rare in the public life of our society to hear anything about forgiveness. Let a public figure be caught in a sex scandal, and the press cries out to have him banned from public office for the rest of his life. Let a petty dictator trumpet his military might, and the world wants him erased from the globe. We find it difficult to know what forgiveness might mean in these contexts. Even in our personal lives, the dictum "don't get mad, get even" probably carries much more weight than Jesus' admonition to turn the other cheek. Only recently has the psychological literature begun to recognize the importance of forgiveness—of others and of oneself—to the process of personal healing, recovery, and growth.[18] Theologians have long been concerned with the meaning of forgiveness, of course, and many pastors are familiar with how difficult it is to encourage their parishioners to forgive and forget. But small groups are a place where people can learn how to forgive. How does this happen?

A woman whose group helped her learn to forgive others described very valuably how this process works: "Sometimes I'm angry with somebody because they've done something very hurtful to me. If I talk about it [in the group], and they say 'Yeah, gee, that is really bad what they've done to you,' then I can put it aside and say to myself 'forget carrying around all this anger.' A couple of times different people have pointed out that's kind of why God tells us to forgive people because if you carry around that anger, it eats you up and it's not healthy. And I think God enables us to be happier people by saying 'forgive,' because if you carry it around, it will just eat away at you and you will be the one who suffers, not the other person. So I think [the group] has helped me come to the point in my life where I can say, 'Okay, it's okay to be angry, but don't carry it around in here. Let go of it.'"

This woman is describing an attitude change. Anger is the natural response when we feel we have been wronged, but admitting we are angry is often difficult, especially when our religious upbringing teaches us that anger is wrong or sinful. The first thing the group provides is enough acceptance that you can admit to yourself that you are angry.

Then, having admitted it, you get it off your chest, you externalize it, and you give yourself some distance from it. You can breathe easier as a result.

Forgiveness of this kind is facilitated in small groups not so much by people in the group saying "I'm sorry" to one another, but (as this example suggests) by venting their anger to the group about some person outside the group until they gain some distance from that person. Ironically, groups nurture this process in two ways, both of which require individuals to shoulder more responsibility rather than less. In the first place, individuals learn to recognize that part of the problem is theirs. Then, individuals also realize that it is in their interests to forgive the targets of their anger. An example of realizing that part of the problem is yours was given by Frank in discussing his divorce. "I left my wife and I was convinced that most of the problems in our marriage were because of her, most of the problems in my life were because of her. This woman was a royal pain. And she was a good woman, it's just that she drove me crazy. I didn't hate her, I just wanted her to die. I used to hope that she would just go die. And now we have a reasonably good relationship and when our kids do stuff, she's there and I'm there and she wrote us a note when we got married, when my present wife and I got married." He said the group he is involved with has "said to me that it is my responsibility to forgive her. It's absolutely essential that I forgive her. And I can see that my attitude has changed one hundred percent. Absolutely a hundred percent."

Frank also gave an example of how, even when the problem is not yours, you can recognize that forgiveness (or at least emotional detachment) is in your self-interest. "My present wife's ex-husband is, I think, an active alcoholic. He abused the kids. He still emotionally abuses my step-daughters. The man's a jerk. He's a psychiatrist and I think should have his license taken away. I think his death would probably not be any great loss to life. I mean, the guy drives me up the wall. My youngest step-daughter is in therapy around her issues with her dad. She really struggles with that. The Saturday before Easter, he threatened to stop paying for therapy, he really jerked her around, she was going crazy, I got really angry. That was the week before Easter. The Saturday before Easter he was coming to see the kids and he was not supposed to come in the house and it all got crazy and I was insane. I don't know when I've been so angry. I wanted to kill. I left the house and walked around town and I was stomping and storming and I was acting like about an eight-year-old having a temper tantrum. He's done numerous things since we've been married that have really driven me right up the wall. I don't like him and I think he's evil. The Friday after Easter I was in and I, and I'm still storming. I was in a twelve-step meeting and read the eighth step and everybody's talking about the paragraph in the eighth step where it says we are supposed to forgive all those who have wronged us, whether the wrong is real or imagined. And I sat there and realized that if I—I mean, this guy probably goes home and sleeps well. I lose sleep, he's probably fine. And I realized that what I need to do if I am going to be peaceful and serene is to forgive him. And that step meeting Friday night changed my entire outlook on this guy."

For Frank, the group made him stop and think. It made him realize that forgiving this man was in his own best interest. The other way in which groups facilitate this process is by showing people how to forgive themselves. The realization that others are willing to forgive, to accept, and not to criticize means that the individual also can lighten up. The following example illustrates the kind of acceptance that many group members said they had discovered: "When I first came to the group, I was there I guess about two or three months and I had this overwhelming guilt and was scared almost that people were going to find out my past, that they were going to find out that I had had a baby and wasn't married, and it was just tormenting me. I don't even know how the discussion got brought up, but we were doing a book that applied to our everyday Christian walk. One way or another I just brought it up, and I just kind of cried and blurted this out. I was really scared. I didn't know if I was going to be accepted any more, if I was going to be told not to come back (because that's what had happened in our other church). And I had two phone calls from women who were there that morning that the same thing had happened to them and that there was nothing to be ashamed of, that everybody has a past, and I received either a letter or a card from almost everybody there, just saying that they loved me, and they knew me *for me* and that no matter what I had done, there was nothing that could not be forgiven, that God had already forgiven me and to just go on and not worry about it. I still have them. I have the cards and the letters and stuff and that was one of the best things that ever happened to me there."

Forgiveness received also becomes an obligation to pass on to others. As a kind of epilogue to her story, the same woman related: "There was a girl recently in church, she's in high school, who had a baby, and now I'm doing that to her. I send her cards and letters and I've invited her here with her baby and stuff, because I just had such a warmth and acceptance that now, in turn, I'm doing that to somebody else."

We need to consider whether these examples illustrate the same understanding of forgiveness expressed in Jesus' words from the cross ("Father, forgive them, for they know not what they do") or whether forgiveness in small groups is somehow taking on new connotations. Certainly there are longstanding religious teachings suggesting the importance of acknowledging one's anger and taking responsibility for it. Having a safe context in which to vent your wrath can be valuable. Feeling accepted by fellow group members can be an important part of learning to forgive yourself. But forgiveness of this kind also can be shallow and self-serving. It may prove much easier to forgive yourself than to forgive others. And it may be easier to forgive others silently, or within your group, than to face them in person and to tell them they are forgiven.

INVOLVEMENT IN CHURCH

Many church leaders hope that small groups will be a means of getting people more involved in the wider activities of their churches. If church leaders are honest, they may recognize that they desire this involvement for programmatic reasons. After all, churches can minister to their communities more effectively if their members are willing to devote time and money to the church's programs. But good church leaders probably are motivated by deeper concerns as well. Small groups can become insular, focusing their members' attention only on themselves. Involvement in wider church activities can be a way of overcoming this insularity. Most small groups, moreover, function only as a part of the larger spiritual body rather than intending to be the entire body themselves. Their functions are by nature limited. Most of them, for example, do not include worship or choral music or preaching among their activities. Most do not administer the sacraments or try to instill a deeper understanding of the role of sacraments in spiritual regeneration. Most do not maintain a professional staff to help meet the specialized needs of the community. These activities can be performed better by encouraging group members to be involved in larger religious organizations.[19] Some of the weaknesses of small groups that we have noted in previous sections stem from the specialized nature of these groups. To the extent that small groups encourage

Table 8.3

RELIGIOUS VIEWS BY WHETHER FAITH HAS CHANGED

Percentage of Group Members Who Say Each of the Following Among Those Who Think Their Faith Has or Has Not Changed

Mostly Agree	Faith Influenced	
	Yes	No
My religious beliefs are very personal and private	50	72
My spirituality does not depend on being involved in a religious organization	51	73
The clergy are generally no more spiritual than other people	46	47
A lot of churches are really out of date	37	44
All churches are pretty much alike	17	26
It doesn't matter what you believe, as long as you are a good person	38	77

their members to be involved in the wider activities of religious organizations, some of these weaknesses perhaps can be overcome.

We saw in chapter 2 that many group members, just as in the wider society, have a privatized view of faith; namely, a view that emphasizes the individual spirituality of the person rather than the role of organized religion. We cannot say from the survey data whether the deepening spirituality that people experience in small groups encourages them to move away from this privatized view. There are, however, some indications that people who say their faith has been deepened in small groups have a less privatized version of faith than those who say they have experienced no change. Specifically, group members who say that their faith has changed are less likely than other group members to say their religious beliefs are very personal and private (see table 8.3). They are also less likely to say that their spirituality does not depend on being involved in a religious organization. They seem to take a somewhat more positive attitude toward churches (by denying, for example, that churches are out of date). And they appear to be less relativistic in their religious views (by denying that all churches are

Table 8.4

ACTIVITY BY WHETHER FAITH HAS CHANGED

Percentage of Group Members Who Say Each of the Following Among Those Who Think Their Faith Has or Has Not Changed

	Faith Influenced	
	Yes	*No*
Attend religious services at least weekly	78	37
Church/synagogue has become more important in the last five years	73	35
Have three of more close friends in their congregation	69	50
Involved in at least one special activity, program, or committee in their church	76	47
Involved in three or more special activities, programs, or committees in their church	29	10

pretty much alike and that it doesn't matter what you believe as long as you are a good person). They are, however, just as likely as other group members to say that clergy are no more spiritual than other people. This view, of course, need not be considered a negative statement about clergy or churches. It can reflect an understanding of spirituality that recognizes its manifestations among people in all walks of life.

The survey also shows a connection between having experienced a deepening of one's spirituality in a small group and being involved in other church activities. Specifically, small-group members who say their faith has been influenced are more likely than other small group members to say their church or synagogue has become more important to them over the past five years, to attend religious services at least once a week, to say that they have three or more close friends in the congregation, and to be involved in special activities, programs, or committees in their congregation (table 8.4). These relationships, with the exception of the one involving close friends in the congregation, remain statistically significant when length of time in the group, religious orientation (conservative or liberal), and whether the group was sponsored by a church or not are taken into account. Further results from the survey concerning the relationships between group membership and church involvement are presented in chapter 11. For now, though, it is important to emphasize that small groups are not as insular as some of their critics have suggested. To be sure, they may become the focal point of their members' religious involvement and thus alter the character of their spirituality, but most small groups, it appears, are not inhibiting their members from participating in other religious activities. Their members can thus experience the benefits of worship, serving others, and hearing the lessons presented by clergy and teachers, even if these are not part of the group experience itself.

Many of the people we talked to in person explained that they were quite actively involved in their congregations. They often denied, however, that they had become more involved because of being in their small group. They were already involved and figured they would still be involved even if the small group didn't exist. As one man noted, "If the group didn't exist, I would be somewhere else in the church doing similar kinds of things." A number of people, though, told us that their small group had become a vehicle for becoming involved in other church activities. They might hear about a need because someone in their group mentioned it. As leaders, they sometimes were pressed into service on other church committees. The most common reason for becoming more involved, though, was that someone in their group had asked them to do something. And when asked, they felt more of a responsibility to say yes because they knew the individual who was asking them personally. In discussing how the members of her small group helped each other, for example, a Chicago woman observed, " When two of the guys in our small group were Buildings and Grounds chairpeople, I think the rest of us tried really hard to help them on the church workdays." If two or three people in the group are already on other church committees, the small group can thus become a way of expanding their efforts. Fellow group members are less likely to say no because they feel a personal obligation, not to help the church as an abstract entity, but to help someone they know personally.

Whether spirituality is defined in terms of church programs or whether it is defined more generically as a relationship to God, and whether it entails reading the Bible or simply experiencing forgiveness and acceptance in one's life, therefore, small groups do make a difference in the spiritual lives of a large majority of those who participate in them. People find small groups attractive in the first place because they have an abiding curiosity about the sacred. Once involved, the majority also feel their faith has in some way been deepened. They feel closer to God, more interested in prayer, and more interested in the Bible. Their faith becomes more interesting to them, more relevant to their personal needs, and more practical in guiding their daily lives.

In these ways, small groups are influencing Americans' relationship to the sacred. They are not simply creating community. They are claiming to provide insights about God. For an increasing number of Americans, small groups are the carriers of what it means to be spiritual. But for some people, spirituality is domesticated at the same time that it is reinforced. Prayers are answered, less through miraculous intervention by the supernatural than in small ordinary ways that take on significance chiefly because the group says they are significant. Biblical knowledge does not increase, but forgiving oneself becomes easier and sharing one's faith becomes tantamount to living a good life. The meaning of spirituality becomes closely associated with the group. As one person put it, "It's just you and me here, just flesh and blood. There's no magic show." Sacredness ceases to be the *mysterium tremendum* that commands awe and reverence and becomes a house pet that does our bidding. God becomes a source of advice and comfort, and the proof of God's existence becomes the group. Because the reality of the sacred depends on God's relevance to our lives, God becomes easier to understand and God's actions become smaller, modifying our attitudes and calming our anxieties, rather than moving mountains.

But a domesticated view of the sacred has always been worrisome to the saints and sages who have struggled most deeply with its meaning and implications. And the possibility that small groups are encouraging this kind of faith is troublesome to at least some religious leaders today. As one person, a woman who currently leads several small groups but who has also spent years learning to pray and meditate and who has learned much from early religious writings, explained: "A really important second- or third-century statement from one of the early church councils means a lot to me. It says that anything we say about God is more untrue than it is true. Which is not a reason to say nothing, because we're human beings. But let's be real straight on that. We don't know! We're called to radical trust and to the mystery of God."

9

WHAT MATTERS?

Group Processes and Individual Spirituality

The evidence in the last chapter gives ample reason to believe that small groups can—and often do—have an impact on the spiritual lives of their members. But what is it about small groups that makes this difference? Is it the fact that they study the Bible? Is it the love members show toward one another? Does it depend on members holding each other accountable? Does it require group leaders to function as role models? Is it some combination of all these factors? Or do some of them matter more than others?

Religious leaders will want to know the answers to these questions because they are interested in fostering spirituality There is a considerable—and growing—literature on how to use small groups to promote spirituality. And different segments of the small-group movement are oriented toward different ideas of how to do this most effectively. A group like Logos Fellowship (chapter 5), for example, tries to cultivate spirituality by having a strong leader who can provide authoritative answers to the questions group members may raise. John's men's group, in contrast, has no authoritative leader, but believes strongly in each member holding other members accountable for the ways in which they put their faith into practice. Donna's Bible study group illustrates yet another style. In her group, the women mostly try to model faith by caring deeply for each other and providing mutual support and affirmation. Frank's AA group follows yet another approach. It does not try to cultivate spirituality directly, but, by encouraging its members to recognize their need for a higher power to overcome alcoholism, often has this effect.

These various approaches are not mutually exclusive. A group does not have to favor one at the expense of the others. Moreover, one group may be more effective, given its membership, by adopting a particular style, while another group is better served with a different approach. There is, nevertheless, considerable debate within the small-group movement about which approaches are better. Much of this debate hinges on the question of how much authority should be imposed on small groups, on the one hand, or how much autonomy they should have, on the other hand. The former view is rooted in more traditional models of teaching. It suggests that didactic instruction is best. Thus, an authoritative leader who earns the respect and admiration of the group and a clearly defined method of Bible study are preferred. The alternative view suggests that people learn best from each other. In this view, a warm, caring atmosphere and trusted peer relationships within the group are likely to be most effective in nurturing spirituality. The evidence obtained through our research, focusing as it does on a large number of group members, provides a basis for saying whether any of these various approaches is more effective than the others.

There is, however, another reason for being interested in this evidence. We saw in the last chapter that small groups are not only encouraging people to think more about their spirituality but also to practice spirituality in ways that may have weaknesses as well as strengths. Biblical knowledge may not be enhanced, but members may feel closer to God and thereby figure that they can understand God's ways. They may not study theology, but feel certain nevertheless that the Bible is true. They may not experience miracles, but believe firmly that their faith makes their lives easier. If small groups are domesticating the sacred in these ways, we can understand better why this may be happening by looking more closely at which characteristics of groups have the greatest impact on spirituality.

WHAT MATTERS TO PARTICIPANTS

Our survey again gives us an initial sense of what matters to participants. We asked all group members the following question: "In getting help from the group, how important has each of the following been to you—very important, fairly important, not very important, or not at all important?" We intentionally did not ask whether each of the activities on the list had contributed to the person's spiritual development. We wanted to see whether those whose faith had been influenced mentioned different activities from those whose faith had not been influenced. That way, we could see not only what group members thought was important, but also whether these activities did help explain why some people experience spiritual development in groups more than others.

The results are summarized in table 9.1. What stands out is that the informal, interpersonal dynamics of group life are considered important more often than anything else. The love and caring that people see enacted in the group especially is what they feel has helped them the most. Studying particular lessons from the Bible comes out significantly lower than any of these interpersonal characteristics. Having a role model to admire and look up to seems to be considered important less often as well. On the basis of this evidence alone, we might conclude, therefore, that groups should worry less about the

Table 9.1

ACTIVITIES THAT HELPED MEMBERS

*Percentage of All Group Members Who Say Each
Is Very or Fairly Important*

People in the group giving you encouragement	86
Hearing other members share their views	85
Seeing love and caring acted out in the group	84
Seeing how to apply ideas to your life	80
Having a leader who could answer your questions	80
Having one person in the group who you could discuss things with	79
Hearing people tell stories about what worked and what didn't work for them	78
Having someone in the group that you admire and try to be like	58
Studying particular lessons from the Bible	54

content of their Bible studies (if they have them) and focus more on meeting the emotional and physical needs of their members.

Another way to look at these results, though, is to say that they tell us very little about what makes groups helpful. The low response to studying lessons from the Bible may be because a significant number of groups do not study the Bible. Most of the other responses are important to the overwhelming majority of group members.

Were we to crank out more complicated statistics on these results, we would learn more, but only a little bit more. When people whose faith has been deepened by their group are compared with others whose faith has not been influenced, for example, we learn that the former regard all these activities as having been more important to them than the latter. There are some small differences: the importance of studying Bible lessons seems to discriminate best between those whose faith has deepened and other members. But this finding probably is not surprising. Seeing how to apply ideas is also a particularly important factor, it appears, in the deepening of faith. Coupled with studying Bible lessons, this result tells us something about the kind of study that may be most important. That is, Bible studies that focus on personal applications seem to have more impact on members' faith than Bible studies that emphasize abstractions. Seeing love and caring acted out emerges as another strong correlate of saying one's faith has been influenced, as does having someone in the group to confide in. Well-prepared leaders and someone to admire make a positive difference as well, but relative to the other statements, rank at the bottom of the list. All these relationships are statistically significant even when the length of time people have been in their groups, their religious orientation (conservative or liberal), and whether or not their group is sponsored by a church are taken into account.

If we are to understand how small groups influence their members spiritually, we must, however, move to a different kind of analysis. Knowing that the survey has helped us identify some key aspects of groups that are considered helpful by most group members—and more often so by members whose faith has been influenced—we can take up each of these group characteristics in greater depth. We can tease out what is going on best by listening to group members themselves and by reporting on what we observed in the groups we studied. We also can use the survey data to tell us if some of these characteristics are more important for certain people than they are for others.

SEEING LOVE IN ACTION

The most distinctive feature of the contemporary small-group move-ment is its emphasis on support. Insofar as the small-group movement is also concerned with spirituality, it suggests that the sacred is pur-sued best not by reading about it, by meditating privately, or by listen-ing to lessons and sermons, but by being part of a close-knit group that can put faith into practice. In this view, the quality of love in a group is the decisive element in fostering deep spirituality. Of those whose faith had been deepened as a result of being in a small group, a substantial majority (67 percent) did indicate that "seeing love and caring acted out in the group" had been very important to them—a higher percentage than for any other group characteristic listed in table 9.1. Statistical analysis of the survey revealed that seeing love enacted was very strongly associated with the likelihood of members saying their faith had been influenced by their group, even when dif-ferences in gender, age, education, religious tradition, and views of faith were taken into account. In short, there seems to be evidence that groups do better at fostering spirituality when they also do a good job of caring for their members. What, then, did people mean when they said they had seen love and caring in their group? And how did this contribute to the deepening of their spirituality?

For readers who may think that the answer to these questions is obvious, let us be clear on two points. First, love is central to Judeo-Christian understandings of spirituality, but it is not restricted to those contexts either. In a society as secular as ours, it is quite possible to see people caring for one another and make no connections at all between that caring and spirituality. Just because a physician has a good bedside manner, for example, we do not leap to the conclusion that he or she is acting out of a deepened sense of spirituality. So we must ask how the demonstration of caring in small groups leads to a deepening of members' faith. Second, once we make that connection, we still have to consider the various ways in which it might be made. For instance, one possibility might be that seeing a deed of kindness intellectually reminds us of a biblical teaching about love. A very dif-ferent possibility might be that seeing a deed of kindness emotionally leads us to feel closer to God.

What we learn both from our interviews and our survey is that our society has a strong tendency to think of love and caring within a reli-gious framework of some kind. Although it is certainly possible to think of love and caring in purely secular terms, we generally do not.[1] The example of a physician is revealing. We do not attribute a physician's caring to spirituality because that caring is part of a paid, professional role. We also tend not to think of caring for one's children or spouse in religious terms. The reason is that family provides a more obvious framework to make sense of that kind of caring. Small groups, of course, do not allow us to explain the caring that takes place in either of these ways. They do not involve professional services and they generally extend beyond members' immediate families. Small groups are just gatherings of people who happen to show a great deal of love and caring toward each other. To be sure, the participants receive, perhaps as much as they give. But we generally make room in our thinking for some degree of self-interest in any kind of caring activity.

The connection between caring and some notion about religion also exists in our wider society. When asked who in the world best illustrates caring, for example, people tend to mention Mother Teresa of Calcutta more often than anyone else. Also frequently mentioned are other religious leaders—the pope, Billy Graham, or a person's own pastor.[2] Small groups, however, make it even more likely that this connection will be made. With so many of them sponsored by religious organizations, it is hard not to think of caring as having something to do with faith. Even the groups that are not sponsored by religious organizations so often include discussions of a higher power or of spirituality that the connection is likely to be present there as well.

Judging from the way people in small groups talk about it, having some religious frame of reference in mind does two things as far as caring is concerned. It increases the chances of caring having an impact on one's faith, and it sensitizes people to the importance of caring in the first place. For example, in the survey, people who belonged to church-based groups were more likely to say that seeing love and caring acted out in their group was very important to them than were people who belonged to different kinds of groups. The reason wasn't just that the groups were different, however. People who said religion was very important to them or who attended church a lot were also more likely to give the same response, no matter what kind of group they were in.

Small groups, therefore, are one of the significant ways in which a connection between caring and faith is dramatized in American culture. People can think of caring and assume that it occurs purely for self-interested reasons or that caring is mainly what professionals do. They can look at the churches and be cynical, saying that churches are oriented only toward fancy buildings and high salaries for the clergy. But small groups make people think of caring and spirituality in the same context. They know from their own experience or that of their friends that people do find support and affirmation in small groups. They also know that many of these groups are sponsored by religious organizations and that they include prayer or Bible study, or at least some reference to a higher power.

The answer to the question of how caring influences members' faith is more complex. Some people did find their faith challenged intellectually. John, the physician, was one such person. He had such a strong desire to do what he thought God wanted him to do that being admonished by a member of his men's group was something he could regard as an act of love. Someone might say to him, John, are you not spending enough time with your wife, and he would realize intellectually that he was remiss in this area of his spiritual life. As a result, he would go home and try to do better. In this way, his spiritual life was deepened by becoming more disciplined.

It was more typical, however, for group members to feel their spirituality being deepened by the emotional experience of being a party to caring in their group. Caring was often described as a feeling—such as warmth, closeness, togetherness, or well-being—and this feeling in turn made people sense, quite often intuitively, that God was somehow more real, alive, present, or available to them than before.[3] In other words, spirituality was deepened not so much by an event that motivated people to go out the next day and live better lives; it was deepened by an experience of divine presence, by a sense that one was accepted by God or perhaps submerged in God's love.

This heightened awareness of God was very decisively influenced by the group process. As people shared their problems or just their thoughts, and as they empathized with others, they ceased feeling so alone. Rather than feeling they were distinct individuals, they momentarily dropped the boundaries separating themselves from others and felt more a part of something larger than themselves. There seemed to be a kind of spirit in the group that they were participating in, but one that was more powerful than they.

The example that perhaps stands out most clearly among all the people we talked to was the observation of one woman in a twelve-step group who described how she had felt at a recent meeting. "When I sit amongst the group and I listen to what people have to say," she mused, "I feel very strongly a movement of my own spirit, so it's I suppose what one would call a mediation, but I have a very strong sense of God being present for me in that context." Emphasizing that this sense occurs at a heart level and that it involves a realization of the fullness of life, she continued: "I have a very strong awareness of the presence of God in that context, so it's a spiritual experience for me. One could say God is there whether you're aware of it or not, but my awareness of that presence for me makes it happen at a heart level. And not every time. This past time in particular I found that everything people said was just kind of like going through my whole body. I thought 'Holy smokes.' I feel I'm opening up a lot more to feeling things than I did before."

"Holy smokes" is a good way of putting it. The feeling in the group is powerful, but vague. It is hard to describe, something that many members are reluctant to describe. It comes from the fact that members are concerned about one another. There is an atmosphere of acceptance. Members are disclosing their intimate thoughts and feelings. For example, at the Silver Chase Meeting one evening a young man who had been attending the group for several years admitted to feeling that he probably had been the victim of incest as a child. A woman in the group cried silently, explaining how hard she was struggling to learn how to accept herself. Others listened attentively, some nodding, as if to say they had experienced the same things. It was not hard to feel that there was a spirit present in the group. Some of the members clearly felt that they were in the presence of God.

And do such feelings remain at the level of warm cozies? Perhaps. But sensing God's presence is sometimes the first step toward trying to understand more fully the nature and mysteries of God. Frank's journey to spirituality through AA is a good example. Once he realized that God was interested in him, he wanted to probe more deeply into his spiritual life than either AA or any of the churches he had known could provide. Fortunately for him, some other people in the community who had been involved in AA felt the same needs. So they started a weekly meeting to focus exclusively on one of the twelve steps (step 11) that reads: "We sought through prayer and meditation to improve our conscious contact with God as we understood him, praying only for knowledge of his will for us and the power to carry that out." Every Sunday afternoon, week after week, the group gathered to read, reread, and discuss that simple statement. The group did this for five years!

Demonstrating love and caring, then, is certainly one of the important ways in which group members can contribute positively to one another's spiritual growth. Of course, some people can benefit more easily from this sort of activity than others. In the survey, people who described themselves as deeply religious, who said they were on a spiritual journey, and who saw themselves as extroverts or "people persons" were significantly more likely than their counterparts to say they had benefitted by seeing love and caring acted out in their group. In other words, members who fit in, abided by group norms, and shared themselves were likely to benefit. Members who were suffering from health problems, depression, or sadness were also more likely to give this response. In contrast, people who described themselves as rugged individualists, ambitious, or career oriented were less likely than others to say they had benefitted in this way. So were those who said they were bothered by worries about money. For these people, it was probably harder to share in the first place and to see that the group could help them.

The likelihood of people experiencing love and caring, nevertheless, apparently can be increased by incorporating certain activities into the group. Of all the activities asked about in the survey, prayer turns out to contribute most to the likelihood of people experiencing love and caring in their groups. This fact is all the more significant because prayer and Bible study often go hand-in-hand and, as we shall see, Bible study contributes powerfully to most kinds of spiritual development in small groups. But when the two are examined simultaneously, prayer, rather than Bible study, is associated with seeing love enacted in one's group.

Donna's women's group provides an example of how prayer draws the connection between caring, on the one hand, and spirituality, on the other hand. Sometimes the connection is quite direct; for example, one woman prayed that God would help her find a babysitter for later in the week and after the meeting two women in the group volunteered to help out. But in many instances the connection is less direct and therefore more interesting. For example, the group had been praying for several weeks about an elderly woman who was in poor health. The woman was not a member of the group or an immediate relative of any of the members. But each week the group included her in their prayers. They would discuss her case, asking if anyone knew how she was doing. Then, during the prayer time, one member would be assigned to pray specifically for her. "Our dear heavenly father," the group member prayed one week, "we just praise you this morning that you have given each of us the time today to come to praise your name, to ask for prayer, and to allow us to communicate to each other what our needs in particular are today, just grateful that we have this chance to do it. And Father, during this prayer time we lift up to you Millicent Hardy in the twilight years of her life. Father, be with that family, be with her especially, keep her nerves calm, her spirit calm, knowing that you are in charge, and grant her the comfort and the peace that she needs." It was the kind of prayer that made every member of the group feel a little better. They knew that if they were in the same situation, the group would be praying for them, and that God would keep their nerves calm, too.

Group members testify that prayers like this help them to remember that God is real. They believe that God will help them when the chips are down. Spirituality is important because it is a way to have peace and to face difficult situations. The value, they feel, is that people in the group really do care for them—and do so enough to talk about them and remember them in prayer. Their faith is strengthened by knowing that the group can be counted on and by believing that God will take care of them.

The way in which the sacred is domesticated must also be recognized, however. Group members seldom prayed for anything that might be too difficult (in their view) for God to handle. They did not pray that God would heal Mrs. Hardy, for instance, only that she would be calm. In other cases, they prayed for wisdom to decide what to do, but not that God would show them the right answer. They gave praise in abundance, but focused mostly on how happy they were about something that had gone right. They thanked God for what he had done for them, but less often remembered to be thankful that God was real even when he did not serve their interests. Their sense that God was a pragmatic being who would help them out of bad spots also put their faith on shaky ground. One group leader, for example, pointed out how troublesome it was for group members to assert God's existence on the basis of having miraculously found a parking space. "I want to say, well, does that mean that God is not loving me when I don't get a parking space? Does it mean that God is punishing me and not loving me if I get cancer or if my husband is killed in a car accident? Does that mean that God loves me less because those things happen? Come on now, let's think a little more deeply!"

THE ROLE OF THE LEADER

More than half (56 percent) of all group members whose faith had been influenced by their group said that it had been very important to them to have a leader who could answer their questions. There was also a significant statistical relationship in the survey between saying one had received help from the group leader and saying that one's faith had been deepened by being in the group. These facts help put some of the things we have said in previous chapters about leaders in a broader perspective. Leaders, as we have suggested, generally function best when they are sensitive to the dynamics of the group, steer the discussion, encourage members to participate, and help to keep things running smoothly rather than dominating the discussion themselves. But some members also look to leaders for advice. They want them to be more experienced, more knowledgeable, better informed.[4]

Who are these members? The profile is relatively clear. They tend to be less well educated, from lower income groups, and older than other members. They are more likely to be women than men. And because of regional traditions, they are somewhat more likely to be located in the South than in other parts of the country. Because churches often have encouraged members to look toward clergy or lay leaders for answers, group participants who are members of churches are also considerably more likely to take this stance than are people who are not members of churches. Sunday school classes and Bible study groups in which the dissemination of information is an explicit goal are more likely to include members who look to leaders for answers than groups aiming simply for open discussion among all participants. Groups that practice the charismatic gifts, such as speaking in tongues, are more likely to include members who give such responses. As might be expected, groups that require members to study something in advance are also more likely to include people who say it is important to them to have well-prepared leaders who can answer their questions.

The role of leaders as sources of information and advice, therefore, must not be overlooked as a factor in the spiritual development of group members. One of the reasons that many group members look to their leaders is that they do not feel comfortable approaching the clergy with their questions. Given the social profile we have just considered, clergy are likely to be much better educated than many of the parishioners most attuned to seeking answers from leaders. There may be personal barriers associated with these educational differences. Moreover, growing numbers of people attend large churches, perhaps with memberships of a thousand or more, so they may not know the clergy personally. One pastor, for example, talked about rushing to the mortuary recently to be with a family in his church who had called him because the wife had just been murdered. He said he was glad to be there, but realized he had never met the family before and couldn't remember what any of them looked like, even though they had attended his church for more than a year. Other members, for whatever reasons, may not feel comfortable asking busy pastors for their time. For people unaffiliated with churches or at the fringes of their congregations, this discomfort may be a special problem. In comparison, the group leader is more likely to be known personally and is more likely to be accessible because of the informal interaction of the group.

A participant in one of the groups we studied put it this way: "As an adult, you somehow don't go running to the pastor every time you have a question about something." Partly, she feels he's too busy. Partly, she also isn't looking for the kind of answers she feels he would be able to give. She says she isn't trying to learn answers for an exam. So she mostly likes to read and study things that will have practical consequences for her life. That's why she likes her small group. They discuss topics that apply to her daily life. She especially appreciates the chance to hear what the leader has to say because the leader is a woman who has gone through many of the things she is now experiencing. Something specific the leader says will stay with her during the coming week. Perhaps it is advice about something to read, or perhaps it is just reassurance; in either case, it helps her grow in her spiritual life.

In talking to group leaders, we discovered that most of them do see their role this way. They are facilitators, not teachers. They may be leading a study of the Bible or of some other book, but the idea is to draw out practical implications, not to impart knowledge. As one leader explained, "It's not supposed to be real heavy Bible study like you'd get if you went to seminary or something. It's more like, 'What does this passage say to me, how does it affect my life, what do I think about this,' that kind of thing, not the real heavy theological stuff."

To say that leaders are facilitators is not to suggest, however, that they have no special role to play other than keeping the discussion on track. In the small groups we studied that had spirituality as an explicit aim, leaders were often regarded by other members as someone who had attained a higher-than-average level of spiritual maturity. Where leaders were selected by the pastor or by a church committee, there was often an explicit rule that said: go after the more spiritually mature people when looking for a leader. In other cases, the idea that a leader should not only be a good talker but also someone with spiritual depth was an informal sentiment among group members. We heard a number of people say, for example, that it would be nice to have more leaders in their group, but that this was impossible because most of the members weren't spiritually mature.

There is, in short, a kind of spiritual pecking order in most groups. The position in the pecking order may mean that the person has to be older and have learned how to apply his or her faith to a wider range of life experiences, such as rearing children or facing illness and grief. It may mean that the person has somehow learned how to be kind and encouraging to other people. It may mean that the person knows more about the Bible or is more involved in church work than most people. Whatever it means, the spiritual pecking order not only provides an informal definition of spirituality for the group to emulate, it also gives the leader some authority from which to speak. Even if the pronouncements are about nothing more consequential than what is a good movie to see, the leader's statements may carry more weight because they are associated with spiritual maturity.

Leaders, of course, often supply answers to group members inadvertently as well. They do so in subtle ways, perhaps less by what they say than by how they say it or by what they do not say. The effect is to control spirituality, channeling it in certain directions, preventing it from spilling out of its banks and flooding the valley. The following incident illustrates how leaders can influence spirituality in this way. A woman in her late twenties who had been attending a Bible study group for more than three years became increasingly interested in the mysteries of prayer and found a book she very much liked that discussed the importance of listening to God. She believed the listener could be instructed by God, not audibly, but through a kind of imprinting on her conscience. From her experience in the group, though, she knew it would be unacceptable to share her belief. "What do you mean, do you hear voices?" was what she knew people would say. So she broached the subject obliquely, just commenting in the group that it was a good idea to listen to God (everyone nodded) and that she sometimes thought of herself as putting her head in God's lap (a few smiles). She didn't say any more and neither did anyone else. Finally, the leader broke the silence, steering the group's thoughts away from the brink of unexplained mysteries by affirming the importance of sitting still and enjoying a few "quiet moments" with the Lord.

The problem that arises with this sort of channeling of spirituality is that members may not feel that their point of view truly has been understood or appreciated. In this case, "I didn't feel rejected," the woman recounted later, but "they didn't take it the way I meant it." She felt the group was unwilling to delve more deeply into the spirituality of prayer. She sensed the group was maintaining a kind of facade. In retrospect, it would have been more effective for the leader to have discussed the matter further rather than simply letting it drop.

The relationship between leadership and spirituality, then, is different in practice from what much of the theoretical literature on leadership suggests. Leaders seldom cultivate spirituality by providing definitive answers to spiritual questions. The climate of contemporary culture militates against that model. The respect that some leaders earn depends more on the fact that they have had certain experiences and can tell stories about how God helped them. That quality is what group members are after. So the leader is respected for already having attained some of these benefits. Other leaders are respected because they gently facilitate the discussion and avoid the role of authority figure entirely. But in these cases, the leader also plays an unanticipated role. The leader guides the discussion away from thorny issues. These issues might disrupt the tranquility of the group, but they also might lead to deeper spiritual insights. Leadership, therefore, may work in such cases to keep the group on track, but not to overcome the more limited ways in which it approaches spirituality.

HAVING A CONFIDANT

If there is a single key to the spiritual development that takes place in groups, it is not so much the dynamics of the whole group or the information given by the leader, but the one-on-one relationships that develop between pairs of individuals in the group. They become special friends, find they have even more things in common than they do with other members of the group, and provide role models for each other.[5] Sometimes one person becomes a mentor for the other one, but it is more common that each provides a mirror for the other. It isn't that one looks up to the other as an ideal, but that each can see the human qualities in the other and find some things they admire and others they want to avoid.

The role of the confidant has generally been overlooked in the literature on small groups. The reason is that small groups are supposed to be different from friendships. They are groups, after all, and it is their group-ness that is important. They have leaders, goals, structure, lessons, and planned activities. Religious leaders especially have emphasized this aspect as the key to spiritual development in small groups. What may be happening, however, is something quite different. Small groups help people grow spiritually by becoming excuses for friendships to develop. Finding it difficult to make friends in the wider community, people join small groups. Then, after a few weeks, they find a special person with whom they can share their ideas and interests. Their spirituality is shaped as much by this one other person as by the formal activities of the group.

The secret of this kind of relationship is often just that: an intangible quality, a kind of chemistry that cannot be reduced to any formula. But people often recognize that deep similarities in background and basic lifestyle are the ingredients for this chemistry to happen. In Donna's case it was another woman who had children just about the same ages as hers: "We both have very small children. We both have boys. She has three small boys, two, three, and four years old. I have a two-year-old and a four-year-old. So I can relate when she tells me how frustrating it is to rear these children; I have the same frustrations with my children."

Another woman explained in some detail why she had developed a special friendship with a member of her group. "Mary and I both come from dysfunctional homes. She is daring enough, so to speak, to delve into her relationship with the Lord and stretch it past [the church's] philosophy. She relates to the Lord a lot like I do. If she is making a choice, say, of buying four apples or three apples, it's something she'll give to the Lord, and that's very much like myself. We both believe that he cares from the very smallest thing to the largest thing in our lives and that it's not silly to bring them to him. Things like that have really drawn us together."

These examples illustrate how some shared experience or background characteristic can become the basis for a deeper, spiritual bond. The confidant is likely to be affirming, to provide assurance that one's views are not completely weird. But a confidant can also be a valuable source of instruction and practical advice. The same woman observes: "Mary has been a type of a mentor in a way, even though she's not that much older than myself. She's a little bit more experienced in the fact that she has three children and she's dealing with some of the aspects of older children. She's been through some stages that I'm going through now, she's been through it already. But yet at the same time she's going through it again, because she has a baby the same age as mine, so that's encouraging. I've called her up upset, 'My baby is just screaming upstairs, he won't go to sleep,' and she says, 'Well, do you feel you should get him?' And I said no, and she'll say, 'Well, leave him there.' And she'll encourage me to not feel guilty and to leave him there. And she'll share a story how she's left her son to cry for an hour because she just knew, as his mother, that it wasn't right to go pick him up. That's the type of relationship Mary and I have had."

The confidant relationship contributes to spiritual development not so much because one person teaches the other certain doctrines or beliefs, but because both individuals discover they share a common destiny in life. This commonness gives them courage to face life, to make it through the day; it is not a matter of religious belief, but of practical faith, of conviction that life is good, and of security, so that one can accept oneself. Donna, for example, explained it this way: "I have learned that we're not in a boat by ourselves, that we all experience moments of torment and moments when you think, 'I cannot take one more moment of this,' you know, you're just slamming cabinets and carrying on like a maniac and you think, 'What is wrong with me? Why can't I deal with these children like an adult?' But we all have moments like that, or days like that. And it helps to know that you're not totally failing your children."

Among all group members in our survey, 42 percent said having a confidant had been very important to them. This figure rose to 51 percent among those who said that their faith had deepened as a result of being in their group. This means, of course, that having a confidant, while important to many people, is not necessarily a crucial factor for everyone.

Having a confidant is most likely to be important, the survey reveals, to people in anonymous groups, singles groups, and other self-help groups. Having a confidant also seems to be especially valued by group members who are worried about health problems, figuring out what's important in life, or experiencing difficulties with their work. People who say having a confidant has been important to them are also quite likely to say they have benefitted from the encouragement they have received from their group.

These findings need to be emphasized. They suggest that having a confidant may be especially important in groups that are not oriented primarily toward Bible study, prayer, and other religious activities. As we shall see in a few pages, Bible lessons play such an important role in these kinds of groups that having a confidant, while still valued, tends to pale by comparison. When such activities are absent, having a confidant is likely to be all the more important.

It makes sense that having a confidant would be important to people struggling with addictions or experiencing various worries in their lives. But is having a confidant also relevant to the process of spiritual discovery? One indication that it is comes from the individuals we have just considered. In each case, the confidant was most helpful in giving practical advice, such as reassurance about how to be a good mother. That reassurance, however, provided a foundation for sharing concerns about faith as well. Another indication comes from the survey. Among all group members surveyed, there was a positive relationship between having a confidant in one's group and saying one's faith had been deepened. This relationship held when length of involvement in the group, religious orientation, and whether the group was church-based or not were taken into account. The survey also provided an additional, particularly intriguing piece of evidence. When the relationships between various personal traits (discussed in chapter 7) and having a confidant were examined, the strongest relationship of all turned out to be with being "on a spiritual journey." Group members who described themselves in this way were much more likely to say they had benefitted from having a confidant than were group members who did not describe themselves in this way.

The positive value of having a confidant would seem, on balance, to be considerable. If faith is a journey, it helps to have a fellow traveler. The presence of this person makes it possible to go forward. The danger is that the blind will lead the blind. A confidant, like any friend, is likely to share many of our personal biases. The confidant may be no better read, no more thoughtful, or no more spiritually mature than the next person. Thus, the reassurance that an individual receives may be comforting, but not particularly conducive to growth. If small groups function mainly as a place for such relationships to develop, then their contribution may in many cases fall short of what their leaders desire.

SOMEONE TO ADMIRE

The confidant is someone special, a close friend in the group to whom an individual can relate privately, but there is a different kind of role model in some small groups as well. This is the person everyone looks up to. Sometimes it is the group leader. Often it is a person who is especially active in the group, perhaps a longstanding member, perhaps an older member, but always somebody who inspires others, somebody who serves as a model of good behavior.

"She's so open, she's so much herself. She takes risks. She knows who she is. She is content in who she is." These were the words one woman used to describe a member of her group whom she especially admired. She could scarcely contain her enthusiasm. "All the things that have happened to her and all the mistakes that she has made—she could very well have let it drag her down. But instead she has chosen to let God use her and chosen to be vulnerable for us and give to us whatever it is that she has." At times, the woman says, she wonders if she is acting the way she should, but then she looks at this other woman and decides, yes, it is okay just to be yourself. "She has her little niche that the Lord wants her to be in, and she has a great ministry, which gives me the encouragement to think that he can use even me. She's human. She is not Miss Poised Grace or whatever. She is human, but yet Christ flows through her. She's just real. She's confident. She's not embarrassed as to who she is."

Anyone who has been in a small group probably knows somebody like this. They are hard not to admire. In spiritual matters, they set a standard of excellence. If being yourself is the important issue, then they exemplify what it means to be yourself. If spirituality means knowing how to live placidly in the midst of adversity, then they show how to do this. They are like Jesus to his disciples. They are the mentors, fulfilling the biblical mandate of older women teaching younger women and older men teaching younger men.

So much has been written about the importance of such role models that we might suppose they are one of the most powerful ways of all in which spiritual development occurs in groups. Yet our research does not confirm this expectation. Of those whose faith had been deepened by their experience in the group, only 33 percent said "having someone in the group that you admire and try to be like" had been very important to them—the smallest percentage for any of the items listed. Statistical analyses of the data also showed that when other factors were taken into consideration, having someone to admire was not significantly related to having experienced a deepening of one's faith in general or having grown spiritually in the various ways we discussed in the last chapter.

Upon reflection, the reason for this finding is perhaps obvious.

Someone to admire can set a standard of spiritual perfection, but it is likely to be an unattainable standard. You may aspire to it as an ideal and yet find it impossible to reach in practice. In part, the difficulty is not knowing how this person reached this point in the first place—a problem that can be mitigated to some extent by candid disclosures of personal struggles in the group. In part, the trouble is also that a role model of this kind may be hard to approach at a deep, intimate level. They may be too threatening. Or they may have too much invested in maintaining an image of self-confidence and competence.

It is not surprising, therefore, that the confidant appears to play a more meaningful role in spiritual formation than the role model. People can ask questions more freely of someone they feel close to than of someone they put on a pedestal. Groups do better, it seems, when they encourage informal interaction among their members and help them to find at least one other person with whom they can discuss things openly than when they showcase the merits of someone who can only be looked up to by all the rest. Several of the people we talked to underscored this point effectively by noting how spiritual development in their groups had been stifled by such star gazing. Especially when the stars are given more attention than others, group members are likely to sit back, feeling incompetent, hoping to do better, but failing to take responsibility for their own lives.

ACCOUNTABILITY

People who are involved intensely in groups designed to foster discipleship talk a lot about accountability. They mean opening their lives for inspection, like John does when the men in his group go over their personal calendars and checkbooks with each other. Their desire is to lead a consistent life in which every activity is governed by higher spiritual principles. They also mean taking responsibility for each other. Their group contract involves something like an honor code. They are duty bound to respect the advice of the group but also to take responsibility for each other, doling out advice when they think it is needed.

Other groups, perhaps most, do not have checklists or required reporting but rely more on the well-honed conscience of group members to police themselves. The group's existence reminds them that having a relationship with God on a daily basis is important. They may be encouraged to read the Bible and pray in preparation for group meetings. More likely, they are presented with subtle cues that say this is what must be done in order to be close to God. For example, one woman explains, "As a young mother, you're just totally absorbed in the fact that you've got to find free time. As a younger teenager or even younger married with no children, you pretty much come and go as you please. That's the first thing the group really inspired me to do, that I couldn't just let it go. I couldn't just say, 'Lord, I'm tired and I know you know I'm tired, so I know you understand that I'm not picking up your Word today. Or even a verse.'"

A confidant can provide specific advice, and a person can be accountable to a single individual, like a friend, or a pastor. In groups, pairs of individuals often develop this kind of mutual responsibility, as we have seen. But groups hold people accountable in another important way. What makes something a group is not so much that you know each member in the group, but that these members also know each other. If your friends did not know each other, a diagram of your relationships would look like a series of lines radiating out from a single point. But if these friends also know each other, a diagram would look more like a circle, with each point connected to every other point within the circle.

An elementary school teacher in Los Angeles who had been in a group at her church but who had dropped out several years ago drew a nice contrast between these kinds of relationships: "I used to be in this group of people who met weekly and that was a specific circle of friends where we really did help each other out, sharing problems, sharing whatever. Now my friends are more linear. I'm friends with this person and I'm friends with that person, but I don't have a circle of friends who sort of know each other right now."

The difference is that a circle provides for more internal accountability than a series of linear relationships. If your friends don't know each other, you can (even without thinking about it) play up one side of yourself to this friend and a different side to someone else. One friend, for example, can be a confidant on spiritual issues; another can share babysitting but have no spiritual points of intersection at all. When your friends all know each other because they are in the same group, you are more likely to experience the tendency toward personal consistency that fellow believers refer to as discipleship. Your friends can compare notes to see if you are treating them all the same. They can decide whether you need advice. For them to all get along with each other, they are likely to agree on certain principles themselves. And this agreement will minimize your chances of being pulled in widely differing directions. Clearly this kind of group can have a powerful influence over an individual. People who want a high degree of discipline and coherence in their lives are likely to find such groups attractive, while people who want more room for spontaneity and diversity are likely to feel uncomfortable in these settings.

We did not include a statement about accountability in our survey like the ones reported earlier in table 9.1. We did see in that table, however, that many group members say it has been especially important to them to receive encouragement from people in their group. We also know that saying this is very closely related with saying one's faith has been deepened by being in the group. It is also closely associated with giving one's group high marks for holding its members accountable.

According to the survey, the kinds of groups that do the best job of holding their members accountable are therapy groups and women's groups. In contrast, members of Sunday school classes generally rate their groups low on this trait. Insofar as accountability encourages spiritual formation, then, its role may be especially important for certain kinds of groups in which other factors generally associated with faith development matter less. This possibility is also suggested by the fact that people in meditation groups and in twelve-step groups generally rate their groups high on accountability, taking other activities into account. Members of groups that speak in tongues and individuals from non-Protestant backgrounds do so as well. The same conclusion is suggested by the self-descriptions of individuals who rate their groups high on accountability: people who claim to be on a spiritual journey, people who describe themselves as "free spirits," those who are bothered by loneliness, and those who say they are "very private" persons. For many people like this, the pull of group encouragement may be especially important because their own tendency is too much to rely on themselves.

STUDYING THE BIBLE

On the surface, it makes sense that studying the Bible would be the best way for small groups to nurture spirituality. But some of what we have considered thus far suggests that we should not take this possibility at face value. If people are really being guided by confidants, for example, small groups may be fostering an intuitive spirituality rather than one grounded in biblical traditions. We have suggested that spirituality in small groups is often oriented more toward gratifying individual needs than gaining deeper biblical understanding. Yet a majority of small groups include Bible study among their activities. We are left, then, with a puzzle. What kind of Bible study is it if these are the consequences?

About half of all members who say the group has deepened their faith say "studying particular lessons from the Bible" has been very important to them. Among members of Bible study groups, this proportion rises to about two-thirds. Statistical analysis also reveals that studying the Bible is the single activity that discriminates best between those whose faith has been influenced by their group and those whose faith has not been influenced. When the effects of a whole variety of group activities (such as praying, sharing, providing emotional support, and focusing on special needs) are all considered simultaneously, studying the Bible generally has the strongest statistical effects of all. It is also the best predictor of most of the specific effects people attribute to their groups, such as answers to prayer, openness and honesty with others and with oneself, the ability to forgive others and oneself, feeling closer to God, and being able to share one's faith. In the last chapter we already saw some of the ways in which group participation encourages people to become more interested in the Bible. Here, we want to consider briefly how the process of studying and discussing Bible lessons in groups contributes to spiritual development.

"I would read the Bible and it didn't make any sense. I was very frustrated. Just really confused. And disillusioned." This is how Karen, whom we met in a previous chapter, began her story in trying to explain how group Bible study had contributed to her spirituality. "Before I knew it, I was right back into my old insecurities. The Lord must've known that I was really feeling pretty bad. I was right back into the same things I'd been in before, which did include drugs and alcohol. Guys and whatever. Just the basic escape things. But I was so sick of it. I was so sick of it, I was disgusted with myself, I was totally, totally ashamed. I had tasted a little teeny bit of joy in giving my life to the Lord and then I was beginning to believe it wasn't real. So I remember writing (I loved to write) and I remember writing to the Lord, actually it was 'to whom it may concern,' what is life really all about and just poured out all my feelings and how I really desperately did want to figure out who Jesus was if there was any way possible."

When Karen found a Bible study group, she was, as these comments suggest, highly motivated. Like so many of the people we talked to and observed, she had experienced a kind of dramatic spiritual awakening, what others described variously as a time of feeling especially close to God or having a sudden insight into the nature of God. But then, as it did for many people, the emotional thrill of this moment passed, leaving a desire to somehow get back to that special time. Believing that the Bible might hold the key, they tried to study it on their own.

The reason group study worked better than individual study for many people was that it disciplined their efforts. Busy schedules diverted their attention, but having a specific time to meet each week helped to ensure that they spent a little time reading the lesson. Group leaders and pastors, of course, have often stressed the value of such discipline. But, we found, there was a lot more to spiritual development than discipline alone.

The process of reading and discussing the Bible in the group was terribly important. For many people, it was important because they were better able to see the central idea or main principle in a biblical passage. It was also important because these principles could then be recast into more practical language. Being fundamentally interested in themselves, they found the Bible relevant because it addressed their own problems. Finally, the group discussion helped to legitimate the truth of what was being studied. That is, people came away with the feeling, not that they had studied a set of facts, but that they had seen something that "made sense" or "worked" in their own contexts.

Social scientists have often noted the importance of social interaction for underscoring the plausibility of beliefs and ideas. Some notion an individual thinks of and never tells anyone else may seem like little more than a personal opinion. But something that gets discussed from a variety of angles is likely to seem real (just as the chair you are sitting on seems real) because there is agreement about it and it exists independently of what any one individual may think.[6]

This phenomenon was what we observed in groups. Ideas from the Bible became more real for two reasons. They were there in print, in the first place, and everyone knew they were there. In other words, the act of sitting in one another's presence and looking at the same words from the printed page helped underscore the existence of biblical ideas, certainly compared with hearing in some vague way that the Bible (somewhere) said such and such. But the more important reason was that the ideas were generally reinforced by the personal experiences of people in the group. Asked if an idea made sense, usually people would say, yes, that it made sense to them at least because they had tried it, or they had thought about it, or even that at one time they had asked somebody about it and received an answer that satisfied them.

"Sometimes we only get one or two things done, and other times we go right through the book. But it brings out a lot." The speaker is Karen again, talking about the Bible study she participates in every week. She says the other women "bring a lot of color to it in their experiences and stuff. It's neat. It's neat that, like, even just one Bible verse could mean six different things, and everyone just throws into the batch their interpretation, and it's amazing that God's word can come so alive." What makes it come alive? "Because people are all talking about it."

The key point that our research suggests about Bible study, then, is that the group process counts, not simply the raw content of the lesson being studied. If spiritual development were only a matter of exposing people to a certain body of ideas, getting them to read the Bible on their own, or inviting them to listen to sermons, these activities might function just as effectively as small groups. But the reinforcement that comes from considering ideas as a group gives them added significance. We return to this point again in the next chapter in discussing the role of stories in small groups.

We are now in a better position to understand one of the findings we considered briefly in the last chapter. Group members who say they have benefitted from studying Bible lessons are also more likely to take the Bible literally and to say it is free of any historical or scientific errors. These relationships hold up when we take into account the gender, age, and education level of respondents, their denomination, how important religion is to them, and whether their group studies the Bible. Believing that the Bible should be taken literally, word for word, and that it is "inerrant" typically have been regarded as traits of *fundamentalists*.[7] These were among the beliefs, in fact, that defined the fundamentalist movement when it emerged at the end of the last century, and they continue to be the rallying cry of fundamentalist groups within the Southern Baptist Convention, among independent Baptists, and in other small Protestant sects.

Studies of the American public reveal, however, that the literal inspiration and inerrancy of the Bible are beliefs held by many more people than just a small fundamentalist fringe. In one national survey, for example, 32 percent of the public said "the Bible is the actual word of God and is to be taken literally, word for word" was the statement that best expressed their feelings about the Bible (when asked to choose among five alternatively worded statements). Among active church members, this figure was 37 percent.[8] That number is considerably higher than the 10 or 12 percent who actually identify themselves as fundamentalists.

Our own survey shows that among small-group members an even larger proportion believes in the literal inspiration and inerrancy of the Bible. Among all group members, 38 percent say the statement about taking the Bible literally is true, while 37 percent say the statement about the Bible containing errors is false. Among small-group members who also happen to be members of a church, these figures rise to 43 and 41 percent respectively. And half of all members who belong to church-based small groups give these responses. In other words, small-group members are perhaps 10 to 15 percentage points more likely than the public at large to emphasize the literal inerrancy of the Bible.

Why do so many people in our society believe in the literal inspiration and inerrancy of the Bible? Science, liberal theology, and humanistic perspectives in higher education have all challenged these views of the Bible for more than a century. As science, education, and the secular media have gained prominence in American culture, these challenges have become widely disseminated. There is even considerable evidence that these challenges have eroded traditional views of the Bible. For example, in our own survey, only 30 percent of the college educated said the Bible was free of errors, compared with 40 percent of those with no college education. The fact that nearly one college graduate in three who is in a small group believes in biblical inerrancy, however, is still the point that bears explaining.

Our in-depth interviews and observations suggest an explanation. The wide scope of the small-group movement in the United States is one of the most powerful forces preserving these traditional understandings of the Bible. These groups, we have already observed, do not sit around reading higher criticism or trying to find explanations for potential inconsistencies in the Bible. They are devoted to finding practical applications of biblical principles. The Bible is to be taken literally, and it is inerrant, not because it provides an air-tight metaphysical account of the universe but because its words are borne out in the daily experience of group members. What they talk about in their groups—what their discussions lend plausibility to—are specific rules for the conduct of everyday life: love your neighbor, blessed are the meek, let not your heart be troubled, pray without ceasing. Group members say it makes sense to take these words literally because they apply so clearly to ordinary behavior. They know from the testimonies of people in their group, moreover, that these words are true.[9]

The role of studying the Bible in small groups, therefore, leads to a quandary, but also provides a solution to that quandary. The quandary is that Bible studies in small groups seem to be a major source of biblical conservatism in our society. But if so, how can this observation be reconciled with our observation that groups promote a more domesticated version of the sacred? Surely biblical conservatism would be an indication of the strength of tradition, not a sign of its erosion. The answer is that people in small groups are biblical literalists because of they way in which they have domesticated the sacred. That is, the proof of the Bible's veracity is now the fact that I loved my neighbor yesterday and it made me happy, or that I was meek to my boss and he was nice to me in return. As long as the Bible works, it is literally true. And group meetings provide an occasion for people to report how the Bible worked for them.

Small groups, then, foster spirituality, and they do so in many cases by encouraging their members to study the Bible. As a result, members find the Bible to be of relevance to their lives. They read it, discuss it, and try to apply it to their personal needs. It seems real, credible, because other members say they followed its advice and found it to be useful. Religious leaders who sponsor small groups as a way of cultivating spirituality must, therefore, be reassured that the process works. But, if group experience is the ultimate authority that proves the truth of the Bible, then they must also worry that they have perhaps set loose a force they cannot contain. Certainly group experience can be used to legitimate other truths as well.

WORKING THROUGH CRISES

One other dimension of group process is so important to spiritual development that it cannot be ignored, even though it differs from the dimensions we have considered thus far. An activity like studying the Bible is something group leaders can plan. Being a well-prepared leader falls into this category as well. Showing love or encouraging supportive friendships may have to be nurtured more indirectly, but they can still be nurtured. Much of what contributes to an individual member's spiritual development, however, is associated more with what is happening in that person's life outside the group than it is with the group process itself. Thus group members must be sensitive to these external factors as well.

Of these wider circumstances, the one that came through time and time again as people talked about their faith was the role of personal crises. Previous research has shown that personal crises are sometimes an important reason why people begin to grow in their faith.[10] Losing your job, for example, means not only the loss of income, but also the loss of a significant piece of your identity and security. When a crisis of this kind occurs, it can encourage you to think more deeply about the meaning and purpose of life. The process is painful, but the result is often a sense that your faith has been deepened.

It is just as likely, however, that personal crises lead people to be less committed to their faith.[11] Perhaps they had never really thought about why they believed in God. When things started going badly in their marriage or at work, therefore, they suddenly found they could no longer believe in a child-like image of God that had no relevance to the bad times in life. They needed to see love and support in a visible way and even to receive advice about how to think about God, in order to grow in their faith.[12]

Small groups contribute to the relationship between personal crises and faith development in two ways. They provide the setting in which people can be honest about their own crises, reflect on their pain, and face up to the questions with which they are struggling rather than denying that life has its problems. They also bring people into contact with others who are experiencing crises or perhaps with others who can testify to the spiritual growth they have experienced as a result of crises.

One member of a house church provides an example of someone who was able to face his pain by being in a small group. "Several of us had crises in our lives at the same time," he recalls. "And the group became a place where you didn't have to pretend you had everything together as a person. You could just come and say, 'Here's where I am. This is the part of me that hurts. I need your help, I need to understand what God wants me to do in this case.' And so we got to talking about real issues that were really affecting us. There were some times I would come and just cry, just say 'Here's what happened this week and I'm really hurting.' I think it was God using some real painful experiences in my life which for the first time in my life I couldn't solve, because I've always been very successful and here was the first time in my life I was not succeeding."

The power of personal testimonies given by people who have grown spiritually as a result of deep trauma in their lives has always been recognized by the church. For centuries people have told how God saved them from a life of sin, put them back on the right track, and helped them find peace and happiness. The only problem now is that many churches have become so respectable that people dare not admit that they have ever done anything was ever wrong. Church becomes a place to serve on committees and show off one's social skills, not to tell how being at wit's end necessitated learning about God. For this reason small groups play a vital role: they make it acceptable to tell about pain and confusion.

In some groups there is an explicit belief that spirituality has to be experienced in the group because the established churches have lost touch with the painful side of life. Frank, the man who found God in AA, illustrated this view quite clearly when he remarked: "I see the churches as kind of playing games. They're not really serious. I heard a woman last Saturday at the AA picnic—84 years old (sober 44 years)—talk more eloquently about God than many, many, many clergy I've heard preach." He thinks people in AA have experienced their need for God in a deeper way than most preachers. "I openly admit that if I'm going someplace to talk to people about God, I'll go to an AA meeting. If I want to talk about spirituality, I will go to AA. I won't find it in a church." He believes the churches fundamentally no longer understand spirituality because they do not understand brokenness and despair. "Without knowing despair, how can one know recovery?" he asks.

Others take a less jaundiced view of the churches. But the small group restored their self-esteem and showed them how to accept themselves rather than the clergy or the Sunday morning worship services. In many cases, this process has more to do with getting through the day, with experiencing happiness in ordinary ways, than it does with deep philosophical questions. One woman, for example, said the result of being in a Bible study group was mainly "I like myself better and because of that I have more self-confidence." Elaborating, she observed: "I take better care of myself. I got my hair cut. I go out now and I'll buy nicer clothes. I'll care what I look like. Even on Sundays, I would put any old skirt or a dress on and never look in the mirror, never to see what it looked like on me, and now I care what I look like. I'll buy earrings to match my clothes and put on a little bit of makeup, things that I just didn't care about before."

In such cases, even without bringing God into the picture, learning to accept oneself becomes the key to functioning more responsibly from day to day. A member of a twelve-step group provided another example: "I know a guy who has struggled with his wife. I mean, I have seen him in agony in meetings because of his wife. Because of their relationship, not because of anything she did. And mostly about his anger and how he has emotionally beaten up on her and the kids. And I have seen him over a period of a year, maybe two years, really become a reasonably good husband and father. There's nothing magic. The group told him that he was okay and the group told him that he really was a good father and the group reminded him that he really shouldn't do what he knew he shouldn't do. The group didn't tell him anything he didn't know. They just reinforced what he already knew."

But in many cases, working through personal crises also produces the kind of self-confidence that says, yes, I'm okay, not because I'm doing the right things, but because God sustains me through it all. As the man from the house church group put it, "There's areas of failure in my life that are okay. I know that God cares for me through failure. That approval, self-image, whatever, is not based upon success or achievements or other people's opinions, but it's based on God's care for us."

The responses given to our survey add credence to the belief that working through personal crises may be a significant way in which spiritual development takes place. When factors such as age, church attendance, and the type of group one attends were taken into account, there was still a positive relationship between the number of personal issues people said they were bothered with and the likelihood of them saying their faith had been deepened as a result of being in their group. Worries about health were especially related to feeling that one's faith had been deepened, but so were loneliness, guilt, and anxiety.

The most important finding from the survey, however, was that faith development seems to be much more commonly associated with personal crises for people in nonchurch groups than it is for people in church-sponsored groups. For those in nonchurch groups, faith development was associated with a wide variety of personal crises, including problems with one's work, family problems, and worries about money. For those in church-based groups, health problems, loneliness, and guilt were the only kinds of personal problems associated with faith development. For the former, the relationships were always statistically stronger as well.

Why would this be the case? When results are teased out from a wide variety of data in the survey, the answer that emerges is this: Members of church-based groups are already more likely to be oriented toward trying to develop their faith. In good times as in bad times, they feel they are supposed to be working hard to improve their faith. Being in a group helps them do this, but it does so in a fairly orderly way. Members of nonchurch groups are more varied in their interests. Some are quite interested in spiritual development, others are not at all interested. Being outside of a religious context, the reasons some are interested in spiritual development depend much more on their personal experiences. When things go badly, they are more likely to perceive an interest in spirituality. Being in a group often helps them along with their spiritual journey. But the process is less predictable, less orderly. It depends to a greater extent on warmth and encouragement from the group. When those are present, the individual with personal problems is especially likely to feel better. And feeling better about oneself makes it more possible to feel that there may be some goodness, some divine love, in the universe after all.

As with the other dimensions of spirituality we have considered, the relationships among crises, caring in small groups, and Americans' quest for the sacred are fraught with ambiguities. On the one hand, people who have experienced deep turmoil in their lives may need the security of small groups in order to believe that God exists. On the other hand, the comforts provided by small groups can focus so much on individual needs that the sacred canopy collapses around our own shoulders. It becomes a security blanket that serves us well as long as we do not ask too many questions about it.

Gaining that sense of God's care—the feeling that things are somehow working out in the way God wants them to—is seldom easy. Were someone to stop and reflect on all the suffering, hatred, malnutrition, and exploitation in the world today, it might seem that God's care is remote indeed. For the average middle-class American, bracketing out those problems may be facilitated by affluence, ample health care, and adequate food and clothing. But the sense that God is basically a loving, caring, trustworthy friend still requires an act of faith. And, as social scientists would insist, it requires an appropriate setting as well. Small groups provide such a setting. They temporarily shield the individual from loneliness and despair or from large impersonal institutions. By constructing an artificial world, they arrange for interaction to be sufficiently brief, sufficiently personal, and sufficiently free of economic or bureaucratic encumbrances for a sense of caring to be experienced, at least temporarily. By associating spirituality with the group process, the group reinforces the sense that God is also a loving being. A sense of confidence that things will work out for the best thus can emerge. It comes as a result of the sharing and prayer that is central to most small groups. Quite often it is greatly facilitated by the telling and retelling of stories as well. It is this subject to which we turn in the next chapter.

10

THE POWER OF STORIES

Narrative and Spiritual Growth

Asked to recount a story she had told recently in her group, Karen recalled how she had shared a memorable experience that happened to her on a retreat. "Someone in the group had shared how deeply ashamed she was of herself. I was a couple of people later in sharing, but I addressed the issue of shame too, because shame is something that I've become very aware of. It plays a major part in my own life. I shared that in therapy I had identified a particular area of shame and asked my therapist, 'Is this it? Is this the major shame?' and he said, 'No, I think it's one, but I think basically the soul feels shame when it's not allowed to develop into what it's meant to be.' I personally call that soul shame. And I talked about that and I talked about an experience I had on retreat of trying to look inward to find my own beauty and having a very hard time and being very uncentered, and all of a sudden I thought, 'Look outward for it. Look at what's beautiful outside yourself.' It was so powerful. I did, I looked, and it was the night sky and it was *so* beautiful, and I *saw* that. Then the next day I had a similar experience, and the idea of that maybe even being a mirror for myself, but it had to be a balance, I couldn't always keep looking inside, I needed to look outward. I do that with people. I do it when I'm afraid. If I'm afraid, instead of panicking and reverting to isolation, I'll say, 'What is beautiful here?' and a lot of times I'll see it and then it moves me out of standing in fear so I can deal with that cause of the fear. So that was what I shared this past time, and that was for me of a spiritual nature."

THE TERMITE STORY

One of the things that troubles Fred most when he leads his group is that they answer his questions too quickly. "Does Jesus care?" "Of course he cares." They just feed back answers they've heard somewhere and don't think about how these answers apply in their lives. When that happens, he tries to get them to think more concretely. "I will bring up a story where I'm wrestling and try to relate it a little bit more to the subject matter at hand and then reopen it, 'How are you wrestling with this?'

"One of those stories that we really were wrestling with—that we were talking about and people were going through with us—was our house, the roof was rotting. We had wooden shingles, they're called cedar shakes, on the roof and they were rotting out and we got real bad termites. Somebody had buried lumber or something and they got into the lumber and they were coming up in my furnace room. My furnace room kind of sits outside of the house and it has a dirt floor and they were coming up inside of that. They got into it, they ate out a whole back wall and then got up into the ceiling. And then in my study there was a hatch of termites. I mean, they were all over the place. And we'd really been praying because we didn't want to go through major renovations on our house. We just didn't think it was wise to sink all that money into the house and remortgage, but I think we found our answer. If we didn't remove those termites, nobody was going to buy the house. Remove the termite damage. Our house was terribly nonfunctional upstairs. It was built really kind of weird. And so we decided that that's what we needed to do and I think the termites were our answer.

"When they finally hatched out in our roof upstairs, we knew we had to do something about it. So we had the whole second story taken off and then the place remodeled upstairs, rebuilt. And being out of the house for five weeks, living with my mother-in-law, the things that we went through there, trying to really do our jobs here. And it just seemed like we were always, always on the go and busy and tired, and how God brought us through some pretty strenuous times and led us to making some good decisions.

"I think that people got involved. We used to have the fellowship at our house, and so they knew what needed to be done there. [My wife] and I are people that like to live in moderate means, and I believe in the scripture that says 'Let your moderation be known to all men.' Be a moderate people, not people of extremes and excessive anywhere. And to live that, it seemed to us to be an excess to go through this great thing. But we really felt it's what God wanted us to, and I think that people felt us wrestling with it and really seeking God. It felt like we got an answer and they got an answer at the same time."

THE CAKE STORY

"I guess my biggest conflict in life, as you already know," ventured Donna, "is my in-laws. So I guess the most recent thing that happened to me was when my sister-in-law and I were planning a birthday party for my mother-in-law. And my sister-in-law is the 'favored' daughter-in-law because she converted to Russian Orthodox. And that's been hard to deal with kind of, too. But I do my best to make things happy and peaceful in the family. We were planning a birthday party and at the time my sister-in-law and I did not have much money. We were kind of feeling the crunch of the recession and decided to do things ourself at home. And I offered to bake a cake for her birthday. And she said, 'Okay, that would be fine.'

"But then I got a call back that she didn't think that was such a good idea. That my mother-in-law would prefer a store-bought cake over one of my home-made cakes. And it really hurt my feelings, I guess, in that I thought it would be special to make something home-made. And I guess I repeated the story recently in the group. And just to get some of their feedback, like 'What would you say if someone said that to you? How would you react?' My reaction was, 'Oh.' And instead of saying, 'Well, gee, don't you think it would be nicer if, you know, we made a home-made one?' And I kind of did try to say something like that, but she persisted and said, 'Well, I talked to Grandmom,' meaning my mother-in-law's mother, 'and she agreed also that a bakery-bought cake would be nicer.'

"I told this story to our group and a couple of the people could really relate to it and said, 'Gee, that's almost rude to tell somebody that they'd like a bakery cake over your own.' I just guess I wanted to hear, 'Boy, wouldn't you be offended or hurt if somebody did that to you?' And the agreement was that it was kind of rude to do and that they should have just let it go and not persisted and called me back and canceled my cake. And I didn't make the cake. I let them buy the cake and then I paid for the cake. And that's another thing I didn't want to do was the expense of it.

"I felt better sharing about it, but I think the thing is, like I said before, you need the Christian point of view from people, like you don't want to be a doormat in certain areas of your life, but also you want to be strong but not rude back. Because I don't want to lower myself to— So I felt better after telling it, just because they gave me a few ideas on what they thought about it. And it's always nice for me to hear what other people think about problems."

These stories are quite mundane. But they illustrate clearly the type of discourse that characterizes most small groups. To be sure, there is the occasional story of child abuse, incest, or being spared an untimely death. Yet the ordinary experience of Americans is the subject of group discussions, far more than it is the occasional trauma or miracle. These stories are the connective tissue that holds small groups together. The fact that they deal with ordinary events means that most individuals can contribute something. Few members are likely to be intimidated because they have nothing special to share. Through storytelling individuals turn their own experiences into a collective event. They preserve their individuality but at the same time find community in the similarities between their stories and those told by others in their group.

Storytelling has become the dominant mode of discourse in small groups for several reasons. One is that relatively few groups function as classes in which a set of abstract principles is transmitted from the leader to the participants. Even Sunday school classes, as we have seen, increasingly try to encourage comments and discussion from the group rather than following a systematic lesson plan. Thus it is expected that members will share something from their lives, especially when spirituality is required to be practical. Small groups also, for the most part, are not intended to forge an explicit consensus around some point or to hammer out a compromise that all members can live with, such as a policy-making body might be. Their operating norm is instead that each member should contribute something from his or her unique perspective. This practice, of course, means that personal opinions are highly valued. But these opinions also must be validated in some way; otherwise, they lack seriousness and strike group members as being a waste of time. Linking opinions to personal experience is the safest method of providing such validation; at least nobody can dispute that this event was something the person experienced. To present an opinion, therefore, members typically tell stories about something that happened to them. Doing so is also legitimated by an assumption that such sharing is good for the soul. Other people may learn from the stories they hear. But, more importantly, the storyteller is able to vent some feeling that needs to come out. By expressing these feelings, the storyteller is better able to detach from them or to gain a new insight about the experience. The role of the listeners thus is to listen and to be accepting. The stories can be ordinary because they are still part of the storyteller's experience, they disclose something of that person's private life to the group, and they do not have to have a particular moral slant or be linked to some preconceived notion of the truth.

Stories may for these reasons be commonplace, but they are also powerful. They shape individuals: as people tell their stories, they become these stories. As the group encourages certain stories to be told, it shapes the identities of its members. Stories also provide the main vehicles by which the sacred is communicated and transformed. Sacred texts are composed largely of stories. When groups study these texts, it is the stories, much more than the genealogies, the poetry, or the prophecies, on which they focus. They compare their own stories with these sacred narratives. In the process, they also turn the sacred into something that is less mysterious, less transcendent, perhaps even less grand, because it is part of the most mundane experiences of their lives.

The role of stories in groups is, therefore, another lens through which we can look in order to understand better what the small-group movement says about our society. As a place where stories are told, support groups provide an occasion for rounding off the rough edges of our individuality, transforming us into communal beings. Yet, it is the nature of stories to preserve our individuality, for each story is ours alone and is subject to our own interpretations. The stories told in groups tend much more to be about individual members rather than being stories of the group. They also permit individuals to arrive at their own understandings of truth rather than requiring agreement about a list of absolute principles. Spirituality, then, becomes a matter of subjective interpretation, even though it is fostered by the collective presence of the group. Mundane experiences are elevated by connections with sacred stories. But the sacred is also diminished by being translated into the narratives of termites and cakes.

THE WAY LIFE IS

For much of the past two centuries, scholars have tried to understand human existence through abstract models and systems; they have regarded stories as an outmoded way of thinking that is more characteristic of primitive folklore than of modern culture. But in recent years that view has begun to change. We are no longer confident that science, metaphysics, philosophy, or systematic theology can answer our questions about the nature of human existence. As a result, many experts on human behavior are now suggesting that stories encapsulate something fundamental about the way life is.[1]

Harvard psychologist Jerome Bruner has suggested in a recent essay, for example, that the stories we tell about ourselves are not only a way of remembering the past but an essential component of the way in which we enrich, interpret, and guide our behavior and our moral commitments. "We seem," he writes, "to have no other way of describing 'lived time' save in the form of a narrative."[2] This is a significant admission from a man who earlier in his career had argued that the transition from childhood to adult life was marked basically by a shift from stories and fantasies and symbols to rational, denotative, and conceptual thinking.

Of particular importance for our purposes are two aspects of Bruner's argument: first, that life, as Oscar Wilde observed, imitates art; and second, that art, especially in this case, is constructed to reflect the deepest rules and assumptions of our cultural tradition. The first of these assertions is important because it indicates that stories are not told simply to pass the time or to make us feel good; stories become the models we use to shape our subsequent decisions and behavior. The second assertion points to the fact that we tell different stories depending on what we believe and particularly on what we have heard others tell. This means that groups in which stories are told can play a powerful role in bringing to life the stories we may read in scripture, in biographies, or in novels and that these stories in turn shape the narratives we tell about ourselves, which then influence how we think we should act in the future.

Religious leaders, of course, generally have been more comfortable paying special attention to stories all along. Although the drive for abstract theoretical knowledge greatly influenced religious thinking in the last century, too, some of the best theoreticians in the religious world recently have been paying closer attention to the importance of stories. Mindful not only of the fact that Jesus and the prophets told stories, but also that the Bible is composed largely of stories, they have argued that spiritual insight may be especially amenable to the narrative form.[3] The value of analogies, metaphors, myths, and narratives is being discussed by theologians and ethicists, whereas a generation or two ago such discussions would have diminished the importance of stories.

If storytelling is gaining greater credence among secular scholars and religious leaders alike, one of the reasons may be that stories are especially valuable for adapting people to the fluid circumstances in which we live. Storytelling, after all, is a way of reconstructing ourselves. When we are in a new situation, we need to make sense of it. We may also need to make new sense of who we are—that is, of our self-identity—in each new situation. A story provides us with an account of how we arrived here, where we were before, and what the differences are. Stories about journeys are particularly suited to this task. Storytelling is also a way of gaining information about our surroundings. We read stories in the newspapers for such purposes. In personal life, we tell our own stories in order to elicit feedback and to prompt our peers to disclose who they want to be and who they want us to be. When there are few absolutes, stories also become a way of securing agreement about reality in delimited contexts. My story reflects my particular point of view. You can tell yours to reveal how your experience has been similar to or different from mine.

STORYTELLING AS A FEATURE OF GROUPS

The literature on small groups suggests that storytelling is a widely encouraged practice in these settings. Certainly it was in the groups we studied. Alcoholics Anonymous groups encourage members to tell their stories of addiction and recovery as a way of coming to terms with the realities of their own lives. Therapists have long regarded the healing process, whether in individual counseling or in groups, to involve the creation, as Bernice Neugarten has remarked, of "a meaningful life story from a life history."[4] The personal testimony has been standard fare in fundamentalist and evangelical circles for years. Spiritual direction centers have become another setting in which storytelling has received much emphasis in recent years. Among others, Raymond Studzinski has written, for example, that spiritual direction can be thought of as a "restorying" of life so that the past is better understood and the future more fully realized.[5]

In this view, the role of the group is to further spiritual development by encouraging individuals to recall the past more vividly through the telling of stories and by collectively helping them to interpret their stories. Life is said to be enriched in the process as individuals discover new layers of meaning in their personal experience. The act of repeating a personal account may reveal new insights. In addition, the individual may also gain insight into the nature of the divine, perhaps by sensing a moment of hope or redemption or by recognizing that his or her own story is part of some larger sacred tradition. In the process, the believer engages in "discernment" or, as theologian William Spohn explains, "The story . . . makes a normative claim. . . . It is not just any story, but one which claims our lives by asserting that it must be the truth of those lives. This is the story which reveals in a definitive way God's intentions for the world and for us."[6]

Just how common is it to tell stories in small groups? Among members of all kinds of small groups, three-fourths say they have told stories about some experience in their life at some time or another in their group. About the same number say they have compared their own experiences with stories told by other members of their group. So the telling of personal stories is certainly a common feature of small groups.

More specific kinds of stories also play a prominent role in many groups. For instance, nearly two-thirds of all group members say they have discussed stories from the Bible or from some other book in their group. More than half have discussed things that happened to them as children in their groups. One person in two claims to have discussed the story of the Good Samaritan in his or her group. And nearly this many say they have discussed the biblical parable of the Prodigal Son.

Among persons whose faith has been influenced by their groups, the role of stories seems to be even greater (see table 10.1). Five out of six of these people have discussed stories from the Bible or from some other book. Four out of five have told their own stories and heard others tell their personal stories. And more than two-thirds have discussed the Good Samaritan and Prodigal Son stories.[7]

To understand better the role of stories in groups, why they are important, and how they may contribute to spiritual development, let us consider some specific examples in greater detail.

STORIES AND PRAYER

People in groups tell stories about themselves in the course of discussing other topics, such as a book on child rearing or a recent novel

Table 10.1

THE ROLE OF STORIES

Percentages Who Have Done Each of the Following in Their Groups Among Group Members Whose Faith Has Been and Has Not Been Influenced

	Faith Influenced	
	Yes	No
Discussed stories from the Bible or some other book	84	26
Told stories about some experience in your life	82	59
Compared your own experiences with stories told by other members of the group about themselves	80	55
Compared your own experience with stories you have read about or discussed in the group	74	40
Discussed the story of the Good Samaritan in the group	73	16
Discussed the story of the Prodigal Son in the group	67	12
Discussed things that happened to you as a child	63	39

they have read. But in many of the groups we studied, stories came up most frequently and with the greatest candor as part of the time the group devoted to prayer. Personal stories were raised with such frequency that we need to consider what it is about prayer that is so conducive to the sharing of stories. Consider the following example.

In one of the groups we studied, a young woman who was a regular member of the group suffered complications early in the third trimester of her pregnancy. To prevent a premature delivery, the obstetrician placed her in the hospital where she received intravenous medication to control contractions. At each meeting of her group the members prayed that God would keep the mother healthy, allow her baby to grow to term, and help her to maintain a cheerful attitude. The expectant mother was not able to tell her story directly to the group, but other members, in contact with her during the week by phone, reported on how she was doing. After six weeks, but still five weeks from term, the mother delivered—twins, each about five pounds.

The women regarded this outcome as a miracle. Had the babies been born much earlier, they might not have been healthy. Had they been carried to term, they would have been much harder to deliver. The day the group received the news, they recounted the entire experience again (retold the story) and then made it an item for praise during their time of prayer. They thanked God for being so wonderful in answering their prayers. Later, they often told the whole story again, noting that God does not take away people's problems but sustains people in hard times and helps them to grow in the process.

The key to understanding the relationship between prayer and stories lies in the fact that this episode became an item for praise. What is a praise item? This group's leader defines it this way: "Any time God has answered prayer, but also other things that have gone well." A praise item is in fact the story that defines the episode as one that has gone well. This is especially apparent when on the surface things have not gone well.

For example, the same woman gave a further illustration of a praise item. "My [90-year-old] dad was involved in a car accident. He was having mini-seizures, but he would not stop driving. And we kept saying, 'Dad, somebody is going to get hurt!' We were very afraid that my father was going to cause major injuries, possibly death, to an innocent party. My dad did have an accident. He did have a seizure while he was driving, blacked out totally. But it was about a 1,000 feet from his house, not even, maybe 500, up the top of the hill. He ran into a tree. My mother had not been able to catch him and be ready in time to go out the door with him. She never wears her seat belt. She wasn't in the car. My father had his seat belt on. He was hurt but not severely. He had bruises, so he was uncomfortable. Our praise was that God had accomplished two things. He had gotten my father off the road permanently without a major family conflict. And God accomplished this without serious injury to anyone and nobody else involved. That was a praise item."

Let's dissect what is going on here. Stories obviously can take almost any direction. This story, for instance, could have been a tale of woe. But the context in which stories are told limits how they can be told. A story told on a comedy program on television has to be told in a way that makes it seem funny; a story reported on the evening news has to be told in a way that makes it seem significant or unusual enough to be newsworthy. In the present case, the general context is the Bible study group, the more specific context is its time of prayer, and the particular framework in which the story is embedded is the praise item, which, as we have seen, means the story has to be told in a way that shows how things have gone well and that God had something to do with it. What the story accomplishes, then, is a reinterpretation of what happened. Rather than being bad that a 90-year-old man was injured, it is good that he is off the road without having seriously injured himself or anyone else.

If a story is essentially a narrative that moves certain characters from one point in time to another, then the basic movement in stories like this is from a problem situation to a state in which the problem has been resolved. Problem: expectant mother is in hospital; solution: healthy babies are born. Problem: aging father won't quit driving; solution: aging father is forced to stop driving. The problem, in fact, implies the solution. It would not work, for example, to tell a story that went: problem, aging father is having mini-seizures; solution, aging father is having even worse seizures. In other words, what specifically is identified as the problem in the story becomes something that can be resolved at the end of the story.

Why is it important to know this pattern? We might suppose that this sort of movement is a characteristic only of stories that are intended as praise. But a closer look at other stories told in groups reveals that this is just a more distinct example of a much more general pattern. Think again about the three stories at the beginning of the chapter. In the night sky story, the problem is being unable to overcome shame by looking inward for beauty; the solution is looking outward and finding beauty in the night sky. The termite story is a rambling narrative that seems not to have much of a point at all, except that the storyteller brings the logic of it together near the end: being a "moderate" person, it seemed "excessive" to renovate his house and add a whole second story (the problem: an apparent violation of the biblical injunction to live moderately); the termites provide an explanation for this behavior (solution: God works in mysterious ways). The cake story moves in the same direction. The problem: feeling offended but wondering if it was legitimate to feel that way; solution: having others in the group validate one's feelings.

Stories like this are important because they perform a theological function and a psychological function. The theological function is resolving doubts one might have about the goodness of God. When people believe firmly in the goodness of God (as most Americans do), an invasion of termites is not only an unsettling financial experience, it raises the question, how can God allow something like this to happen to me? An individual's imagination can run off in all directions in trying to deal with a question like this: maybe I've done something awful, maybe God is punishing me, maybe God really isn't good, maybe there is no God. Those are the kinds of thoughts people can have in private. But having to tell the story in a group forces the individual to tell it in a certain way, to look for the silver lining, as it were, and, in so doing, to emphasize that God is good after all. The psychological function is straightforward. A person is likely to feel better knowing that what at first seemed bad actually had a good ending.

There is, however, a danger to be considered. I have intentionally stressed the fact that our stories are an interpretation of what happened, not simply a factual report of the events. Our ability to interpret experience is what makes us human, what gives us power over our feelings and our responses. But groups that encourage people to interpret their experiences in a particular way may make it very difficult for people who do not happen to think that way to feel accepted. The group with the expectant mother, for example, included two other women who were experiencing very painful emotions. Both told stories about their struggles to the group and candidly discussed their fears and their shortcomings. One generally talked about her pain, but then concluded her stories with some comment about the progress she was making. The group liked her and encouraged her; as one woman noted, "the progress she's made in spite of everything is very reassuring that there is hope for all of us." The other woman was not able to sense progress. Her problems seemed monumental to her. The group tried to be understanding and accepting toward her, too, but they found it difficult. "Sometimes I just want to tell her to grow up" was how one of the members expressed her feelings.

In short, the stories we heard in the groups we studied were overwhelmingly stories with happy endings. This was not because the stories had good consequences for their characters, but those who told them interpreted them that way. As these interpretations were given, group members were encouraged to feel better—about themselves and about the goodness of life. Many, judging from our survey, did feel better and have a more optimistic outlook on life. But this norm for storytelling also made it hard for people whose stories did not seem to end happily to tell theirs. Some of them gravitated to twelve-step groups where it was more acceptable to tell stories filled with pain and anguish. Those who stayed in church-based groups were more likely to bend their stories to fit the group norm.

SOCIO-BIOGRAPHY: THE PERSON AS STORY

This last example brings us to another very important point about the role of stories in groups. People in groups do not simply tell stories— they become their stories. That is, as far as the rest of the group is concerned, the identity of any particular member of the group becomes almost synonymous with the personal stories that member tells. And that process in itself can have a significant impact on the way in which individuals think about themselves.

This process has long been recognized in the therapeutic literature. For example, pioneering psychiatrist Henry Stack Sullivan wrote some years ago that "in group treatment, memories are used largely to elucidate why people act, how they feel, and how they react to one another, consciously and unconsciously [and as a result] the memories one has in [a] group are part of the chain of action, discovery, and interaction."[8] The telling and retelling of personal memories has also become standard fare in a wide variety of other groups. It is helpful to have a concrete example.

A man who had attended the same group every week for more than a decade responded in an interesting way when he was asked to tell some story from the group that particularly stood out in his memory. Instead of relating a narrative about some specific event, he described each member of his group as if they were the stories. "Heather tells us about how vulnerable she is when she's not doing all the things she's used to doing." She struggles with becoming more dependent on friends and on God, he says, as opposed to being an achieving, controlling person. Daniel's story is always about God, what God is, and whether God is interested in him. "It's sort of an ongoing story that he tells." Another couple have an ongoing story they tell the group about their marital problems. One member's story revolves around his unhappiness in one career and switching to another. The man himself says his story is always pretty much the same, too. It mostly has to do with wanting to become a better person, wondering how to do that, and fearing that becoming a better person may not make any difference in the larger scheme of things.

This response was simply a more elaborate version of what many group members reported. They couldn't single out a specific story they'd heard because their fellow members tended to tell the same story over and over. Every week it was the story all over again about the impending divorce, the conniving ex-husband, the struggle to stay sober, the search to know God more intimately. But, of course, the story wasn't exactly the same from week to week. What made it seem like a single story was the fact that each week there was a new episode. The latest development could be understood only in the context of previous episodes and interpretations. In short, the discourse of small groups was like a daytime soap opera. All the episodes were connected.

They were connected because the storyteller was not engaged only in relating the news; the storyteller was involved in the hard work of reconstructing an identity. Each episode needed to be integrated into an ongoing story that included an evolving interpretation of the person's past, present situation, and future. Storytelling was thus an important feature of the symbolic interaction through which a member related his or her multiple and varied roles to the others, thereby forming an identity that was more stable, central, and well integrated than any of these separate roles.[9]

Students of the subject call this process the construction of a *socio-biography*.[10] It is biographical in the sense that it involves creating a story of one's life, a kind of narrative about one's origins, formative experiences, and defining characteristics. It is a social process because it involves storytelling in public. Rather than simply imagining the past privately, an individual tries out various versions of his or her story in a group setting, receives feedback from the group, and incorporates that feedback into subsequent episodes.

We can now draw together a number of the themes we have been considering in this and in several of the previous chapters. Storytelling in groups is the key to understanding why people come to feel comfortable in groups, why they so often feel that group participation is an intensely spiritual experience, and why spirituality is so often regarded as a journey. Feeling comfortable in a group comes about as a result of developing a socio-biography that reflects both the member's own and the group's input. What a person chooses to share in a group becomes ever more important to that person's identity. The group's affirmation of this identity reinforces and legitimates it. Often this transformation happens in subtle ways. It is nevertheless a powerful influence. For example, an individual tells a story about a particular experience. That experience is but one of the thousands of experiences that make up the person's life, and even telling it simplifies what happened. The group then remembers that story, thinks of the person in that way, and interprets subsequent stories he or she may tell by linking them with this story. The group reinforces certain facets of the person's identity, and gradually he or she begins to act that way. Spirituality is involved because the stories told are deemed to be about life and therefore about fundamental power, goodness, authority, justice, love, and other attributes associated with the concept of God. This is what people mean when they say they are learning to apply their knowledge of God. In the telling and retelling of their stories, they assimilate ideas about God into their understanding of their own identity. In the process, they become more like God, modelling their behavior after the stories they read about in sacred texts. In the same process, however, God also becomes more like them. They are worried about termites and cakes. So they assume God is, too. The story of Jesus dying on the cross becomes a story about feeling depressed one day and then feeling better the next. And the group is an important part of the process. Stories are told, not once, but repeatedly and over long periods in groups. This is why storytelling unfolds episodically; it reflects on itself as well, transforming spirituality from a static concept into a journey. The next step in the journey is never taken empty-handed but with the baggage that previous storytelling has provided.

The same man who described his fellow group members as stories provided a clear statement of why these stories play such an important role in his spiritual journey. "It's very helpful to me to have somebody tell me about their life honestly and about God in their life," he says. The reason is that he can then "watch the process." He can see God working and, not only that, but the effects of this working in someone's life. For example, he sees God healing his friend Heather and liberating her from the need to be in control all the time. Because he knows Heather personally, he can understand God better by imagining that if he were God, he would want to be doing the same thing. "If I was God, I'd want her to feel that she's lovable and good and fine the way she is." In his friend Daniel's case, he can also sense God at work. "It's almost like he's paying attention to his muse for the first time in his life. I feel like that's God working in his life, really freeing him up."

What we see in specific stories that become items for prayer is repeated, writ large in the longer-playing stories that become associated with individuals' lives in groups. There is still the omnipresent movement from problems to solutions, with all its attendant positive and negative functions. But what helps overcome the worst excesses of these stories in the short-run, what keeps them from requiring everyone to view the world through rose-colored glasses, is that the individual-as-story implies an episodic telling and retelling of events. The journey may inevitably be one of progress. Yet there can be a continuing struggle with pain and brokenness at the same time that minor victories are experienced along the way.

MY STORIES AND OUR STORIES

Most of the stories told in support groups are about the experiences of individual members. One of the most curious features of group storytelling is that each person can tell a unique story that strongly asserts his or her individual identity, and yet the group as a whole comes away feeling closer together, having experienced a sense of commonness or community oneness.[11] How is this possible?

If we look closely at some of the stories people recounted, paying particular attention to their choice of words, we see that both the content and the form of these stories makes a difference. The content is generally of an experience that people can identify with. The form recasts the experience in a way that makes it more common than it was.

The content of stories told in groups generally includes some experience that the storyteller assumes is common to other group members. Quite often, as the survey reveals, it is a story about one's childhood. Everyone can relate to the toy that broke or to a story about feeling close to some special friend, parent, or grandparent. John, for example, liked to tell his group about how things were in the small church in which he was raised. Donna's favorite story involved a gift her grandparents gave her when she was thirteen. Karen's group loved to talk about their pregnancies. In twelve-step groups, the stories of alcoholism, pain, and despair can be told because such experiences are the basis of the group's existence. Even in more diverse groups, stories about personal feelings increasingly seem to be the common currency. Everyone can understand to a degree when someone tells a story about being afraid or angry. For example, Frank's stories of anger with his ex-wife commonly evoked nods of understanding from his AA group.

When such stories strike a chord that resonates closely with another member's experience, they become the basis for special insight, empathy, and the formation of a confidant relationship. One woman related that another woman in her group had told how as a young girl she and her brother would check the hood of their father's car to see how long he had been home in order to guess whether he had been home drinking and was dangerous. This story made an impact on the listener because she, too, was from a dysfunctional background and realized there was a kindred spirit in the group. "It really touched me," she said. "It drove home to me what she had lived through." Asked if the story had also been helpful to her, she explained: "It's helpful to hear this kind of story because a lot of times in a church you don't hear about the dysfunctional families." She said the story had helped her relate to this woman better, too: "It helped me to pray specifically for her, rather than just as a category."

"I remember the night," another woman said. "There were only five of us—and I was talking about what it felt like to feel like an untouchable person, that nobody in my whole life had ever been demonstrative or affectionate, and that made me in many ways feel like I wasn't a touchable person. And then another member of the group addressed that same topic in his life and after it was over I just said to him could I have a hug, and I don't think I would've done that if that hadn't come up. That was very powerful and meaningful. I reached out to that person because of what we were talking about and good things came out of that."

Apart from the content, the form a story takes can also do much to reinforce a sense of common destiny among group members. One of the reasons why stories about personal feelings promote a sense of group-ness is that these stories are often told in the same way children tell secrets. The message communicated is that the listeners are privileged. They share a common bond because they know something others do not know. Feelings are especially good for this purpose because they are regarded in our culture as disclosures of something within. We do not reveal them easily to strangers or to business associates. We keep them inside us. To talk about feelings in a group, therefore, is to divulge something hidden to the privileged few.

John, the physician, offered a revealing example of how such disclosures of personal feelings can sometimes lead to greater openness, intimacy, and a willingness to share in the group. "Someone shared about their struggles with their marriage and how they were really—had struggled soon after they were married with their, you know, their relationship and that kind of thing. And so there was discussion. What that does is give permission then for you—I mean, when people expose areas of brokenness in their lives, it gives you much more legitimacy to expose your areas of brokenness. And so when that happened, suddenly we found all the fractured couples in the group. Had that not happened, I think that we still wouldn't know about those fractured relationships that we want to encourage and help."

The group leader also can play an important role in translating individual stories into community property. Discussions can be prefaced with statements such as "We are here to learn from each other." Prayers often serve this purpose as well. After each individual has expressed some unique need, for example, the prayer time may package these statements with phrases like "We come to you God" or "Lord hear our prayers." The group leader also may interject connective tissue after an individual member's story; for example, "well, I'm sure we can all relate to that."

Even though stories forge a common bond among group members, storytelling need not conform to a mold that makes all the members feel like they are telling the same story. As we have seen, groups develop a division of labor, as it were, such that each person has a unique role to play by virtue of his or her special stories. One person is best at telling the divorce story, for example, another may be best at pounding his fists and conveying anger or injustice when he tells his story.

Many of the people we talked to were quite aware of what it took to be good storytellers in their groups. They realized there were certain topics that could or could not be discussed. For example, it might be appropriate to discuss incest if one had experienced it as a child, but not if one were committing it as an adult. They also realized that storytelling is a collective process. One person might tell a story in order to get a certain point across. But then someone who disagreed or who wanted to make a different point could retell the story or add a personal episode, drawing strong enough connections to make it seem as if the point were going to be the same, but then leading the story in a new direction.

Here is an example from Karen. "We were talking about making our houses pleasurable for our husbands when they come home. And I guess I get frustrated with that conversation because it comes up a lot, and the other side of it is not presented. Mostly all they say is we need to wait on the way we're feeling and minister to our husbands when they come home. And I don't agree that that's always the case. There are times when they need to put their feelings on hold and minister to us when they come home. It's a balance. I had commented that it is a balance. You need to feel each other out. Every day is going to be different. And I shared the story of one day when the kids were just off the wall and I needed to entertain them. I sat down in the living room floor, I had every single toy that these children must've owned in the middle of the floor, and my house is never like that when my husband comes home. He came home and I had to laugh at the expression on his face when he turned the corner. But the funny part was, to tell you how this place was, my mother had come home within an hour of that time with the same expression on her face. So the point I was saying is that you need to be flexible. That was just something of my home that I had shared." By introducing this story into the discussion, Karen was able, she felt, to significantly alter the overall conclusion that the group was drawing. Rather than always putting their own needs on hold, the women came away from the group having heard that it was important to take care of themselves as well.

Stories, then, can be about a person's unique experiences, but they can be told in a way that reinforces common bonds in the group or that challenges the group consensus. It is important for group members and observers of the small-group phenomenon alike to be aware of these subtle processes. The group's power over its members often is not expressed so much in overt statements, such as "Do it this way, or else," as in subliminal messages associated with the use of collective pronouns, or nods of approval that come from telling certain stories, rather than others.

STORIES ABOUT THE GROUP

Even though groups can exercise power over their members, the more common failing in American society is probably that members participate in groups for their own benefit and seldom come to identify with the group as a corporate entity at all. This failing is perhaps most easily overcome when groups become sufficiently embedded in their members' experience that people can relate narratives about the group itself. In this sense, the wonderful thing about groups is that they not only provide the occasion for telling stories, they also become the source of stories. Memorable things happen in the group. We fix the event in our memory by putting it into story form. Then we can pull it out, showing ourselves (or whoever may be listening) that this is what good people should be like and, indeed, make the point that we have experienced this ourselves in a group of good people.

How a group chips in to help somebody who is undergoing a time of trial is an especially rich source for story material. Such events are like the crises a community experiences, like a flood or a cyclone, when we see people at their best, helping one another unselfishly. Here is an example from Donna: "There was a person who was already in the group when I joined it, who was losing her mother of cancer. And I remember being really touched about that because her mother was far away and she couldn't come every week to the group. But when she did, we kind of dropped everything for her. And we would never discuss the book when she was there. We would only discuss her, what she was going through and how she was feeling for the entire time. And I thought that was a really— I thought that the people in the group were very sensitive to others' needs and very aware of how other people are feeling and what their needs are. And I thought that was very touching to see everything kind of come to a halt for somebody else."

The story can also be about a happier, even frivolous time. John, for example, told this story about his group: "We have a relationship that allows us to be, not foolish, but playful with each other. And the experience that I'm thinking of is where we broke down into groups at a party and used one of the persons as a Christmas tree and decorated them. I mean, some very dignified people became very undignified. Those are times when you just *really*, I mean, you know that you have a relationship because you wouldn't do that with just anyone."

The important thing is that the experience is deviant, not something that happens in ordinary life. Consequently, it helps define the distinct identity, the specialness of the group. For this reason, parties and holiday celebrations contribute a great deal to group life. As we have seen from our survey data, small groups often include parties, eating together, or helping their members celebrate birthdays and anniversaries among their activities. As in life generally, these activities help to define special moments.

In addition to the special moments that are planned, memorable events sometimes just happen in groups. These, too, become the source of stories that can be told and retold to illustrate the corporate identity of the group. "Images come to mind" was how one member of the Silver Chase meeting put it. Especially vivid to her were images of summer evenings when it was too hot for the group to meet inside the church, so they would move outside: "Some of the hot nights sitting out in the graveyard, under the lights, getting bit by mosquitoes. I'd bring the bug spray with me and pass that around. I think sometimes when the group got very, very big. I remember some neat experiences where I'd go upstairs and join the smaller group up there. The trauma I experienced when the construction happened and they moved us out of our room, got moved into a different room, and it's funny how much a creature of habit I am that I couldn't sit in a parlor."

What makes these experiences notable is that they break the normal routine sufficiently to cause deep emotion. Not studying the designated lesson or not meeting in the usual room becomes an occasion when the divine seems to be especially present. Group members feel closer to each other than usual. The transcendent breaks into their midst. This, paradoxically, is why the combination of structure and informality contributes to the vitality of small groups. Structure provides routine, but informality allows the group to break with routine, thereby experiencing something more memorable and significant.

Stories about the group, however, may also reinforce a sense of orderliness and rationality that provides a safe haven from life rather than a genuine experience of the divine. Philip Slater in his study of therapy groups has noted that the members of these groups quickly developed myths that helped them make sense of their experience together, comforting stories that said in effect "what seems like an uncontrolled and frightening chaos to ignorant mortals is really an orderly game." In the groups Slater studied, these myths often focused on imagined psychological principles, the machinations of a mastermind leader who had planned everything in advance or on the magic of the group process.[12]

In the groups studied for this book, stories emerged that functioned in similar ways, although their content was quite different. Some of the stories emphasized the security of the group contract; that is, they gave evidence that the group would pitch in to help members who might be in some kind of trouble. Other stories seemed intended to show that some unconscious, benevolent hand was guiding the group. Rather than talking about planning and leadership, for example, members would tell about how "things just worked out for the best" or how the group had evolved and grown in unexpected ways.

Few stories recalled episodes of group failure, when the process broke down, when nobody showed up, or when someone stormed out with hurt feelings. Few stories even told of misfortunes happening to group members that were not also the occasion for divine blessings, human courage, and unanticipated good fortune. Thus, the group stories became manifestations of the kind of orderly, secure worlds in which group members wanted to live. It was for this reason that some members especially cherished the stories they could tell about breaks in the routine. Occasionally, such breaks opened their vistas just a crack, allowing them to sense the raw mystery lurking beneath the orderliness of everyday life.

STORYTELLING AND TEXTS

Thus far we have considered storytelling in groups as a kind of free-form activity. As we have seen, there is an underlying pattern involving the identification of a problem and the movement toward its resolution. In this sense, people in groups pattern their stories after the stories they have heard other people tell. Otherwise, it would appear, the stories are infinitely malleable, depending on the storytellers' varied experiences. That impression, however, is somewhat misleading. In addition to giving members opportunities to tell their own stories, groups also provide occasions for retelling stories found in written texts and for comparing personal experiences with these stories. The most common text, as we have seen, and the one that has the greatest impact on spirituality, is the Bible. "The linking of a story of an individual with a Great Story," as Andrew Greeley has written, becomes for many people one of the most significant ways in which small group members gain "the experience of grace."[13]

Of course, it is valuable in many cases for group members to hear familiar Bible stories again. Often they have heard these stories since earliest childhood, but have perhaps not thought about them seriously as adults. By thinking about these stories again, people are forced to consider their relevance to adult needs and experiences. Sometimes the truth of biblical principles is reinforced in the process.[14]

A man who had learned Bible stories as a child in Catholic schools gave an insightful example of how hearing these stories again in his prayer fellowship helped him to understand better their value: "I've recognized that there's a lot more to it than what I was taught by the nuns, most of whom I realize probably didn't even have college degrees in these little schools that I had. And they were teaching stuff that *they* learned in fifth grade. A lot of Bible stories tend to be of the sort, 'Think of only others, don't think of yourself.' 'Do unto others as you would have them do unto you.' But they forget the 'as you would have them do unto you' part of it. So I think I've examined some of that stuff. I look at some of those phrases, some of the stories, in a new light."

The biblical narratives, repeated in group discussions, provide templates for interpreting the meaning of personal experiences. By doing so, the narratives become more deeply understood and more available for practical application. "One of the drawbacks of sermons, no matter how rich they may be," writes pastor Dale Galloway, "is that they do not lend themselves to feedback and discussion. In the home cell meeting, questions are asked and dialogue and discussion take place. There's not only the knowledge in the hearing of the Word of God, there is the practical application of it to the daily life."[15]

"We did a book on women of the Bible," recalls Karen. "We compared biblical passages about women in the Bible and related them to today." Doing that, she explained, forced her "to kind of relate it to my own personal life." A man who had experienced something similar in his Sunday school class provided the following illustration: "During a recent class we talked about issues of brokenness. And people shared from their life issues of brokenness and we compared them to people in the Bible, like David struggling over a lot of his broken issues of being crowned king and then having Saul chase him for years and his indiscretions with Bathsheba. What does all that mean? And so we templated a lot of the broken experiences of our lives with those in the Bible and said, 'Well, what does that mean?'"

A pastor involved in an AA group said the connection between the stories he heard at meetings and the stories he knew in scripture was very close. Indeed, he often tried to make the connection in his preaching and his personal counseling. He was especially drawn to the parallel between the Exodus story and the process of recovery from addiction. "I use the story of God leading and having Moses lead the people out of slavery into the wilderness and into the promised land. I use that all the time as a story of recovery. I talk about that all the time. Here at church on Maundy Thursday we had a seder. The guy that I sponsor is Jewish and he and I developed a Passover meal, without a lot of food. And I talked about how God has led us all out of slavery."

Relating biblical narratives to personal experience also becomes a way of driving home the principles contained in these narratives. Such principles are seldom learned once and for all, like riding a bicycle. Instead, they require periodic attention. Hearing others talk about how a particular story has proven personally valuable can be a powerful reminder. "I think often to hear something once is kind of a light-bulb moment," a member of one group observed, "but unless one hears it many, many times, it may not be something that we incorporate into our lives. So awareness is one thing and incorporation is another. The group has helped me to incorporate awareness maybe more than actual awareness itself, because people will say things that are not necessarily a new idea to me, but it reminds me, yes, this is what I need, this will help me at this moment in my life."

The telling and retelling of stories in groups, finally, is often valuable in its own right. Raw experience is often difficult to remember; it needs to be organized in our minds for us to know what it means. Having to tell a story to a group forces people to organize their experience. "Even something I'll say," remarked one woman, "will remind me to do it the following week." As an example, she recalled: "I was telling the group about how one can stand in love or one can stand in fear, and most people fear their love. And the task is seemingly to try and love your fear and how does one do that. As human beings we will be afraid. And just in saying that and naming that, I was able then following that, myself, to immediately say to myself when I would feel myself drawing back from someone or a situation and say, 'You're afraid. What are you afraid of here, what are you going to do about it?' So it's helped."

Another member of a group recalled being asked as part of a group ice-breaking activity to think about his last birthday and tell briefly what had been the most meaningful part of that day, including an explanation of why this had been especially meaningful. He said he had resisted the task because he had a warm feeling tucked away in his memory about the overall experience of his last birthday. To pull out one thing and call it the most meaningful, he felt, would be to disrupt the way he wanted to remember his birthday. In retelling the story some twenty years after the incident in the group, he revealed, nevertheless, what a powerful effect telling stories in groups can have in the shaping of memories. Despite his desire to retain a warm feeling about the entire day, this story was what he remembered.

Readers with little first-hand exposure to the small-group movement should, above all, recognize that support groups have become an important place in our society for the telling of stories. Many observers have argued that storytelling is a lost art, declining with the erosion of extended families and close-knit neighborhoods and being replaced by soap operas and sitcoms—stories imposed on us by the mass media. But small groups allow people to tell their own stories and to do so creatively. Many groups also provide templates or master narratives from sacred texts. These stories give individuals a way of connecting their personal experiences with larger sacred traditions. In the process, individuals perceive the spiritual significance of their personal experiences and grow in their spiritual journeys. Readers who have participated in support groups probably will have already experienced how stories may contribute to their personal enrichment in these ways.

Yet pitfalls also must be recognized. The storytelling associated with kin groups and neighborhoods in the past was often a way of passing on long traditions about the collective experiences of a particular people. People told stories about their ancestors, about times of trial, and about moments of moral realization. The stories told currently in small groups are much more likely to be about personal journeys. To the extent that they tap common experiences—say, of childhood, of anger, of illness, or of grief—they unite their listeners. But the group is not a people with a history. It is a transient gathering, a place where nomads meet to share temporary insights. The stories told in these settings help us adapt to the more transient ways of our society. In the best of circumstances, they may help us understand the pain of fellow strangers or the common feelings of people from backgrounds very different from our own. They cannot substitute for the stories that parents should be passing on to their children or the stories that nations, ethnic groups, or religious communities must tell in order to preserve their traditions.

The ways in which spirituality is molded by the storytelling of small groups is also a product of our times, and the storytelling that takes place in groups helps, in turn, to reshape our ideas of the sacred. In small groups, everyone is an expert. There is no need to listen to wise persons or sages, no need to study what others have said about sacred stories in order to discern their definitive meanings. Each story has multiple meanings. One person's interpretation is as good as another. If a sacred story elicits an example from my own experience, so much the better. Finding practical applications, after all, is what our religious leaders encourage us to do. In the process, truth can be adapted much more readily to complex circumstances. We can agree to disagree— because our stories are all different. And yet we can also agree tacitly that our stories must have happy endings. If our stories make us feel better, they are worth repeating. If they do not, we would rather not hear them. Our stories, therefore, permit us to see how the sacred can be part of our daily experience, but they may also prevent us from probing more deeply into the nature of sacred truth or its mysteries.

For this reason, a number of the group leaders we spoke to

expressed some concern about the current direction of the small-group movement. They saw its value for promoting spiritual renewal, but they also recognized that this spirituality could be superficial. One leader, for example, said the prayer requests that emerged in her group were largely off the top of people's heads—just to have something to say—rather than reflecting deep issues in their lives. To combat this tendency, she asked her group to pray silently for 45 minutes at the start of each meeting. Another leader found the groups he was responsible for worked best when he let them do what they wanted. But some of the groups soon turned inward, practicing a form of spirituality that focused entirely on their own needs. As an antidote, his church started several new groups to promote involvement in outreach to the wider community. Another leader remarked, "Ten years ago, we thought small groups were an easy way to cultivate spirituality; now we realize a lot of hard work is required!"

PART FOUR

THE SOCIAL SIGNIFICANCE OF THE SMALL-GROUP MOVEMENT

11

SERVING THE COMMUNITY

Group Membership and Public Commitment

If engagement with ourselves does not push back horizons so that we see neighbors we did not see before, then we need to examine the appointment kept with self. If prayer does not drive us out into some concrete involvement at a point of the world's need, then we must question prayer. If the community of our Christian brothers does not deliver us from false securities and safe opinions and known ways, then we must cry out against that community, for it betrays.

—Elizabeth O'Connor[1]

One can be in a study group and come to the conclusion that providing clothing for overseas relief is needed. But until one engages in a clothing-collection project . . . such an attitude may not represent a solid commitment.

—Jack Corbett and Elizabeth Smith[2]

Talk to clergy about small groups and nine times out of ten the comments will be favorable and enthusiastic. The dissenting voice will raise concerns about the wider involvements of group members. Talk to social scientists about small groups and the response is likely to be considerably more mixed. "Don't these groups turn people's attention toward their own problems, leading them to be oblivious to the needs of others?" is a common way of framing the issue.

There is ample reason to voice this concern. Millions of people in our society suffer from poverty, malnutrition, inadequate housing, homelessness, debilitating health problems, and other serious needs. In the wider world, these needs are even more acute. The time and energy of those with resources must be shared freely with those who lack the vital necessities of life. Increasingly, governments are refusing to shoulder these responsibilities, so the voluntary efforts of individual citizens become all the more important. How, then, is it conscionable for so many people to spend so much time within their own small groups attending to their own needs when the needs of others are so great? Can these groups be motivated to serve the wider community as well as their own members?[3]

INGROWN OR OUTGOING?

Social critics have long been divided about the larger social signifi-cance of small groups. At the end of the nineteenth century, industri-alization and migration to large cities had grown to such proportions that observers wondered if the social fabric could withstand much more. City dwellers did not know their neighbors the same way rural villagers did. What struck most migrants to the city was how different they were from everyone else. They could, of course, band together with others who, say, did the same kind of work. Guilds, for example, had long provided people in similar jobs with a way of associating with one another. Professional organizations might serve a similar function. Hanging out at the same tavern could provide camaraderie, too. Or neighbors could join a brass band or cycling club. They could even attend the same church. But would any of these groups lift their sights above their own kind? Wouldn't society fragment into thousands of small, ingrown organizations?[4]

The alternative view had been expressed by Alexis de Tocqueville when he visited the United States earlier in the nineteenth century. Noting the extent to which small community associations already dot-ted the American landscape in the 1830s, de Tocqueville entertained the possibility that these organizations were perhaps the key to Ameri-can democracy. The reason, he argued, is that such groups empower people to be concerned about larger social issues. The local garden club might be interested mainly in pretty flowers, but its meetings at least encourage members to become acquainted with their neighbors. In the process, they learn leadership skills, discover the importance of electing officers and conducting business in an orderly fashion, and perhaps even wind up discussing politics and economics in addition to their usual activities.[5]

In the present context, both of these perspectives can be taken toward the vast numbers of small groups that seem to be flourishing in our society.[6] On the one hand, it seems reasonable to argue that small groups focus so much attention on the emotional needs of their members that they could not possibly encourage broader interests. A majority of them focus on Bible study and prayer—activities, as we have seen, that often deal mainly with questions of how to make it through the day, how to be patient with one's children, how to feel good about oneself, how to worry less and trust more. Other groups explicitly rule out discussions of social and political issues. Twelve-step groups, for example, generally ban such topics from meetings unless they come up in conjunction with the specific addictions or dysfunctions on which the group is focusing. A very small percentage of groups claim community service or political concerns as their primary reason for existence.

On the other hand, de Tocqueville's argument about empowerment could also be applied to most contemporary small groups. If they focus on members' addictions, their role in overcoming these addictions may empower people to lead more productive lives in the wider world. A group that devotes most of its time to studying the Bible could nevertheless discover in those discussions a rationale for being concerned about the needy and the poor. Meeting with other young mothers an hour a week with child care provided may be essential for keeping up on what others are thinking about community issues. Or a group that sparks members' interest in their church may also encourage them to become involved more actively in the volunteer efforts of their church.

SURVEY RESULTS

A partial answer to the question "ingrown or outgoing?" is provided by the responses to a question in the survey that asked, "As a result of being in this group, have you done any of the following?" A list of ten activities followed, eight of which dealt with various kinds of helping activities and two of which focused on involvement in churches or synagogues.

The results indicate that three-quarters of all small-group members have "worked with the group to help someone inside the group who was in need"—a larger percentage than for any of the other activities listed (see table 11.1). On the surface, this finding might suggest that small groups are indeed ingrown, helping their members more often than they help anyone else. Just because the needy person who happens to be helped is a member of the group, of course, does not mean the need is any less real. The chances are, from what we saw in chapter 6, that these needs were emotional rather than physical. But we also saw that meals, child care, and even financial assistance are not uncommon among group members. It is mainly the other ways in which group members say they have been influenced by their groups, however, that point toward wider effects beyond the group itself.

Nearly two group members in three say they have "worked with the group to help other people in need outside of the group." Almost as many claim to have donated money to a charitable organization (other than their church or synagogue)—allegedly because of their group. More than half say they have "become more interested in peace or social justice" as a result of their group. At least four group members out of every ten have become more interested in social or political

Table 11.1

SOCIAL CONSEQUENCES OF GROUP PARTICIPATION

Percentage of Group Members Who Say They Have Done Each of the Following as a Result of Being in Their Group

Worked with the group to help someone inside the group who was in need	74
Worked with the group to help other people in need outside of the group	62
Donated money to a charitable organization, other than your church or synagogue	57
Became more interested in peace or social justice	56
Became more interested in social or political issues	45
Became involved in volunteer work in your community	43
Changed your attitudes on some social or political issue	40
Participated in a political rally or worked for a political campaign	12

Table 11.2

CONSEQUENCES FOR CHURCH INVOLVEMENT

*Percentages Who Say They Have Done Each of the Following
as a Result of Being in Their Group Among Members
of Church-Based and Nonchurch Groups*

	Church Based Group Members	Nonchurch Group Members
Taken a more active part in other programs sponsored by your church or synagogue	61	12
Increased the amount of money you give to your church or synagogue	50	13

issues, changed their social or political attitudes, or become involved in community volunteer work. One in eight claims to have participated in a political rally or worked for a political campaign as a result of being in their group.

The survey also lends further support to the evidence in chapter 8 suggesting that greater interest in, acknowledgement of the importance of, and involvement in church activities was one result of group participation. Among all group members, 40 percent said they had taken a more active part in other programs sponsored by their church or synagogue, and 34 percent said they had increased the amount of money they gave to their church or synagogue, both as a result of being in their group.

These figures, however, differ dramatically depending on whether or not people are members of church-sponsored groups. Among those who are members of such groups, six in ten say they have become more active in their church or synagogue and five in ten say they have increased their level of giving. For religious leaders who have encouraged small groups as a means of invigorating local congregations, these findings should, of course, come as welcome news.

The implications of small groups not sponsored by churches or synagogues are less clear. As shown in table 11.2, about one member in eight who is not part of a church-based group claims to have become more active and to have given more to a church or synagogue as a result of the group. We do not know, however, what proportion of these members has become less active or decreased the level of giving.

Overall, the survey results seem to indicate that small groups generate a substantial amount of caring and interest that extends beyond the boundaries of the group. Thus, de Tocqueville's argument that small groups empower people for community involvement seems more nearly correct than the arguments of contemporary naysayers. Yet, the survey results also help us to reconcile the two perspectives. De Tocqueville's view assumes that groups are small enough to make discussion and interaction possible, yet large enough to convince their members that they can make some difference in the wider community. The critics' view assumes that groups may be so small that they isolate, rather than empower. In short, *size* is the key factor.

Size is, indeed, an important factor. Groups that have more than 20 members are significantly more likely to be made up of people who say they have been influenced in the ways shown in table 11.1 than are groups of fewer than 10 members. People in the larger groups, for example, are 14 percent more likely to say they have done volunteer work as a result of being in their group than people in the smaller groups. The former are 13 percent more likely than the latter to have become more interested in peace and justice. And they are 12 points more likely to have participated in a political rally or campaign.

The effect of size, it appears, is chiefly to increase the likelihood that members will develop wider interests that extend beyond their group—and even beyond their church—rather than increasing all types of activity. Members of larger groups do not differ very much from members of smaller groups, for instance, in saying they have helped someone within their own group or in saying that they have become more active in their church. One important exception to this pattern, though, is that members of larger groups are significantly more likely than members of smaller groups to say they have increased their financial giving to their church.[7]

Different kinds of groups are more likely to influence their members' attitudes and behavior in different ways, of course. But people do not have to be in a special interest group to have their political views changed. Nor is it necessary to be in a peace fellowship to be challenged about issues of peace and justice. Group projects to help the needy evolve from other group activities, just as the political influences of small groups do. We can better understand the nature of these effects and how they come about if we consider each kind of effect in greater detail.

ENCOURAGING A CHARITABLE LIFESTYLE

Small groups have an enormous advantage in being able to help other people because members can divide up the work. This division of labor has been the secret of volunteer efforts from the beginning.[8] One person might not be able to help even one needy family, but if a number of people from the community chipped in a few dollars apiece or a few hours a week, their collective efforts could make a huge difference. Small groups can take on projects in the same way. What no individual or single family could accomplish, the members of the group can more easily accomplish together.

George is a member of a covenant group at the Baptist church he attends in a suburb of Chicago. The group meets regularly for fellowship and Bible study, but there is another important clause in the covenant that binds it together: "There are four families, ours being one of them, who have covenanted to help this lady who has multiple sclerosis. We have said that, relatively speaking, we would help to take care of her no matter what. When this lady has gotten ill she has generally stayed in our home because logistically it was easier, but the other families have been support families."

This case would be an example of a project undertaken collectively by the group to help someone outside of the group. In other cases, the group may not function collectively but actively encourages individual members in their efforts to help others. John, for example, does a lot of volunteer work, including a "docs for kids" program to raise money for handicapped children. His men's group isn't involved in this collectively, but they do encourage him and each other to do things in their own way.

Probably the most important way in which small groups influence the wider community is by freeing individuals from their own insecurities so that they can reach out more charitably toward other people. People who are overcome by their own problems tend to be too afraid of what may happen to risk helping others. They may fear being rejected or failing. They may feel their time, and even their money, must be safeguarded. Being in a small group can give them greater confidence in themselves and in the future.[9]

Frank has experienced this kind of transformation. "AA has changed my attitude towards everything about life, including money," he says. "When I was drinking, I was always scared to death that I wouldn't have enough money. And I never gave money anywhere. Never. I could never give money because I was always scared to death."

When Frank started attending AA regularly, he remembers his sponsor challenging him to think differently about money. "When I'm broke, I mean just *broke*, what I need to do is take 10 percent of my income and save it for myself and take 10 percent of my income and give it away. And so I decided to try, because he'd been around 20-some years and I had begun to learn by then that how I lived my life didn't work very well and it seemed to work better the other way. And I started giving away some and saving some, with 10 percent both places being a goal. And I've discovered that as I've given away more, I somehow seem to have more. So yeah, it's changed my attitude. I give more money to the hungry and all that."

Another woman experienced a similar transformation. Being in a twelve-step group had made it possible for her to do volunteer work at a shelter in the inner city. "If you don't love yourself," she explained, "it's pretty hard to love your neighbor. And I think that's a lot of what's going on in the group. So, yeah, I'm able to be more open and to reach out more because of that work and other work."

In many cases, the transformation is much more subtle. Being in a small group has an almost indiscernible influence. Studies of volunteers in other settings, for example, show that they struggle deeply with their motives, wondering whether they are doing the right thing, whether they have the time and talents, and so on.[10] All these worries can become a real hindrance to getting out and doing something. One reason small groups encourage community involvement, therefore, is that they prompt people to quit thinking and start acting.

Sometimes they do this by pressing people for a decision. Sometimes they supply words that resolve some of the questioning in which people are engaged. Sometimes they merely up the ante, so to speak, saying, yes, you may not have time, but this is really urgent. For instance, Karen told how she had decided to become a "Pal" (like a big sister) for the Pioneer Girls organization at her church. "Lizzy," she said, "is in charge of getting the Pals and she comes to Bible study, I guess more often than not. I had read about it in the church newsletter and I thought I would really like to do that. But I was afraid of overcommitting because I was committing to the choir, too. It was like 'Wow, how can I get involved in all these things?' So I wanted to be careful I didn't get involved in too much stuff. I thought, well, a Pal is really not that big a responsibility. Maybe I'll do it. But then I think subconsciously I said no, I don't think I will do it, because I was afraid I wouldn't be a good one. That perfectionist in me says either do it all or don't do it at all. And then when Lizzy brought it up as a real need at the Bible study, I thought well, if it's really a need, I'm not going to not do it for that reason."

How typical are these experiences? In addition to the data from our own survey, we can demonstrate that small-group participation is conducive to volunteer service by considering evidence obtained in a major national study of volunteerism. In 1988, Independent Sector, Inc., the national consortium in Washington, D.C., that represents nearly all large nonprofit organizations in the United States, commissioned the Gallup Organization to conduct a survey of the American public to examine in detail the kinds of voluntary activities in which people were engaged. This study was one of the most exhaustive surveys ever done on this topic.[11]

Unfortunately, this survey asked only a few questions about religion and none about participation in small groups. Several years after results of the study had been published, though, I discovered something about it that had never been revealed. Like so many surveys, this one had included questions paid for by other sponsors. As it turned out, one of those sponsors had asked a number of questions about religion, including one on small groups. By obtaining the original data from both sponsors, I was thus able to match the identification numbers of individuals in the two in order to see how these individuals' participation in small groups was related to their volunteer activity.[12]

Out of approximately 2,000 people surveyed, 21 percent said that in the last two years they had attended a "prayer group, Bible study, or other religious group which meets somewhere other than a church." About half this number said they had done so regularly, and half had participated only occasionally. The study makes it possible, therefore, to compare regular participants in this kind of group, occasional participants, and those who had not participated.

One question indicating the differences among these three groups asked people how important "giving time through volunteer work to charitable and religious organizations" was to them as a personal goal. Of the regular participants in small religious groups, 65 percent said this goal was "absolutely essential" or "very important." In comparison, 51 percent of the occasional participants gave the same responses, whereas only 29 percent of those who had not participated in small groups gave these responses.

The importance of giving money to charitable causes seemed to be related to small-group participation in the same way as the priority people attached to donating their time. Seventy-five percent of the regular participants in small groups, for example, said it was absolutely essential or very important to them to "make contributions to charities, institutions, religious organizations or causes you agree with." In comparison, 60 percent of the occasional participants in small groups gave the same responses, as did only 42 percent of those who had not participated in small groups.

These differences could be attributable to the fact that both statements included something about religion. It would not be surprising if people involved in religious small groups also valued giving time and money to religious causes. Another statement showed clearly that religious commitment differed sharply between those in these groups and those not involved: 92 percent of the regular participants and 87 percent of the occasional participants said "making a strong commitment to your religion or spiritual life" was absolutely essential or very important, compared with only 55 percent of those not in small groups.

We can easily get beyond this objection, though, by looking at the survey questions asking about volunteer efforts actually donated to organizations. The survey presented respondents with a list of 10 different kinds of volunteer organizations, plus a category of "multi-purpose human welfare" agencies and one for volunteer activities done "informally or alone." This list made it possible to see if participants in small groups donated time only to religious organizations or to other community agencies as well.

As expected, group participants were more likely than nonparticipants to donate time to religious organizations. By a margin of 56 percent to 14 percent, regular participants in small groups were more likely to have done volunteer work in a religious organization during the past twelve months than were people not involved in small groups, and occasional participants scored in between (31 percent had donated time).

On all the other items, regular participants in religious small groups also were more likely to have done volunteer work than were nonparticipants in these groups. This pattern was true for volunteer work donated to educational organizations, health organizations, social service and welfare organizations, civic associations, recreational organizations, arts and cultural organizations, work-related organizations, political organizations, and multipurpose human welfare organizations, and volunteer work done informally or alone. Occasional participants in small groups were also more likely to have done volunteer work in all these kinds of organizations than people not in small groups. And (with a few exceptions), regular participants were also more likely to be involved in volunteer work than occasional participants.

But what about being in a small group encourages people to be more active in community organizations and charitable work? Some might argue that certain kinds of people become involved in both. For example, women have often provided the backbone of America's volunteer efforts, and as they are also somewhat more likely to be involved in small groups than men, perhaps the connection between volunteerism and small groups is just an artifact of gender differences. Similar arguments might be made about differences attributable to age, social class, or region of the country. A statistical examination of the effects of these other factors, however, showed that none of them explained away or reduced the relationship between being in a small group and doing volunteer work.

If the key factor is being in a religiously oriented small group, though, what about this participation encourages people to become involved in other kinds of community service? Any of the following are among the possibilities:

- People in groups have been raised with more religious and, therefore, caring values in the first place.
- People in small fellowship groups are exposed to needs and opportunities for volunteer service because they belong to churches.
- People in small fellowship groups take their faith more seriously, so they are more interested in serving others.
- People in small fellowship groups are more doctrinally committed to Jesus and therefore try to follow his example of loving others.
- People in small fellowship groups have experienced God's love more deeply, so desire to show this love to others.
- People in small fellowship groups come into contact with other people, are more people-oriented, and learn about opportunities to serve in other ways.

With the survey data we have just been considering, we can go part of the way toward sorting out these various possibilities. We can do so by examining the relationships between volunteer work and various measures of religious commitment. We can also compare these relationships for different kinds of volunteer work and for different religious groups. Our strategy is to see which measures of religious commitment, including participation in small fellowship groups, help us to distinguish most clearly between those who become involved in volunteer work and those who are not involved.

The first thing we learn from this statistical sleuthing is that small group participation does make a difference and that it makes more of a difference than any other measure of religious commitment. To be precise, participation distinguishes between volunteers and nonvolunteers better than any of the following: how important religion was to people as they were growing up, how often they attended religious services while growing up, how important religion is to them now, whether they believe Jesus is God, whether they feel they have committed their lives to Jesus, whether they are a church member, how often they attend religious services, whether they pray, and whether they have had a deep religious experience. For example, when predicting whether people will do volunteer work for social service and welfare organizations, being in a small fellowship group predicts about twice as strongly as any of these other factors.

Second, we learn that early childhood religious training is also important. One of the significant reasons why people do volunteer work as adults is that they attended religious services while they were growing up. And, of course, people in small fellowship groups were also more likely to have attended religious services as children. So some—but by no means all—of why small fellowship groups are conducive to community service is that these people were already conditioned as children to hold religious values and to care for other people. It does appear, however, that the critical factor is having attended religious services, not simply having come early to the view that religious values are important. People's recollections of how important religion was to them as children, at least, are not significantly related to whether they are now involved in volunteer work.

Third, people in small fellowship groups do not seem to be involved in community service simply because they are joiners or because they hear about service opportunities through their churches. If that were the case, church membership and church attendance would be good predictors of volunteer involvement. But they are relatively weak predictors.

Fourth, small-group participants do not seem to be more involved in community service because they take their faith more seriously than other people. Neither the importance that people attach to having a deep religious faith nor the fact that they pray helps us to distinguish between those involved in volunteer work and those not involved.

Fifth, commitments to specific doctrines about Jesus also do not seem to explain why small-group participants become involved in community service. Neither the belief that Jesus was God rather than merely a human leader nor feeling that one has committed one's life to Jesus helps separate people who are involved in community service from those who are not involved.

Sixth, it does appear, however, that having had some kind of profound religious experience or spiritual awakening is a major reason why people in small groups become involved in community service. What probably is happening, judging from the comments of people we talked to, is that a spiritual awakening made them think more deeply about the meaning of life and their reasons for living. Having had such an experience scored second only to being in a small group as a predictor of involvement in social service and welfare organizations, and it was even slightly better than small-group participation as a predictor of informal volunteer effort.

Finally, this last finding also helps us understand something about the special role of small groups. If we want to know why people go out on their own, informally, to help others, it helps to know that they have had a personal religious awakening. But if we want to know why that interest in helping other people takes the form of an organized activity, such as a social service organization, it helps more to know that someone was also in a small group. In other words, individual religious awakenings lead to individual caring activities; group participation leads to more organized efforts.

For religious leaders, these results have mixed implications. If the goal of small groups is to nurture spirituality, then religious leaders need to be concerned about the doctrinal content of these gatherings. They should encourage group members to understand the Bible and teachings about the divinity of Jesus, for example, whether these teachings happen to encourage volunteering or not. If the goal, however, is mainly to promote service to the wider community, doctrine appears less important. Religious awakenings and getting people involved in a small group appear to be all that matter. The fact that many small-group members do not seem to be gaining a very deep understanding of their spirituality may seem less important, therefore, because these people are at least learning to love their neighbors. Judging from some of the results presented in previous chapters, the two goals also may work at cross-purposes in some groups. Most religious groups seem to be able to cultivate spirituality and encourage volunteer activities in the community. But some that focus heavily on one or the other of these goals may find it hard to accomplish the other. Above all, religious leaders who want church members to become more active, not only in their churches but in serving the wider community, should recognize that small groups can be a valuable vehicle for accomplishing these aims.

For readers interested in understanding the social significance of the small-group movement, the implication of these results is relatively straightforward. Small groups have an overall positive effect on involvement in wider community activities. Despite the fact that most small groups, as we have seen, focus on the emotional needs and interests of their members, they nevertheless nudge people to become involved in helping friends and neighbors who are not members of their group and to play an active role in voluntary agencies. Critics can still argue that these groups promote a self-help ideology that expects social betterment to come about through volunteerism and individual initiative rather than supporting major changes in social structure or reform programs initiated by government. Nevertheless, the critics who charge that small groups are engaged only in a narcissistic obsession with their members' own feelings appear to be wrong. Small groups are strengthening community attachments rather than encouraging their members to focus only on themselves.

SERVICE TO AND THROUGH THE CHURCH

The Independent Sector survey also sheds some additional light on the kinds of activities small-group members are likely to be involved with in their churches. We saw in that survey that 56 percent of the people who were regular participants in small fellowship groups had donated time to religious organizations (probably their churches) in the past year, compared to only 14 percent of the people who had not participated in fellowship groups. Those 56 percent were then asked what kinds of things they had done. These responses show that the most common activities in which members of small fellowship groups are engaged are as follows (the figures in parentheses are the percentages of regular group participants who had done each activity within the past 12 months):

- Teaching Sunday school classes (26 percent).
- Assisting the clergy (18 percent).
- Serving on boards or committees (13 percent).
- Deacons (9 percent).
- Fund raising (6 percent).
- Cleaning (6 percent).
- Choir (5 percent).
- Church ushering (5 percent).
- Parish visitation (4 percent).
- Nursery and babysitting (4 percent).

These are all supportive activities that contribute not only to the church but to its ability to serve the wider community. These findings underscore what we have already observed in previous chapters about the relationship between small-group participation and involvement in other church programs. Small-group members are clearly one of the main resources on which churches are able to draw in meeting the needs of their communities.

Some caveats, however, should be kept in mind by any religious leaders who may attempt to develop small groups in a deliberate effort to enhance their programs and church finances. One is that increased involvement in church programs and increased giving are restricted largely to small-group members who are already actively involved in their churches. There is little evidence from our study that small groups by themselves are an effective way of mobilizing dormant members. Another caveat is that small groups seem to heighten involvement and giving among religious conservatives better than among religious liberals. Because liberal churches already have been losing members relative to conservative churches, they may have to work harder at developing small-group programs to stay even. (In the next section, we consider the political implications of these differences between religious conservatives and liberals.) Finally, the possibility that group involvement may lead people away from the churches must also be considered. If interests in volunteer work and political activity are stimulated by some of these groups and at the same time levels of anticlericalism and religious privatism remain high, some small-group members undoubtedly will leave the churches for other endeavors.

It is also worth considering carefully the implications of these results for church growth. Because our study was conducted at only one point in time, it is impossible to say anything directly about the role of small groups in fostering church growth. A recent study by Daniel V. A. Olsen, however, suggests the importance of raising some critical questions about the long-term effectiveness of small groups as a church growth strategy.[13] In studying more than 700 attenders of Baptist congregations, Olsen found that the cultivation of friendships in these congregations seemed to work against church growth. The reason was that church members reached a "saturation level" beyond which they found it difficult to incorporate larger numbers of people into their friendship networks. They had, as it were, enough friends already. Newcomers found it difficult to feel at home in these churches.

Small groups, as we have seen, promote having more friends in one's congregation. Judging from Olsen's research, this fact may have negative implications for long-term church growth. Starting from ground zero, small groups may overcome anonymity and build friendships that make the congregation a more vibrant community. But it may be difficult to promote small groups after the point at which people feel they already have enough friends. Some pastors to whom we spoke seemed to agree with this assessment, noting from their own experience that it had become more difficult after a time to expand the number of small groups in their churches.

An alternative possibility, however, is also worth entertaining. Small groups may be the solution to the kind of cliquishness that Olsen observed. If long-term members already have friends to spare, then intentionally forming groups in which newcomers can meet fellow newcomers may be a useful strategy. This possibility, of course, presupposes that a decent supply of newcomers is already at hand. Whatever the situation, then, small-group programs clearly must be tailored to the needs of particular congregations, rather than being assumed to provide an effective strategy for church growth in all contexts.

These last observations do not mean that church growth strategists should abandon small groups as a means of revitalizing the churches. They do suggest, however, that religious leaders need to think carefully about the limits of small groups. To date, the small-group movement has enjoyed considerable success in encouraging greater involvement in religious organizations. A next round of efforts by religious leaders, nevertheless, may need to be different. Greater attention than before may be needed to encourage group members to branch out and become involved in community activities rather than becoming ingrown. New kinds of groups may be needed to attract dormant church members. If there is a saturation point, other ministries besides small groups may be needed to elicit the participation and nurture the spirituality of those who are not interested in small groups.

HOW SOCIAL ATTITUDES ARE SHAPED IN GROUPS

In the groups we studied, social and political issues frequently came up, not so much as formal topics for discussion, but informally—for example, during dessert or in the course of book discussions, Bible studies, or prayer requests. Most of the people we talked to in person, however, said their own views were not changed as a result. They found it interesting to hear that some people were in favor of strong military action and others were against it, for instance, but just concluded that people had a right to hold different opinions. Where small groups clearly make a difference is not so much in changing opinions as in reinforcing ones that are deeply rooted in a person's lifestyle.

Donna's descriptions of her group made it clear that one of the common bonds, perhaps as basic as anything else, was the conviction that staying home to raise your children is important and that you shouldn't feel bad about yourself if you didn't have a career. "I think a lot of women in there feel like they are not looked up to because they chose to stay home with their children. That lots of times a career woman will kind of say, 'Oh, that's all you do? Isn't that boring?' It kind of makes you feel like you're not as good as they are because *they* have a career and you might not. Now there's been talk of that because that happens from time to time if you go to a party or you're in a different mixing of people that you run up against all different kinds of people who have all different kinds of views. I would say that people in there highly value the time they spend with their children during the day. That they would not trade that. That they feel like, and it's one of my opinions too (slight laugh), I'm a little bit opinionated in that, that I would not let somebody else— I would do just about anything to *not* let somebody else raise my kids in a day care situation, that I want to be the primary care giver. I think a lot of them would think that way. Because that's been discussed."

In John's group, discussions of current events are common because the group's purpose is to relate their faith to all areas of their lives. For example, "when Kuwait was invaded, and the leaders met in September and said, over the next six months, what are the issues we're going to discuss? Are we going to discuss a book of the Bible or are we going to discuss a topic? One of the things they said is we need to discuss the Persian Gulf war and what does that mean. And so that we discuss those issues. I know a person in the class who wants to discuss the New Age movement, what does that mean? And our relationship to it and what our personal response should be, as we touch it in our lives, what should that mean. So that we discuss politics, philosophy, economics, war."

In other groups, political topics generally were dealt with in a more casual manner. It was not so much that anyone said, "What do we all think about abortion?" It was more that people expressed their views in an offhand manner. Sometimes it was an admiring comment about a particular author or public figure. Sometimes it was just a piece of information, cited authoritatively, that let the rest of the group know some person or point of view was legitimate.

Karen gave the following example. "Sometimes issues will come up, like the school, the educational system. When it's voting time sometimes. If it's on 'Focus on the Family,' if there's something political in there, sometimes that'll be mentioned in the group. Dr. [James] Dobson's a great political activist. He runs a program, 'Focus on the Family,' on the Christian radio station. It's on many Christian radio stations; it's on ours in this area."

The small group functioned, in her case, in exactly the way that communication specialists have long suggested such groups might. Mass communication, like Dobson's radio program, reach wide audiences, but seldom have any impact by themselves. The reason is that individuals are bombarded with too much information of this kind. According to the "two-step" theory of communication, such information becomes effective when it is reinforced by people you know personally.[14] For Karen, the small group brought Dobson's program to her attention and gave her an opportunity to discuss Dobson's ideas with other like-minded individuals.

Like-mindedness is often the key. Group members, as we have seen, typically pride themselves on their tolerance of diversity. And yet there may be certain issues on which everyone thinks alike. In many of the church-sponsored groups, it is simply assumed that religious faith and church-going are good things. Consensus also prevails in many groups on the value of self-help. People should take responsibility for them-selves, and, with a little help from their friends, get by. They should not look to government programs for assistance. Nor should anyone pay much attention to significant differences in economic resources or in opportunities to get ahead. Many groups also take for granted that sharing the intimate details of one's feelings and being guided by these feelings are positive values. These issues do not have to be dis-cussed at length. When they come up, everyone just nods knowingly. The impression is strong: This is an issue about which we all agree.

Karen again provided a vivid example. "Sometimes we talk about the education system and that's very key to us since our children are beginning to reach that age. There's a lot of talk about home school-ing your children or sending them to Christian schools, as opposed to the public schools, things like that. The abortion issue is not really dis-cussed so much because we all agree. There's just really nothing to dis-cuss other than sadness about what's happening." Elaborating, she observes: "I don't think there'd be a single person there that wouldn't be prolife."

Does this example suggest that the small-group movement may be a significant political force in our society? It would be rash to general-ize from this one case. Certainly small groups differ in their political orientations. As we have seen, many group members say their interest in peace and social justice has increased, and these issues are generally considered liberal issues, unlike the antiabortion issue about which Karen's group was so unified. Nevertheless, there is some reason to believe that small groups, on balance, reinforce conservative political orientations in our society more than liberal political perspectives.

One reason for believing this is the evidence we have considered in previous chapters about the religious orientations of group members. As we have seen, many more group members claim to hold conserva-tive religious orientations than liberal orientations. Furthermore, the most active group members tend to believe in the literal inspiration and inerrancy of the Bible, and group processes in many Bible study and prayer fellowships seem to reinforce these beliefs. The relevance of this for politics is that many studies in recent years have found strong relationships between religious conservatism, including biblical literalism, and politically conservative orientations such as opposition to abortion, to pornography, to homosexuality, and to other policies such as weapons reduction proposals or initiatives to bolster welfare programs.[15]

More to the point, our own survey also shows that group members are likely to define their political views much in the same way they do their religious orientations. Among members who describe themselves as religious conservatives, for example, 79 percent also describe themselves as political conservatives. In contrast, only 21 percent of those who say they are religious liberals describe themselves as political conservatives. Furthermore, members who say their group is very important to them and who attend regularly are more likely to list themselves as political conservatives than members who are less involved. Members of church-based groups are also more likely to be political conservatives than are members of nonchurch groups.

If tacit agreement is indeed a significant way in which political beliefs are reinforced, then it is also important that many more individuals say they are members of groups in which political conservatism is the norm than say they belong to politically liberal groups. Among all group members, 22 percent say they belong to the former, compared to only 7 percent who say they belong to the latter. The survey also suggests that there is a stronger overlap between religious conservatism and being in a politically conservative group than there is among liberals. Among religious conservatives, for example, 37 percent say they are in a group composed mostly of political conservatives, whereas among religious liberals, only 16 percent say their group is composed mostly of political liberals.

In pointing out these patterns in the survey, my intention is neither to decry nor applaud them. It is simply to suggest that, for better or worse, small groups in our society probably are not entirely neutral on political matters. The "for better" implication is that de Tocqueville was probably right when he suggested that voluntary groups strengthen democracy by making people more interested in their civic responsibilities. At a time when worries are being widely expressed about citizens withdrawing from participation in public life, any activity that actually encourages greater interest in public issues may be a healthy sign.[16] Certainly there has been much evidence in recent years of the role of house churches, base communities, and other spiritually oriented cell groups in fostering democratic movements in Eastern Europe and in Latin America.[17] The "for worse" side of the equation is negative, of course, only for those who may not be in a position to voice their views as effectively as others. Political liberals, it appears, are clearly at a disadvantage relative to political conservatives in being able to draw on the small-group movement to mobilize sentiment and political involvement. But, as we have also seen, small groups are widely democratic in the sense of being distributed broadly throughout the major sectors of society. It takes resources to run them, but the resources are relatively small and certainly not the monopoly of any social segment. Blacks and Hispanics, for example, have been quite active in organizing small groups, just as White Anglos have been. Political and religious liberals probably could use small groups to greater advantage than they have to date. It is also possible to join groups, or to start ones, that explicitly rule politics out of order.

The danger that many observers of our society have emphasized is that politics divides religion, and religion divides politics, when the two are brought together. In other words, political conflict over an issue such as abortion can make it harder for religious communities to unite people of all different ideological persuasions. That danger is less likely to exist in small groups, especially when such groups are composed entirely of political conservatives or of political liberals. But small groups, divided into like-minded ideological camps, can make it harder for larger communities, such as congregations, to function amicably.

What mitigates these divisive tendencies in small groups is partly the fact that a majority of them bring together people of various political orientations. In addition, if their survey responses can be trusted, people in small groups overwhelmingly claim, as we have seen in previous chapters, that disagreements with other members have been minor and that their understanding of people with different views has grown.

Increasingly, the goal of small groups also appears to include promoting such understanding explicitly. In a world torn by political, racial, ethnic, and religious conflicts, small groups perhaps can become a staging ground for seeking reconciliation. One man, a national leader in the small-group movement, articulated this goal clearly when he remarked: "Coming out of the various small-group movements, not just in the church but outside the church, is a *surfacing* of some common values." Small groups, he believed, might be one place "where the American public could again really agree about *something*." Using words that sounded remarkably similar to those of de Tocqueville a century and a half ago, he added: "Democracy, as many people have been arguing, depends upon some kind of consensus about the good, or at least on some notion of how we're going to compromise when we don't agree about the good. We are so individualistic that we have the potential of imploding. I'm not horriblizing, I'm just saying what I really think is the problem. And one of the possible ways of dealing with that is through these common experiences. They might lead us at least to be part of the process. That's the big dream!'"

REPRODUCING THE SMALL-GROUP MOVEMENT

If small groups are having an impact on the wider society in the ways we have considered, we must ask whether the members of these groups are doing anything to perpetuate the small-group movement. It could be, for instance, that the impact of groups on members' lives and on the wider community is substantial at the moment but that little is being done to ensure the long-term survival of the broader movement. Alternatively, there may already be mechanisms in place to ensure not only the survival, but the growth, of this movement.

In previous chapters we have already seen some of the mechanisms that are likely to keep the small-group movement alive. Churches and other religious organizations are fully behind such groups, at least for the time being. They are providing meeting space, study guides, information networks, and other resources. Beyond the churches, self-help clearinghouses are spreading the word about the locations and purposes of groups. Seminars at the national and regional levels for training leaders have been launched with increasing frequency in recent years.

All this, ironically, could backfire. As we saw in chapter 5, the less structure the better, as far as member satisfaction is concerned. Too many planners, leaders, and experts could turn the small-group movement into a bureaucracy much like large corporations, large churches, and large government agencies. Nothing would be as likely to dampen enthusiasm at the grass-roots level as this development. The question that must be asked, therefore, is whether anything is happening at the grass-roots level to perpetuate the small-group movement.

From what we have been able to learn from our survey, the answer is clearly yes. Group members are spreading the word to their friends, inviting people they know to attend their groups, and getting new members to join. In the survey, for example, 78 percent of all current members said they had "discussed the group with friends who were not involved in it." Seventy percent said they had "invited a friend to attend the group." Fifty-seven percent said they had "had a friend, who was not a regular participant, visit the group." And 44 percent said they had "been responsible for someone new joining the group." In addition, one member in nine had helped start a new group. All of these activities help in recruiting new members and in ensuring the continuity of small groups.

Further analysis of these results indicates that long-term members are more likely than other members to have done all these things. In other words, members do not seem to turn increasingly inward the longer they belong to their groups; instead, they experience more opportunities to invite their friends and draw new people into their groups. In addition, members seem equally likely to engage in these activities whether their group is part of a larger religious organization or whether it lacks such sponsorship.

The survey also suggests that small groups extend naturally into family settings, just as they do into friendship networks. For instance, 48 percent of all members say they have attended their group regularly with their spouse or with some other family member. About the same proportion (45 percent) say they have been encouraged by a family member to attend the group. Four members in 10 say they have taken a family member who was not a regular participant along with them to the group. In contrast, only 12 percent say they have had disagreements with a family member about whether they should attend the group.

These responses mean two things. First, informal friendship networks and family ties are being used to reproduce the memberships of small groups. That is, new people are being invited and encouraged to join. As current members move away, die, or perhaps lose interest, new members thus will be present to carry on the activities of small groups. Indeed, this had been the experience of many of the groups we studied in depth. Some of them were as large and as active as they had been five or ten years earlier, even though most of their original members were no longer present. Second, these same responses indicate, again, that small groups are not an insular phenomenon in our society. Group members do not attend meetings by themselves and then never talk about these meetings. Were that the case, the broader social impact of small groups would certainly be diminished. Instead, most group members talk about their groups in other social contexts and bring people from these contexts to visit their groups.

These findings bring us full circle to something we considered in chapter 2. There, we saw that small groups are distributed fairly evenly across all segments of the American population—rich and poor, black and white, men and women, South and North, and so on. That pattern suggested a strong potential for these groups to influence the wider society. The 10 people who might be in a group in one neighborhood could influence the 15 people who might not be in a group. We see now that this potential is quite real. As long as group members keep inviting their friends, the small-group movement seems likely to remain a vital feature of American society.

But the movement is, as I have argued, also at a crossroads. If it currently encourages its members to take part in wider community activities, it is nevertheless faced with pressures that may discourage it from doing so in the future. These pressures include the activities that make small groups desirable and that perpetuate them: focusing a great deal of their attention on the emotional needs of members, emphasizing that each individual is ultimately responsible for resolving his or her own problems, nurturing a concept of the sacred that emphasizes what God can do for the individual, and encouraging members to draw their friends and family into the shelter of their groups. As the movement ponders its future, it must at least recognize that the continuing involvement of its members in other public affairs will require deliberate attention. An ethic of caring that extends beyond the group must be cultivated, issues of peace and justice must be kept on the agenda, and a spirituality of sacrifice will need to be brought into juxtaposition with conceptions of personal gratification.

Movement leaders and observers of the movement must also be clear about the kind of community participation it encourages. At present, membership in small groups appears to go hand in hand with taking a more active role in one's church and with volunteering in other community agencies. A spirit of volunteerism and an emphasis on individual caring are the themes that unite these various forms of participation. Individuals are thereby encouraged to think about others and to temper their own selfish interests by considering needs in the wider community. In the process, however, the individualism that worries many critics of our society may not be very much modified. Voluntary service can still be performed with minimal commitments of time and energy, it can focus chiefly on the church or school programs that primarily benefit one's own children, and it can be engaged in for reasons of career advancement or for personal gratification alone. Small groups are places where the nature of these commitments and motivations can receive thorough examination. Only by focusing explicit attention on the character of community and on the needs of the wider society are small groups likely to realize their potential for creating a genuine sense of community.

12

ENVOI

The Shared Journey, Spirituality, and the Social Role of American Religion

In this concluding chapter, I want to draw together a number of the conclusions that have emerged in previous chapters and return to the issues of community and spirituality that I raised at the outset. I also want to present a more personal assessment of the small-group movement. I am prompted to do so by a recent encounter with someone who had read one of my previous books. "The frustrating thing for me," he admitted, "was that you kept your 'scientific objectivity' throughout the book. By the time I got to the last chapter, I was hoping to find out what you *really* thought!" Well, what do I really think about small groups? What are their strengths? Their weaknesses? Would I want to be in one myself? Would I encourage my friends to join them?

These are important questions. In trying to answer them, I am mindful of the fact that individuals differ enormously in their needs and interests, in how much support they already have, in their attitudes about spirituality, and in the amount of time they have to devote to new activities. When I was a college student, I had both the time and the need for small groups, and my participation in them during those years contributed greatly to my capacity to get on with life and to discover more deeply who I was. In midlife, faced with tremendous time pressures and wanting to spend as much time as I can with my wife and children and with close friends, I do not feel as much of a

341

need to participate in a small group. I can imagine myself becoming quite actively involved in them at some point in the future. That being the case, there are nevertheless some generalizations worth considering.

The result of conducting research on small groups has been largely to reinforce my feelings about their importance, both for the specific individuals who are a part of them and for American society as a whole. Perhaps this is a natural consequence of spending several years of one's life studying anything. But most of the findings I have discussed in previous chapters point toward the overall significance of small groups, and there are certainly positive consequences to be emphasized as well. Consider some of these points again.

1. Forty percent of the American public is currently involved in some kind of small group. For those of us who look around and take our cues from others (don't we all do this?), it is easy to conclude that something important must be happening if this many people are involved. Some readers may of course disagree that this is a significant proportion of the population. I was surprised, however, that the figure is this high. The standard theories had led me to believe either that Americans were so individualistic that they would not be interested in being involved or that other forms of community were still strong enough that there would be no need for people to join these groups. For this reason alone, the fact that so many people are involved seems striking. Clearly, based on membership figures alone, the small-group movement has become a profoundly important phenomenon in American society. Millions of people are meeting regularly with small groups of like-minded individuals to find caring and support. Whether we are involved ourselves or whether we are critical bystanders, we must reckon with this movement if we are to understand the present character of our society.

2. The people who are involved in small groups are not terribly different from those who are not involved. That is, small-group members come from all walks of life and from all segments of American society. They include men and women, older people and younger people, people of different incomes, and people from different racial, ethnic, and religious backgrounds. Their members are involved because of an interest in religion, or because someone invited them, or because they heard about a group at church, or because they wanted friends, or because they were already well integrated in their neighborhoods. They want help with emotional problems or loneliness or their spiritu-

al life. But they are not some exceptional (weird) fringe of the population with whom the average person would not want to—or could
not—identify. Their members are quite normal, quite average, and the
fact that they are involved in support groups has become quite common as well.

3. Small groups in American society are enormously diverse. They
focus on different issues, follow different formats, vary in how they are
organized, and draw together people from a wide variety of backgrounds. Some groups are intensely religious, others are not. Some
groups are for women only, some are for men only, and some aim
explicitly to include both men and women. Some are highly structured, others are free-form. They are able to draw such a large segment
of the American population because they cater to the diverse interests,
needs, and lifestyles of the public. For most potential participants this
fact would probably be regarded as a plus. Speaking for myself, if I had
to spend my only free evening a week in "fellowship" with a group of
stodgy social scientists, I might decide I'd rather take hemlock. If I
knew I could mix with some people in my community who were interested in peace and social justice, I would be much happier. If I knew I
could move on to something else when my interests changed, I would
be that much happier as well. In short, the variety of small groups,
coupled with the ease of moving into and out of them, enhances their
appeal. We are, after all, a mobile society, not only in the ways we
move ourselves around, but also in the ways in which our interests and
orientations adapt to new situations. Small groups allow us to find
something suitable to our tastes at a given moment and then to move
on when our interests change.

4. At the same time, small groups are fairly stable and are taken
quite seriously by most of their members. To be sure, they are fluid
and diverse, but they are not one-night stands. People participate in
them for long periods of time, often for as long as five years. Most participants meet regularly—weekly, biweekly, or monthly, generally for
several hours at a time. They develop long-lasting friendships in these
groups. They disclose their personal lives to each other and they discuss their basic values. For people seeking community, small groups
are thus a way of finding some genuine caring and companionship. For
me, this, too, is an attractive feature. I recognize, on the one hand,
that my own interests change; so it is comforting to know I could
move from group to group. But, on the other hand, if I felt that every
group I joined was going to be like a revolving door, I'd have second

thoughts. I'd hope people there would stay for a while. How else could I get to know them? It isn't easy making new friends. If I made the effort of joining a group, I'd probably want to stay around a while. I'd feel better knowing others were deeply committed to the group, too. This, again, was a result that surprised me. I assumed that small groups might be quite ephemeral. The fact that they are not suggests to me that they are more deeply planted in the social landscape than their critics may have assumed.

5. Small groups provide encouragement and a wide variety of other services to most of their members. People who participate regularly say they are highly satisfied with their groups, and they give them especially high marks for providing encouragement, for allowing them to discuss their ideas openly, for accepting different points of view, and for cultivating trust among their members. In a society characterized by norms of achievement, and thus by prevailing feelings of inadequacy, this reassurance certainly is one of the features that makes small groups attractive. To be sure, they do not provide the deepest support conceivable and they do not substitute for other agencies or insurance plans or services. But they do a good job of providing emotional support. I wouldn't expect them to clean my gutters if I were too busy to do it myself. But I'd certainly vote for anything that I could count on regularly to tell me I'm okay, that I'm a member of the human race, that we all have certain fears and doubts, and that we don't have to bear these alone. I recognize, of course, that some of this encouragement can be superficial. For many people, it might seem odd to join a group with the explicit aim of gaining some support. Yet, as one group member remarked, the feelings turn out to be pretty much the same, whether one seeks them out or they just happen.

6. It does not take a great deal of special knowledge or skill to make a small group function well. However, you would never guess this by reading the huge stacks of how-to books on small groups. These books make it sound like only a well-trained leader could make a group function smoothly. There is some truth to this view. Groups can be badly misled. They can certainly fall apart from mismanagement. Yet the important finding is that caring and informal friendships are the key to an effective group, not following some elaborate management plan. In my view, that is good news. Frankly, I get enough administrative structure in my work life. I have to know all sorts of things that the average person cares nothing about to do my job. I wouldn't want to be in a small group that depended on all that. It makes me feel better about

them to know that they work well mainly in spite of such structures rather than because of them. Indeed, the secret to the movement's success is that it has emphasized smallness, informality, and first-hand personal relationships. Members, therefore, feel important; they can take pride in their groups, experience a sense of ownership, and gain satisfaction when the group functions well.

7. Small groups do not, for the most part, compromise the individuality of their members. We saw, for example, that there are strong norms of tolerance in most groups and that people work out an informal contract with their groups that allows them to be who they are, to talk about their own needs and interests, and to receive personal affirmation. Some people, of course, want a group that will tell them how to live. I probably am not atypical, though, in asserting candidly that I don't. I want the freedom to be myself. I want to state my own views and still feel I'll be accepted. To be honest, I've got to be getting something out of the group, too. Otherwise, it's hard to maintain my commitment. Admittedly, the desire for individual autonomy of this kind has been the subject of much criticism in the academic literature of late. It is a desire that needs to be kept in check. Yet it does seem to me that small groups are successful and that they are better able to meet the needs of their members because they respect individual autonomy. They are, in this sense, thoroughly American. They are widely attractive because they fit well with the emphasis on individualism that has been so prominent in American culture.

8. Many small-group members feel spiritually nurtured by their groups. They have been drawn to attend in the first place because they wanted to be more disciplined in their spiritual lives. They perhaps grew up in a religious tradition, and now, as adults, feel the need for some group with whom they can discuss their religious values. As a result of their participation, they feel closer to God, better able to pray, more interested in reading the Bible or other religious texts, and more confident that they are acting according to spiritual principles that emphasize love, forgiveness, humility, and self-acceptance. Again, not everyone has a deep need to grow spiritually; some people may have no interest in spirituality at all. But so many people in our society do have this need that I find myself feeling positive toward groups that seem, in some way, to be meeting this need. Besides, spirituality can be defined quite broadly and the wide variety of small groups that claim to foster spirituality make it possible to do so. I might not have an interest in learning the details of I Corinthians at the moment, but

learning about forgiveness, attaining some healing in my relationships, and achieving a better understanding of divine love or a deeper awareness of myself—some of those aims might be quite attractive. Whether one is religiously oriented or not, therefore, it is important to understand that the small-group movement has become a significant force in American religion.

9. Small groups make a difference to the spiritual lives of their members mostly by demonstrating love, by nurturing intimate relationships, and by giving people an opportunity to tell their stories. As an educator, I can understand why. I doubt very much that my students are fundamentally shaped by the lectures I give. They are more shaped by the experiences I help to facilitate—discussions of important issues, hearing one of their peers struggling with a new insight, or finding people on campus to use as role models. In this respect, small groups work a lot like families. I suppose I'd be less impressed with them if they depended only on leaders who knew all the answers or on the abstract knowledge gained from book learning. Much of what happens in small groups is, of course, not as intense or as basic as the socialization that occurs in families. But small groups do provide a context in which people can rethink themselves and their values. The stories they tell help them to do so. They piece together narratives that make sense of the changes they have experienced. Many small groups also encourage members to compare their own stories with the narratives available in sacred texts. In the process, they are inspired to lead better lives than they might otherwise lead. The sacred texts become real to them as they try to apply these stories to their lives.

10. The members of small groups are quite often prompted to become more active in their communities, to help others who may be in need, and to think more deeply about pressing social and political issues. These findings came as a surprise to me. I had expected small-group members to be turned inward, devoted to their own emotional needs to the point that they would have no time or interest in politics or civic affairs. I must admit that I would worry if I thought these groups caused people to focus only on their inner emotional needs or to spend their time only with members of their own groups. I would also worry if the evidence showed that these groups pulled people away from their families or caused divisions with their loved ones. But the evidence was largely favorable, suggesting that small groups may help to integrate people with their families or neighborhoods and to make them more aware of the wider society. In this sense, small groups

cultivate community, not only by encouraging people to share their thoughts and interests with a few other people within their groups, but also by linking group members with others in their neighborhoods and by motivating them to become more involved in volunteer agencies, in their churches and synagogues, and in broader social and political debates.

The preceding points are some of the reasons why the research results have led me to take a generally positive view of small groups. I should also say (hearing skeptical voices about to speak) that none of these conclusions was necessitated by the way I conducted my research. I did not start with an assumption that small groups would mostly have positive consequences. Indeed, I recognized from the outset that small-group members might bias the results by reporting more favorable experiences than might truly be the case. Thus, I devised all sorts of ways to build in comparisons and to do statistical tests, and I deliberately looked for (and asked my fellow researchers to look for) ways in which small groups might not be working so well.

Having mentioned many of the positive aspects of small groups, however, I would be remiss not to emphasize some of the ways in which these conclusions can be overstated. I hasten to do so, frankly, because there is an enormous amount of boosterism in the literature on small groups and among their leaders. Rather than simply adding to the chorus of rah-rah's, we need to recognize some of the limitations of small groups. One of these is that small groups can be regarded mistakenly as a panacea for all our needs. Another is that small groups can be harnessed too readily to the interests of church growth advocates. A related problem is that a "god of the group" mentality can emerge. Still another has to do with a pecking-order syndrome in groups. After considering each of these limitations, I will return to some thoughts about the larger significance of small groups for spirituality and for the well-being of our society.

PANACEA?

There are many reasons why people may turn to small groups to find community and why religious organizations may look to these groups to solve all their problems. If community is breaking down and if the family is no longer as reliable as it once was, then small groups can fill some of the gap. If Americans are becoming more reluctant to sit and listen to sermons in large church auditoriums, the home studies and prayer fellowships may be more attractive. Groups are adaptable to the more diverse interests that are present in most medium- to large-sized congregations. They can thus serve as little congregations within these larger multipurpose religious organizations. They perhaps can meet some of the needs that seem to have become a burden in our society as well. For example, support groups that help their members recover from alcoholism or other addictions contribute positively to the overall health of society. They are also a way for lay members to regain a sense of their own spiritual destiny rather than having it spoon-fed to them by a clergy they may no longer trust or admire. One pastor was quite frank about this advantage in comparison with the more traditional programs of his church: "Our Sunday school has been deteriorating for years. We have people visit, and then shy away because it doesn't suit their interests or it just doesn't work for them. The problem is usually the minister who has problems adjusting between participant and expert. Now, with the small groups, we have them set up as loosely as possible to fit all types of Christian interests."

But small groups are no panacea. They cannot solve all the problems of the churches, let alone of American society. Take the sad situation of most of our public schools today. What can small groups do? Certainly a group of men and women who meet on Wednesday evenings to study the Bible can become a crucible in which sentiment about the local schools is stirred up. Someone concerned about an issue coming before the next school board meeting can ask the group to pray about it. As the group prays, they become aware of the issue. Perhaps after the meeting they ask the concerned member how they can help. The Bible study helps mobilize people to attend the school board meeting. Still, that cannot be the whole story. The Bible study played a role because one member was already aware of the issue. The newspapers were important in communicating information about the issue. Other community organizations were important. Had the Bible study group been the only game in town, its members would have been insular, isolated from other issues. Other people were spending their spare time serving on the school board—perhaps so much of it that they had no time to be in a Bible study. To make a real difference, some people might have to run for political office or to campaign for a new slate of officials.

This example may be extreme. On just about any issue one might raise, however, the same arguments about the limitations of small groups can be made. A person has a serious problem with alcoholism?

Self-help groups may be part of the answer, but group meetings will not help much unless sponsors are on call day and night, and the help of physicians and therapists may also be sorely needed, as are laws regulating the sale and consumption of alcohol. Someone wants to grow spiritually? The Wednesday Bible study can be a time of growth and encouragement, but that person will have to spend time in prayer and devotional reading outside the group as well. Sermons, books, and personal advice from the clergy are likely to play a valuable role. People have lost their jobs? A small group can give them emotional support—something that may be badly needed when self-esteem is linked so closely to having a good job. A small group oriented particularly to job seeking can also provide professional advice. But small groups are scarcely the answer to unemployment in the society as a whole.

In my view, a balanced assessment of small groups requires careful consideration of what they can and cannot do. The concept of "mediating groups" that has been advanced by some social scientists seems like a particularly helpful way of sorting out these differences. Small groups mediate (stand in between) the individual, on the one hand, and the massive institutions of which our society is composed, on the other hand. They cannot substitute for what the individual must do. For example, they cannot tell the individual exactly what to do when faced with a tough moral decision. They can only provide guidance and encouragement. For all their help in overcoming loneliness and in providing friendship, small groups also cannot substitute for the private lives that people normally experience in families. At the other extreme, small groups cannot be expected to solve the problems of our nation's schools, eliminate poverty, provide jobs, tackle the national debt, or formulate foreign policy. On all these issues, small groups make a difference primarily by supporting individuals, by helping them lead their lives more effectively, and by nurturing individual-level contacts that may lead to action of some kind on a larger scale.

CHURCH GROWTH

Like so many things in life, one of the greatest virtues of small groups can also become one of their worst vices. Books and articles by the score have championed the small group as an effective method of reviving dead churches and making them grow into larger churches. This desire for expansion is only natural: believers over the centuries have felt it their mission to bring others into the church, and ambitious pastors with high career aspirations know that the way to succeed is by adding numbers to their ranks.[1] Small groups can be an attractive method for achieving that goal. As one pastor calculated, a congregation divided into small groups of six members each could easily double within five years, if each group added only one member a year.   As evidence that such hopes are not unfounded, discussions of small groups always get around sooner or later, as we have seen, to the example of Dr. Cho's church in South Korea. It grew to more than a half million members—all because of small groups. Every pastor seems to have a personal anecdote that proves the same point.

The problem is an inversion of means and ends. What is the ultimate goal? Caring and supportive communities in which people can grow spiritually as they experience the love of others? Or a successful megachurch that boosts its image in the community and its pastor's salary at the same time?[2]

In some cases these two goals may work together, hand in hand. Small groups energize people to carry out other valuable tasks being performed by a large church. And a large church makes it possible to give people a richer offering of small groups.

But conflict between these goals is also likely. If caring and love is found in small intimate groups of a dozen or fewer individuals, then the megachurch concept of thousands of people jammed like sardines into a huge auditorium bears no relation at all to the real level at which community is found. Administrators may have grander designs for preaching services, community action, moral politics, and the like, but they should be careful not to undermine the small group in pursuing their agendas. Siphoning off every promising leader once every six months in order to start new groups is certainly going to work against the functioning of the groups that already exist. Consuming the scarce time of every possible member to run larger programs and committees will leave these people without the time to participate in the supportive groups they so vitally need.

These trade-offs can be seen by looking closely at the seemingly harmless example of churches growing by asking small groups of six to add one member a year. In the first place, any group of six in a typical U.S. neighborhood in which the average family moves at least once every three years probably will have to replace two of its members every year just to stay even. To add another means a fifty percent turnover each year and a stable base of only three continuing members. How realistic is it to expect deep ties capable of providing intimate support in a group like this?

Astute religious leaders will recognize that small groups must be allowed to develop and mature at their own pace. Nothing is likely to be more disruptive than to have an ambitious member of the clergy setting growth goals that group leaders are expected to meet. Group participants are less likely to be influenced by these intrusions. But if their groups are reduced to being muscles in the great growth monster, they are likely to become too sinewy and tough to accomplish their primary function. They will become too structured, too instrumental, and too much an extension of a pastor's plans to enlarge the congregation to be concerned about members' needs and to unfold in a way that members feel is compatible with their own interests.

Even when small groups do not become the instruments for achieving religious leaders' career ambitions, it is also evident that they can become a source of pride—pride that often emerges when religious leaders start comparing notes with each other. There is, after all, a deeply ingrained sense of competition in American religion, just as there is in sports, business, and politics. Clergy are each other's closest competitors. It is easy for Pastor X to look at Pastor Y and say, "Well, my church is certainly better than his."

If Pastor X has lots of small groups and his church is growing, he may be convinced that his church is better than Pastor Y's. As one pastor we talked to remarked, deflecting a question about the hallmarks of a successful group to give a short disquisition on why his church was better than others in town, "We are conservative and evangelical, and basically drawing the type of people who are tired of the mamby-pamby of traditional mainline churches who refuse active teaching and the glory of the New Testament. People who come to our church are hungry. They are wanting fellowship and wanting to get serious within the church, and many of them are driving twenty to thirty miles into town to get it." In his view, the real truth was to be found at his church; others were just offering social gatherings and prestige. "If that is what they want—the prestige of being a member of such and such church—there are plenty of other places like that within the city. There is good business elsewhere is what I tell them."

If one talks with Pastor Y, whose church is not running small groups and growing, one gets a quite different, but sometimes equally defensive, story. In one community, for example, the pastor was keenly aware that his church was largely unsuccessful in sponsoring small groups, compared with a sister congregation belonging to the same denomination on the opposite end of town. In his view, small groups probably are bad because they undermine the unity of the church by causing people to go in different directions.

There is, of course, some truth in this remark. Small groups can be a divisive element, and they can cause grief for the pastor if people start forming their own opinions and challenging the authority of the central command. But this freedom is probably why small groups have so long been such a vital element of spirituality at the grassroots. Here people at least can be themselves and pay attention to their own needs and the needs of others they know and care about rather than worrying about the professional and bureaucratic aspirations of the clergy.

GOD OF THE GROUP

There used to be a saying about "the God of the gap"—a phrase meaning that many people squeeze God into the narrow margins of their lives, focusing most of their attention on material things, preferring to understand life in secular terms, and turning to God only when the totally unexplainable or catastrophic happens. Judging from the statements of public leaders, the God of the gap is still very much alive. But another idolatrous, limiting conception—the God of the group—may be even more prominent.[3]

The God of the group is a deity that can fully accept only those who seek his presence "in community." Woe to the poor introvert who feels depleted in the presence of others and needs time alone to replenish her energy: get her involved in a group! Shame on the poor soul who is too busy making ends meet to spend time in a group: force him to rethink his priorities! Do we want to grow in our spiritual journeys? Let us quit these lonely meditations and join a group. Do we want to identify the true models of spiritual life and leadership in our churches and synagogues? Look to the active members of small groups.

This attitude clearly reflects a narrow, know-it-all view of how spirituality is best cultivated. It turns people who find God in other ways into second-class citizens. Taken to the extreme, it also robs the church of many who might otherwise feel at home within its walls, but who feel diminished compared to those who populate small groups. A Catholic priest expressed this concern especially well: "I don't think that small groups are for all of the parish. The church should be big enough to support the needs of the individual, and that includes breaking down into small groups if that is what people need and express what they want. But under no circumstances should people involved in these small groups be deemed the elite of the church just because they have this extra involvement."

Historically, the Judeo-Christian tradition has always embraced a wide range of devotionalism and practical piety. Mystics have been venerated, even though they largely kept to themselves. People who found God in the quiet of their rooms at night were regarded as no less spiritual than those who prayed aloud in the temples and meeting halls. Indeed, Jesus admonished his followers not to make a public display of their humble petitions to God. It is well to remain mindful of this admonition.

Small groups can facilitate self-understanding, piety, and a life of obedience to God. But they also can brand others as second-class citizens of the kingdom of heaven. Religious leaders especially need to remember the multiple ways in which they can minister to spiritual seekers. Some will be too busy to become involved in small groups. Others, for whatever reasons, may find it more profound to discover the sacred in books, through helping the needy, or in the mirror of nature. A woman we talked with who had worked as a spiritual director for the past 15 years underscored this point very strongly by observing that "everything in life should be a source of spiritual direction, not just small groups."

THE PECKING ORDER SYNDROME

A closely related problem often occurs within groups. Not only do faithful group members feel better than others who are not members, they also feel superior to those in their own groups who do not conform or who have not been down the road for as many years as they have. Frank's remarks about people in AA who annoy him are indicative of this syndrome. He is, as we have seen, an extraordinarily warm and caring individual. He would give his life to help others stay sober. But when he is candid with himself he also admits there are people in AA who rub him the wrong way. Why? Listen to the way he describes what he doesn't like about the meeting he attends: "Recently there are some young people there, and I don't like how they whine. You know, I really don't need to hear the 20-year olds talk about how tough life is with mom and dad." He also complains about new people who are "frustrating because they talk about how tough life is in the first 30 days of sobriety." When asked if anyone particularly annoyed him, he admitted: "There's a guy in the group who's early on in recovery and he thinks he's got it all figured out." This man has been sober for perhaps ninety days. Frank says, "I will reach out and I will spend time with him. I've made offers to talk any time he wants to talk, but I really don't need to hear his lectures about how the program works."

This is a clear example of the implicit pecking order that develops in virtually all groups.[4] Those who have followed the group's norms faithfully for a number of years know more than those who have not. Sometimes, as in Frank's case, they have experienced deep pain. Their growth has not come easy. It bothers them when younger or less experienced people try to pose as their equals.

Anything a group values can become the basis for a pecking order of this kind. In AA and other twelve-step groups, length of time in recovery is a known fact, something people find ways to disclose as they talk in the group, and it is often taken as a sign of maturity and wisdom. In evangelical groups a pecking order may be based on one's ability to quote scripture from memory or on the regularity of one's prayer life, the number of people one has witnessed to about the gospel, having read the latest book by a favorite evangelical author, or being constantly filled with the gifts of the Holy Spirit. Other groups may establish a pecking order around experiences in the civil rights movement, the number of peace demonstrations members have attended, the use of politically correct or inclusive language, how many church committees they have been asked to chair, talent in singing, or skepticism toward people whose faith is too "simple-minded."

No group can totally escape an implicit pecking order. To champion certain values is to discuss them positively in the group and to reward those who achieve these values with praise, positions of leadership, or other tokens of respect. Not to reward such efforts would be to deny the values the group holds dear. But most groups also believe in the importance of trust, acceptance, and even equality among their members. Groups work better when everyone feels respect and is able to contribute. It is essential, therefore, for groups to work hard at balancing their implicit pecking orders with signals of mutual trust.

TOWARD A DEEPER SPIRITUALITY

One thing remains clear: small groups in the United States are prevalent largely because the American people have a deep interest in spirituality. Whether this interest is properly focused, whether it is a profound longing to know God, or whether it is in some way obsessive are questions that have been much debated. As I have just argued, it is important to remember that spirituality can and does occur in deeply significant ways outside of small groups. At the same time, several points are worth emphasizing about the ways in which it manifests itself in small groups.

First of all, spirituality within small groups themselves is extraordinarily diverse. Some of it is focused squarely on gaining biblical knowledge. For other people, the important questions concern applying this knowledge to their daily lives. Others have trouble with biblical language entirely, but believe that a higher power of some kind—or transcendence within themselves—can animate their lives. Small groups, on balance, probably do more to reinforce a very conservative, literal approach to religion than to undermine such an approach. And yet, plenty of groups have liberal theological inclinations and unorthodox views of all kinds. As a result, anyone fearful that the small-group movement is channeling American religion in some untoward direction perhaps can rest somewhat easier.

Diversity is clearly one of the reasons why the small-group movement has been so successful. American religion has long been known for its denominational and confessional pluralism. Small groups take this pluralism one step further. A person is no longer limited simply to deciding whether to be a Baptist, a Lutheran, or a Catholic. Indeed, making the transition from one to the other might be so uprooting that it would be easier to stay at home on Sunday mornings. With dozens of small groups meeting in their neighborhoods, individuals trying to identify a comfortable spiritual niche can shop around more easily. Perhaps another group in the Baptist church takes its denominational heritage less seriously. Perhaps an ecumenical group at another church focuses on prayer and Bible study and dismisses the importance of denominational distinctions entirely. To join a new group, you do not have to go through a new members class, study church history, undergo rebaptism, or incur a moral obligation to help pay the pastor's salary. You simply have to show up, meet a few friendly individuals, and then quit attending a few weeks or months later if the chemistry hasn't been right. In short, diversity helps religious organizations adapt to a more competitive market situation. Small groups are like product lines. The American automobile industry would have folded shop long ago had it continued to make only the family sedan.

Sports cars, pick-ups, and minivans helped retain consumer interest. Small groups, offering diverse definitions of spirituality, do the same thing for the religious market.

The negative, flip side of this diversity is also worth emphasizing, however. Respect for diversity easily can lead to a Milquetoast religion in which any view is regarded as highly as any other view. The danger of this happening is even greater in the spiritual marketplace than it is in the automobile industry. An automobile is at least a material product that is delivered from the assembly plant pretty much in one piece. People may order one color or gadget rather than another, but (other than the few who patronize customizing shops) most purchasers drive their car the way they receive it. Religious beliefs are much more malleable. Small groups are not like dealerships that transmit prefabricated goods from factory to consumer. They are more like customizing shops, creating their own versions of spirituality. Moreover, each member of the group can walk away with an individualized, distinctive version—largely because spirituality remains personal and subjective. Even when group members discuss their religious beliefs, they may link them so closely with personal experience that it becomes difficult for anyone else to disagree. Heretical or half-baked views can be the result, as well as religious orientations that are self-congratulatory and self-justifying. What can counter this tendency, of course, is the more intensive spiritual mentoring and theological training that members receive in their churches and synagogues. Some of this training influences small groups directly—through clergy involvement, the study guides used, and the input of knowledgeable members. But diversity can become the prevailing value. And ideas about spirituality can as easily be influenced by television, the latest movies, popular writers, the neighborhood gossip, personal moods, and the dynamics of group interaction.

Tolerance of other perspectives may be difficult to encourage and a worthy task to pursue, but it is easy compared to the hard work of finding a common ground and of forging a reasoned consensus about what is true and worthy and good. As one pastor observed, "We need to move beyond tolerance and seek common ground based on the very nature of humanity and the very nature of who God is." Unless religious leaders devote serious attention to these tasks, including careful consideration of their basic theological principles, therefore, small groups can simply be a way in which spirituality is adapted to the vagaries of a secular society.

A second point worth emphasizing is that spirituality in small groups, for all its diversity, is very much a collective enterprise. To understand how small groups are redefining spirituality, we must, therefore, take very seriously the fact that people are meeting and interacting with one another. At its worst, the small group can be a matter of the blind leading the blind. At its best, it consists of members holding each other accountable, stepping in when personal discipline weakens, providing mentoring, and nurturing each other toward greater insight and mutual responsibility. Faced by the prospect of piety turning increasingly inward, religious leaders can take comfort in the fact that small groups—perhaps more than anything else—encourage private beliefs to be shared publicly and to be acted on in ways that others can see. Giving voice to one's religious views in a small group is certainly a more open, dynamic process than listening to a sermon on Sunday mornings. Talking is itself important. People remember more of what they say than of what they read or hear. And working within a small group to feed the hungry and clothe the naked is certainly a "corporate" expression of faith to a greater extent than offering a silent prayer for the needy or dropping a check in the mail.[5]

The fact that small groups encourage discussions of spirituality—and that caring is so often evident—is one reason why religious leaders have been looking to the small-group movement to revitalize America's churches and synagogues. But, from the vantage point of such leaders, controlling the small-group movement may be like trying to hold a tiger by the tail. The movement is successful because it encourages grass-roots participation. It focuses members' attention on each other's needs and on helping people they know personally. Whether small groups also can engender greater interest in denominational policy disputes, for example, or whether these groups will reinforce the distinctive theological teachings that clergy would like them to understand are different questions. Some members are already interested in church policy and theology. But the larger movement may be doing more to redefine religious organizations than to revitalize them.

As we have seen, small groups frequently orient their members toward thinking of spirituality less in terms of ecclesiastical tradition, less in terms of theological knowledge, and more in terms of practical experience. Small groups encourage many members to regard biblical wisdom as truth only if it somehow helps them to get along better in their daily lives. Groups generate a do-it-yourself religion, a God who makes life easier, a programmed form of spirituality that robs the sacred of its awe-inspiring mystery and depth. The "application" that a group member draws for his or her life becomes more important than whether that application is grounded in truth. Each believer becomes capable of deciding which combination of beliefs to emphasize and does so mainly by drawing on personal experience rather than by paying any special attention to the clergy or to the collective, historic wisdom of the church. In simplest terms, the sacred comes to be associated with small insights that seem intuitively correct to the small group rather than wisdom accrued over the centuries in hermitages, seminaries, universities, congregations, and church councils.

Collective interaction notwithstanding, it is also worth emphasizing how private and how inwardly focused the spirituality expressed in small groups often is. People join them because of emotional needs bubbling up within their own psyches. They talk about their own experiences and their personal problems. They are interested in their own spiritual growth. And they come away feeling better about themselves. All of these developments are laudable. They may enable people to reach out to the needs of others. But it is a sad commentary on our society that so many people believe themselves to be in such desperate straits that they cannot serve others without spending so much time on themselves.

If we approach small groups strictly from the vantage point of the individual, we might come away with a fairly positive view of their functioning. As a social scientist, I can decry the cultural conditions that have made us obsessed with ourselves. I can point to the ways in which our economic system reinforces a logic of self-interest or the ways in which uncertainties in family life lead to frail self-identities that require a great deal of emotional work. As an individual, I myself cannot escape these larger cultural forces, I can only try to patch my life together as best I can. Small groups are a powerful way to do this. They help me understand myself. And in the process, I am assisted by concepts of forgiveness, mercy, strength, and responsibility that grow out of religious tradition. Spirituality becomes part of the process of self-understanding.

Approaching the small-group movement from the standpoint of its place in American society, however, requires a somewhat different perspective. You can, of course, make the same analysis you do at the individual level—and then multiply it by 200 million. Thus, if small groups help individuals cope with their lives, surely the movement is helping the society as a whole. But as a social scientist, I must ask different kinds of questions: Do small groups simply maintain the status quo? Do they create the kind of community that can hold a massive society such as ours together? And do they contribute to its long-term betterment?

The question about small groups maintaining the status quo always emerges in the context of political criticisms. It is much like the question posed periodically about athletic contests: don't the Super Bowl or the World Series just take our minds off the serious problems in our world and cause us to be complacent? What sort of energy might be released if all the people who spend their Wednesday evenings studying the Bible became interested in world hunger or decided to send petitions to their legislators about some issue?

Such possibilities are certainly intriguing. The problems facing our world are so severe that energy of this kind could be valuably devoted to fighting them. We need to acknowledge that small, informal groups may divert attention from larger social issues. But we must also be practical enough to know that a utopian redirection of energy will never happen. What can happen is a small investment of time and effort. And that will happen only through existing social networks. Small groups may need to be prodded more in that direction, but at least they provide the groundwork for such prodding to take place.

Do small groups provide the glue that holds our society together? To a considerable extent, yes. Of course, they permit traditional communities to be abandoned, as I have suggested. They make it possible for the individual to be modular, to shift identities and loyalties as circumstances may dictate. But at any given moment, these groups do connect individuals with one another. The ties are personal, sometimes deeply so, and they connect a vast segment of the society directly through group memberships, while many others are the occasional beneficiaries of these connections. To be sure, what really holds American society together in large measure are the business transactions, the jobs, the voting, the lobbying, the schools, the universities—all the massive institutions we read about in the newspapers. But most of those institutions encourage individuals to act entirely out of self-interest. They promote competition. They cause us to think in terms of individual rights and to engage in arms-length relationships. Were they all that held American society together, the world would indeed be a bleak place in which to live.

Small groups, in contrast, allow people to know one another at a more intimate level. They provide contexts in which doubts and fears, personal aims and aspirations, grief, joy, and the minor victories of everyday life can be shared. They function well because they provide at least some of the intimacy that families and friendships and neighborhoods have always provided. They draw people out of themselves and help round out their personalities. In addition, they connect people to the wider society. The community they develop among their members becomes part of a wider community as they help others, participate in their churches and synagogues, and work together on community projects.

Small groups enrich the wider society, not so much by eradicating it of social ills or by fostering a better way of governing ourselves. They enrich social life by linking the individual to larger social entities and by bringing a personal, human dimension to public life. They allow people to be themselves, to be vulnerable, to be weak, to be emotionally distraught, to be recovering from addictions, and yet to participate in the collective life of our society.

Because of small groups, spirituality can become one of the primary ways in which the common good is enriched and ennobled. If the sacred is being redefined, turned on its authoritarian head, made more populist, practical, and experiential, it is nevertheless being adapted to modern social conditions in a way that allows it to remain relevant. Spiritual needs are always personal. People experience them as a desire to know God or to feel accepted by some power larger than themselves. But when they band together with others to explore these needs, they become more aware of their common destiny. Their groups become part of the larger social fabric. As they engage in their own distinct spiritual journeys, they seek to know themselves as individuals, and in the process they also discover community.

COMMUNITY IN A LIBERAL SOCIETY

In the final analysis, small groups clearly hold significant potential for maintaining, or even enhancing, the role of community in contemporary society. Whether this potential is realized, however, depends on the ability of movement leaders, participants, and interested outsiders to nudge these groups in the right direction. Certainly small groups inherently tend to focus exclusively on the personal needs of individual members, thus working at odds with the enterprise of building effective communal ties. To see what may need to be encouraged, we must again consider briefly how small groups are similar to (and dissimilar from) families.

Families constitute the clearest example of communitarian social structures, not simply because their members interact with each other regularly and sometimes intimately but because families have a well-institutionalized place in the wider society. To be a member of a family is to incur certain legal and culturally recognized rights and responsibilities. These include such expectations as being married to only one spouse at a time, registering marriages and births with the state, deriving claims to the pooled and separate assets of various family members, paying for the support of minor children, and so on. In these ways the individual is not only given warm, intimate support but is connected systematically to the larger institutions of our society. Families, it might be noted, are hardly unique in this respect. Religious congregations, for example, typically file formal charters that provide them with legal recognition, follow certain by-laws in acquiring and maintaining property, and hire professionals charged with looking after their collective interests.

Small groups are not entirely devoid of such corporate ties. Many are formally chartered by sponsoring religious organizations or by national federations that have legal status and that suggest rules of operation for member units to follow. Nevertheless, small groups have a far more transient relationship to their institutional environment than do most other forms of community. Based almost entirely on the wishes of their immediate participants, they are more like informal circles of friends than families or churches. They do not bind their members to one another legally or financially, nor do they link individuals with the wider legal, governmental, or economic structures of our society. Failure to attend regularly is tantamount to no longer being part of the group, whereas poor attendance seldom means dismissal as a member of a family.

This characteristic of small groups, I have suggested, makes them especially suited to the complex social environment of the contemporary United States. Having so much of their lives hemmed in by legal statutes, many people find the opportunity to associate freely with kindred spirits a welcome change. Knowing that advice given or received, for example, is not subject to professional norms and, therefore, cannot invite malpractice suits is a refreshing change of pace. In addition, small groups may provide some of the same services that are available in the economic marketplace but at cheaper rates or on an informal system of barter. For instance, for the price of spending an enjoyable evening each week with their groups, people can purchase inexpensive "insurance" against such contingencies as needing a sitter for their children in case of a family emergency or needing an extra pair of arms for moving the piano.

Viewed in a positive light, it might be reasonable to suggest that small groups provide the ideal solution to the debate that has been raging for some time about how best to achieve a healthy society. Communitarians, on the one hand, argue that market relations and the liberal state are fundamentally at odds with the familial and neighborly relationships that have characterized good societies in the past. Liberal political theory, in contrast, attaches less importance to communities and argues instead that modern market and governmental structures are most conducive to a good society. Small groups seem to have adapted rather well to the fragmenting conditions that worry communitarians, but show more capacity to perpetuate community than most liberals would believe possible.

If small groups have such potential, it nevertheless makes sense to pay special attention to the forces that must remain in balance for them to function effectively. On the one hand, their freedom must be protected zealously. Efforts by government or religious agencies to control them would be as detrimental as such efforts have always been when directed at the family. External support in the form of medical care, schools, or tax incentives can help the family but must not determine what it should do from day to day. Leadership, coordination, and meeting space can be provided to small groups, but their regular activities must be permitted to vary. At the same time, small groups need to be encouraged to behave as groups rather than as aggregations of individuals. Setting goals for the group can be one way of transcending purely individual interests. Projects in which group members work together to help others outside the group help reinforce community as well as assisting those being served directly. Greater efforts to keep in touch with absent members may be needed to give a greater sense of longevity to such groups. Small groups, moreover, should not be private enclaves that hide out, as it were, in the interstices of society and call on their members only to provide informal encouragement or simply nudge them to do volunteer work that depends entirely on personal whim. Small groups should, like families, link their members to the institutional structures of the wider society as well. Being part of formal religious organizations is one way to do this. Making commitments to help community organizations might be another option. Above all, frank discussion of collective values is needed, especially when these values include community.

If small groups extend planning, rational calculation, and formal organization into the private spaces of our lives, they can at least provide opportunities for concerned members to shape and remold the directions in which the small-group movement is leading. Having leaders, small groups can be led; having goals, new agendas can be specified. At present, the movement commands enormous resources. It is a vast resource itself. It can be used for cynical, self-serving purposes. Or it can be discussed, improved, and turned more seriously toward enhancing the common good. Which direction the movement will go still remains in our hands.

Because it is neither unified nor centrally organized, responsibility for the direction of the small-group movement must come from many different sources. Clergy, both at the parish level and in national offices, must bear much of the responsibility because of the extent to which support groups are currently located in local churches. Therapists, mental health specialists, and directors of self-help associations must also take a close look at where the movement currently is heading. At the grass-roots level, group members and their leaders have a critical stake in shaping the movement. And, more broadly, public opinion leaders in the mass media and in colleges and universities, as well as the public at large, must play a role in interpreting and guiding the movement.

Religious leaders need to be concerned especially with the quality of spirituality being encouraged by the small-group movement. They are likely to favor the further expansion of small groups because these groups seem to stimulate thinking about the sacred and, for the most part, motivate members to become more actively involved in attending their churches, participating in church activities, and supporting these programs financially. But religious leaders should also be concerned about the ways in which small groups may be redefining spirituality. If it is acceptable, as some religious leaders suggest, to encourage a brand of faith that "scratches people where they itch," it is nevertheless troublesome if the sacred becomes nothing more than a magnificent backscratcher. By promoting the small-group movement, clergy inadvertently can reinforce an attitude toward spirituality that says, in effect, "if it works for me, it must be true."

Perhaps the best antidote to such a redefinition of spirituality is for the churches to include small groups as part of a broader, multipurpose program of ministry. Such a program should present a balanced assortment of opportunities for learning, worship, and service, as well as fellowship. Small groups should not be the principal activity of the church nor the program that receives greatest emphasis in terms of pastoral time or lay involvement. They should be oriented toward fellowship and caring, but their members should be encouraged to participate in classes and to seek religious instruction in other settings, they should take part in worship services and the sacraments, and they should be encouraged to be of service through their work, in their neighborhoods, and through volunteer activities. Religious leaders should be cautious in using small groups instrumentally to meet targeted levels of church growth. Larger churches are not necessarily better churches. Nor are small groups the secret of success in all settings. An emphasis on numeric success requires special caution, moreover, when "whatever works" to achieve this goal comes to be seen as more worthy, or even as being closer to the truth, than other activities whose results may be more difficult to measure. Religious leaders need to take careful stock of what they want the church of the twenty-first century to be and to ask whether small groups can become vehicles for preserving ancient truths and for deepening theological wisdom or whether these groups will only make spirituality more palatable to a secular society.

Leaders of the self-help movement and of the wide variety of special interest groups that have only loose connections with religious organizations should be especially concerned about the contribution that these groups can make in the future to the health of American society. To date, many of these groups have played an important role in supporting individuals through painful processes of recovery from alcoholism, bereavement, dysfunctional family backgrounds, and other traumatic personal experiences. The self-help movement is, however, presently at an important juncture in its history. Critics argue that the recovery movement has begun to feed on itself, perpetuating some of the problems it purports to solve and overselling the extent to which addictions, codependency, and other dysfunctions characterize the American people. The research presented here demonstrates clearly that the small-group movement is much larger and far more diverse than its recovery or self-help components. The latter play an important role in helping people who face emotional crises but should not be the model used to interpret the broader small-group movement. Continuing efforts to provide information and to remain conversant with trends in the fields of mental health, counseling, and medicine, and with state and federal agencies must be emphasized. At the same time, greater efforts must be made to encourage interaction between secular and religious leaders in the small-group movement, especially because of the resources religious organizations have at their disposal. Both the secular and the religious components have a critical role to play but must guard against emulating the other too closely or trying to compete too directly.

At the grass-roots level, members and leaders of small groups need to be aware that they are part of a massive phenomenon that has the potential to change American society—for good or for ill. In thinking about how to make their groups function more effectively, participants must be mindful of both the strengths and limitations of small groups. These gatherings are occasions for sharing and for receiving encouragement. They are not adequate substitutes for family, friends, or other long-term personal relationships, nor can they serve in place of community organizations or government programs concerned with the social, moral, political, and economic needs of society. Leaders need to be aware that small groups' function is best fulfilled when structure is kept in the background. Too many plans, goals, and tightly organized agendas will kill the spirit that animates small groups. Members, in contrast, need to be more aware of implicit group norms that drive people away or that prevent needs from being openly discussed. Periodic evaluations can play an important role in any healthy group. Members need to consider why they are attending, whether they are merely participating in order to feel good about themselves, and whether there are larger needs or issues that their group should be addressing.

Opinion leaders and the wider public also need to be aware of the prominent place that the small-group movement has come to occupy in American society. Ours is by no means a nation of isolated individualists whose tastes are guided entirely by self-interest and consumerism. The small-group movement is testimony to our continuing quest for community. For many millions of Americans, it provides friendships, forums for discussing values, and links with wider institutions. The movement should not be dismissed as being somehow artificial or ineffective. It, nevertheless, should be understood as a distinct product of our times. We want community, but nothing very binding. We want spirituality, but we prefer the sacred to serve us instead of requiring our service. To date, we have probably gotten more from the small-group movement than we have been encouraged to give in return.

The journey on which many in the small-group movement have embarked has now brought the movement to a crossroads. It has accomplished much over the past quarter century. But, like all movements, it mirrors the shortcomings of its host environment. For the future, we need to think carefully about ways in which the movement may contribute to the shaping of a better society. It is a resource. If deployed effectively, it can encourage deeper reflection about ourselves and our relationship to the sacred. It can motivate its members to engage in volunteer activities and in public service. It can probably be prompted to take a greater role in working for peace, justice, and other social reforms. It can also prompt us to think harder about what kind of community we seek, and how to attain it.

Appendix A
METHODOLOGY

The Sample

The sampling procedure used for the survey followed standard Gallup Organization practices for the selection of a general adult population sample. This procedure is similar to that used in in-person surveys such as The Gallup Poll, a description of which can be found in all reports published by the Gallup Organization and from which the following wording has been adapted. The sampling procedure is designed to produce an approximation of the adult civilian population, eighteen years and older, living in the United States, except those persons in institutions such as prisons or hospitals.

The design of the sample is that of a replicated, probability sample down to the block level in the case of urban areas and to segments of townships in the case of rural areas. The sample design includes stratification by these seven size-of-community strata, using 1990 census data: (a) incorporated cities of population 1,000,000 and over; (b) incorporated cities of population 250,000 to 999,999; (c) incorporated cities of population 50,000 to 249,999; (d) urbanized places not included in (a)–(c); (e) cities over 2,500 population outside of urbanized areas; (f) towns and villages of less than 2,500 population; and (g) rural places not included within town boundaries. Each of these strata are further stratified into four geographic regions: East, Midwest,

South, and West. Within each city size–regional stratum, the population is arrayed in geographic order and zoned into equal sized groups of sampling units. Pairs of localities are selected in each zone, with probability of selection and each locality proportional to its population size in the most current U.S. census, producing two replicated samples of localities.

Within each subdivision so selected for which block statistics are available, a sample of blocks or block clusters is drawn with probability of selection proportional to the number of dwelling units. In all other subdivisions or areas, blocks or segments are drawn at random or with equal probability. In each cluster of blocks and each segment so selected, a randomly selected starting point is designated on the interviewer's map of the area. Starting at this point, interviewers are required to follow a given direction in the selection of households until their assignment is completed.

A total of 160 representative sampling locations was drawn for the present survey. Interviewers assigned to each location were instructed to screen households until seven persons in groups and six persons not in groups had been interviewed. This procedure yielded a total of 1,021 interviews with individuals in groups and 962 interviews with individuals not in groups. All interviews were completed between November 4 and November 18, 1991.

Because the sample is stratified, each of the 160 sampling locations is assigned equal weight in determining the composition of the overall sample. The incidence of small-group members in each sampling location is determined by dividing the number of interviews completed with small-group members in that location by the total number of interviews completed in that location (interviews with group members, interviews with nonmembers, and interviews terminated as a result of the screening process). Across all sampling locations, the average incidence of group members is 40 percent.

Weighting the Sample

The sample of completed interviews was weighted in two steps to bring the demographic characteristics of the final sample into alignment with the demographic characteristics of the continental U.S. adult population. The first step eliminated the disproportionality of group members in the final sample. Group members were oversampled for this study to ensure that the final sample would contain a sufficient number of completed interviews (at least 1,000) in that category. This oversampling results in persons in groups being disproportionately represented in the final sample. In this weighting step, these people are weighted down to their correct proportion as determined through the screening process. The second step used demographic and regional parameters from the U.S. Census Bureau's Current Population Survey as target parameters to bring the final sample of completed interviews into alignment with the regional distribution of population and the age, sex, education, and race distributions of the continental U.S. population of adults. The weighting variables have also been multiplied by a constant to ensure that the total number of weighted cases and the number of completed interviews (1,983) are the same. For results based only on group members, a different constant is used to ensure that weighted cases and the number of completed interviews with group members (1,021) are the same.

Table A.1 presents a comparison of percentages and numbers for the weighted and unweighted data for interviews completed among persons in groups. Table A.2 presents similar comparisons for interviews completed among persons not in groups. The tables show that the chief undersampling that occurred in the data collection process was among men in groups, people in groups living in small towns and rural areas, people both in groups and not in groups with high school educations or less, and people both in groups and not in groups between the ages of 18 and 34. Conversely, oversampling occurred mainly among persons age 50 and older, among persons with college educations, among blacks, and for people in groups, among women, people living in the Midwest, and people living in large cities. The weightings adjust these proportions to more nearly approximate their distribution in the U.S. population.

Although total numbers of weighted and unweighted cases are the same among both those in groups and those not in groups, the weighting procedure necessitates adjusting discrepancies within the various subcategories. Because of these discrepancies, statistical measures of significance (such as Chi-square) are not always accurate. These inaccuracies are likely to be greatest when variables are being examined that may be systematically related to differences in age or education. All analyses discussed in the text that involve inferences about statistical associations are based on comparisons of relevant statistics using both weighted and unweighted numbers.

Table A.1

COMPARISONS OF WEIGHTED AND UNWEIGHTED
DATA FOR INDIVIDUALS IN GROUPS

	Weighted		Unweighted	
	Percentage	*Number*	*Percentage*	*Number*
Total	100	1020	100	1021
Male	42	424	38	386
Female	58	596	62	635
Age 18–34	32	328	24	243
Age 35–49	27	278	31	316
Age 50 and over	39	401	44	450
High school or less	49	501	44	445
Some college	28	288	29	296
College graduates	22	231	27	278
White	85	867	83	848
Black	11	11	14	140
Other	3	32	3	28
Large city	29	299	31	315
Medium city	36	362	38	387
Small town/rural	33	341	29	298
East	24	243	23	232
Midwest	25	259	29	296
South	22	221	21	219
West	26	265	27	274

Sampling Tolerances

In interpreting the survey results, it should be borne in mind that all sample surveys are subject to sampling error—that is, the extent to which the results may differ from what would be obtained if the whole population had been interviewed. The size of such sampling errors depends largely on the number of interviews. Table A.3 may be used in estimating the sampling error of percentages reported herein. The computed allowances have taken into account the effect of the sample design upon sampling error. They may be interpreted as indicating

Table A.2

COMPARISONS OF WEIGHTED AND UNWEIGHTED DATA
FOR INDIVIDUALS NOT IN GROUPS

	Weighted		Unweighted	
	Percentage	*Number*	*Percentage*	*Number*
Total	100	960	100	962
Male	50	479	50	485
Female	50	481	50	475
Age 18–34	40	382	31	299
Age 35–49	26	251	29	280
Age 50 and over	33	316	39	372
High school or less	57	548	53	511
Some college	25	243	26	252
College graduates	17	159	20	188
White	86	826	84	804
Black	10	100	13	126
Other	3	26	3	26
Large city	29	275	30	286
Medium city	34	326	37	353
Small town/rural	34	325	30	287
East	24	232	24	231
Midwest	27	257	28	265
South	25	245	23	222
West	24	227	25	242

the range (plus or minus the figure shown) within which the results of repeated samplings in the same time period could be expected to vary, 95 percent of the time, assuming the same sampling procedures, the same interviews, and the same questionnaire.

The table would be used in the following manner: Say a reported percentage is 40 for a group that includes approximately 1,000 respondents. Go to row "percentages near 40" in the table and go across to the column headed "1,000." The number at this point is 4, which means that the 40 percent obtained in the sample is subject to a sampling error of plus or minus 4 points. Another way of saying it is that

Table A.3

RECOMMENDED ALLOWANCE FOR SAMPLING
ERROR OF A PERCENTAGE

In Percentage Points (at 95 in 100 Confidence Level)

	Sample Size				
Percentages Near	*1000*	*750*	*500*	*250*	*100*
10	2	3	3	5	7
20	3	4	4	6	10
30	4	4	5	7	11
40	4	4	5	8	12
50	4	4	5	8	12
60	4	5	5	8	12
70	4	4	5	7	11
80	3	3	4	6	10
90	2	3	3	5	7

very probably (95 chances out of 100) the true figure would be somewhere between 36 and 44, with the most likely figure being the 40
obtained.

Most percentages presented in the text are based on the entire sample of group members. Thus, the column headed 1,000 gives a reasonable approximation of the sampling error to which these figures are
subject. Other percentages and statistical relationships discussed in
the text have been subjected to Chi-square or F-test measures of statistical significance. All relationships meeting a probability of 0.05 on
these measures are considered statistically significant.

Method of Data Analysis

For bivariate relationships involving the entire sample of group members or relationships involving no more than one control variable (such
as type of group, gender, or age), cross-tabular analysis was used with
Chi-square as the preferred measure of statistical significance and
gamma as a measure of the degree of statistical association for ordinal
variables. Multivariate statistical analysis of the data generally involves
stepwise discriminant function analysis.

Discriminant analysis is an ideal method of analysis for data such as that obtained in the present study. It empirically differentiates among two or more groups in the data using multiple variables to differentiate between these groups. Another way to say this is that discriminant analysis allows us to make predictions about the likelihood of respondents giving one answer to a question rather than a different answer on the basis of how respondents answer several other questions in the survey. For example, suppose we want to know what differentiates between respondents who are satisfied with their groups and respondents who are not satisfied. We let these two categories of satisfaction be the dependent variable (what we want to explain) in our analysis. We then examine simultaneously the relationships between this dependent variable and a variety of predictor (independent) variables, such as gender, age, frequency of church attendance, and how long the person has been attending his or her group. Discriminant analysis tells us if each of these variables is a statistically significant predictor of satisfaction, taking into account the effects of all the other variables in the model. It also tells how strongly each of these variables is related to the dependent variable.

As with all statistical procedures, certain assumptions are invoked when discriminant analysis is used. These are: that no predictor variables can be linear combinations of each other, that the covariance matrices for each group must be approximately equal, and that each predictor variable must be measured at the interval level. In using discriminant analysis, we have avoided violating the first of these assumptions by a default in the stepwise selection of predictor variables (disallowing the simultaneous entry of variables that are very closely correlated). We have assessed the extent to which the second assumption may be violated by using the Box's M test. The third assumption is generally not met with any kind of survey data; however, we have, as in most multivariate applications, sought to minimize its importance by using binary (dummy) predictor variables or items that at least involve ordinal levels of measurement. Researchers have generally found discriminant analysis to be a very robust procedure with regard to unequal covariance matrices and discrete data.

We assessed the fitness of the various discriminant functions by testing their significance with a Chi-square statistic, by evaluating the Wilks's lambda statistic (an inverse measure of association), by examining the relative eigenvalues (indicating the proportion of explanation provided by one function relative to other functions), and by inspecting the squared canonical correlation. For each variable in the discriminant function, we assessed its relative strength by examining the standardized canonical discriminant function coefficients. A common rule of thumb is to treat any coefficient of 0.30 or higher as meaningful.

A comparison of functions generated using the stepwise procedure and functions generated without this procedure revealed that standardized coefficients generally resembled each other quite closely. The stepwise procedure was used for the reason cited previously and to avoid introducing insignificant variables into final models. Two step procedures were used when a series of control variables needed to be introduced prior to the main test variable under consideration.

Some of the results were also validated by subjecting the same sets of variables to multiple regression analysis. Because of dichotomous dependent variables in most cases, many of which were sufficiently skewed to violate assumptions about homoschedasticity, the discriminant procedure was preferred. In a few cases, factor analysis was also employed for exploratory purposes in order to determine which variables tended to measure the same concepts or dimensions. Because the meaning of particular items is often lost when multiple items are combined, items were introduced in the analysis singly rather than as components of scales. For the same reason, discriminant models were kept parsimonious, either by examining one test variable at a time (with standard controls in each model) or by restricting models to those evaluating the relative strength of each item in a list of similarly worded items.

Reporting of the Data

Because the study is based to a significant extent on qualitative data from in-depth interviews and field observations as well as on quantitative data from the survey, only a small number of quantitative tables have been included in the text. The decision to minimize the amount of such information was also predicated on the fact that the book is oriented toward a diverse audience that includes nonspecialists as well as statistically trained specialists. The text does summarize the main results of a vast amount of statistical analysis. Further results and details have been reserved for the methodological notes on each chapter that follow in this appendix.

In what follows, the significance and strength of various relationships is summarized. These relationships are based on computer analyses that yielded in excess of 30,000 pages of quantitative results. Because of the sheer magnitude of these results, it did not seem feasible to present the numbers corresponding to specific conclusions about standardized coefficients, gammas, Wilks's lambdas, and so on. What we did attempt to include is enough description of how we arrived at our results (what variables were included and what kinds of analysis were performed) that someone with sufficient interest could replicate our procedures.

To facilitate the possibility for replication, the full text of the survey instrument has been included in appendix B. We have not tried to refer to questions, here or in the text, by number, but have described the questions in sufficient detail that the reader can locate them in the questionnaire to determine exactly how they were asked. Many of these questions, it might be noted, are suitable for administration in particular groups (some researchers have already done so). Copies of the data themselves can be obtained on diskette by writing to the George H. Gallup International Institute, 100 Palmer Square, Princeton, New Jersey 08540, and asking for the 1991 Lilly-Small Groups Survey. Our own analysis was performed using the Statistical Package for the Social Sciences (SPSS).

Chapter 2: The Quest for Community

In addition to the demographic patterns reported in chapter 2, the following conclusions emerge when pairs of demographic variables are examined: Women are more likely to be involved in small groups than are men in all age categories and in all regions of the country. Older people are somewhat more likely to be involved in small groups than are younger people, controlling for gender, education, and region. College graduates are more likely than those with lower levels of education to be involved in small groups, controlling for other factors. The population category least likely to be involved in small groups is men who have lived in their communities less than three years (only 23 percent), while the category most likely to be involved in small groups is college educated men and women age 50 or older (56 percent).

Other demographic patterns that may be of interest to some readers include the following: Women, older people, residents of small towns or medium-sized cities, and people who have lived longer in their communities tend to have been in their groups longer than average.

Younger people and people who have lived in their communities fewer than three years, however, are more likely to attend their groups frequently (once a week or more). Among all group members, women, people between ages 35 and 49, blacks, and those in the lowest income brackets are the most likely to say their group is extremely important to them. The fact that these demographic variables are associated in different ways with group membership, length of involvement, frequency of attendance, and importance of the group, it should be noted, gives added support to the claim that small groups are not a phenomenon restricted chiefly to a certain segment of American society.

In addition to the information on community presented in tables in the chapter, some further cross-tabulations were examined. These give some initial sense of the relationships between participation in small groups and meeting needs for community. When the items in table 2.3 were considered in relation to depth of involvement in groups, for example, more deeply involved members were generally more likely to say their needs for these kinds of community had been fully met. The measure of involvement used here was the same as in table 2.4: a comparison between the three-quarters of group members who said their group was very important to them and the quarter who said their group was not very important to them. This measure proved to be the best single-item indicator of level of involvement in the data. Because expectations and available meetings varied considerably from group to group, for example, frequency of attendance at group meetings did not provide as clear a measure of involvement. When those who said their group was very important were compared with those who said it was not this important, the former were 7 percentage points more likely to say their need for community was fully met on the emotional support item, 24 points more likely on the group with similar beliefs item, 5 points more likely on the friends with similar values item, 12 points more likely on the sharing item, 10 points on the bailing out of a jam item, 6 points on the never critical item, 26 points on the spirituality item, 7 points on the coworker item, 12 points on the depression item, and 7 points on the community item (there was no difference on the neighbors item).

These results were examined further using discriminant analyses to distinguish levels of importance of their groups among members and frequency of attendance at group meetings, controlling for age, gender, and church membership. For importance, statistically significant relationships were obtained for all the community items but one (cooperative coworkers); for frequency of attendance, for six of the eleven items.

On spirituality, another indication of its relationship with small-group involvement comes from a question asked of both group members and nonmembers: "How interested are you at present in developing your faith or spirituality?" Among current group members, 80 percent said they were either very interested or fairly interested. In comparison, only 55 percent of nonmembers gave these responses. That a desire for spirituality may prompt people to join small groups in the first place is also suggested by the fact that among nonmembers, 76 percent of those who said they would like to be in a small group gave these responses about spirituality, compared with only 48 percent of those who said they would not like to be in a small group.

Discriminant analysis of the relationships reported in table 2.4 confirmed that importance of the group and frequency of group attendance are significantly associated with not regarding one's religious beliefs as private, not saying that one's spirituality depends on no religious organization, not saying that all churches are alike, and disagreeing with the statement that beliefs don't matter as long as one is good, all controlling for age, gender, and church membership.

It will, of course, be of interest to some readers to know why some people are involved in small groups in the first place and why others are not. That question, however, is not our primary interest. As already shown, group members are not very much different than nonmembers on most social characteristics. As we will see, they can be distinguished in terms of other personal characteristics; with the exception of their religious involvement, though, few of these characteristics add much to our understanding The reason is that group members are virtually as diverse as American society. It is, therefore, more important to understand this diversity and to learn what we can about how groups function, why some of their members are more satisfied than others, and how spirituality may be influenced by participating in such groups.

More specifically, to estimate the capacity of various social characteristics to explain why some people become involved in small groups and others do not, several discriminant analyses were performed, demonstrating that years lived in one's community, age, education, family income, and gender all have significant effects. All of these variables, however, accounted for only 5 percent of the variation between group members and nonmembers. Additional discriminant models were examined that included data on a number of lifestyle characteristics. The following factors all had significant positive effects on the likelihood of being in a small group: being in counseling, taking classes of any kind, being in a fitness or exercise program, being a member of a professional organization, having an informal group of friends, reading the Bible, reading other religious books, meditating, and watching religious programs on television. Raising small children and reading novels for a pastime had negative effects. Taking the demographic factors into account, none of these activities explained more than an additional 6 percent of the variance. A model that included all significant demographic and lifestyle variables explained only 16 percent of the variance between group members and nonmembers.

A substantive interpretation of the various demographic and lifestyle characteristics that distinguish between group members and nonmembers suggests that people become members, not because of isolation or social deprivation, but because of other social ties, networks, and interests that expose them to small groups.

Chapter 3: Exploring the Options

The typology of groups presented in chapter 3 (summarized in table 3.2) was created by using some of the group descriptions shown in table 3.1. The following procedure was followed: first, define as Sunday school class all those who say yes to the description Sunday school class and who say their group is part of the formal activities of some church or synagogue; second, of the remainder, identify Bible study groups as all those who say yes to the descriptions Bible study group, prayer fellowship, house church, or covenant group; third, of those remaining, define as self-help groups all those who say yes to the description self-help group; finally, let special interest groups be a residual category.

A subtypology of Bible study groups was generated through a series of factor analyses. One factor analysis was performed using a list of twenty activities that group members could indicate were included in their group or not. Another was based on a list of 11 items concerning group structures and characteristics. Another was based on a list of 16 descriptions that members were asked to respond to. A final factor analysis was conducted using all these items. In each case, only the responses of persons who were in groups that in some way were identified as Bible studies, prayer fellowships, house churches, or covenant groups were included. The subtypes of groups presented in the chapter notes are derived from the factor analysis that included all of the foregoing items. A varimax rotation that converged after 17 iterations was used. In addition to the factors identified as types in the chapter, several other factors emerged that did not have substantive meaning, such as a factor identifying all groups that have business meetings and elected officers and one that identifies all groups that provide emotional support or that focus on special needs.

The differences discussed in the chapter between Bible study groups and Sunday school classes are based on discriminant analyses, where the dependent variable was being classified as a member of one or the other of these kinds of groups, and where various sets of predictor variables were introduced simultaneously to determine which ones remained significant and produced the strongest discriminating effects. It is worth noting that the failure to mention a variety of other factors in the text means that these variables did not distinguish between Sunday school and Bible study group members; for example, most group activities and group structures, most member motivations, and most self-descriptions did not differ.

A similar method (discriminant analyses) was used for determining which variables distinguished most strongly between the members of Bible study groups and self-help groups and between those in self-help groups and in special interest groups.

Chapter 4: A Good Place to Begin

All data pertaining to this chapter are reported in chapter 4.

Chapter 5: Making It Work

Comparisons of the various organizational characteristics among the four major kinds of small groups, as determined from the survey, show the following: Leaders are present in 94 percent of Sunday school classes, 90 percent of Bible study groups, 81 percent of self-help groups, and 92 percent of special interest groups. A stated goal or purpose is present in 84 percent of Sunday school classes, 81 percent of Bible study groups, 90 percent of self-help groups, and 85 percent of special interest groups. A formal name is present in 67 percent of Sunday school classes, 65 percent of Bible studies, 85 percent of self-help groups, and 86 percent of special interest groups. An agenda or schedule is present in 72 percent of Sunday school classes, 68 percent of Bible study groups, and 80 percent of self-help and special interest groups. Elected officers are present in 52 percent of Sunday school classes, 42 percent of Bible study groups, 61 percent of self-help groups, and 67 percent of special interest groups. Business meetings are present in 51 percent of Sunday school classes, 40 percent of Bible study groups, 58 percent of self-help groups, and 61 percent of special interest groups. Something to study in advance is present in 72 percent of Sunday school classes, 66 percent of Bible study groups, 41 percent of self-help groups, and 25 percent of special interest groups. Child care is present in 49 percent of Sunday school classes, 25 percent of Bible study groups, 16 percent of self-help groups, and 12 percent of special interest groups. A membership fee is present in 9 percent of Sunday school classes, 11 percent of Bible study groups, 30 percent of self-help groups, and 46 percent of special interest groups. A formal contract is present in 12 percent of Sunday school classes, 14 percent of Bible study groups, 28 percent of self-help groups, and 22 percent of special interest groups. And a fixed term after which the group disbands is present in 11 percent of Sunday school classes, 15 percent of Bible study groups, 12 percent of self-help groups, and 13 percent of special interest groups.

Conclusions presented about the relationships among variables are based largely on stepwise multivariate discriminant analyses of three different measures of member satisfaction: the distinction between members who said they were extremely satisfied with their group and all other members, the distinction between members who said they were either extremely satisfied or very satisfied and all other members, and those who scored above the mean and those who scored at or below the mean on a scale based on members' evaluations of their group on the twelve items shown in table 5.2. Because the second of these three measures produced results very much like the first, we have restricted the discussion in the text to the former. In each model, the following variables were introduced in step 1 in order to take into account differences in member characteristics that might be associated with expressing higher or lower degrees of satisfaction: gender, age, frequency of attendance at religious services, and frequency of participation in the group. In separate models, additional variables were then introduced in step 1. Activity variables, such as praying, studying the Bible, and eating together, were introduced in one set of models. Structure variables, such as having a stated agenda or elected officers, were introduced in another set of models. And function variables (shown in table 5.2) were included in a third set of models. The variables that emerged as statistically significant predictors of the several measures of satisfaction in step 2 are thus generating effects net of all other variables in the same model.

When the responses of all group members were examined, group activities that produced significant effects in the model predicting extremely satisfied responses were: speaking in tongues, following a twelve-step program, focusing on an addiction, practicing meditation, discussing books, and eating together. Working on projects together had a negative effect in this model. As predictors of at least very satisfied responses, group activities that proved significant included: engaging in sports or working on hobbies together, discussing books, eating together, focusing on a specific need or problem, and doing things for the community. Discussing social or political issues had a negative effect in this model. And for the composite rating scale, high scores were significantly influenced by: practicing meditation, following the twelve-steps, speaking in tongues, and eating together.

Group structure variables that were statistically significant in the various models were as follows: for extreme satisfaction: having a name, having a term after which the group disbands, and child care; with negative effects from having a leader, an agenda, and a stated goal; for at least very satisfied: having a name, having a term, and having a purpose; with negative effects from having a leader and having an agenda; and for the rating scale, having a name, having a term, and providing child care; with negative effects from having a leader and having elected officers.

The group function variables producing significant effects in the models, respectively, were: for extreme satisfaction: having people who trust each other, making newcomers feel welcome, having members faithfully attend, drawing everyone into the discussion, and meeting emotional needs; and for at least very satisfied: making me personally feel appreciated, having people who trust each other, and faithful attendance. Because the rating scale was based on these items, it did not make sense to examine them as both dependent and independent variables in the same model.

The foregoing models were repeated for members only of each of the four main kinds of groups: Sunday school classes, Bible studies, self-help groups, and special interest groups. The same controls were introduced in these models. These results are featured in the chapter.

The final sections of chapter 5 (on trust, faithful attendance, and welcoming newcomers) are based on analyses of variables that discriminate between excellent ratings on each of these items and less favorable ratings. Statements in the chapter about differences among types of groups are based on discriminant models in which each of the four main group labels (Sunday school classes, Bible study groups, self-help groups, and special interest groups) were introduced simultaneously as predictors. These results were also checked by repeating the analyses using all the group labels discussed in chapter 2. The results parallel those reported earlier in the chapter based on the typology of groups.

For all the other results in these sections, discriminant models were examined in which gender, age, church attendance, and frequency of group attendance were held constant. Separate models were examined for each dependent variable in which one of the following independent variables was introduced: whether the group had been in existence for at least five years or not, whether it was sponsored by a church or not, how long the respondent had been involved in the group, how often the group met, group size, whether the group was composed of people of different ages or mostly the same age, whether most members came every time or not, whether it was composed of members of various religious views or of similar religious views, whether group activities included sharing problems or not, and whether the respondent listed having been invited by a friend as a reason for being in the group.

These models were also used to predict variations in member evaluations of how well their group functioned in terms of making them personally feel appreciated. Self-help and special interest groups produced positive coefficients in the model with the various group labels, while Sunday school classes and Bible study groups were not significant in the model. Groups in existence for a longer time and church-based groups produced negative coefficients. Religiously homogeneous groups, groups in which members shared problems, and groups in which members had been invited produced positive coefficients. Size, how often the group met, and whether most members attended every time were not significant predictors of members feeling appreciated.

Chapter 6: Getting and Giving Support

The claim made in chapter 6 that small groups may be more effective in supporting people with certain kinds of needs than those with other needs is suggested by an examination of the strength of relationships between the severity with which people say they are bothered by various problems and their likelihood of saying they have received encouragement from their group. Using the gamma statistic as a simple measure of the strength of these relationships, the strongest relationships were for being bothered by loneliness, depression, and health problems. Somewhat weaker relationships appeared for being bothered by guilt, anxiety, and family problems. The weakest relationships were for work problems, money problems, and figuring out what's important in life.

Church-based groups and nonchurch groups appear to provide somewhat different kinds of support to their members. Judging from the results of a discriminant analysis using the various measures of support to distinguish between the two kinds of groups, the former are most different from the latter in terms of being more likely to help their members feel they are not alone, helping them when someone is sick, taking them meals, and providing child care; the latter are most different from the former in helping their members overcome addictions. Despite the fact that physical assistance is somewhat more common in church groups than in nonchurch groups, member satisfaction in church groups is still most strongly associated with emotional care rather than physical assistance. Among members of church-based groups, feeling like one was not alone had the strongest net effect on member satisfaction, followed by receiving help with an emotional crisis, help in celebrating something, and help in making decisions.

Chapter 7: Balancing Self and Others

The meaning of the various self-descriptions discussed in chapter 7 was examined by performing a factor analysis on these items using a varimax rotation procedure. The analysis yielded four clusters: (a) "loners," defined most strongly by needing to spend a lot of time alone and describing themselves as loners, and including those who said they were private persons or introverts, (b) the "ambitious," defined by being career oriented and highly ambitious and by calling themselves leaders, (c) "extroverts," defined by using this term to describe themselves and by calling themselves a people person, and (d) the "spiritual," defined by describing themselves as a deeply religious people and by saying they were on a spiritual journey. These results help mainly to confirm that people were using these labels in conventional and consistent ways.

The factor analysis also casts doubt on some assumptions about the meaning of individualism. The phrase "rugged individualist" was expected to cluster with the loner/private person category, but instead was most strongly associated with the extrovert/people person cluster. The phrase "free spirit" was also most strongly associated with this cluster. One interpretation of these results may be that individualism connotes the kind of personal strength that goes along with feeling comfortable with other people and with being oneself around other people, whereas the loner image connotes less individual strength or certainty about who one is.

The fact that people in small groups are willing to describe themselves as rugged individualists or as free spirits, therefore, seems less surprising given this meaning of these terms. These are people who apparently gain individual strength from being around other people. What is more striking is the extent to which small-group members include those who describe themselves as loners and as private people who need a lot of time by themselves.

The factor analysis nevertheless does support the idea that these various labels are tapping some distinct personal styles or value orientations. An alternative view, for example, might suggest that everyone is a mixture of all these traits (e.g., a people person who still needs time alone). But if that were the case, it would have been difficult to sort these items into such neat categories; everything would have been related to everything else. The differences, of course, are relative. But it appears that small groups do include substantial numbers of people who are loners as well as many who are extroverts.

The relationships between length of time in a group and kinds of problems experienced are substantiated by an analysis that used all the problems to discriminate members who have been in their groups for longer periods of time from those who have not been involved as long. Longer-term members are more likely to say they have had disagreements and been troubled by the group expecting too much of them; shorter-term members, by finding it hard to be open in the group, by not being understood by the group, and by not being able to find time for the group.

Some of these problems also differ significantly between men and women: women are more likely than men to say they feel pressured, misunderstood, and uncomfortable; men are more likely than women to say they have been reluctant to share in their groups.

Chapter 8: The Spiritual Dimension

Examples presented in chapter 8 of statements in the survey that correlated most closely with saying that one's faith had been influenced by participation in one's group include feeling closer to God, answers to prayer, more love for others, the Bible becoming more meaningful, and better able to share one's faith. A discriminant analysis relating all the items shown in table 8.1 with saying that one's faith had been influenced confirmed that the five items just listed were all positively related to saying one's faith had been influenced at a statistically significant level. Feeling closer to God was by far the most strongly related. With all the items considered simultaneously, statements such as feeling better about oneself, more open with oneself and with others, having relationships healed, and better able to forgive oneself and others were only weakly related with saying one's faith had been influenced or not significantly related at all. A substantive interpretation of these findings is that people in groups for the most part tend to define faith or spirituality in fairly conventional terms having to do with God, prayer, love of others, the Bible, and sharing one's faith. Other consequences of group participation, such as self-acceptance and better relationships with others, are more likely to be regarded as byproducts or consequences of spirituality rather than core elements of spirituality. There is, of course, variation in these meanings of faith among different kinds of groups. Some of these variations are considered in chapters 8 and 9. The variation is, however, not as great as some might suspect. For example, when separate discriminant analyses were performed for members of church-based groups and members of nonchurch groups, feeling closer to God remained the most strongly associated predictor of saying that one's faith had changed in both instances. Among members of church-based groups, change in faith was significantly associated with a somewhat larger number of statements, including love for others, answers to prayer, openness with self, and the Bible becoming more meaningful. Among members of nonchurch groups, change in faith was moderately associated with saying that one was better able to share one's faith. What these differences suggest, substantively, is that faith in church settings carries a richer or more complex set of connotations, including feeling close to God, whereas in nonchurch groups it focuses more exclusively on feeling close to God.

In addition to the cross-tabular data presented in tables 8.2, 8.3, and 8.4, the relationships between having one's faith influenced by the group and attitudes toward the Bible and involvement in church were examined using stepwise discriminant analysis. The correlates of saying that one's faith had been influenced by the group were measured by introducing length of time in the group, religious orientation (conservative or liberal), and whether the group was sponsored by a church or not as control variables in step one of each model. Then in step two, each of the variables at issue concerning the Bible and church were introduced respectively into separate models. With these controls, significant but relatively weak positive relationships appeared between saying one's faith had been influenced and statements about the divine inspiration of the Bible, taking the Bible literally, believing the Bible to be inerrant, and knowing that the statement about Acts being in the Old Testament was false. The statements about Jesus being born in Jerusalem and the Bible being a book of rules were not significant related to saying one's faith had been influenced by the group.

With the same controls in each model, saying one's faith had been influenced by the group was significantly, but weakly, associated with rejecting the statements about religious convictions being private, about spirituality not depending on any religious organization, about churches being out of date, about all churches being alike, and about beliefs not mattering as long as one tries to be good. The statement about clergy being no more spiritual than anyone else was not related with saying one's faith had been influenced by the group at a statistically significant level. Frequency of church attendance was very strongly associated with saying one's faith had been influenced by the group, as was saying one's interest in church or synagogue had increased in the past five years. Being involved in three or more special activities or committees in one's congregation was moderately associated with saying one's faith had been influenced by the group. Having three or more friends in the congregation was not significantly related to saying one's faith had been influenced.

Chapter 9: What Matters?

The relationships between the items in table 9.1 and saying that one's faith had been influenced by the group were examined with multivariate methods. Using stepwise discriminant analysis, alternative models were tested to determine how well they discriminated between persons who said their faith had changed as a result of being in their group and persons who said their faith had not changed. Because (as discussed in chapter 8) virtually all persons who said their faith had changed indicated that it had deepened either a lot or a little, the idea of faith being deepened is generally referred to in the chapter. In the first step of each discriminant analysis, number of years in the group, religious orientation, and whether the group was sponsored by a church or not were introduced as predictor variables. Of these, the last had a very high standardized canonical discriminant function coefficient, religious orientation (conservative or liberal) showed a moderate relationship (indicating that conservatives were more likely to have experienced a deepening of their faith), and number of years in the group had only a weak relationship. In the second step of each model, one of the items in table 9.1 was added as a predictor variable. In each of these models, the added item was statistically significant. Studying particular Bible lessons and seeing how to apply ideas had the highest coefficients, followed by seeing love acted out, having a confidant in the group, hearing others share, having people tell stories, and receiving encouragement from people in the group. Well-prepared leaders and someone to admire were significant, but relatively weak, predictors.

The correlates of seeing love enacted were examined by performing various discriminant analyses to determine which items in the survey distinguished best between group members who said seeing love and caring acted out in the group had been very important to them in getting help from the group and those who said this factor had been fairly important, not very important, or not at all important. This distinction, again, was strongly associated with the likelihood of individuals saying their faith had been influenced by being in the group. This relationship was significant in a model that also included the effects of gender, age, education, religious preference, and view of faith. Each of these control variables was also significantly associated with the dependent variable, indicating substantively that women are more likely than men to say seeing love and caring acted out has been important to them, as are older people, those with lower levels of education, Protestants, and those who believe they must work hard at their faith.

Using discriminant analysis, the group labels (kinds of groups) that have the strongest positive effects on the likelihood of seeing love and caring acted out are (in order): Bible study groups, therapy groups, prayer fellowships, anonymous groups, covenant groups, and self-help groups. A substantive interpretation of these results is that each of these kinds of groups is more likely than average to include members who say seeing love and caring acted out has been very important to them in getting help from their group. Because all group labels were included in the analysis, this result takes account of the fact, for example, that some therapy groups may also be Bible study groups, and vice versa.

The self-descriptions that predicted importance of seeing love enacted were (ordered by strength of the standardized coefficients): deeply religious, on a spiritual journey, extrovert, and a people person. Negative coefficients were obtained for rugged individualist, career oriented, and ambitious. In interpreting the negative coefficients, it is perhaps helpful to observe that needing to spend time alone yielded a positive coefficient and describing oneself as a loner or an introvert were not significant in the model. In other words, while outgoing people may be more likely to experience (or value) caring in the group, inward-oriented people are not unlikely to value caring by virtue of those traits themselves. Being preoccupied with ambition or success appears to be the decisive negative factor.

The correlates of leadership were examined using the statement "having a leader who could answer your questions." Discriminant analyses were performed on the data to determine what other variables produced statistically significant differences between respondents who said this had been very important to them in getting help from the group and respondents who said this had been fairly important, not very important, or not at all important. When all group labels (kinds of groups) were used as predictor variables, those that produced the strongest positive effects were (in order): Bible studies, therapy groups, singles groups, and house churches. The only type of group that showed a negative association with this statement was men's groups.

The relationship between leadership and saying one's faith had been influenced was examined with a multivariate discriminant model that included gender, education, age, religious preference, importance of religious while growing up, and view of faith as controls. In this model, all the control variables were related moderately to the leadership variable, and having had one's faith influenced by the group was related strongly to the leadership variable. The significance of importance of religion while growing up is notable, suggesting that persons with deep religious involvement as children may be conditioned to look toward leaders for answers.

The type of leadership that may be most effective in groups can perhaps be inferred indirectly from a discriminant analysis using the other statements in table 9.1 as predictor variables and the statement about the importance of leadership as a dependent variable. The predictor variable that produced the strongest effect was the statement about "people in the group giving you encouragement." The second strongest effect was that produced by the statement "having someone in the group that you could admire and try to be like." Both of these qualities, of course, may be especially desirable in the group leader.

Having a confidant was measured in the survey by the statement "having one person in the group that you could discuss things with." Persons who said this had been very important in getting help from the group were compared with persons who said this had been fairly important, not very important, or not at all important, using discriminant analysis. When 16 group labels (from chapter 2) were introduced simultaneously as discriminating variables, the labels with the highest coefficients (in order) were: anonymous group, singles group, self-help group, and support group (all with coefficients of 0.30 or more). House church and Bible study group had positive, but weaker, coefficients. Youth groups had a negative coefficient. All the other kinds of groups had either statistically insignificant or weak coefficients.

"Having someone in the group that you could admire and try to be like" was the statement used for the results reported in the section on someone to admire. The observation in the chapter about this statement not being a significant predictor of spirituality is based on an analysis of the joint relationships between all the items in table 9.1 and the likelihood of someone saying their faith had been influenced by their group. When having someone to admire is examined without controlling for these other factors, it does show a significant relationship with one's faith having been influenced. This relationships is also statistically significant when age, gender, education, religious preference, the importance of religion while growing up, and view of faith are controlled. Substantively, these results mean that admiring someone in the group may appear to encourage faith development, but it is more likely that faith development is really being facilitated by other factors, such as seeing love in the group or studying the Bible.

Accountability was examined by comparing people who said their groups did an excellent job of holding its members accountable with those who gave their groups lower ratings. We used this question because we did not include a question in the survey that was comparable to the ones listed in table 9.1. A discriminant analysis using the items in table 9.1 to predict this variable, however, showed that the strongest predictors were "people in the group giving you encouragement" and "seeing how to apply ideas to your life." In other words, accountability and encouragement seem to be related dimensions of group experience.

The relationship reported in the chapter between rating one's group high on accountability and being in a group that practices meditation, uses the twelve steps, and practices speaking in tongues, it should be noted, is based on a model that also includes whether or not the group tries to hold its members accountable. With one possible exception (women giving higher ratings to their groups on the whole than men), the results reported in this section appear to mean that members have benefitted more than average from their group holding them accountable rather than giving their group high marks despite their own personal experiences.

Chapter 10: The Power of Stories

The significance of storytelling in small groups also can be seen clearly when the various kinds of storytelling shown in table 10.1 are considered jointly: 87 percent of all group members had experienced storytelling in their group in at least one of these ways; 81 percent, in two or more of these ways; 74 percent in three or more ways; 63 percent in at least four of these ways; and 50 percent in five or more ways.

When the relationships between having had one's faith or spirituality influenced by the group and the various items about storytelling were examined simultaneously using discriminant analysis, the item that discriminated best between those whose faith had been influenced and those whose faith had not been influenced was discussing any kind of stories from the Bible or other books. Having discussed the Good Samaritan story also had a strong independent effect. Having discussed the Prodigal Son story and having compared one's own experience to stories read had significant but weaker effects. When members of church-based groups were examined separately, the overall effect of the general item about discussing stories from the Bible or other books was reduced, but the effect of discussing the Good Samaritan story was strengthened. Among members of nonchurch groups, there was a strong effect from discussing stories from the Bible or other books and from discussing the story of the Prodigal Son. Substantively, these results suggest that the effect of storytelling on spirituality is specific to stories that have a religious content and that the storytelling itself makes a difference, rather than just being in a church context. The significance of specific stories is also suggested by the fact that the best predictor of saying one's desire to serve other people outside the group had increased and of saying one's love toward other people had increased in the group was discussing the Good Samaritan story, while the best predictor of having relationships healed was discussing the Prodigal Son story.

Chapter 11: Serving the Community

The results discussed in chapter 11 are chiefly from a question that read "As a result of being in this group, have you done any of the following?" The specific statements to which yes or no responses were given are shown in tables 11.1 and 11.2. The limitation of this question wording is, of course, that respondents may have attributed activities to their group involvement that they would have become interested in anyway or for reasons other than their small group. To compensate for this possibility, we performed two kinds of analysis on the data. We examined each response in relation to measures of group involvement, such as length of involvement in one's group and frequency of attendance, to determine if more active members were more likely to say they had experienced each of these consequences. We also asked some independent questions about related activities, such as church attendance, volunteer work, and interests in politics. The results of these analyses strongly support the claim that active group members are generally more likely to be involved in other community, church, voluntary, and political activities than less active group members. These relationships hold when other differences in respondents, such as age, gender, and level of education, are taken into account. Descriptively, these results support the claim that small-group members are not, by and large, ingrown or focused entirely on their own individual or group problems. Whether group involvement encourages these other activities is more difficult to establish. The qualitative data presented in the chapter shows some of the ways in which group involvement does encourage these other activities, at least for some people.

The results in the chapter from the 1988 Independent Sector survey are based on both cross-tabular and multivariate analysis. Because the survey included oversampling of blacks and Hispanics on some questions but not on others, and because this oversampling necessitated the use of complex weighting procedures, our analysis was based only on data for white respondents (unweighted). The percentages of group members engaged in various kinds of church activities may appear to be relatively small, but when aggregated they are consistent with the proportions in our own survey who claimed to be involved in at least some kind of church program or activity. The percentages for particular activities are likely to be low because the questions were open-ended and coded after the fact.

Cross-tabular analysis of our own data on the likelihood of people saying they had increased their church giving as a result of being in a group reveals that these relationships hold for most subcategories of respondents. In other words, younger and older people, men and women, people with different levels of education, and members of small and large churches alike are all about equally likely to say that their giving has increased. Members of black churches are somewhat more likely to give this response than members of white churches. Respondents who attend church every week are much more likely to give this response than less frequent church attenders. Virtually no church members who attend church only a few times a year say their group involvement has led them to give more to their churches. In other words, group involvement must be accompanied by wider congregational involvement to encourage financial giving. Among all church members, the most striking differences were between religious conservatives and religious liberals: whereas 51 percent of those who identified themselves as religious conservatives said they had increased their giving, this figure was 38 percent among religious liberals and 35 percent among moderates. The potential of small groups to increase giving among liberals (but not among moderates), nevertheless, is suggested by comparisons among Protestants who attend their small group at least once a week: 61 percent of these conservatives say they have increased their giving, but so have 60 percent of these liberals.

Appendix B
THE SMALL GROUPS SURVEY

First, I would like to ask you some questions about the community you live in...

S3. How many years have you lived in your present community?
1   Less than one
2   One to less than two
3   Two to less than three
4   Three to less than five
5   Five to less than ten
6   Ten or more
7   Don't know
8   Refused

S4. Of your closest friends, how many would you say live in your present community?
1   None
2   One or two
3   Three to five
4   More than five
5   Don't know
6   Refused

S5. Are you currently involved in any small group that meets regularly and provides support or caring for those who participate in it?   (Hand respondent Card A if needed for examples.)
1   Yes -- Ask S6
2   No -- Skip to Q7
3   Don't know
4   Refused

CARD A: EXAMPLES OF GROUPS

Youth group
Singles' group
Couples' group
Women's group
Men's group
Bible study group
Prayer fellowship

House church
Covenant group
Self-help group
Anonymous group
Sunday school class
Special interest group
Discussion group
Support group
Therapy group

S6. How many groups like this are you currently involved in?
1   Only one
2   Two
3   Three or more
4   Don't know
5   Refused

Not including the group(s) that you currently belong to...

Q7. In the past, were you ever involved in any small groups that met regularly and provided support or caring for those who participated in them?
1   Yes -- Ask Q8
2   No -- Go to note after Q11
3   Don't know
4   Refused

Q8. How many groups like this would you say you have been involved in as an adult?
1   None
2   One
3   Two
4   Three or four
5   Five or more
6   Don't know
7   Refused

Q9. During the past three years, were you involved in any groups like this?
1   Yes -- Ask Q10
2   No -- Go to note after Q11
3   Don't know
4   Refused

Q10.   How long, during the past three years, were you involved?
1   Less than 6 months
2   6 months to less than 1 year
3   1 year to less than 2 years
4   2 years to 3 years
5   Don't know
6   Refused

Q11.   Were you in a group that focused on religious or spiritual matters?
1   Yes
2   No
3   Don't know
4   Refused

Note: If "Yes -- Current member of small group" in S5, continue; all others, skip to Q69.

Now, on another topic...

(Show respondent Card 1)

Please refer to the responses on this card for the next few questions...

Q12.   Compared to 5 years ago, has each of the following become a lot more important to you (AL), somewhat more important (SM), stayed the same (SS), become somewhat less important (SL), or a lot less important (LL) to you? (READ AND ROTATE A-K)

	AL	SM	SS	SL	LL	DK/RF
A. Prayer	1	2	3	4	5	6
B. Helping other people	1	2	3	4	5	6
C. Political issues	1	2	3	4	5	6
D. Having nice things	1	2	3	4	5	6
E. The environment	1	2	3	4	5	6
F. Spiritual matters	1	2	3	4	5	6
G. Your church/synagogue	1	2	3	4	5	6
H. Studying the Bible	1	2	3	4	5	6
I. Your family	1	2	3	4	5	6
J. Your job or career	1	2	3	4	5	6
K. Money	1	2	3	4	5	6

CARD 1

A lot more important
Somewhat more important
Stayed the same
Somewhat less important
A lot less important

Q13.   Do you, yourself, happen to be involved in any charity or social service activities, such as helping the poor, the sick, or the elderly?
1   Yes
2   No
3   Don't know
4   Refused

(Show respondent Card 2)

Q14.   I'm going to read you a list of personal *needs*. For each one, which statement on this card best describes how well you have met that need. Is this a need you feel you have partly met (PM), fully met (FM), or never experienced (NE)? (READ AND ROTATE A-K)

		PM	FM	NE	DK/RF
A.	Having neighbors with whom you can interact freely and comfortably	1	2	3	4
B.	Being able to share your deepest feelings with someone	1	2	3	4
C.	Having friends who value the same things in life you do	1	2	3	4
D.	Having people in your life who give you deep emotional support	1	2	3	4
E.	Being in a group where you can discuss your most basic beliefs and values	1	2	3	4
F.	Having friends you can always count on when you're in a jam	1	2	3	4
G.	Having people in your life who are never critical of you	1	2	3	4
H.	Being part of a group that helps you grow spiritually	1	2	3	4
I.	Having cooperation, rather than competition, with people at work	1	2	3	4

J. Having people you can turn to
    when you are feeling depressed
    or lonely   1   2   3   4
K. Knowing more people in your
    community   1   2   3   4

CARD 2   Partially met
                 Fully met
                 Never experienced

Now, on another topic...

(Show respondent Card 3)

Q15. Do each of the following phrases describe you, personally, very well
       (VW), fairly well (FW), not very well (NVW), or not at all (NAA)?
       (READ AND ROTATE A-N)

		VW	FW	NVW	NAA	DK/RF
A.	A "rugged individualist"	1	2	3	4	5
B.	A "people person"	1	2	3	4	5
C.	An "introvert"	1	2	3	4	5
D.	An "extrovert"	1	2	3	4	5
E.	A "good neighbor"	1	2	3	4	5
F.	Someone who needs a lot of time alone	1	2	3	4	5
G.	A "free spirit"	1	2	3	4	5
H.	A "loner"	1	2	3	4	5
I.	On a "spiritual journey"	1	2	3	4	5
J.	Highly ambitious	1	2	3	4	5
K.	Career-oriented	1	2	3	4	5
L.	A leader	1	2	3	4	5
M.	Deeply religious	1	2	3	4	5
N.	A very private person	1	2	3	4	5

CARD 3

Describes you...
     Very well
     Fairly well
     Not very well
     Not at all

(Show respondent Card 4)

Q16.   Please look at the descriptions on this card. Which label best describes
        how much each of the following bothers you. For each statement
        would you say it bothers you a lot (AL), some (S), only a little (OAL),
        or none (N)? (READ AND ROTATE A-I)

		AL	S	OAL	N	DK/RF
A.	Worrying about your health	1	2	3	4	5
B.	Trying to figure out what is important in life	1	2	3	4	5
C.	Problems with your spouse or family	1	2	3	4	5
D.	Feeling lonely	1	2	3	4	5
E.	Problems with your work	1	2	3	4	5
F.	Feeling depressed or sad	1	2	3	4	5
G.	Anxiety	1	2	3	4	5
H.	Feeling guilty	1	2	3	4	5
I.	Worrying about money	1	2	3	4	5

CARD 4

Bothers you...
    A lot
    Some
    Only a little
    None

Now, on another topic...

Q17.   How often, if at all, do you attend religious services?
    1   More than once a week
    2   About once a week
    3   Several times a month
    4   About once a month
    5   Several times a year
    6   Once a year or less
    7   Never
    8   Don't know
    9   Refused

Q18.   Are you currently a member of a church or synagogue?
   1   Yes -- Ask Q19
   2   No -- Go to Q26.
   3   Don't know
   4   Refused

Q19.   How many people belong to this church or synagogue? Would you
       say...
   1   Fewer than 100
   2   100 to less than 200
   3   200 to less than 300
   4   300 to less than 500
   5   500 to less than 1,000
   6   1,000 or more
   7   Don't know
   8   Refused

Q20.   How many years have you attended this congregation?
   1   Less than one
   2   One to less than two
   3   Two to less than three
   4   Three to less than five
   5   Five to less than ten
   6   Ten or more
   7   Don't know
   8   Refused

Q21.   Of your closest friends, how many would you say attend this
       congregation?
   1   None
   2   One or two
   3   Three to five
   4   More than five
   5   Don't know
   6   Refused

Q22.   How many special activities, programs, or committees are you
       currently involved with in your congregation?
   1   None
   2   One or two
   3   Three to five
   4   More than five
   5   Don't know
   6   Refused

Q23. Does your congregation encourage people to become involved in small fellowship groups?

1 Yes
2 No
3 Don't know
4 Refused

Q24. Are small fellowship groups part of a plan to make your congregation grow?

1 Yes
2 No
3 Don't know
4 Refused

Q25. Of the people who attend your congregation, would you say that...

1 Most are involved in small fellowship groups
2 About half are involved in small fellowship groups
3 About a quarter are involved in small fellowship groups, or
4 Very few are involved in small fellowship groups
5 Don't know
6 Refused

Ask everyone:

Q26. What is your religious preference?

01 Protestant -- Ask Q27
02 Catholic
03 Jewish
04 Eastern Orthodox
05 Other   -- Go to Q28
06 Mormon
07 Moslem
08 Hindu
09 Atheist
10 Agnostic
11 None
12 Don't know
13 Refused

(Show Hand Card 5)

Q27.   What specific denomination or faith is that?

CARD 5

01 Church of Jesus Christ of Latter-Day Saints (Mormon)

Baptists:
02 Southern Baptist Convention
03 American Baptist Convention
04 National Baptist Convention of America
05 National Baptist Convention, USA
06 Other Baptist (specified)
07 Baptist, don't know which denomination

08 Episcopalian

Lutheran
09 Evangelical Lutheran Church in America
10 Missouri Synod Lutheran
11 Other Lutheran (specified)
12 Lutheran, don't know which denomination

Methodist
13 United Methodist Church
14 A.M.E. Zion Church
15 A.M.E. Church
16 Other Methodist (specified)
17 Methodist, don't know which denomination

Presbyterian
18 Presbyterian Church (USA)
19 Presbyterian Church in America
20 Other Presbyterian (specified)
21 Presbyterian, don't know which denomination

22 United Church of Christ (or Congregationalist or Evangelical and Reformed)
23 Christian Church (Disciples of Christ)
24 Church of the Nazarene
25 Assemblies of God
26 Pentecostal
27 Fundamentalist
28 Nondenominational or independent church

29 Other Protestant (specified)
30 Protestant, unspecified

Q28.   How important would you say religion is in your own life...
1   Very important
2   Somewhat important
3   Not very important
4   Not at all important
5   Don't know
6   Refused

Q29.   How important would you say religion was in your family while you were growing up...
1   Very important
2   Somewhat important
3   Not very important
4   Not at all important
5   Don't know
6   Refused

Q30.   Which of these statements comes closest to your view of religious faith?
1   You have to let faith unfold in its own way, or
2   You have to work hard at developing your faith
3   Both (volunteered)
4   Neither (volunteered)
5   Don't know
6   Refused

Q31.   Do you mostly agree (MA) or mostly disagree (MD) with each of the following statements? (READ AND ROTATE A-F)

		MA	MD	DK/RF
A.	My religious beliefs are very personal and private	1	2	3
B.	My spirituality does not depend on being involved in a religious organization	1	2	3
C.	The clergy are generally no more spiritual than other people	1	2	3
D.	A lot of churches are really out of date	1	2	3

E. All churches are pretty much
    alike   1   2   3
F. It doesn't matter what you
    believe, as long as you are
    a good person   1   2   3

Q32. Have you ever had a religious experience -- that is, a particularly
      powerful religious insight or awakening?
      1   Yes
      2   No
      3   Don't know
      4   Refused

Q33. Would you say you have made a commitment to Jesus Christ, or not?
      1   Yes
      2   No
      3   Don't know
      4   Refused

Q34. In your opinion, is each of the following statements about the Bible true
      (T) or false (F)? (READ AND ROTATE A-F)

		T	F	DK/RF
A.	The Bible is the inspired word of God	1	2	3
B.	Everything in the Bible should be taken literally, word for word	1	2	3
C.	The Bible may contain historical or scientific errors	1	2	3
D.	According to the Bible, Jesus was born in Jerusalem	1	2	3
E.	The book of Acts is in the Old Testament	1	2	3
F.	The Bible is a detailed book of rules that Christians should try to follow	1	2	3

Q35. On a scale from 1 to 6, where "1" is "very conservative" and "6" is
      "very liberal," where would you place yourself in terms of your
      religious views?

Very conservative   Very liberal   DK/RF

          1   2   3   4   5   6   7

Q36.   Using the same scale, how would you define your political views, where "1" is "very conservative" and "6" is "very liberal"?

Very conservative   Very liberal   DK/RF

1   2   3   4   5   6   7

(Read:)   Next I would like to discuss the small group that you spoke about earlier that meets regularly and provides support or cairng for those who participate in it.   If you are currently involved in more than one such group, please think about the group that you are most actively involved in.

Q37.   How long have you been involved in this group?
1   Five years or longer
2   Three to less than five years
3   One to less than three years
4   Less than one year
5   Don't know
6   Refused

Q38.   How often, on the average, does this group meet?
1   More than once a week
2   Once a week
3   Once every two weeks
4   About once a month
5   Less than once a month
6   Don't know
7   Refused

Q39.   How often, do you, personally, attend group meetings?
1   More than once a week
2   Once a week
3   Once every two weeks
4   About once a month
5   Less than once a month
6   Don't know
7   Refused

Q40.   How long does an average meeting of the group last?
1   Less than an hour
2   About an hour
3   About an hour and a half

4 About two hours
5 More than two hours
6 Don't know
7 Refused

Q41.   How many people usually attend the meetings of this group?
1 Five or less
2 Six to ten
3 Eleven to fifteen
4 Sixteen to twenty
5 Twenty-one to thirty
6 More than thirty
7 Don't know
8 Refused

Q42.   Are these people:
1 Mostly your age
2 Mostly younger than you
3 Mostly older than you, or
4 Of all different ages
5 Don't know
6 Refused

Q43.   Is the group made up of...
1 All women
2 Mostly women
3 About equal numbers of men and women
4 Mostly men, or
5 All men
6 Don't know
7 Refused

Q44.   In their religious views, is the group...
1 Mostly conservative
2 Mostly middle-of-the-road
3 Mostly liberal, or
4 A mixture of liberal and conservative
5 Don't know
6 Refused

Q45.   On political issues, is the group...
1 Mostly conservative
2 Mostly middle-of-the-road

3   Mostly liberal, or
4   A mixture of liberal and conservative
5   Don't know
6   Refused

Q46.   Is the group...
1   All white
2   Mostly white
3   About evenly mixed
4   Mostly nonwhite, or
5   All nonwhite
6   Don't know
7   Refused

Q47.   Would you say that...
1   Almost everyone in the group comes every time, or
2   A lot of people do not come every time.
3   Don't know
4   Refused

Q48.   Does the group do any of the following activities? Does the group
(READ AND ROTATE A-T)?

		YES	NO	DK/RF
A.	Study or discuss the Bible	1	2	3
B.	Pray together	1	2	3
C.	Discuss religious topics	1	2	3
D.	Eat together	1	2	3
E.	Sing together	1	2	3
F.	Let people share their problems	1	2	3
G.	Work on projects	1	2	3
H.	Discuss social or political issues	1	2	3
I.	Discuss books	1	2	3
J.	Do things for the community	1	2	3
K.	Do sports or hobbies together	1	2	3
L.	Have parties	1	2	3
M.	Provide emotional support	1	2	3
N.	Follow a "twelve-step" program	1	2	3
O.	Focus on an addiction	1	2	3
P.	Practice meditation	1	2	3
Q.	Engage in physical exercise	1	2	3
R.	Practice speaking in tongues	1	2	3
S.	Focus on a specific need or problem	1	2	3

T.	Hold members accountable	1	2	3

Q49.   How long has the group been in existence?
   1   Less than a year
   2   One year to less than two years
   3   Two years to less than three years
   4   Three years to less than five years
   5   Five years or more
   6   Don't know
   7   Refused

Q50.   Does the group have any of the following? (READ AND ROTATE A-K)

		YES	NO	DK/RF
A.	Business meetings	1	2	3
B.	Elected officers	1	2	3
C.	A contract people have to agree to	1	2	3
D.	An agenda or schedule	1	2	3
E.	Child care	1	2	3
F.	A leader	1	2	3
G.	Something to study in advance	1	2	3
H.	A stated purpose or goal	1	2	3
I.	A term after which it disbands	1	2	3
J.	A membership fee	1	2	3
K.	A name	1	2	3

Q51.   Would any of these descriptions apply to your group? (READ AND ROTATE A-P)

		YES	NO	DK/RF
A.	Youth group	1	2	3
B.	Singles' group	1	2	3
C.	Couples' group	1	2	3
D.	Women's group	1	2	3
E.	Men's group	1	2	3
F.	Bible study group	1	2	3
G.	Prayer fellowship	1	2	3
H.	House church	1	2	3
I.	Covenant group	1	2	3
J.	Self-help group	1	2	3
K.	Anonymous group	1	2	3
L.	Sunday school class	1	2	3
M.	Special interest group	1	2	3
N.	Discussion group	1	2	3

O.	Support group	1	2	3
P.	Therapy group	1	2	3

Q52. Does the group usually meet...
1   At a church or synagogue
2   In a community building or town hall
3   At one member's home
4   At various members' homes on a rotating basis, or
5   Some other place
6   Don't know
7   Refused

Q53. Was each of the following a reason why you became involved, or not?
(READ AND ROTATE A-I)

		YES	NO	DK/RF
A.	Feeling like you didn't know anyone in your community	1	2	3
B.	Having problems in your personal life	1	2	3
C.	Being invited by someone you knew	1	2	3
D.	Hearing about it through your church or synagogue	1	2	3
E.	Needing emotional support	1	2	3
F.	Being in another group like it previously	1	2	3
G.	Wanting to become more disciplined in your spiritual life	1	2	3
H.	Experiencing a crisis in your life	1	2	3
I.	The desire to grow as a person	1	2	3

Q54. How important is this group to you personally?
1   Extremely important
2   Very important
3   Fairly important
4   Not very important
5   Don't know
6   Refused

(Show respondent Card 6)

Q55. Would you rate the group as excellent (E), good (G), fair (F), or poor (P) on each of the following? [NA = Not Applicable] (READ AND ROTATE A-L)

		E	G	F	P	NA	DK/RF
A.	Draws everyone into the discussion	1	2	3	4	5	6
B.	Respects all different points of view	1	2	3	4	5	6
C.	Addresses important issues	1	2	3	4	5	6
D.	Members are faithful in attending	1	2	3	4	5	6
E.	Makes me personally feel appreciated	1	2	3	4	5	6
F.	Leaders are well prepared	1	2	3	4	5	6
G.	Everything works smoothly and efficiently	1	2	3	4	5	6
H.	Members hold each other accountable	1	2	3	4	5	6
I.	Meets emotional needs	1	2	3	4	5	6
J.	Helps other people outside the group	1	2	3	4	5	6
K.	Makes newcomers feel welcome	1	2	3	4	5	6
L.	People trust each other	1	2	3	4	5	6

CARD 6   Excellent
Good
Fair
Poor

Q56. On the whole, how satisfied are you with the group?
1   Extremely satisfied
2   Very satisfied
3   Somewhat satisfied
4   Somewhat dissatisfied
5   Very dissatisfied
6   Extremely dissatisfied
7   Don't know
8   Refused

Q57.   Has the group ever helped you, personally, in any of the following
ways? (READ AND ROTATE A-K)

		YES	NO	DK/RF
A.	Helped you through an emotional crisis	1	2	3
B.	Gave you encouragement when you were feeling down	1	2	3
C.	Made you feel like you weren't alone	1	2	3
D.	Helped you make a difficult decision	1	2	3
E.	Loaned you money	1	2	3
F.	Helped you out when someone was sick	1	2	3
G.	Brought meals for your family	1	2	3
H.	Helped you celebrate something	1	2	3
I.	Provided you with physical care or support	1	2	3
J.	Provided you with babysitting or child care	1	2	3
K.	Helped you overcome an addiction	1	2	3

Q58.   Groups are never perfect. Have you ever experienced any of the
following in this group? (READ AND ROTATE A-L)

		YES	NO	DK/RF
A.	Feeling shy or reluctant to share your feelings	1	2	3
B.	Feeling uncomfortable	1	2	3
C.	Feeling like you didn't quite fit in	1	2	3
D.	Disagreeing with other members of the group	1	2	3
E.	Feeling pressure from the group to do something	1	2	3
F.	Finding it hard to make time for the group	1	2	3
G.	People in the group expecting too much from you	1	2	3
H.	Feeling like the group didn't understand you	1	2	3
I.	Not feeling appreciated by the group	1	2	3
J.	Feeling like you couldn't really be open and			

		YES	NO	
	honest with the group	1	2	3
K.	Feeling that people in the group were criticizing you	1	2	3
L.	Feeling the group was invading your privacy	1	2	3

Q59.   From being involved in this group, has your faith or spirituality been influenced?

1   Yes -- ASK Q60
2   No -- GO TO Q61
3   Don't know
4   Refused

Q60. Would you say it has....(READ 1-4)

1   Deepened a lot
2   Deepened a little
3   Become less important, or
4   Changed in some other way
5   Don't know
6   Refused

Q61.   As a result of being in this group, which of these, if any, have you experienced.... (READ AND ROTATE A-O)

		YES	NO	DK/RF
A.	Answers to prayers	1	2	3
B.	Healings of relationships	1	2	3
C.	A new depth of love toward other people	1	2	3
D.	Feeling closer to God	1	2	3
E.	Less interested in people outside your group	1	2	3
F.	Conflict with people in your group	1	2	3
G.	More understanding of persons with different religious perspectives	1	2	3
H.	More open and honest with other people	1	2	3
I.	More open and honest with yourself	1	2	3
J.	Feeling better about yourself	1	2	3
K.	The Bible has become more meaningful to you	1	2	3
L.	Better able to forgive others	1	2	3
M.	Better able to forgive yourself	1	2	3
N.	Has helped me share my faith with others outside the group	1	2	3

O. Has helped me to serve people outside
    the group   1   2   3

Q62. In getting help from the group, how important has each of the
      following been to you? Very important (VI), fairly important (FI), not
      very important (NVI), or not at all important (NAAI)? (READ AND
      ROTATE A-I)

		VI	FI	NVI	NAAI	DK/RF
A.	Studying particular lessons from the Bible	1	2	3	4	5
B.	Hearing other members share their views	1	2	3	4	5
C.	Seeing how to apply ideas to your life	1	2	3	4	5
D.	Having a leader who could answer your questions	1	2	3	4	5
E.	People in the group giving you encouragement	1	2	3	4	5
F.	Having one person in the group that you could discuss things with	1	2	3	4	5
G.	Someone in the group that you could admire and try to be like	1	2	3	4	5
H.	Hearing people tell stories about what worked and what didn't work for them	1	2	3	4	5
I.	Seeing love and caring acted out in the group	1	2	3	4	5

Q63. Have you sensed God's presence in the group... (READ 1-4)
    1 Many times
    2 A few times
    3 Only once, or
    4 Never
    5 Don't know
    6 Refused

Q64. Have you ever done any of the following? (READ AND ROTATE A-
      J)
                                                       YES   NO   DK/RF
A. Attended this group regularly

		YES	NO	DK/RF
	with your spouse or some other family member	1	2	3
B.	Taken a family member who was not a regular participant along with you to the group	1	2	3
C.	Had disagreements with a family member about whether you should attend the group	1	2	3
D.	Been encouraged by a family member to attend the group	1	2	3
E.	Invited a friend to attend the group	1	2	3
F.	Had a friend who was not a regular participant visit the group	1	2	3
G.	Been responsible for someone new joining the group	1	2	3
H.	Discussed the group with friends who were not involved in it	1	2	3
I.	Helped start a new group	1	2	3
J.	Invited someone to attend your church or synagogue	1	2	3

Q65.   Is this group part of the regular activities of any church or synagogue?
   1   Yes -- ASK Q66
   2   No -- GO TO Q67
   3   Don't know
   4   Refused

Q66.   Is the group... (READ AND ROTATE A-G)

		YES	NO	DK/RF
A.	Something one of clergy helped to start	1	2	3
B.	Under the supervision of one of the clergy	1	2	3
C.	One of a number of such groups at this church or synagogue	1	2	3
D.	Composed mostly of members of this church or synagogue	1	2	3
E.	Part of the church's or synagogue's plan to grow	1	2	3
F.	Connected to the church or synagogue that you, personally, belong to	1	2	3
G.	Using plans, lessons, or other materials provided by a church or synagogue	1	2	3

Q67.   Many small groups are places where people discuss stories they read, tell stories about themselves, and listen to others tell their stories. Tell me if you have done each of the following in your group.   (READ AND ROTATE A-G)

		YES	NO	DK/RF
A.	Told stories about some experience in your life	1	2	3
B.	Discussed things that happened to you as a child	1	2	3
C.	Discussed stories from the Bible or some other book	1	2	3
D.	Compared your own experience with stories you have read about and discussed in the group	1	2	3
E.	Compared your own experiences with stories told by other members of the group about themselves	1	2	3
F.	Discussed the story of the Good Samaritan in the group	1	2	3
G.	Discussed the story of the Prodigal Son in the group	1	2	3

267.   As a result of being in this group, have you done any of the following? (READ AND ROTATE A-K)

		YES	NO	DK/RF
A.	Become involved in volunteer work in your community	1	2	3
B.	Taken a more active part in other programs sponsored by your church or synagogue	1	2	3
C.	Worked with the group to help other people in need outside of the group	1	2	3
D.	Worked with the group to help someone inside the group who was in need	1	2	3
F.	Become more interested in social or political issues	1	2	3
G.	Changed your own attitudes on some social or political issue	1	2	3
H.	Become more interested in peace or social justice	1	2	3
I.	Participated in a political			

	rally or worked for a political campaign	1	2	3
J.	Donated money to a charitable organization, other than your church or synagogue	1	2	3
K.	Increased the amount of money you give to your church or synagogue	1	2	3

(All in Q68, Go to Q73)

ASK THESE QUESTIONS TO PEOPLE WHO ARE NOT IN A GROUP:

Q69. Would you like to be involved in some kind of small group that meets regularly and provides support or caring for its members?
1   Yes - Ask Q70
2   No - Go to Q73
3   Don't know
4   Refused

Q70. How likely is it that you will join a group like this within the next year? Is it...
1   Very likely
2   Fairly likely
3   Fairly unlikely, or
4   Very unlikely
5   Don't know
6   Refused

Q71. Do you have a specific group in mind that you would like to join?
1   Yes
2   No
3   Don't know
4   Refused

Q72. If you were to join a small group like this, would it probably have...
1   A religious focus, or
2   Some other focus
3   Don't know
4   Refused

(Ask all:)

Q73.   Are you part of any circle of friends who sometimes do things to help
each other out?
1   Yes - Ask Q74
2   No - Go to Q75
3   Don't know
4   Refused

Q74.   Does this circle of friends do each of the following? (READ AND
ROTATE A-I)

		YES	NO	DK/RF
A.	Support each other emotionally	1	2	3
B.	Work on projects together	1	2	3
C.	See each other socially	1	2	3
D.	Have any regular meetings	1	2	3
E.	Give each other gifts	1	2	3
F.	Live in the same neighborhood	1	2	3
G.	Know each other from high school or college	1	2	3
H.	Provide child care for each other	1	2	3
I.	Help each other financially	1	2	3

Q75.   How interested are you at present in developing your faith or
spirituality? Are you...
1   Very interested
2   Fairly interested
3   Fairly uninterested, or
4   Very uninterested
5   Don't know
6   Refused

Q76.   Are you currently involved in any of the following? (READ AND
ROTATE A-L)

		YES	NO	DK/RF
A.	Raising small children	1	2	3
B.	Raising teenagers	1	2	3
C.	An athletic team, fitness program, or exercise program	1	2	3
D.	Counseling or therapy	1	2	3
E.	Taking classes of any kind	1	2	3
F.	A professional organization that you attend meetings of	1	2	3
G.	A group of friends or			

	neighbors that get together			
	informally	1	2	3
H.	Reading novels	1	2	3
I.	Reading the Bible	1	2	3
J.	Reading other religious or			
	spiritual books	1	2	3
K.	Meditating	1	2	3
L.	Watching religious programs			
	on television	1	2	3

D1. AGE: Please tell me how old you are. (record actual age)

00 (Refused)   99   99+

D2. EDUCATION: What is the highest level of education you have
                    completed?
   1   Less than high school graduate (K-11)
   2   High school graduate (12)
   3   Some college
   4   Trade/technical/vocational training
   5   College graduate
   6   Post-graduate work/degree
   7   Don't know
   8   Refused

D3. RACE: (Record)
   1   White
   2   Black
   3   Some other

D4. ETHNICITY: Are you, yourself, of Hispanic origin or descent,
                     such as Mexican, Puerto Rican, Cuban, or other
                     Spanish background?
   1   Yes
   2   No
   3   Don't know
   4   Refused

D5. OCCUPATION: What is your current occupation?
   01 Other
   02 Don't know
   03 Refused

04 Unemployed
05 Blank
06 Student
07 Housewife
08 Retired/disabled
09 Professional/managerial
10 Secretarial/clerical
11 Services/labor
12 Sales/retail
13 Farmer/rancher
14 Military

D6. CHILDREN: Are there any children under the age of 18 currently
                       living in your household?
1   Yes
2   No
3   Don't know
4   Refused

D7. IF YES: How many children are...
    A. Less than six years old: _____
    B. Between 6 and 12 years old: _____
    C. Between 13 and 17 years old: _____

D8. Which of the following best describes the place in which you live?
    1   A large city or metropolitan area (over 500,000 people)
    2   The suburb of a large city or metropolitan area
    3   A medium city or suburb of a medium city (100,000 to 500,000
        people)
    4   A small city
    5   A small town
    6   A rural area
    7   Don't know
    8   Refused

(Hand respondent Card 8)

D9. INCOME: Would you please give me the letter of the group which best
             represents the total annual income, before taxes, of all the
             members of your immediate family living in your household?
    CARD 8
    01 Under $10,000
    02 $10,000 - $14,999

03   $15,000 - $19,999
04   $20,000 - $24,999
05   $25,000 - $29,999
06   $30,000 - $34,999
07   $35,000 - $39,999
08   $40,000 - $44,999
09   $45,000 - $49,999
10   $50,000 - $54,999
11   $55,000 - $59,999
12   $60,000 - $64,999
13   $65,000 or more
14   Don't know
15   Refused

D10.   Does your household have a telephone?
1   Yes
2   No
3   Don't know
4   Refused

D11.   GENDER: (Record)
1   Male
2   Female

NOTES

Chapter 2. The Quest for Community

1. Mark A. Noll, Nathan O. Hatch, George M. Marsden, David F. Wells, and John D. Woodbridge (eds.), *Eerdmans' Handbook to Christianity in America* (Grand Rapids, Mich.: Eerdmans, 1983). One of the most useful overviews of the role of religion in American history.

2. This part of the story is captured magnificently in Nathan O. Hatch, *The Democratization of American Christianity* (New Haven, Conn.: Yale University Press, 1989).

3. Even the traditional image of revival meetings focusing chiefly on individual piety is being challenged by new historical studies emphasizing its links to the corporate rites and services of churches; see for example Leigh Eric Schmidt, *Holy Fairs: Scottish Communions and American Revivals in the Early Modern Period* (Princeton, N.J.: Princeton University Press, 1989).

4. Justo L. Gonzalez, *The Story of Christianity*, 2 vols (New York: Harper & Row, 1984). A readable history of Christianity (volume 1 focuses on the early Christian church through the Middle Ages, volume 2 on the Protestant Reformation to the present) that demonstrates repeatedly how small groups sustained and revitalized individuals' commitment to their faith.

5. George Gallup, Jr., *Faith Development and Your Ministry* (Princeton, N.J.: Princeton Religion Research Center, 1985). Based on an extensive national survey carried out in cooperation with the Religious Education Association of the United States and Canada, this 78-page report documents the extent to which people are currently interested in developing their faith and some of the practical ways in which religious organizations might help to meet these needs. Available from the Princeton Religion Research Center, P.O. Box 628, Princeton, NJ 08542.

6. For an overview of the role of religion in contemporary U.S. society, see my book *The Restructuring of American Religion: Society and Faith Since World War II* (Princeton, N.J.: Princeton University Press, 1988). Comparisons between the U.S. and other advanced industrial societies can be found in David Harrington Watt, "United States: Cultural Challenges to the Voluntary Sector," in *Between States and Markets: The Voluntary Sector in Comparative Perspective*, edited by Robert Wuthnow (Princeton, N.J.: Princeton University Press, 1991), pp.

243–287. Other chapters in the same volume provide evidence on the strength of religion in Japan, England, Germany, France, and other countries.

7. On the recent rise of interest in religion as an academic topic, see Ellen K. Coughlin, "Social Scientists Again Turn Attention to Religion's Place in the World," *Chronicle of Higher Education* (April 1, 1992), A6–A8.

8. The decline of community has been a perennial theme in the social sciences at least since Ferdinand Tönnies, *Community and Society*, trans. by Charles P. Loomis (New York: Harper & Row, 1963; originally published in 1887). For a dispassionate empirical discussion of the ways in which community is and is not changing in American society, see Claude S. Fischer, "Ambivalent Communities: How Americans Understand Their Localities," in *America at Century's End*, edited by Alan Wolfe (Berkeley and Los Angeles: University of California Press, 1991), pp. 79–91.

9. These points are emphasized in Paul Leinberger and Bruce Tucker, *The New Individualists: The Generation After the Organization Man* (New York: HarperCollins, 1991). Based on hundreds of qualitative interviews, this is a major study providing contrasts between social patterns in the 1950s and the 1980s. It is, however, written for a popular audience and many of its claims would require further substantiation.

10. David Riesman, Nathan Glazer, and Reuel Denney, *The Lonely Crowd: A Study of the Changing American Character* (New Haven, Conn.: Yale University Press, 1950). See also David Riesman, *Individualism Reconsidered* (Glencoe, Ill.: Free Press, 1954).

11. For a recent empirical study, see David Hummon, *Commonplaces: Community Ideology and Identity in American Culture* (Albany: State University of New York Press, 1990); the literature on urbanism and its impact on social life more generally is reviewed in Suzanne Keller, *The Urban Neighborhood* (New York: Random House, 1968), and Claude S. Fischer, *The Urban Experience*, 2d ed. (San Diego, Calif.: Harcourt Brace Jovanovich, 1984).

12. Robert J. Sampson, "Friendship Networks and Community Attachment in Mass Society: A Multilevel Systemic Model," *American Sociological Review* 53 (1988), 766–779; Charles E. Connerly, "The Community Question: An Extension of Wellman and Leighton," *Urban Affairs Quarterly* 20 (1985), 537–556; and Carol J. Silverman, "Neighboring and Urbanism: Commonality Versus Friendship," *Urban Affairs Quarterly* 22 (1986), 312–328.

13. Herbert J. Gans, *Middle American Individualism: Political Participation and Liberal Democracy* (New York: Oxford University Press, 1988). Clearly written exposition by a former president of the American Sociological Association of the social sources and consequences of the emphasis on individualism and the breakdown of community in American society.

14. In my research on caring, I found in a national survey I conducted in 1989 that 37 percent of the public feel they could not count on their immediate neighbors if someone in their family became ill and they needed help; about the same proportions said they could not count on relatives in their extended family or members of a church or synagogue; see *Acts of Compassion: Caring for Others and Helping Ourselves* (Princeton, N.J.: Princeton University Press, 1991), p. 11.

15. Robert C. Fuller, *Ecology of Care: An Interdisciplinary Analysis of the Self and Moral Obligation* (Louisville, Ky.: Westminster/John Knox, 1992), p. 92.

16. Gordon Kaufman, *Theology for a Nuclear Age* (Philadelphia: Westminster Press, 1985), p. 60.

17. Thomas Luckmann, *The Invisible Religion: The Transformation of Symbols in Industrial Society* (New York: Macmillan, 1967). A classic discussion that examines the major social forms of contemporary religion, how these forms are being challenged by modern society, and the ways in which religious convictions are increasingly becoming matters of private belief.

18. The same point was forcefully argued about the same time in Peter L. Berger, *The Sacred Canopy: Elements of a Sociological Theory of Religion* (Garden City, N.Y.: Doubleday, 1967).

19. Robert N. Bellah, Richard Madsen, William M. Sullivan, Ann Swidler, and Steven M. Tipton, *Habits of the Heart: Individualism and Commitment in American Life* (Berkeley: University of California Press, 1985). Based on in-depth interviews with middle-class persons in several regions of the country, this widely praised book examines the extent to which utilitarian individualism and expressive individualism have eroded public commitment in many areas of our lives. For a counterargument, see Andrew M. Greeley, "Review of *Habits of the Heart*, by Robert N. Bellah et al.," *Sociology and Social Research* 70 (1985), 114. See also the essays in Charles H. Reynolds and Ralph V. Norman (eds.), *Community in America: The Challenge of Habits of the Heart* (Berkeley and Los Angeles: University of California Press, 1988).

20. Bellah, et al., *Habits of the Heart*, p. 236.

21. James Davison Hunter, *Evangelicalism: The Coming Generation* (Chicago: University of Chicago Press, 1987), especially chapter 5. Hunter makes this point with reference to young evangelicals in the United States. His discussion draws heavily from the insightful work of John Murray Cuddihy, *No Offense: Civil Religion and Protestant Taste* (New York: Seabury, 1978).

22. George Gallup, Jr., *The Unchurched American—10 Years Later* (Princeton, N.J.: Princeton Religion Research Center, 1988).

23. Among the many analyses of changes in the clergy and in perceptions of clergy authority, see John Seidler and Katherine Meyer, *Conflict and Change in the Catholic Church* (New Brunswick, N.J.: Rutgers University Press, 1989).

24. Ibid.

25. See Kurt W. Back, *Beyond Words: The Story of Sensitivity Training and the Encounter Movement*, 2d ed. (New Brunswick, N.J.: Transaction Books, 1987). Recently updated, this book (originally published in 1972) remains one of the best introductions to the history of the small-group movement in secular settings during the 1960s.

26. Steve Barker, *Good Things Come in Small Groups: The Dynamics of Good Group Life* (Downers Grove, Ill.: InterVarsity Press, 1985). especially chapter 1. One of the most useful brief introductions to the role that small groups can play in nurturing spirituality.

27. On the social organization of early Christians, see especially John G. Gager, *Kingdom and Community: The Social World of Early Christianity* (Englewood Cliffs, N.J.: Prentice Hall, 1975); and Wayne A. Meeks, *The First Urban Christians: The Social World of the Apostle Paul* (New Haven, Conn.: Yale University Press, 1983).

28. Antecedents of the contemporary small-group movement have been traced too

often to warrant repeating here in detail; see, for example, Donald F. Durnbaugh, "Intentional Community in Historical Perspective," in *The House Church Evolving*, edited by Arthur L. Foster (Chicago: Exploration Press, 1976), pp. 18–30; and James A. Davies, "Small Groups: Are They Really So New?" *Christian Education Journal* 5 (1984), 1–12.

29. For a brief overview of the Sunday school movement, see Sydney E. Ahlstrom, *A Religious History of the American People* (New Haven, Conn.: Yale University Press, 1972), pp. 741–742.

30. A brief history of the recent growth of the self-help and recovery movement is given in John Steadman Rice, *A Disease of One's Own: Psychotherapy, Addiction, and the Emergence of "Co-Dependency"* (Princeton, N.J.: Princeton University Press, 1993), chapter 1.

31. Riv-Ellen Prell, *Prayer and Community: The Havurah in American Judaism* (Detroit: Wayne State University Press, 1989).

32. Estimating 25 members per average group is conservative because it means dividing the total number of individual participants by a larger number, thus yielding a smaller number of groups.

33. This estimate comes from a variety of sources, including religious censuses conducted periodically by the National Council of Churches and, most recently, a large-scale study of congregations conducted by Independent Sector; see Virginia A. Hodgkinson, *From Belief to Commitment* (Washington, D.C.: Independent Sector, Inc., 1989).

34. Providing a single estimate of the scope of the small-group movement is understandably more difficult than the casual observer of this phenomenon might wish. Readers who may think the conclusion presented in the text (that half the adult population is part of this movement) too high can find support for their skepticism in the fact that as many as a quarter of current group members may not be very deeply committed to their groups (as indicated by infrequent attendance or saying the group is only "fairly important" or "not very important" to them). It is also the case that the 40 percent who claim to be in such groups in the present study is higher than percentages found in some other studies. For example, in a national survey conducted by telephone as a pilot for the present study, only 29 percent responded affirmatively to the same question about group membership. In a 1992 survey that I conducted among the U.S. labor force, the same question yielded "yes" responses from 26 percent. The explanation for these differences seems to be the fact that in the present study respondents were shown a list of groups that perhaps clarified the range of groups that might be considered relevant. This list may have particularly influenced persons who attend Sunday school classes to respond affirmatively. There are also arguments to be made, however, that support high estimates of the level of involvement in small groups. In the U.S. labor force survey, for example, a separate question about regular attendance at Sunday school classes yielded a figure of 18 percent, and 19 percent of the labor force claimed to be involved in some kind of religious fellowship group. Other surveys conducted by the Gallup organization have consistently found at least 20 percent of the public claiming to be involved in Bible study groups. These figures are all comparable to ones that will be discussed in the next chapter. In the present study the possibility that some respondents may have answered yes without

being in a group is contradicted by the fact that very few respondents then gave don't know or inconsistent responses to detailed questions about their groups. We will also report data on involvement in informal circles of friends and neighborhood gatherings that, if added to the present figures, would suggest even higher levels of involvement in small groups.

Chapter 3. Exploring the Options

1. Clyde H. Reid, *Groups Alive—Churches Alive: The Effective Use of Small Groups in the Local Church* (New York: Harper & Row, 1969), especially chapter 1. Limited to groups sponsored by churches, this book nevertheless discusses the various functions small groups can play and suggests the variety of groups that may be formed to fulfill these functions. Chapter 1 includes brief overviews of educational, administrative, social action, mission, spiritual growth, and therapeutic groups.
2. *Yearbook of American and Canadian Churches* (Nashville, Tenn.: Abingdon Press, published annually). Compiled by the Office of Research, Evaluation and Planning of the National Council of the Churches of Christ in the U.S.A., 475 Riverside Drive, New York, NY, 10115, these volumes contain a wealth of relevant statistical information on Sunday schools, membership, and giving patterns among denominations, summaries of opinion polls, and names and addresses of personnel in charge of activities such as education, youth services, and lay ministries.
3. William Bean Kennedy, *The Shaping of Protestant Education: An Interpretation of the Sunday School and the Development of Protestant Educational Strategy in the United States, 1789–1860* (New York: Association Press, 1966); Lewis J. Sherrill, *The Rise of Christian Education* (New York: MacMillan, 1950); Robert W. Lynn and Elliott Wright, *The Big Little School: Sunday Child of American Protestantism* (New York: Harper & Row, 1971); Gerald E. Knoff, *The World Sunday School Movement: The Story of a Broadening Mission* (New York: Seabury, 1979).
4. Some of the most important contributions to the recent literature on religious education include Mary Boys, *Education in Faith: Maps and Visions* (San Francisco: Harper & Row, 1989); Mary Boys (ed.), *Education for Citizenship and Discipleship* (New York: Pilgrim Press, 1989); Don Browning, David Polk, and Ian Evison (eds.), *The Education of the Practical Theologian* (Atlanta: Scholars Press, 1989); Robert Browning and Roy Reed, *The Sacraments in Religious Education* (Birmingham, Ala.: Religious Education Press, 1985); Craig Dykstra, *Vision and Character* (New York: Paulist Press, 1981); Thomas Groome, *Christian Religious Education* (New York: Harper & Row, 1980); Joseph Hough and John Cobb, *Christian Identity and Theological Education* (Atlanta: Scholars Press, 1985); John Westerhoff, *Building God's People* (New York: Seabury Press, 1983); and Barbara Wheeler and Joseph Hough, *Beyond Clericalism: The Congregation as a Focus for Theological Education* (Atlanta: Scholars Press, 1988).
5. Overviews of the history, rationale, and objectives of the Bible study movement written by leaders of the movement include: William Bangham, *Journey into Small Groups* (Memphis, Tenn.: Lay Renewal Press, 1974); Paul Yonggi Cho, *Successful Home Cell Groups* (Los Angeles: Logos International, 1981); Dennis Den-

ning, *We Are One in the Lord: Developing Caring Groups in the Church* (Nashville. Tenn.: Abingdon Press, 1982); Michael Dibert and Frank E. Wichern, *Growth Groups: Key to Christian Fellowship and Spiritual Maturity in the Church* (Grand Rapids, Mich.: Zondervan, 1985); Roberta Hestenes, *Using the Bible in Groups* (Philadelphia: Westminster Press, 1985); Ron Nichols, et al., *Good Things Come in Small Groups* (Wheaton, Ill.: Inter-Varsity Press, 1985); Charles M. Olsen, *Cultivating Religious Growth Groups* (Philadelphia: Westminster Press, 1984); and Evelyn Whitehead and James Whitehead, *Community of Faith: Models and Strategies for Building Christian Communities* (New York: Seabury, 1982).

6. Adapted from Karen Hurston (Church Growth Association) and Bob Fulton, "Types of Home Groups," in Roberta Hestenes and Careth Weldon Icenogle, *Building Christian Community Through Small Groups: A Syllabus for the Doctor of Ministry Seminar* (Pasadena, Calif.: Fuller Theological Seminary, 1990), p. 85.

7. Margaret Poloma, *The Charismatic Movement: Is There a New Pentecost?* (Boston: Twayne, 1982).

8. Of course not all Bible study groups are the same. Numerous typologies of Bible study groups have been put forward in the published literature, but no effort has been made, using information from group members, to classify such groups. Our data lend themselves to distinguishing among the following types of groups, all of which include some kind of religious or spiritual activity, such as studying the Bible, prayer, and discussing religious topics. *Bible studies* include members who call their groups "Bible studies," include studying the Bible and discussing religious topics among their activities, generally study something in advance, and often pray or sing together. *Cohort groups* include members who define their groups primarily in terms of age, gender, or marital status, such as singles' groups, youth groups, men's groups, or women's groups; otherwise, their activities are quite diverse. *Support groups* include members who consider their reason for meeting primarily to be support, discussion of common interests, or self help; their activities are also quite diverse. *Twelve-step groups* include members who (in this case) study the Bible together and pray together but meet primarily to focus on an addiction, follow the twelve steps to recovery, and often include meditation among their activities. *Task groups* include members who may include Bible studies, prayer, or religious topics among their activities, but who meet primarily to work on projects and to do things for the community. *Sports groups* include members whose groups have some religious focus but whose activities are oriented primarily toward sports, physical exercise, or other hobbies, and who generally meet for a limited term after which the group disbands. *Therapy groups* include members of groups that have some common religious orientation but that meet primarily for therapeutic purposes and often consider themselves a type of "anonymous' group. *Covenant groups* include members who use this label to describe their groups, who enter into a contract with one another, and who agree to hold each other accountable in their Christian lives (the term house church is empirically associated with this cluster as well). *Couples groups* include members who usually attend their groups as couples, often providing child care, and sometimes meeting as offshoots of Sunday school classes; otherwise, their activities are quite diverse. *Prayer fellowships* include members who use this label to describe their groups and who meet primarily for prayer, but who often include Bible study

and singing as well. While many of the specific types of groups that have been identified in the literature appear on this list, it is also worth noting that the variety of groups represented here is even more diverse that most published typologies recognize. Bible studies that focus on twelve-step activities, for example, are particularly important, not only because of their distinctiveness, but also because leaders in the Bible-study movement at the national level have been paying increasing attention to the twelve steps in recent years. Cohort groups, therapy groups, and sports or exercise groups may also be worthy of closer consideration. They defy the stereotypic image of a Bible study group composed of staid middle-class women and men sitting together studying sacred texts. They suggest that Bible study can be effectively combined with such activities as therapy and physical exercise. At the same time, it should be emphasized that typologies can be quite misleading. Although we were able to identify these distinct types of groups in our data by using a version of factor analysis that forces such patterns to emerge, we also found that group members generally do not make much of such distinctions. As far as they are concerned, they attend a group that calls itself a Bible study, or they go to the "Tuesday night" group, or the group "that meets at the Smith's" and know they generally pray and study the Bible together.

9. John W. Ellas, *Church Growth Through Groups: Strategies for Varying Levels of Christian Community* (Houston: Center for Church Growth, 1990), p. 124.

10. Robert E. Slocum, *Maximize Your Ministry* (Colorado Springs, Colo.: NavPress, 1990), p. 270.

11. Mark Twain, *The Adventures of Tom Sawyer* (New York: Grossett and Dunlap, 1946; originally published in 1875), p. 45.

12. Edward J. Madara and Abigail Meese, *The Self-Help Sourcebook: Finding and Forming Mutual Aid Self-Help Groups*, 3d ed. (Denville, N.J.: American Self-Help Clearinghouse, Saint Clares-Riverside Medical Center, 1990), p. 10.

13. Alfred H. Katz and Eugene I. Bender, *Helping One Another: Self-Help Groups in a Changing World* (Oakland, Calif.: Third Party Publishing, 1990), chapter 2. This book provides a wealth of information on self-help movements of all kinds. It is available by direct order from the publisher: Box 13306, Montclair Station, Oakland, CA 94661.

14. The published literature on self-help groups is immense; much of it accessible only through specialized bookstores or directly from specialty publishers. Some of the books and pamphlets that attempt to give an overview of the self-help movement include Jean-Marie Romeder, *The Self-Help Way: Mutual Help and Health* (Ottowa: Canadian Council on Social Development, 1990); Alfred Katz and Eugene Bender, *Helping One Another: Self-Help Groups in a Changing World* (Oakland, Calif.: Third Party Publishing, 1990); Alan Gartner and Frank Reissman, *The Self-Help Revolution* (New York: Human Sciences Press, 1984); Phyllis R. Silverman, *Mutual Help Groups: Organization and Development* (Beverly Hills, Calif.: Sage, 1980); and Barbara Yoder, *The Recovery Resource Book* (New York: Simon & Schuster, 1990). Somewhat dated, but still valuable, are the following collections: Leonard Borman, Leslie Borck, Robert Hess, and Frank Pasquale (eds.), *Helping People to Help Themselves: Self-Help and Prevention* (New York: Howarth Press, 1982); Morton A. Lieberman and Leonard D. Borman, *Self-Help Groups for Coping with Crisis* (San Francisco: Jossey-Bass, 1979); Alan Gartner

and Frank Reissman, *Self-Help in the Human Services* (San Francisco: Jossey-Bass, 1977); and Alfred H. Katz and Eugene I. Bender (eds.), *The Strength in Us: Self-Help Groups in the Modern World* (New York: New Viewpoints Press, 1976).

15. Of the major types of groups, Sunday school classes are the ones most likely to be divided into such subcategories as women's, men's, couples', singles', and youth groups. About a third of all Sunday school classes are also described as women's groups, about a quarter are described as men's groups, a third are described as couples' groups, and one in five as a singles' group. Among Bible study members, about a third describe their group as a women's group, compared to fewer than a sixth who say their group is a men's group. Surprisingly few Bible study groups (only a tenth) are considered couples' groups by their members, suggesting that a majority of these groups are probably open to adults of all ages and marital status. Of the members of self-help groups, approximately 40 percent belong either to a women's or men's group; few of the remainder are designated exclusively for couples, singles, or youth. Special interest groups closely resemble self-help groups in these ways.

16. Irvin D. Yalom, *The Theory and Practice of Group Psychotherapy* (New York: Basic Books, 1969); M.A. Lieberman and Irvin D. Yalom, *Encounter Groups: First Facts* (New York: Basic Books, 1973).

17. William H. Whyte, Jr., *The Organization Man* (New York: Simon & Schuster, 1956).

18. For a valuable overview of the relationship between personal fulfillment and small communities in the 1960s and early 1970s, see Peter Clecak, *America's Quest for the Ideal Self: Dissent and Fulfillment in the 60s and 70s* (New York: Oxford University Press, 1983).

19. Theodore Roszak, *The Making of a Counter Culture: Reflections on the Technocratic Society and Its Youthful Opposition* (Garden City, N.Y.: Doubleday, 1969), especially pp. 5–16.

20. Kurt W. Back, *Beyond Words: The Story of Sensitivity Training and the Encounter Movement*, 2d ed. (New Brunswick, N.J.: Transaction Books, 1987), p. xi.

21. The theme of differences as a positive feature of urban life has recently been emphasized in Richard Sennett, *The Conscience of the Eye: The Design and Social Life of Cities* (New York: Knopf, 1990).

Chapter 4. A Good Place to Begin

1. This finding helps put other research that has focused entirely on home groups into perspective; for example, C. Kirk Hadaway, Stuart A. Wright, and Francis M. Dubose, *Home Cell Groups and House Churches* (Nashville, Tenn.: Broadman, 1987).

2. On the arrangement of physical resources, such as chairs, tables, lighting, and so on, a useful discussion is available in Adele Mittwoch, "The Once-Weekly Groups," in *The Practice of Group Analysis*, edited by Jeff Roberts and Malcolm Pines (London: Routledge, 1991), pp. 83–95.

3. For example, see Mary Douglas and Baron Isherwood, *The World of Goods* (New York: Basic Books, 1979), p. 32.

4. Drucker has made this claim in a number of speeches and essays; see especially the more general argument in Peter F. Drucker, *Management: Tasks, Responsibilities, Practices* (New York: Harper & Row, 1974).
5. See Patrick J. Brennan, *Re-Imagining the Parish: Base Communities, Adulthood, and Family Consciousness* (New York: Crossroad, 1990), especially chapter 3, for a summary of Dr. Paul Cho's cell group approach to small support groups in the church. Other chapters discuss base communities, small groups concerned with addictions, leadership in small groups, and the role of these groups in fostering faith formation and commitment to social justice.
6. Ibid., p. 50.
7. Church leaders interested in benefitting from some of the plans for small-group ministries that have been developed by local churches may be especially interested in Tom Kiedis, *Lay Pastor Manual*, an unpublished collection of materials available from Palm Beach Community Church, 3970 RCA Blvd., Suite 7009, Palm Beach Gardens, FL 33410.
8. An example of the serendipity approach is Lyman Coleman, *Beginning a Serendipity Group: Six Sessions to Get Acquainted* (Littleton, Colo.: Serendipity House, 1991). This is a 43-page guide filled with ice-breakers, short lessons, discussion questions, and other helpful hints for group leaders working primarily from a religious perspective. It also lists more than 50 other booklets for small groups ranging from specific Bible studies to topics such as stress, money, family, careers, marriage, parenting, addiction, and codependency. Available from Serendipity, P.O. Box 1012, Littleton, CO 80160, or 1-800-525-9563.
9. Roberta Hestenes, *Using the Bible in Groups* (Philadelphia: Westminster Press, 1983). This is a widely used guide for small-group leaders that includes chapters on the rationale for small groups, how to start and lead them, methods of group Bible study, and building relationships in small groups.
10. Theses produced from doctorate of ministry projects are also a rich source of models that have been tested in local church settings and are designed for use in particular denominational contexts; see, for example, Thomas Alva Litteer, *Pastor's Role in Church Renewal and the Development of Lay Ministry Through Home Fellowship Groups* (Unpublished D.Min. Dissertation, Fuller Theological Seminary, 1990); John Thomas Kort, *How One Church Discovered Its Approach to Evangelism by Formulating a Statement of Evangelism Through a Small Group Study of Selected Evangelism Methods and Approaches* (Unpublished D.Min. Dissertation, Princeton Theological Seminary, 1990); Bruce William Bunker, *Christian Ministry in the Workplace: A Covenanted Journey of Reflection with Laity* (Unpublished D.Min. Dissertation, Hartford Seminary, 1989); Clarence Raymond Pritchard, *Preaching Linked with Small Groups as a Means of Increasing the Understanding and Application of Biblical Truth* (Unpublished D.Min. Dissertation, Talbot School of Theology, Biola University, 1989); and Colin Goode, *Congregational Development Through Lay Leadership of Small Groups at Trinity Episcopal Cathedral, Little Rock* (Unpublished D.Min. Dissertation, Fuller Theological Seminary, 1990).
11. One prominent example is J. Keith Miller, *A Hunger for Healing: The Twelve Steps as a Classic Model for Christian Spiritual Growth* (San Francisco: HarperSanFrancisco, 1991).

12. Numerous theological defenses of small groups have been written in recent years; indeed, most guides for leaders of Bible studies and prayer fellowships begin with a discussion of the Biblical basis of small groups. The variety of treatises on this subject is evident among the following: Robert Banks, *Paul's Idea of Community: The Early House Churches in Their Historical Setting* (Grand Rapids, Mich.: Eerdmans, 1980); Dietrich Bonhoeffer, *Life Together* (San Francisco: Harper & Row, 1976); Paul D. Hanson, *The People Called: The Growth of Community in the Bible* (New York: Harper & Row, 1986); Gareth Weldon Icenogle, *Biblical, Theological and Integrative Foundations for Small Group Ministry* (Pasadena, Calif.: Fuller Theological Seminary, Unpublished Doctoral Dissertation, 1990); and Gerhard Lohfink, *Jesus and Community* (Philadelphia: Fortress Press, 1989).

13. Published statements on the role of small groups in revitalizing churches and facilitating church growth can be found in John W. Ellas, *Church Growth Through Groups* (Houston: Center for Church Growth, 1990); Richard Peace, *Small Group Evangelism* (Downers Grove, Ill.: InterVarsity Press, 1985); John N. Vaughan, *The Large Church* (Grand Rapids, Mich.: Baker, 1985); and C. Peter Wagner, *What We Are Missing* (Carol Stream, Ill.: Creation House, 1973).

14. Some systematic evidence on the kinds of congregations most likely to sponsor small-group programs has been collected among Presbyterian churches; see Jackson W. Carroll and David A. Roozen, "Congregational Identities in the Presbyterian Church," *Review of Religious Research* 31 (1990), 351–369; and for Catholic parishes, see David C. Leege, "Parish Organizations: People's Needs, Parish Services, and Leadership," *Notre Dame Study of Catholic Parish Life*, report no. 8 (1986), 1–12.

15. Monica Maske, "The Work of God: Churches Offer Seminars, Support Groups for the Jobless," *Newark Star-Ledger*, March 18, 1991; this article reports several examples of clergy and laity providing facilities, switchboards, professional expertise and other resources to help found groups supporting the unemployed.

16. Peter Steinfels, "Clerics Wonder Whether Religion Can Learn Lessons from Recovery Program for Addicts," *The New York Times*, April 28, 1990; this article discusses the growing interest among religious leaders in twelve-step and other recovery groups. It quotes leaders who are concerned about patriarchal language and insensitivity to wider questions of social justice in these groups as well as ones attracted to the humility, honesty, and acceptance found in many such groups.

17. The history of Alcoholics Anonymous has been documented in a number of books, including Ernest Kurtz, *Not-God: A History of Alcoholics Anonymous* (San Francisco: HarperHazelden, 1979); David Robinson, *Talking Out of Alcoholism: The Self-Help Process of Alcoholics Anonymous* (Baltimore, Md.: University Park Press, 1979); David R. Rudy, *Becoming Alcoholic: Alcoholics Anonymous and the Reality of Alcoholism* (Carbondale: Southern Illinois University Press, 1986); and Norman Denzin, *The Recovering Alcoholic* (Beverly Hills, Calif.: Sage, 1987).

18. On the religious aspects of Alcoholics Anonymous, see especially David R. Rudy and Arthur L. Greil, "Is Alcoholics Anonymous a Religious Organization?: Meditations on Marginality," *Sociological Analysis* 50 (1988), 41–51; Oliver Whitley, "Life with Alcoholics Anonymous: The Methodist Class Meeting as a Paradigm," *Journal of Studies on Alcohol* 38 (1977), 831–848; and Michael Petrunik, "Seeing the Light: A Study of Conversion to Alcoholics Anonymous," *Journal of Voluntary Action Research* 1 (1972), 30–38.

19. Nathan, Hurvitz, "The Origins of the Peer Self-Help Psychotherapy Group Movement," *Journal of Applied Behavioral Science* 12 (1976), 283–294; a brief overview of the religious origins of the contemporary self-help movement.

20. Edward J. Madara and Barrie Alan Peterson, "Clergy and Self-Help Groups: Practical and Promising Relationships," *Journal of Pastoral Care* 41 (1987), 213–220; presents evidence on the relationships between self-help groups and religious organizations in New Jersey and discusses how clergy may become involved in self-help groups as a referral source, an initiator, a provider of meeting space, a supporter of groups sponsored by their own denominations, or by starting self-help groups for clergy themselves.

21. Steinfels, "Clerics Wonder."

22. Virginia A. Hodgkinson, Murray S. Weitzman, and Arthur D. Kirsch, *From Belief to Commitment: The Activities and Finances of Religious Congregations in the United States: Findings from a National Survey* (Washington, D.C.: Independent Sector, 1988); O'Connell's statement is included in the preface to this report.

23. Among the series of inter- and non-denominational study guides that have been developed specifically for use in small groups are the *Fisherman Bible Study Guides* published by Harold Shaw Publishers, Box 567, Wheaton, Ill. 60189 (phone: 708-665-6700); the *Lifeguide Bible Study Series* published by InterVarsity Press, Box F, Downers Grove, Ill. 60515 (phone: 708-964-5700); and the *Lifechange Bible Study Series* published by NavPress, P.O. Box 35001, Colorado Springs, CO 80935 (phone: 800-366-7788).

24. See for example *How to Start a Neighborhood Bible Study*. A handbook, cassette tape, and study guide are included. Thirty-one other guides are also available, as well as a newsletter and leadership training seminar, from Neighborhood Bible Studies, Box 222, Dobbs Ferry, NY 10522, or 914-693-3273.

25. For example, "The Small Group Letter," which appears as an insert in *Discipleship Journal*, and specialized periodicals such as *Leadership* and the *Christian Education Journal*.

26. One example is Edward J. Madara and Abigail Meese, *The Self-Help Sourcebook: Finding and Forming Mutual Aid Self-Help Groups*, 3d ed. (Denville, N.J.: American Self-Help Clearinghouse, Saint Clares-Riverside Medical Center, 1990). This 170-page booklet contains listings of 800 numbers for hotlines concerned with various issues, names and addresses of all major self-help clearinghouses, and a directory of national, regional, and municipal organizations promoting self-help groups.

27. Four such examples that came to my attention as I was writing this are Kathleen Doheny, "Support Groups May Help Older Men Cope with Diabetes," *Los Angeles Times* (March 24, 1992), E10; and Renee Twombly, "Duke Study Finds Friends, Money Affect Mortality," *Duke University News* (January 22, 1992), 2 pages; and Jane E. Brody, "Maintaining Friendships for the Sake of Your Health," *The New York Times* (February 5, 1992); and Redford Williams, "Prognostic Importance of Social and Economic Resources," *Journal of the American Medical Association* 267 (1992), 520–524.

28. On the definition of the voluntary sector, and for a discussion of its recent growth in the United States, see Alan J. Abramson and Lester M. Salamon, *The Nonprofit Sector and the New Federal Budget* (Washington, D.C.: Urban Institute Press, 1986); Robert H. Bremner, *American Philanthropy*, 2d ed. (Chicago: University of

Chicago Press, 1988); Ralph M. Kramer, "The Future of the Voluntary Agency in a Mixed Economy," *Journal of Applied Behavioral Sciences* 21 (1985), 377–391; Walter W. Powell, (ed.), *The Nonprofit Sector: A Research Handbook* (New Haven, Conn.: Yale University Press, 1987); and Jon Van Til, *Mapping the Third Sector: Voluntarism in a Changing Social Economy* (New York: Foundation Center, 1988).

29. Elizabeth Long, "Textual Interpretation as Collective Action: Local Reading Groups and Moral Reflection," unpublished paper presented at the Rice University Center for Cultural Studies, 1989; Elizabeth Long, "Local Reading Groups and American Literary Culture: Preliminary Results from an Ethnography of Reading," unpublished paper presented at the Princeton University Colloquium Series on Religion, Culture, and Society, 1989.

30. Beth Ann Krier, "Excess Baggage: People-Pleasers Carry a Suitcase Full of Woes, but That's About All Co-Dependency's Leaders Can Agree On," *Los Angeles Times* (September 14, 1989).

31. According to John Steadman Rice, *A Disease of One's Own: Psychotherapy, Addiction, and the Emergence of "Co-Dependency"* (Princeton, N.J.: Princeton University Press, 1993), chapter 1, John Bradshaw's *Homecoming: Reclaiming and Championing Your Inner Child* was the eighth best-selling nonfiction hardcover in the United States in 1991 (Bradshaw has been a major proponent of self-help and recovery groups); Melody Beattie, another proponent, has had best-selling books near the top of the charts almost continuously since 1987; Health Communications, Inc., a publisher specializing in self-help and recovery titles increased its sales from less than $1 million in 1983 to $14 million in 1988; and a number of other publishing houses have attempted to gain entry to this lucrative market.

Chapter 5 Making It Work

1. Among the vast number of guidebooks written by experts on small groups, see especially Jeffrey Arnold, *The Big Book on Small Groups* (Downers Grove, Ill.: InterVarsity Press, 1992); Neal F. McBride, *How to Lead Small Groups* (Colorado Springs, Colo.: NavPress, 1990); Arthur R. Baranowski, *Creating Small Faith Communities* (Cincinnati, Ohio: St. Anthony Messenger Press, 1988); and Judy Hamlin, *The Small Group Leaders Training Course* (Colorado Springs, Colo.: NavPress, 1990).

2. C. Kirk Hadaway, Stuart A. Wright, and Francis M. DuBose, *Home Cell Groups and House Churches* (Nashville, Tenn.: Broadman, 1987), chapter 8, provides an excellent, empirically informed discussion of the varieties, functions, and dysfunctions of leadership and authority in small groups.

3. John Adair, "Training Leaders," in *Training in Small Groups: A Study of Five Methods*, edited by B. Babington Smith and B. A. Farrell (New York: Pergamon Press, 1979), pp. 5–18.

4. On explicit and implicit goals, see Theodore M. Mills, *The Sociology of Small Groups* (Englewood Cliffs, N.J.: Prentice Hall, 1967), pp. 80–82.

5. The literature on dissatisfaction and dissolution appears to be rooted more in studies of shorter-term task groups than in studies of the kinds of groups under consideration here; for example, see Roy B. Lacoursiere, *The Life Cycle of Groups:*

Group Developmental Stage Theory (New York: Human Sciences Press, 1980). The formal characteristics discussed in the chapter also differ to some extent by type of group. Leaders are most common in Sunday school classes and in special interest groups; least common in self-help groups. Goals, in contrast, are most common in self-help groups. Having a name is most common in self-help and special interest groups. Having an agenda or schedule is also most common in self-help and special interest groups. Elected officers are least common in Bible studies and most common in special interest groups. Business meetings are also least common in Bible studies and most common in special interest groups. Something to study in advance is most common in Sunday school classes and least common in special interest groups. Child care is most common in Sunday school classes. A membership fee is most common in special interest groups. A formal contract is most common in self-help groups. And a fixed term after which the group disbands does not vary significantly among the kinds of groups (see the methodological appendix for details).

6. It is worth commenting briefly on the ways in which the various kinds of groups differ in terms of their members' evaluations. On the whole, the various kinds of groups do not differ very much in terms of overall levels of member satisfaction. Self-help groups rank slightly above average, and special interest groups a little below average, but the differences are relatively small. On specific characteristics, self-help groups also tend to receive the highest ratings on a number of attributes: respecting different points of view, dealing with important issues, members attending faithfully, meeting emotional needs, helping outsiders, and holding each other accountable. Special interest groups are rated significantly lower than average on meeting emotional needs and having people who trust each other. Sunday school classes and Bible study groups are virtually indistinguishable from each other in terms of how their members rate them on most of these characteristics.

7. The use of subjective assessments of satisfaction in studies of small groups has a long history; see, for example, Elliot Aronson and Judson Mills, "The Effect of Severity of Initiation on Liking for a Group," *Journal of Abnormal and Social Psychology* 59 (1959), 177–181; John W. Thibaut and Harold H. Kelley, *The Social Psychology of Groups* (New York: Wiley, 1959).

8. Phyllis Silverman, "An Introduction to Self-Help Groups," in *The Self-Help Sourcebook: Finding and Forming Mutual Aid Self-Help Groups*, 3d ed., edited by Edward J. Madara and Abigail Meese (Denville, N.J.: American Self-Help Clearinghouse, Saint Clares-Riverside Medical Center, 1990), pp. 14–18.

9. This conclusion is consistent with research relating satisfaction to members' expectations; for example, Thibaut and Kelley, *The Social Psychology of Groups*.

10. For example, see John W. Ellas, *Church Growth Through Groups: Strategies for Varying Levels of Christian Community* (Houston: Center for Church Growth, 1990), p. 61; Dan Williams, *Seven Myths About Small Groups* (Downers Grove, Ill.: InterVarsity Press, 1991), p. 43, states categorically: "Keeping small groups small is essential to keeping them vital. When only a few people band together, then a nurture contract has a chance of being fulfilled."

11. An alternative wording of this conclusion is that trust is a reflection of group cohesion, which in turn depends on the mutual exchange of valued goods among

group members; see Henry Kellerman, *Group Cohesion: Theoretical and Clinical Perspectives* (New York: Grune and Stratton, 1981).

12. Alvin Gouldner, "The Norm of Reciprocity: A Preliminary Statement," *American Sociological Review* 25 (1960), 161–178; reprinted in *Friends, Followers, and Factions: A Reader in Political Clientelism*, edited by Steffen W. Schmidt, Laura Gausti, Carl H. Lande, and James C. Scott (Berkeley: University of California Press, 1977), pp. 28–42.

13. On the role of informal norms in establishing barriers to acceptance, the classic work is that of Muzafer Sherif and Carolyn W. Sherif, *Reference Groups: Exploration into Conformity and Deviation of Adolescents* (New York: Harper & Row, 1964), especially pp. 164–183, 269–273.

14. Carl F. George, *Prepare Your Church for the Future* (Tarrytown, N.Y.: Revell, 1991), p. 99, probably captures a widely held view about the importance of welcoming newcomers when he writes, "Show me a nurturing group not regularly open to new life, and I will guarantee that it's dying."

Chapter 6. Getting and Giving Support

1. Charles Horton Cooley, *Social Organization* (New York: Scribners, 1909), see especially p. 32.

2. Judith Stacey, *Brave New Families: Stories of Domestic Upheaval in Late Twentieth Century America* (New York: Basic Books, 1990), p. 5.

3. Some other empirical studies also indicate positive relationships between group support and various measures of psychological well-being; for example, S. Cohen and T. A. Wills, "Stress, Social Support, and the Buffering Hypothesis," *Psychological Bulletin* 98 (1985), 310–357; K. I. Maton, "Social Support, Organizational Characteristics, Psychological Well-Being and Group Appraisal in Three Self-Help Group Populations," *American Journal of Community Psychology* 16 (1988), 53–77; and K. I. Maton, "The Stress_Buffering Role of Spiritual Support: Cross-Sectional and Prospective Investigations," *Journal for the Scientific Study of Religion* 28 (1989), 310–323.

4. Barbara Sher and Annie Gottlieb, *Teamworks* (New York: Warner Books, 1989), p. 7.

5. Self-help group leaders are also quick to point out the limits of these groups for dealing with serious personal issues. A useful discussion of these limits and the professional resources available for more serious cases is found in Paul G. Quinnett, *When Self-Help Fails: A Guide to Counseling Services* (New York: Continuum, 1991).

Chapter 7. Balancing Self and Others

1. Douglas V. Steere, *On Being Present Where You Are* (Wallingford, Pa.: Pendle Hill Publications, 1967), p. 9.

2. Theodore M. Mills, *The Sociology of Small Groups*, 2d ed. (Englewood Cliffs, N.J.: Prentice Hall, 1984), pp. 136–142, terms this a tension between narcissism and generativity.

3. Two of the more widely read of these studies are Robert N. Bellah, Richard Madsen, William M. Sullivan, Ann Swidler, and Steven M. Tipton, *Habits of the Heart: Individualism and Commitment in American Life* (Berkeley: University of California Press, 1985); and Paul Leinberger and Bruce Tucker, *The New Individualists: The Generation After the Organization Man* (New York: HarperCollins, 1991).

4. Selective perception of more serious proportions has been examined in the classic study by Leon Festinger, Henry W. Riecken, and Stanley Schachter, *When Prophecy Fails* (New York: Harper & Row, 1964).

5. (New York: Rinehart, 1946).

6. On conformity to group norms, Solomon E. Asch, "Effects of Group Pressure upon the Modification and Distortion of Judgments," in *Groups, Leadership, and Men*, edited by H. Guetzkow (Pittsburgh: Carnegie Press, 1951), is still important reading.

7. The metaphor of groups as halls of mirrors is discussed in E. J. Anthony, "The Phenomenology of the Group Situation," in *Group Psychotherapy: The Psychoanalytic Approach*, edited by S. H. Foulkes and E. J. Anthony (London: Karnac Books, 1984), pp. 150–164; L. Zinkin, "Malignant Mirroring," *Group-Analysis* 16 (1983), 113–126; and Jeff Roberts, "Destructive Phases in Groups," in *The Practice of Group Analysis*, edited by Jeff Roberts and Malcolm Pines (London: Routledge, 1989), pp. 128–135.

Chapter 8. *The Spiritual Dimension*

1. J. Keith Miller, *A Hunger for Healing* (San Francisco: HarperSanFrancisco, 1991), p. 6, expresses this idea well when he writes, "Spiritual growth is not . . . to think holy thoughts so that we can experience the presence of the Holy Spirit, but to `exercise ourselves into godliness.'"

2. I do not disagree with many assessments that characterize American spirituality as a rather superficial interest; see, for example, M. Scott Peck, *The Road Less Traveled* (New York: Simon & Schuster, 1978), p. 17. My point is only that the small-group movement is deeply rooted in a segment of the population that takes spirituality much more seriously than this.

3. Extensive use of the allegorical journey described in *Pilgrim's Progress* is made in Keith Miller, *The Taste of New Wine* (Tarrytown, N.Y.: Revell, 1991).

4. This literature is extensive. Among the more readable studies are Daniel Levinson, *Seasons of a Man's Life* (New York: Knopf, 1978); Gail Sheehy, *Passages* (New York: E. P. Dutton, 1976); and George Valliant, *Adaptation to Life* (Boston: Little, Brown, 1977).

5. Useful introductions to these theories and their applications to religious life include Peter Homans (ed.), *Childhood and Selfhood: Essays on Tradition, Religion and Modernity in the Psychology of Erik H. Erikson* (Lewisburg, Pa.: Bucknell University Press, 1978); Bernice Neugarten, *Middle Age and Aging* (Chicago: University of Chicago Press, 1968); and Erik Erikson (ed.), *Adulthood* (New York: Norton, 1978).

6. Lawrence Kohlberg, "Continuities in Childhood and Adult Moral Development

Revisited," in *Life-Span Development and Psychology: Personality and Socialization*, edited by P. Baltes and K. Schaie (New York: Academic Press, 1973); and James Fowler, *Stages of Faith* (San Francisco: Harper & Row, 1981).

7. Jim Plueddemann and Carol Plueddemann, *Pilgrims in Progress: Growing Through Groups* (Wheaton, Ill.: Harold Shaw Publishers, 1990), p. 1.

8. For example, Michael T. Dibbert and Frank B. Wichern, *Growth Groups: A Key to Christian Fellowship and Spiritual Maturity in the Church* (Grand Rapids, Mich.: Zondervan, 1985); and Charles M. Olsen, *Cultivating Religious Growth Groups* (Philadelphia: Westminster Press, 1984).

9. A revealing study, conducted nationally among members of a denomination in which faith is particularly emphasized (Lutherans), revealed that 40 percent said "my trust in God's grace" (the denomination's preferred language) came closest to their own understanding of faith, but 27 percent (the next highest proportion) chose a statement emphasizing works—"a life of commitment to God that I demonstrate by trying to do what is right." Reported in *Views from the Pews: Christian Beliefs and Attitudes*, edited by Roger A. Johnson (Philadelphia: Fortress, 1983), p. 224.

10. Page Smith, *Killing the Spirit: Higher Education in America* (New York: Penguin, 1990), especially chapter 8.

11. On the relationships between small groups and spiritual formation, see especially William Clemmons and Harvey Hester, *Growth Through Groups* (Nashville: Broadman Press, 1975), especially chapters 4 and 5. This book presents a sensitive and informed discussion of the role of *koinonia* in the life of the person of faith and of the role of small groups in fostering openness and acceptance. See also Jack Andre Denys, *Small-Group Stewardship: An Approach to Explore the Feelings of Committed Members* (Princeton, N.J.: Princeton Theological Seminary, unpublished D.Min Thesis, 1984), and Roberta Hestenes, *Using the Bible in Groups* (Philadelphia: Westminster Press, 1983).

12. According to a national telephone survey, "spirituality" means contact with a supernatural world for 8 percent of the American public, a way of life to 5 percent, something about their own convictions and practices to 11 percent, a system of beliefs or doctrines to 46 percent, and a system of morality to 2 percent; 16 percent say they don't know what it means, and 7 percent say it has no meaning. The survey found that "spirituality" is somewhat more likely to connote personal convictions, while "religion" is more likely to connote churches, synagogues, or other organizations, but otherwise the two terms were virtually synonymous in the public mind. I am grateful to Conrad Cherry, director of the Center for the Study of Religion and American Culture at Indiana University, for making these results available to me. The thrust of the discussion in the present chapter is somewhat different, focusing on substantive aspects of spirituality that people were likely to say had changed when they reported that their faith had changed.

13. George Gallup, Jr., *Religion in America: 1992* (Princeton, N.J.: The George H. Gallup International Institute, 1992).

14. Whitehead's terminology is used and expanded upon in John Knox, *Life in Christ Jesus* (New York: Seabury Press, 1966).

15. Margaret M. Poloma and George H. Gallup, Jr., *Varieties of Prayer: A Survey Report* (Philadelphia: Trinity Press International, 1991), p. 129.

16. Paul Yonggi Cho, *Successful Home Cell Groups* (South Plainfield, N.J.: Bridge Publishing, 1981), pp. 57–59.
17. With over a million copies in print, Robert E. Coleman, *The Master Plan of Evangelism* (Tarrytown, N.Y.: Revell, 1972), remains one of the most widely read books that links small-group discipleship with the sharing of faith.
18. For a brief overview of the recent literature on forgiveness, see Clyde A. Bonar, "Personality Theories and Asking Forgiveness," *Journal of Psychology and Christianity* 8 (1989), 45–51; Richard P. Fitzgibbons, "The Cognitive and Emotive Uses of Forgiveness in the Treatment of Anger," *Psychotherapy* 23 (1986), 629–935; Donald L. Hope, "The Healing Paradox of Forgiveness," *Psychotherapy* 24 (1987), 240–244; and Jared P. Pingleton, "The Role and Function of Forgiveness in the Psychotherapeutic Process," *Journal of Psychology and Theology* 17 (1989), 27–35.
19. The relationship between small groups and larger dimensions of the church in a Catholic context is usefully dealt with in Arthur R. Baranowski, *Creating Small Faith Communities: A Plan for Restructuring the Parish and Renewing Catholic Life* (Cincinnati: St. Anthony Messenger Press, 1988).

Chapter 9. What Matters?

1. One reason why love is thought of this way is suggested by Gerald G. May, *The Awakened Heart: Living Beyond Addiction* (San Francisco: HarperSanFrancisco, 1991), chapter 1, in arguing that love always deals with the "why" of life, whereas the efficiency that pervades most of everyday experience in secular settings concerns the "how to" of life.
2. From a national survey I conducted in 1989; reported in Robert Wuthnow, *Christianity in the 21st Century: Reflections on the Challenges Ahead* (New York: Oxford University Press, 1993), chapter 5.
3. This finding is consistent with the arguments of writers who have drawn on Erikson to suggest that faith in adult life (and perhaps personal identity more generally) matures chiefly from establishing caring relationships with others; for example, Robert C. Fuller, *Religion and the Life Cycle* (Philadelphia: Fortress Press, 1988), pp. 66–67.
4. This dimension of leadership is emphasized in Steve Barker, et al., *Small Group Leaders' Handbook* (Downers Grove, Ill.: InterVarsity Press, 1982), pp. 69–71.
5. For a more general discussion of friendship in groups, see Theodore M. Mills, *The Sociology of Small Groups*, 2d ed. (Englewood Cliffs, N.J.: Prentice Hall, 1984), pp. 144–145.
6. The idea of a "plausibility structure" in conjunction with religious beliefs is presented in Peter L. Berger, *The Sacred Canopy: Elements of a Sociological Theory of Religion* (Garden City, N.Y.: Doubleday, 1967), pp. 45–47; the argument is elaborated in Peter L. Berger and Thomas Luckmann, *The Social Construction of Reality: A Treatise in the Sociology of Knowledge* (Garden City, N.Y.: Doubleday, 1966); and in Peter L. Berger, *Facing Up to Modernity: Excursions in Society, Politics, and Religion* (New York: Basic Books, 1977), chapter 1.
7. See Nancy T. Ammerman, "North American Protestant Fundamentalism," in *Fundamentalisms Observed*, edited by Martin E. Marty and R. Scott Appleby (Chica-

go: University of Chicago Press, 1991), pp. 1–66, for a historical approach; and for a statistical approach, see Lyman Kellstedt and Corwin Smidt, "Measuring Fundamentalism: An Analysis of Different Operational Strategies," *Journal for the Scientific Study of Religion* 30 (1991), 259–278.

8. "Literal Belief in the Bible Declining in U.S.," *Emerging Trends* 14 (January 1992), 1. The figures reported in this article are from a Gallup survey conducted in November 1991; that is, at the same time the small-group survey was being conducted. The figures from the two studies, however, are not strictly comparable because of different question wordings and different means of conducting the interviews (telephone versus in person).

9. The importance of group processes in maintaining these convictions is also underscored by the survey. The group activities that most strongly reinforced Bible study were seeing how to apply ideas to one's life, seeing love enacted in the group, and hearing other members share their views. Members who said each of these activities had been important to them were also more likely to say studying particular lessons from the Bible had been important. Not all small groups, of course, regard Bible study as one of their important activities. And within particular groups, individuals themselves may be more, or less, oriented toward Bible study. In the survey, for example, women were somewhat more likely than men to say particular lessons from the Bible had been important to them. Those with lower levels of education, Protestants, and individuals who believed it was necessary to work hard at developing their faith were also more likely to give this response than their counterparts. But these differences were all relatively small. Bible study groups were, of course, the most likely to include people who said they had benefitted from studying particular Biblical lessons. But house churches, covenant groups, Sunday school classes, and even therapy groups were also more likely than average to include such people. Special interest groups were the only type that tended not to include such people.

10. George Gallup, Jr., *Faith Development and Your Ministry* (Princeton, N.J.: Princeton Religion Research Center, 1985), presents survey evidence on the relationship between life crises and believing that one's faith had grown as a result; for a theological discussion from the perspective of two leaders who have been deeply involved in the small-group movement, see Keith Miller and Bruce Larson, *The Edge of Adventure: An Experiment in Faith* (Waco, Tex.: Word, 1974), especially chapters 9, 10, and 11.

11. One study that discovered such a relationship is reported in Stan L. Albrecht and Marie Cornwall, "Life Events and Religious Change," *Review of Religious Research* 31 (1989), 23–38.

12. Fuller, *Religion and the Life Cycle*, p. 62.

Chapter 10. The Power of Stories

1. W. J. T. Mitchell (ed.), *On Narrative* (Chicago: University of Chicago Press, 1981); see especially the introductory essay on the value of narrativity by literary critic Hayden White and the essay on narratives about social dramas by anthropologist Victor Turner. See also Kirin Narayan, *Storytellers, Saints, and Scoundrels: Folk*

Narrative in Hindu Religious Teaching (Philadelphia: University of Pennsylvania Press, 1990), a compelling account of the importance of stories in another religious tradition based on extensive field work in a Hindu village.

2. Jerome Bruner, "Life as Narrative," *Social Research* 54 (1987), 12.
3. Gabriel Fackre, "Narrative Theology: An Overview," *Interpretation: A Journal of Bible and Theology* 37 (1983), 340–352, a useful introduction to recent thinking among theologians about the importance of stories; see also other contributions in the same issue of this journal; Stanley Hauerwas, *Truthfulness and Tragedy* (Notre Dame, Ind.: University of Notre Dame Press, 1977), includes several valuable essays on the role of stories in communicating morality and theology by a leading ethicist; Paul Nelson, *Narrative and Morality: A Theological Inquiry* (University Park: Pennsylvania State University Press, 1987), a scholarly work that demonstrates the close connections between communal contexts, stories, and conceptions of morality, all from a theological perspective; Mark Allan Powell, *What Is Narrative Criticism?* (Minneapolis, Minn.: Fortress Press, 1990), a readable guide that provides help for gaining a greater appreciation of scripture by examining its narrative characteristics; and Meir Sternberg, *The Poetics of Biblical Narrative: Ideological Literature and the Drama of Reading* (Bloomington: Indiana University Press, 1985), for specialists and serious students of Biblical literature, examines the form and content of stories found in the Bible.
4. Bernice L. Neugarten, "Time, Age, and the Life Cycle," *American Journal of Psychiatry* 136 (1979), 893.
5. Raymond Studzinski, *Spiritual Direction and Midlife Development* (Chicago: Loyola University Press, 1985), p. 111.
6. William C. Spohn, "The Reasoning Heart: An American Approach to Christian Discernment," *Theological Studies* 44 (1983), 39.
7. For results of a multivariate analysis of the relationships between storytelling and having one's faith changed, see the methodological appendix.
8. Quoted in Louis R. Ormont, *The Group Therapy Experience: From Theory to Practice* (New York: St Martins, 1992), p. 29.
9. This view of the shaping of personal identity is elaborated in John P. Hewitt, *Dilemmas of the American Self* (Philadelphia: Temple University Press, 1989); George McCall and J. S. Simmons, *Identities and Interaction*, rev. ed. (New York: Free Press, 1978); and Andrew J. Weigert, J. Smith Teitge, and Dennis W. Teitge, *Society and Identity: Toward a Sociological Psychology* (Cambridge, Mass.: Cambridge University Press, 1986).
10. Ken Plummer, *Documents of Life* (London: Allen and Unwin, 1983); John Steadman Rice, "Discursive Formation, Life Stories, and the Emergence of `Co-Dependency': `Power/Knowledge' and the Search for Identity," *Sociological Quarterly* 33 (1992), 333–354.
11. On this process in Sunday school classes, see especially Mary Rose O'Reilley, "The Centered Classroom: Meditations on Teaching and Learning," *Weavings* 4 (1989), 21–31.
12. Philip E. Slater, *Microcosm: Structural, Psychological and Religious Evolution in Groups* (New York: Wiley, 1966).
13. Andrew M. Greeley, *Religion: A Secular Theory* (New York: Free Press, 1982), p. 55.
14. Gerrit Dawson, "Living Stories," *Weavings* 4 (1989), 36–43.

15. Dale E. Galloway, *20/20 Vision: How to Create a Successful Church with Lay Pastors and Cell Groups* (Portland, Ore.: Scott Publishing, 1981), pp. 142–143.

Chapter 11. Serving the Community

1. Elizabeth O'Connor, *Journey Inward, Journey Outward* (San Francisco: Harper & Row, 1968), p. 28.
2. Jack Corbett and Elizabeth Smith, *Becoming a Prophetic Community* (Atlanta: John Knox Press, 1980), p. 17
3. One useful discussion of these issues is that of Amiel Osmaston, *Sharing the Life: Using Small Groups in the Church* (Bramcote, Eng.: Grove Books, 1979), who pays special attention to the distortions that can develop in small groups from paying too much attention to individual needs and group process rather than reaching out to the wider community. See also Anthony Campolo, *Ideas for Social Action* (Grand Rapids, Mich.: Zondervan Publishing House, 1983), especially chapter 5.
4. These were essentially the questions that Emile Durkheim raised in his studies of French society at the end of the nineteenth century, especially in *The Division of Labor in Society* (New York: Free Press, 1933); that troubled him about the role of guilds and professional organizations as means of providing community in *Professional Ethics and Civic Morals* (New York: Free Press, 1958); and that led him to a wider notion of sacred symbolism and ritual in his final work, *The Elementary Forms of the Religious Life* (New York: Free Press, 1965); see also the discussion of Durkheim's view of these issues in Stephen R. Marks, "Durkheim's Theory of Anomie," *American Journal of Sociology* 80 (1974), 329–363.
5. Alexis de Tocqueville, *Democracy in America*, 2 vols (New York: Vintage, 1945).
6. Virtually all small-group manuals address this issue at some point; see, for example, Jim Plueddemann and Carol Plueddemann, *Pilgrims in Progress: Growing Through Groups* (Wheaton, Ill.: Harold Shaw, 1990), pp. 87–88; and Jeffrey Arnold, *The Big Book on Small Groups* (Downers Grove, Ill.: InterVarsity Press, 1992), especially chapter 12.
7. By statistically controlling for other factors, we were able to rule out most possibilities that the correlation between size and wider community involvement was spurious. It is possible, of course, that people with wider interests just happen to join larger groups. The wording of the questions, nevertheless, asked people to say whether or not their group had increased their involvement in these wider activities.
8. Robert Wuthnow, *Acts of Compassion: Caring for Others and Helping Ourselves* (Princeton, N.J.: Princeton University Press, 1991), chapter 7.
9. Still useful on the relationship between personal security and caring for others is the discussion of Abraham Maslow, *Toward a Psychology of Being* (Princeton, N.J.: D. Van Nostrand, 1962).
10. Wuthnow, *Acts of Compassion*, chapters 3 and 4.
11. Some results of this survey are reported in Virginia A. Hodgkinson, Murray S. Weitzman, and Arthur D. Kirsch, *From Belief to Commitment: The Activities and Finances of Religious Congregations in the United States: Findings from a National Survey* (Washington, D.C.: Independent Sector, 1988).

12. This survey formed the basis for George Gallup, Jr., *The Unchurched American—10 Years Later* (Princeton, N.J.: Princeton Religion Research Center, 1988). I wish to thank Virginia A. Hodgkinson, George Gallup, and Dean Hoge for their cooperation in making the data from these surveys available to me. I also wish to thank Tim Clydesdale for his assistance with the merging and analyses of these data.

13. Daniel V. A. Olsen, "Church Friendships: Boon or Barrier to Church Growth?" *Journal for the Scientific Study of Religion* 28 (1989), 432–447.

14. Joseph T. Klapper, "What We Know About the Effects of Mass Communication: The Brink of Hope," *Public Opinion Quarterly* 21 (1957), 453–474.

15. Some of this evidence is presented in Robert Wuthnow, *The Restructuring of American Religion* (Princeton, N.J.: Princeton University Press, 1988); on some of the specific issues that were being contested by the late 1980s, see James Davison Hunter, *Culture Wars* (New York: Basic Books, 1991).

16. For a review of arguments both for and against what has been called the "civil privatism" thesis, see Robert Wuthnow, *The Struggle for America's Soul* (Grand Rapids, Mich.: Eerdmans, 1989), chapter 5. The popular thesis advanced in Robert N. Bellah, et al., *Habits of the Heart* (Berkeley and Los Angeles: University of California Press, 1985), has been challenged in Andrew M. Greeley, "Review of *Habits of the Heart* by Robert N. Bellah, et al.," *Sociology and Social Research* 70 (1985), 114. Clearly, Bellah and his coauthors are arguing that a longer-term and more subtle erosion of public involvement is taking place, but Greeley is correct to point out that many forms of civic participation over the past two or three decades, according to empirical studies, have actually increased.

17. C. Kirk Hadaway, Stuart A. Wright, and Francis M. DuBose, *Home Cell Groups and House Churches* (Nashville, Tenn.: Broadman, 1987), pp. 22–27.

Chapter 12. Envoi

1. One of the more forthright arguments about the relationship between small groups and church growth is presented in Dale E. Galloway, *20/20 Vision: How to Create a Successful Church with Lay Pastors and Cell Groups* (Portland, Ore.: Scott Publishing, 1981).

2. The most thoughtful personal accounts of church growth ministries generally raise these same questions; see, for example, Paul Yonggi Cho, *Successful Home Cell Groups* (South Plainfield, N.J.: Bridge Publishing, 1981), who argues in the opening lines of his book that personal ambition on the part of the pastor is the key to disaster.

3. George McCauley, *The God of the Group: The Influence of Being in a Group on Doing Theology* (Niles, Ill.: Argus Communications, 1975), shows the contribution of group processes to the shaping of theological ideas.

4. Among the first empirical studies to take note of this phenomenon was William Foote Whyte, *Street Corner Society: The Social Structure of an Italian Slum* (Chicago: University of Chicago Press, 1943).

5. It remains puzzling to me that, despite the enormous public and professional interest that has been generated by small groups in recent years, standard textbook treatments of the sociology of religion remain silent on the role of small

groups as a type of religious collectivity, preferring instead to rehash century-old concepts of church, sect, and cult; see, for example, the otherwise very useful texts by Ronald L. Johnstone, *Religion in Society: A Sociology of Religion*, 4th ed. (Englewood Cliffs, N.J.: Prentice Hall, 1992); and Meredith B. McGuire, *Religion: The Social Context*, 3d ed. (Belmont, Calif.: Wadsworth, 1992).

SELECTED BIBLIOGRAPHY

Ahlstrom, Sydney E. A *Religious History of the American People*. New Haven, Conn.: Yale University Press, 1972.

Albrecht, Stan L., and Marie Cornwall. "Life Events and Religious Change," *Review of Religious Research* 31 (1989), 23–38.

Ammerman, Nancy T. "North American Protestant Fundamentalism," in *Fundamentalisms Observed*, edited by Martin E. Marty and R. Scott Appleby. Chicago: University of Chicago Press, 1991, pp. 1–66.

Arnold, Jeffrey. *The Big Book on Small Groups*. Downers Grove, Ill.: InterVarsity Press, 1992.

Back, Kurt W. *Beyond Words: The Story of Sensitivity Training and the Encounter Movement*, 2d ed. New Brunswick, N.J.: Transaction Books, 1987.

Bangham, William. *Journey into Small Groups*. Memphis, Tenn.: Lay Renewal Press, 1974.

Banks, Robert. *Paul's Idea of Community: The Early House Churches in Their Historical Setting*. Grand Rapids, Mich.: Eerdmans, 1980.

Baranowski, Arthur R. *Creating Small Faith Communities: A Plan for Restructuring the Parish and Renewing Catholic Life*. Cincinnati: St. Anthony Messenger Press, 1988.

Barker, Steve. *Good Things Come in Small Groups: The Dynamics of Good Group Life*. Downers Grove, Ill.: InterVarsity Press, 1985.

Barker, Steve, Judy Johnson, Jimmy Long, Rob Malone, and Ron Nicholas, *Small Group Leaders' Handbook*. Downers Grove, Ill.: InterVarsity Press, 1982.

Bellah, Robert N., Richard Madsen, William M. Sullivan, Ann Swidler, and Steven M. Tipton. *Habits of the Heart: Individualism and Commitment in American Life*. Berkeley: University of California Press, 1985.

Berger, Peter L. *The Sacred Canopy: Elements of a Sociological Theory of Religion*. Garden City, N.Y.: Doubleday, 1967.

Berger, Peter L., and Thomas Luckmann. *The Social Construction of Reality: A Treatise in the Sociology of Knowledge*. Garden City, N.Y.: Doubleday, 1966.

Berger, Peter L. *Facing Up to Modernity: Excursions in Society, Politics, and Religion*. New York: Basic Books, 1977.

Bonar, Clyde A. "Personality Theories and Asking Forgiveness," *Journal of Psychology and Christianity* 8 (1989), 45–51.

Bonhoeffer, Dietrich. *Life Together*. San Francisco: Harper & Row, 1976.

445

Borman, Leonard, Leslie Borck, Robert Hess, and Frank Pasquale, editors. *Helping People to Help Themselves: Self-Help and Prevention.* New York: Howarth Press, 1982.

Boys, Mary. *Education in Faith: Maps and Visions.* San Francisco: Harper & Row, 1989.

Boys, Mary, editor. *Education for Citizenship and Discipleship.* New York: Pilgrim Press, 1989.

Bremner, Robert H. *American Philanthropy,* 2d ed. Chicago: University of Chicago Press, 1988.

Brennan, Patrick J. *Re-Imagining the Parish: Base Communities, Adulthood, and Family Consciousness.* New York: Crossroad, 1990. Browning, Don, David Polk, and Ian Evison, editors. *The Education of the Practical Theologian.* Atlanta: Scholars Press, 1989.

Browning, Robert, and Roy Reed. *The Sacraments in Religious Education.* Birmingham, Ala.: Religious Education Press, 1985.

Campolo, Anthony. *Ideas for Social Action.* Grand Rapids, Mich.: Zondervan Publishing House, 1983.

Cho, Paul Yonggi. *Successful Home Cell Groups.* South Plainfield, N.J.: Bridge Publishing Company, 1981.

Clecak, Peter. *America's Quest for the Ideal Self: Dissent and Fulfillment in the 60s and 70s.* New York: Oxford University Press, 1983.

Coleman, Lyman. *Beginning a Serendipity Group: Six Sessions to Get Acquainted.* Littleton, Colo.: Serendipity House, 1991.

Connerly, Charles E. "The Community Question: An Extension of Wellman and Leighton," *Urban Affairs Quarterly* 20 (1985), 537–556.

Corbett, Jack, and Elizabeth Smith. *Becoming a Prophetic Community.* Atlanta: John Knox Press, 1980.

Cuddihy, John Murray. *No Offense: Civil Religion and Protestant Taste.* New York: Seabury, 1978.

Denning, Dennis. *We Are One in the Lord: Developing Caring Groups in the Church.* Nashville: Abingdon Press, 1982.

Dibbert, Michael, and Frank E. Wichern. *Growth Groups: A Key to Christian Fellowship and Spiritual Maturity in the Church.* Grand Rapids, Mich.: Zondervan, 1985.

Douglas, Douglas, and Baron Isherwood. *The World of Goods.* New York: Basic Books, 1979.

Dykstra, Craig. *Vision and Character.* New York: Paulist Press, 1981.

Ellas, John W. *Church Growth Through Groups: Strategies for Varying Levels of Christian Community.* Houston: Center for Church Growth, 1990.

Fischer, Claude S. *The Urban Experience,* 2d ed. San Diego, Calif.: Harcourt Brace Jovanovich, 1984.

Fischer, Claude S. "Ambivalent Communities: How Americans Understand Their Localities," in *America at Century's End,* edited by Alan Wolfe. Berkeley and Los Angeles: University of California Press, 1991, pp. 79–91.

Fitzgibbons, Richard P. "The Cognitive and Emotive Uses of Forgiveness in the Treatment of Anger," *Psychotherapy* 23 (1986), 629–935.

Fuller, Robert C. *Ecology of Care: An Interdisciplinary Analysis of the Self and Moral Obligation.* Louisville, Ky.: Westminster/John Knox, 1992.

Gager, John G. *Kingdom and Community: The Social World of Early Christianity.* Englewood Cliffs, N.J.: Prentice-Hall, 1975.

Galloway, Dale E. *20/20 Vision: How to Create a Successful Church with Lay Pastors and Cell Groups.* Portland, Oreg.: Scott Publishing, 1981.Gallup, George, Jr. Faith Development and Your Ministry. Princeton, N.J.: Princeton Religion Research Center, 1985.

Gallup, George, Jr. The Unchurched American—10 Years Later. Princeton, N.J.: Princeton Religion Research Center, 1988.

Gallup, George, Jr. Religion in America: 1992. Princeton, N.J.: The George H. Gallup International Institute, 1992.

Gans, Herbert J. Middle American Individualism: Political Participation and Liberal Democracy. New York: Oxford University Press, 1988.

Gartner, Alan, and Frank Reissman. Self-Help in the Human Services. San Francisco: Jossey-Bass, 1977.

Gartner, Alan, and Frank Reissman. The Self-Help Revolution. New York: Human Sciences Press, 1984.

Gonzalez, Justo L. The Story of Christianity, 2 vols. New York: Harper & Row, 1984.

Greeley, Andrew M. Religion: A Secular Theory. New York: Free Press, 1982.

Groome, Thomas. Christian Religious Education. New York: Harper & Row, 1980.

Hadaway, C. Kirk, Stuart A. Wright, and Francis M. Dubose, Home Cell Groups and House Churches. Nashville, Tenn.: Broadman, 1987.

Hamlin, Judy. The Small Group Leaders Training Course. Colorado Springs, Colo.: NavPress, 1990.

Hanson, Paul D. *The People Called: The Growth of Community in the Bible.* New York: Harper & Row, 1986.

Hatch, Nathan O. *The Democratization of American Christianity.* New Haven, Conn.: Yale University Press, 1989.

Hestenes, Roberta. *Using the Bible in Groups.* Philadelphia: Westminster Press, 1983.

Hodgkinson, Virginia A., Murray S. Weitzman, and Arthur D. Kirsch. *From Belief to Commitment: The Activities and Finances of Religious Congregations in the United States: Findings from a National Survey.* Washington, D.C.: Independent Sector, 1988.

Hope, Donald L. "The Healing Paradox of Forgiveness," *Psychotherapy* 24 (1987), 240–244.

Hough, Joseph, and John Cobb. *Christian Identity and Theological Education.* Atlanta: Scholars Press, 1985.

Hummon, David. *Commonplaces: Community Ideology and Identity in American Culture.* Albany: State University of New York Press, 1990.

Hunter, James Davison. *Evangelicalism: The Coming Generation.* Chicago: University of Chicago Press, 1987.

Hunter, James Davison. *Culture Wars.* New York: Basic Books, 1991.

Hurvitz, Nathan. "The Origins of the Peer Self-Help Psychotherapy Group Movement," *Journal of Applied Behavioral Science* 12 (1976), 283–294.

Icenogle, Gareth Weldon. *Biblical, Theological and Integrative Foundations for Small Group Ministry.* Pasadena, Calif.: Fuller Theological Seminary, Unpublished Doctoral Dissertation, 1990.

Katz, Alfred H., and Eugene I. Bender, editors. *The Strength in Us: Self-Help Groups in the Modern World*. New York: New Viewpoints Press, 1976.

Katz, Alfred H., and Eugene I. Bender. *Helping One Another: Self-Help Groups in a Changing World*. Oakland, Calif.: Third Party Publishing, 1990.

Kaufman, Gordon. *Theology for a Nuclear Age*. Philadelphia: Westminster Press, 1985.

Kellstedt, Lyman, and Corwin Smidt. "Measuring Fundamentalism: An Analysis of Different Operational Strategies," *Journal for the Scientific Study of Religion* 30 (1991), 259–278.

Kramer, Ralph M. "The Future of the Voluntary Agency in a Mixed Economy," *Journal of Applied Behavioral Sciences* 21 (1985), 377–391.

Keller, Suzanne. *The Urban Neighborhood*. New York: Random House, 1968.

Leinberger, Paul, and Bruce Tucker. *The New Individualists: The Generation After the Organization Man*. New York: HarperCollins, 1991.

Lieberman, Morton A., and Irvin D. Yalom. *Encounter Groups: First Facts*. New York: Basic Books, 1973.

Lieberman, Morton A., and Leonard D. Borman. *Self-Help Groups for Coping with Crisis*. San Francisco: Jossey-Bass, 1979.

Lohfink, Gerhard. *Jesus and Community*. Philadelphia: Fortress Press, 1989.

Luckmann, Thomas. *The Invisible Religion: The Transformation of Symbols in Industrial Society*. New York: Macmillan, 1967.

Madara, Edward J., and Barrie Alan Peterson. "Clergy and Self-Help Groups: Practical and Promising Relationships," *Journal of Pastoral Care* 41 (1987), 213–220.

Madara, Edward J., and Abigail Meese. *The Self-Help Sourcebook: Finding and Forming Mutual Aid Self-Help Groups*, 3d ed. Denville, N.J.: American Self-Help Clearinghouse, Saint Clares-Riverside Medical Center, 1990.

May, Gerald G. *The Awakened Heart: Living Beyond Addiction*. San Francisco: Harper San Francisco, 1991.

McBride, Neal F. *How to Lead Small Groups*. Colorado Springs, Calif.: NavPress, 1990.

Meeks, Wayne A. *The First Urban Christians: The Social World of the Apostle Paul*. New Haven, Conn.: Yale University Press, 1983.

Mills, Theodore M. *The Sociology of Small Groups*, 2d ed. Englewood Cliffs, N.J.: Prentice-Hall, 1984.

Nichols, Ron, et al. *Good Things Come in Small Groups*. Wheaton, Ill.: InterVarsity Press, 1985.

Noll, Mark A., Nathan O. Hatch, George M. Marsden, David F. Wells, and John D. Woodbridge, editors. *Eerdmans' Handbook to Christianity in America*. Grand Rapids, Mich.: Eerdmans, 1983.

O'Connor, Elizabeth. *Journey Inward, Journey Outward*. San Francisco: Harper & Row, 1968.

Olsen, Charles M. *Cultivating Religious Growth Groups*. Philadelphia: Westminster Press, 1984.

Olsen, Daniel V. A. "Church Friendships: Boon or Barrier to Church Growth?" *Journal for the Scientific Study of Religion* 28 (1989), 432–447.

Osmaston, Amiel. *Sharing the Life: Using Small Groups in the Church*. Bramcote, Eng.: Grove Books, 1979.

Peace, Richard. *Small Group Evangelism*. Downers Grove, Ill.: InterVarsity Press, 1985.

Pingleton, Jared P. "The Role and Function of Forgiveness in the Psychotherapeutic

Process," *Journal of Psychology and Theology* 17 (1989), 27–35.

Plueddemann, Jim, and Carol Plueddemann. *Pilgrims in Progress: Growing Through Groups*. Wheaton, Ill.: Harold Shaw Publishers, 1990.

Poloma, Margaret. *The Charismatic Movement: Is There a New Pentecost?* Boston: Twayne, 1982.

Poloma, Margaret M., and George Gallup, Jr. *Varieties of Prayer: A Survey Report*. Philadelphia: Trinity International Press, 1991.

Powell, Walter W., editor. *The Nonprofit Sector: A Research Handbook*. New Haven, Conn.: Yale University Press, 1987.

Prell, Riv-Ellen. *Prayer and Community: The Havurah in American Judaism*. Detroit: Wayne State University Press, 1989.

Reid, Clyde H. *Groups Alive—Churches Alive: The Effective Use of Small Groups in the Local Church*. New York: Harper & Row, 1969.

Reynolds, Charles H., and Ralph V. Norman, editors. *Community in America: The Challenge of Habits of the Heart*. Berkeley and Los Angeles: University of California Press, 1988.

Riesman, David, Nathan Glazer, and Reuel Denney. *The Lonely Crowd: A Study of the Changing American Character*. New Haven, Conn.: Yale University Press, 1950.

Riesman, David. *Individualism Reconsidered*. Glencoe, Ill.: Free Press, 1954.

Rice, John Steadman. *A Disease of One's Own: Psychotherapy, Addiction, and the Emergence of "Co-Dependency."* Princeton, N.J.: Princeton University Press, 1993.

Romeder, Jean-Marie. *The Self-Help Way: Mutual Help and Health*. Ottowa: Canadian Council on Social Development, 1990.

Roszak, Theodore. *The Making of a Counter Culture: Reflections on the Technocratic Society and Its Youthful Opposition*. Garden City, N.Y.: Doubleday, 1969.

Sampson, Robert J. "Friendship Networks and Community Attachment in Mass Society: A Multilevel Systemic Model," *American Sociological Review* 53 (1988), 766–779.

Schmidt, Leigh Eric. *Holy Fairs: Scottish Communions and American Revivals in the Early Modern Period*. Princeton, N.J.: Princeton University Press, 1989.

Seidler, John, and Katherine Meyer. *Conflict and Change in the Catholic Church*. New Brunswick, N.J.: Rutgers University Press, 1989.

Sennett, Richard. *The Conscience of the Eye: The Design and Social Life of Cities*. New York: Knopf, 1990.

Silverman, Carol J. "Neighboring and Urbanism: Commonality versus Friendship," *Urban Affairs Quarterly* 22 (1986), 312–328.

Silverman, Phyllis R. *Mutual Help Groups: Organization and Development*. Beverly Hills, Calif.: Sage, 1980.

Slocum, Robert E. *Maximize Your Ministry*. Colorado Springs, Colo.: NavPress, 1990.

Tönnies, Ferdinand. *Community and Society*, trans. by Charles P. Loomis. New York: Harper & Row, 1963 (originally published in 1887).

Van Til, Jon. *Mapping the Third Sector: Voluntarism in a Changing Social Economy*. New York: Foundation Center, 1988.

Vaughan, John N. *The Large Church*. Grand Rapids, Mich.: Baker, 1985.

Wagner, C. Peter. *What We Are Missing*. Carol Stream, Ill.: Creation House, 1973.

Watt, David Harrington. "United States: Cultural Challenges to the Voluntary Sector," in *Between States and Markets: The Voluntary Sector in Comparative Perspec-*

tive, edited by Robert Wuthnow. Princeton, N.J.: Princeton University Press, 1991, pp. 243–287.

Westerhoff, John. *Building God's People*. New York: Seabury Press, 1983.

Wheeler, Barbara, and Joseph Hough. *Beyond Clericalism: The Congregation as a Focus for Theological Education*. Atlanta: Scholars Press, 1988.

Whitehead, Evelyn, and James Whitehead. *Community of Faith: Models and Strategies for Building Christian Communities*. New York: Seabury, 1982.

Whyte, William H., Jr. *The Organization Man*. New York: Simon & Schuster, 1956.

Williams, Dan. *Seven Myths About Small Groups*. Downers Grove, Ill.: InterVarsity Press, 1991.

Wolfe, Alan, editor. *America at Century's End*. Berkeley: University of California Press, 1991.

Wuthnow, Robert. *The Restructuring of American Religion: Society and Faith Since World War II*. Princeton, N.J.: Princeton University Press, 1988.

Wuthnow, Robert. *Acts of Compassion: Caring for Others and Helping Ourselves*. Princeton, N.J.: Princeton University Press, 1991.

Yalom, Irvin D. *The Theory and Practice of Group Psychotherapy*. New York: Basic Books, 1969.

Yoder, Barbara. *The Recovery Resource Book*. New York: Simon & Schuster, 1990.

INDEX